Bryan Estelle's *The Primary M*
researched and engages solidly v
to an important contemporar,
engagement with society and contemporary issues, particularly
questions of justice, is the source of much division and realignment
within many local congregations. Dr. Estelle engages both historical
and contemporary writers on the topic, as well as offering a thorough
Biblical and Theological walk through key Old Testament passages in
order to make his case. I warmly commend this much needed addition
to the contemporary conversation.

PHIL PROCTOR
Pastor, Sterling Presbyterian Church, Sterling, Virginia

In this timely book Bryan Estelle offers a fresh restatement of the classical
doctrine of the church: it is a spiritual kingdom with spiritual weapons
for a spiritual calling. Citing important voices in the Reformed tradition,
*The Primary Mission of the Church* is a careful and irenic engagement
with recent challenges to the church's spirituality. Estelle demonstrates
how this doctrine, rightly understood, liberates the church from false
hopes and alien agendas even while it equips believers faithfully to fulfill
their callings in the world.

JOHN R. MUETHER
Dean of Libraries and Professor of Church History, Reformed
Theological Seminary, Orlando

# THE PRIMARY MISSION
## OF THE CHURCH

**R.E.D.S.**
REFORMED,
EXEGETICAL
AND
DOCTRINAL
STUDIES

# THE PRIMARY MISSION
# OF THE CHURCH

## ENGAGING OR TRANSFORMING THE WORLD?

# BRYAN D. ESTELLE

SERIES EDITORS J.V. FESKO & MATTHEW BARRETT

**MENTOR**
*Encouraging Christians to Think*

Copyright © Bryan D. Estelle 2022

Paperback ISBN 978-1-5271-0776-2
Ebook ISBN 978-1-5271-0869-1

10 9 8 7 6 5 4 3 2 1

Published in 2022
in the
Mentor Imprint
by
Christian Focus Publications Ltd,
Geanies House, Fearn, Ross-shire,
IV20 1TW, Great Britain.

www.christianfocus.com

Cover design
by Pete Barnsley

Printed by
Bell & Bain, Glasgow

FSC
www.fsc.org

MIX
Paper from
responsible sources
FSC® C007785

# CONTENTS

# Series Preface

Reformed, Exegetical and Doctrinal Studies (R.E.D.S.) presents new studies informed by rigorous exegetical attention to the biblical text, engagement with the history of doctrine, with a goal of refined dogmatic formulation.

R.E.D.S. covers a spectrum of doctrinal topics, addresses contemporary challenges in theological studies, and is driven by the Word of God, seeking to draw theological conclusions based upon the authority and teaching of Scripture itself.

Each volume also explores pastoral implications so that they contribute to the church's theological and practical understanding of God's Word. One of the virtues that sets R.E.D.S. apart is its ability to apply dogmatics to the Christian life. In doing so, these volumes are characterized by the rare combination of theological weightiness and warm, pastoral application, much in the tradition of John Calvin's *Institutes of the Christian Religion*.

These volumes do not merely repeat material accessible in other books but retrieve and remind the church of forgotten truths to enrich contemporary discussion.

MATTHEW BARRETT

J. V. FESKO

# Acknowledgements

*'I will build my church, and the gates of hell*
*shall not prevail against it.'*
Matthew 16:18

Today I listened to an edifying presentation by Vincenzo, a former student, and his dear wife, Judit, as they prepare to head back to Italy in order to plant a Protestant church in a country which is predominately Roman Catholic, with almost zero percent Reformed and Presbyterian churches and only 1.1 per cent Protestant Churches. Vincenzo, raised Roman Catholic and then converted and attending a Pentecostal Church, finally came to understand Reformed theology and ecclesiology. He attended our Seminary and came to understand the true role of works: someone must merit heaven for us, only a perfect human-divine mediator could do so. Finally, he came to understand properly the role of works in salvation. It is all about being saved by grace through faith, and now he desires to take that same gospel back to his fatherland and share it with the spiritually dead people of Italy. I left thinking, 'I love the church and her mission.'

I can think of many times when my kids have asked me why I put up with the difficulties in the church or get up so early in the morning to travel long distances and minister to some far-off congregation, who are without a pastor. My answer? Jesus asked Simon Peter, 'Do you love me more than these?' (John 21:15ff). Peter replied, 'Yes, Lord; you know that I love you.' He said to him, 'Feed my lambs.' This riposte was conducted not just once, but three times! My reply to my grown children was meant to communicate, 'I love Jesus and his church and

11

her mission.' Furthermore, I am constrained by the love of Christ to love her more and more. It doesn't always make sense, especially to human reason; however, it is the love our Lord has placed in my heart. It was the famous American Southern writer, Flannery O'Connor, who described writing a book as 'giving birth to a sideways piano.'[1] I would say that this book was the most difficult delivery of all the writings to which I have given birth. In the process of writing this book, social tumult in my own country and around the world occurred at unprecedented levels, at least in my lifetime. Often the church has been accused of being 'on the wrong side' of issues presented here in this book. Sometimes she has been accused of being silent and therefore allegedly complicit in a whole host of the issues written about below. At times, that may have indeed been true. Nevertheless, she is the duly appointed vehicle of salvation and sanctification for an innumerable host of elect people. I have taken pains to express these in a thoughtful, and hopefully, non-offensive way during this work. It has been agonizing, to say the least.

I'm grateful to the series editors, J. V. Fesko and Matthew Barrett, for their invitation to contribute to the R.E.D.S. series. I am also grateful to the board of Westminster Seminary California for granting me a sabbatical from teaching in the Spring of 2018 so that I could work on this project. The trustees and administration at WSC are truly extraordinary in their efforts to encourage us as faculty to lead the church of Jesus Christ. My wife, Lisa, read a small portion of the manuscript and gave me a thumbs up. Rev. Zach Keele read portions of the manuscript and gave me helpful feedback. An elder in our church, John Earnest, Sr., read the first chapter and gave me some invaluable advice. Craig Troxel read the chapter on the kingdom of God and conveyed his encouragement and response promptly. Numerous conversations with my colleagues at work have helped me sharpen my thinking and also helped me to know better how to respond to those with whom I may find myself in disagreement.

Finally, I dedicate this book to two excellent civil servants who also love the church. Both are former Board members at WSC. Both have

---

1. 'Baboons Differ with Giraffes,' interview with Flannery O'Connor by Celestine Sibley, *The Atlantic Constitution*, February 13, 1957, 24. Reprinted in *Conversations with Flannery O'Connor*, ed. Rosemary M. Magee (Jackson: University Press of Mississippi, 1987).

been, or presently are, ruling elders in Christ's church. First, I wish to recognize Senator Ben Sasse for his exquisite leadership and to thank him for his address to our graduating Seniors on June 9, 2016. Our honorable Senator reminded our graduates to stick to their expertise and God-given craft. Secondly, I wish also to dedicate this book to Brian Miller, who is currently the Special Inspector General for Pandemic Recovery. Although he has held numerous other positions in the civil sphere, he is theologically trained, keeps up on his reading, and tries—with what time allows—to support the church of our Lord Jesus Christ in numerous ways. Thank you for encouraging me in my writing, my publications, and my teaching.

# CHAPTER 1

# The Primary Mission of the Church

*'The standing ordinance of a spiritual Church in the world,
distinct in its origin, in its objects, in its instrumentality,
from the kingdoms of this world, is the grand and public
lesson taught by God as to the fundamental distinction
between things civil and things spiritual.'*

JAMES BANNERMAN

It was the Sunday after the United States had invaded Iraq. I was responsible for part of the worship service at our relatively new church plant in California. We had not called a pastor yet, so the professors from the local theological seminary, who were ministers, were carrying the load of preaching and administering the sacraments. Following the service, I was in a room being interviewed by a visitor to the worship service.

This was no ordinary visitor. He was a newspaper reporter who had come with the goal of observing our worship service so that he could write up a review of our new church in a local paper. His review was called 'Sheep and Goats.' He was Jewish. Our church, which was still a mission work, was a conservative Presbyterian one. He was struck by many things: the refreshments afterwards, but especially the presence of little children in the service sitting well-behaved next to their parents, and the fact that he was not looked at scornfully by the members of our church when the elements were passed for the Lord's supper. After all, he didn't want to partake; this was *our* ritual, not his (besides the fact that I had 'fenced' the table). He was grateful that he felt welcomed even though he did not participate. Apparently, he had not experienced the same courtesy at other Protestant churches he had visited. However, what made one of the biggest impressions upon him was the lack of any reference to politics, political parties, or the war that had just begun with the invasion of Iraq the previous week. I explained that our church was 'apolitical' and although we think it is very important to pray for our civil leaders, as the Apostle Paul had commanded us, we were very careful not to make political comments or even give political impressions in our prayers from the pulpit. As ministers, we conduct our public ministry without reference or bias given to civil leaders, governments and political parties. It is not that we are uninterested in issues of social injustice, but the church corporately was not given the task to address structural injustice. Of course, I explained that does not mean that ministers don't recognize that we are civilians individually, with responsibilities to pay taxes, pray for all our leaders regardless of party affiliation, and to obey the laws of the land as long as we are not coerced to stop preaching the gospel or coerced by the government to perform some other sin. As Guy Waters explains: 'We are not urging the believer's withdrawal from society of social engagement .... We are saying that Christ .... has limited the courts of the church to declaring the will of Christ as revealed in the Scriptures.'[1] However, we are neutral and apolitical when we serve as ministers and as a corporate church. Neither Republican, Democrat, nor Independent. The state and church operate in different orbits. Although their authority derives from the same source— God—we rigorously uphold the spiritual nature of the church and her corporate responsibilities. This was something this newspaper reporter had not observed elsewhere. His experience observing numerous Protestant churches for his job had left him up to this point with an entirely different impression. I explained that what frequently passes for a social gospel is not *the* gospel. He gave us a very good review in the subsequent weeks in the newspaper. I was grateful for the encounter.

This book is about the primary mission of the church. Therefore, in the chapters that follow, I will be defining the church and her mission.

---

1. Guy Prentiss Waters, *How Jesus Runs the Church* (Phillipsburg, NJ: P & R, 2011), p. 70.

16

I will not talk about all the aspects of what a church should be and how it should be run. For example, I write sparsely about officers in the church even though Scripture has a good deal to say about this. Nor will I write very much about the diaconate, although this is another important part of the church's work. I am writing with a particular goal in mind to address some fundamental things about the primary mission of the church that in many places has never been adequately learned or in some cases may have been willfully neglected. But God has not left us bereft of instruction in this area. After all, the origin of the church, together with principles and rules for its government, are all found in the will and determination of God in eternity, as will be discussed below. Does it make any sense whatsoever that he would leave us without his revealed will in such matters for the present church? No.

Before we embark on our study of the primary mission of the church, it is important to get some definitions clear. Much confusion happens in theological discourse because terminological distinctions are not clear early on. First of all, it is important to distinguish between the visible church and the invisible church. The *invisible church*, as defined by the Westminster Larger Catechism, is 'the whole number of the elect that have been, are, or shall be gathered into one under Christ the head.'[2] Therefore, the church exists beyond the level of the local congregation according to this definition. Where disagreements arise is with regard to how this church ought to be governed. In distinction from this is the *visible church*. The visible church is defined as 'catholic or universal under the Gospel (not confined to one nation, as before under the law), consists of all those throughout the world that profess the true religion; and of their children; and is the kingdom of the Lord Jesus Christ, the house and family of God, out of which there is no ordinary possibility of salvation.'[3]

Notice the differences between the invisible and visible church. Waters sets this out succinctly in his wonderfully organized and accessible volume on the church:

> First, the visible church is universal in nature. It is, however, the church as you and I see it in our generation. The invisible church, also universal, is spread across many generations. Second, one is a member of the visible church either by profession of Christianity or by descending from a parent

---

2. Westminster Larger Catechism (WLC 64).
3. Westminster Confession of Faith (WCF 25.2).

who professes Christianity. One is part of the invisible church by the eternal decree of God. Third, the numbers of the visible church increase or diminish. The numbers of the invisible church are fixed and never change. Fourth and particularly important for our consideration, there are some members of the visible church who are not true members of the invisible church.[4]

These categories, visible and invisible church, will be used throughout this book when we refer to the church as visible or invisible.

Another very important point needs to be made right at the beginning. These are Presbyterian and Reformed definitions. In other words, I recognize that a Baptist brother or sister will not agree with these definitions; however, I write as a Presbyterian and this by no means implies that someone who differs with these categories is not a Christian. We should not be so dogmatic as to break communion over this particular issue with our brothers and sisters in Christ who differ from us on these distinctions. Polity, and even the subject of baptism, in this author's opinion, belongs not to the *esse* (essence) of the church but to the *bene esse* (well being) of the church.

Another important topic that will come up frequently below is what is called 'divine right' (*jure divino*) ecclesiastical government, particularly Presbyterianism. The church may not do whatever it deems wise in its polity; rather, there must be a clear sanction in the Bible not only for her worship but for her doctrine and practice. James Bannerman (1807-1868), a leading Scottish theologian, defines *jure divino* government in the following manner:

> The form and arrangement of ecclesiastical government have not been left to be fixed by the wisdom of man, nor reduced to the level of a question of mere Christian expediency, but have been determined by Divine authority, and are sufficiently exhibited in Scripture .... In respect of its government and organization, as well as in respect of its doctrine and ordinances, the Church is of God, and not of man .... Scripture, rightly interpreted and understood, affords sufficient materials for determining what the constitution and order of the Christian society were intended by its Divine Founder to be. In express Scripture precept, in apostolic example, in the precedent of the primitive Churches while under inspired direction, and in general principles embodied in the New Testament, they believe that it is possible to find the main and essential features of a system of

---

4. Waters, *How Jesus Runs the Church*, pp. 11-12.

Church government which is of Divine authority and universal obligation. They believe that the Word of God embodies the general principles and outline of ecclesiastical polity, fitted to be an authoritative model for all Churches, capable of adapting itself to the exigencies of all different times and countries, and, notwithstanding, exhibiting a unity of character and arrangement in harmony with the Scripture pattern. Church government, according to this view, is not a product of Christian discretion, nor a development of the Christian consciousness; it has been shaped and settled, not by the wisdom of man, but by that of the Church's Head. It does not rest upon a ground of human expediency, but on Divine Appointment.[5]

A 'divine right' Presbyterian form of government in the church is often contrasted with a government by *jure humano* (by human right). Bannerman describes the position:

> The form of government for [the] church should be left to the discretion and judgment of its members, and should be adjusted by them to suit the circumstances of the age, or country, or civil government with which they stand connected .... there is no scriptural model of Church government set up for the imitation of Christians at all times, nor any particular form of it universally binding .... Christian expediency, guided by a discriminating regard to the advantage and necessities of the Church at the moment, is the only rule to determine its outward organization, and the only directory of Church government.[6]

Finally, another definition needs brief introduction: Erastianism.[7] This term will occur at various points in this book, especially with regard to the church's relationship to the state and vis-a-versa. A. A. Hodge clearly explains the view:

5. James Bannerman, *The Church of Christ: A Treatise on the Nature, Power, Ordinances, Discipline and Government of the Christian Church*, 2 vols. (London: Banner of Truth Trust, 1960), 2:202. Quoted in Waters, *How Jesus Runs The Church*, p. 43. For one of the most full-bodied explanations and defenses of this view, see *Jus Divinum Regiminis Ecclesiastici, or The Divine Right of Church-Government, Originally Asserted by the Ministers of Sions College, London, December 1646*. Revised and edited by David Hall (reprint, Dallas, TX: Naphtali, 1995). Of historical interest to some readers might be the fact that when Reformed Theological Seminary was begun in 1964, one of the bedrock distinctives on which it was started was *jure divino* Presbyterianism. See Frank Joseph Smith, *The History of the Presbyterian Church in America: The Continuing Church Movement* (Manassas, VA: Reformation Heritage Foundation, 1985), p. 51.

6. Ibid. Quoted in Waters, *How Jesus Runs the Church*, p. 42.

7. The view is integrally connected with Thomas Erastus (1524-1583), a Swiss theologian and physician.

This doctrine regards the State as a divine institution, designed to provide for all the wants of men, spiritual as well as temporal, and that is consequently charged with the duty of providing for the dissemination of pure doctrine and for the proper administration of the sacraments and of discipline. It is the duty of the civil magistrate, therefore, to support the Church, to appoint its officers, to define its laws, and to superintend their administration. Thus in the State Churches of Protestant Germany and England the sovereign is the supreme ruler of the Church as well as of the State, and the civil magistrate has chosen and imposed the confessions of the faith, the system of government, the order of worship, and the entire course of ecclesiastical administration.[8]

During some of the history we will be referring to below, a prominent view of the civil power and ecclesiastical power during the sixteenth and seventeenth century was that the magistrate had authority in church matters as well as civil. This was the case especially with regard to church discipline.[9] The Westminster Assembly debated these views vigorously, but at the end of the day they chose not to embrace Erastianism, but to enshrine the view that there are distinctions between ecclesiastical and civil power.[10]

It is often overlooked in the modern age that quite a bit of what God saw fit to say in his holy Scripture is said to a body of believers, and not just to individuals. Such a claim should delight N.T. Wright, who complains rightly about the reduction of the gospel, that Christians in the West have been too focused accenting individual salvation and going to heaven.[11]

## Why a Spiritual Mission?

Bannerman stated eloquently this great truth about the church of the Lord: the church is a home with a warm hearth for Christians:

> One of the grand offices which the Christian Church has to discharge in the world is thus to be the centre and home of union to believing men, and to become a sanctuary, within which Christians may meet, and enjoy in

8. A. A. Hodge, *The Confession of Faith: A Handbook of Christian Doctrine Expounding The Westminster Confession* (Carlisle, PA: The Banner of Truth Trust, 1869; reprint 1958), p. 298.

9. See the discussion in J. V. Fesko, *The Theology of the Westminster Standards: Historical Context and Theological Insights* (Wheaton, IL: Crossway, 2014), pp. 299-301.

10. Ibid. See below, Chapters 13 and 14 especially.

11. N. T. Wright, *The Day the Revolution Began: Reconsidering the Meaning of Jesus's Crucifixion* (San Francisco, CA: Harper One, 2016).

common their spiritual privileges, and find that those privileges are doubled because shared in common.[12]

However, another of Bannerman's claims, and perhaps the greatest of his life's achievements, was to argue for the separation of the church and the state. It's as if he assumed the position that Christ is ruler of all; however, he manifests his rule in different ways. Christ rules the civil sphere and he rules the ecclesiastical sphere; nevertheless, Bannerman assumes a fine distinction often forgotten in modern times:

> The state, or the ordinance of civil government, owes its origin to God as the *universal Sovereign and Ruler among nations*. The Church, as the visible society of professing Christians in the world, with its outward provision of authority and order and government, owes its origin to *Christ as Mediator*.[13]

Another way of identifying this is that there is the *regnum gratiae* (the 'kingdom of grace') and the *regnum potentiae* (the kingdom of power). The kingdom of power is universal, general or natural – that is, Christ's rule is manifest over the world and its affairs especially through the civil magistrate. Yet, Christ's rule here historically has been understood not in his role as mediator, but as the second person of the Trinity. The 'kingdom of grace' is Christ's rule over the church militant where he governs, blesses, and defends the church in its earthly pilgrimage for the sake of the salvation of believers. These basic categories—that God rules the church as a redeemer (a spiritual kingdom) and rules the state and all other social institutions (the civil kingdom) as creator and sustainer—have been widely held by Reformed thinkers for centuries until the modern period.[14] In addition, until the nineteenth century, there was basically a positive posture towards natural law; until then it was thought that natural law and reason cohered and derived their status 'as Christian authority because of scripture's own revealed word about creation and God's sovereign design therein.'[15]

---

12. Bannerman, *The Church of Christ*, p. 92.

13. Ibid., 97 [emphasis added].

14. See David VanDrunen, *Natural Law and the Two Kingdoms: A Study in the Development of Reformed Social Thought*, Emory Studies in Law and Religion, John Witte Jr., general editor (Grand Rapids, MI: Eerdmans, 2010).

15. Christopher R. Seitz, *Figured out: Typology and Providence in Christian Scripture* (Louisville, KY: Westminster John Knox Press, 2001), p. 60.

Without this bedrock truth, any attempt to describe the primary mission of the church will collapse. Without this skeleton of strong bones, any form we give to the question of what the primary mission of the church is will be flaccid and distorted. This truth, i.e., that God rules over the entire universe, including the church, but with necessary distinctions with regard to how he rules, is a crucial distinction. This axiomatic truth, together with his recognition of the ramifications of the visible and invisible church (more below), had a profound influence on how Bannerman thought about the primary mission of the church. First and foremost, he recognized that the primary function of the church is spiritual. He says, for example, 'The era of the Christian Church is emphatically that of the manifestation of the Spirit; and the administration of the Church is, in its primary character, *a spiritual one*.'[16] For Bannerman, this means the church does have a *primary mission*. He writes in his classic on ecclesiology: 'the Church of Christ has been instituted by Him for the purpose of advancing and upholding the work of grace on the earth, being limited, in its primary object, to promoting the spiritual interests of the Christian community among which it is found.'[17]

Fast forward to the next generation. This same principle was stated eloquently by J.G. Machen, the founder of the denomination in which I serve:

The responsibility of the church in the new age is the same as its responsibility in every age. It is to testify that this world is lost in sin; that the span of human life—nay, all the length of human history—is an infinitesimal island in the awful depths of eternity; that there is a mysterious holy living God, Creator of all, Upholder of all, infinitely beyond all; that he has revealed himself in his Word and offered us communion with himself through Jesus Christ the Lord; that there is no other salvation, for individuals or for nations, save this.[18]

---

16. Ibid., p. 25 [emphasis his].

17. Ibid., p. 98.

18. J. Gresham Machen, 'The Responsibility of the Church in Our New Age,' *The Presbyterian Guardian* 36:1 (January 1967), p. 13. Machen (1881-1937), a Professor at Princeton Theological Seminary, was a staunch defender of Orthodoxy in his day. This led him to found Westminster Theological Seminary in 1929 and the Orthodox Presbyterian Church in 1936. He was born into a home that reflected the aristocratic south (see, D. G. Hart, 'Doctor Fundamentalis: An intellectual biography of J. Gresham Machen, 1881-1937' [Ph.D. dissertation, The Johns Hopkins University, 1988], pp. 27-28). Some of the consequences of this influence will be discussed below in the book.

The church's greatest corporate expression of compassion towards the world is to preach the good news of Jesus Christ. My claim in this book is the same: The church *is spiritual* and its mission *is spiritual*. The church, corporately, should stick to its job description. When she does not, the result is fuzzy boundaries. *When I use the term 'spiritual' in this book, or the phrase 'the spirituality of the church', I am referring to those things that are properly of and properly belonging to the church.*

Even so, it does not follow that this emphasis on the primary mission of the church as spiritual signifies that her business is only with non-physical matters. The power given to the church is spiritual; however, 'That does not mean it is invisible and completely internal, for though Christ is a spiritual king, he rules over both body and soul. His Word and sacrament are directed to the whole person. The ministry of mercy attends to the physical needs of human beings.'[19] Nor does it mean that Christians should neglect the poor, nor turn a blind eye to social injustices (although it might have entailments for *how* the church, or individual members, address those concerns and issues). After all, there are a number of areas both moral and civil where the Bible clearly has something to say. In other words, there are very few 'purely political' issues.[20] Nor does it mean that we should neglect distinct areas of authority that God gave to the church as her primary mission. A brief reflection on preaching, administering the sacraments, administering church discipline, let alone visiting the sick and dying, and providing for the financially destitute within the church hardly resembles a non-material other-worldliness! Truly.

Nevertheless, as Craig Troxel has written, there is an increasing pressure for the church to incorporate concerns for peace and justice, social malaise and injustices, poverty, and so on into the corporate mission of the church.[21] The fact that the primary mission of the church in her

19. Herman Bavinck, *Reformed Dogmatics: Holy Spirit, Church, and New Creation*, Vol. 4, John Bolt ed. (Grand Rapids, MI: Baker Academic, 2008), 4. pp. 414-15.

20. See, e.g., the discussion by David VanDrunen, *Natural Law and the Two Kingdoms*, pp. 264-65.

21. Craig Troxel, 'The World Is Not Enough: The Priority of the Church in Christ's Cosmic Headship,' in *Confident of Better Things: Essays Commemorating Seventy-Five Years of the Orthodox Presbyterian Church*, ed. by John R. Muether and Danny E. Olinger (Willow Grove, PA: Committee for the Historian, 2011): pp. 337-66, especially at p. 362.

corporate capacity is spiritual doesn't excuse an individual Christian from exercising compassion and justice. Far from it. As Troxel continues, individual Christians must not lose sight of their responsibility to show compassion to their neighbors and to be salt and light in the world, especially in times of crisis and natural disasters.[22] But what is justice, biblically defined? This might not be so easily defined and may involve lots of complexity.[23] How some of those kinds of practices are performed in practice will be discussed later in the book; however, first we must discuss theory.

In this book, I assume that 'Theory will color the outcome of the analysis of texts,' especially biblical texts as Jewish biblical scholar Ed Greenstein says.[24] He continues: 'Our very observations, and not only our interpretations, are necessarily shaped by whatever presuppositions, hypotheses, and bodies of knowledge we possess. Our theories guide our selection of evidence, and even our construction of evidence.'[25] Often in biblical studies, as well as in studies of systematic theology, we assume that we are on a similar singular theoretical footing. However, that is not the case. I would maintain that this is especially so in the area of ecclesiology. Greenstein makes a somewhat similar point about the importance of theory in his article on biblical interpretation, especially with regard to the link between one's model and one's method, for he insists, 'if we have different models, and then of necessity different methods—and we do—we can only understand each other in the terms of each other's theories.'[26] In this book, I will take pains not only to describe my ideas about ecclesiology, but the views of others as well. Otherwise, we cannot understand one another, let alone have an intelligent conversation. Or we may downplay genuine disagreements. And disagreement can be a great achievement.

Indeed, the first point in this book is of the utmost importance: as has already been stated, the mission of the church at its very core is *spiritual*. Its birth comes from God, not man. Its source then determines

22. Troxel, 'The World,' p. 363.

23. See, e.g., Zach Keele, 'A Biblical Theology of Justice,' *Modern Reformation* (May/2020).

24. Ed Greenstein, 'Theory and Argument in Biblical Criticism,' *Hebrew Annual Review* 10 (1986): pp. 77-93.

25. Ibid., p. 178.

26. Ibid., p. 173.

its vocation. Its mission corporately is integrally related to its essence, which is spiritual. This Doctrine of Ecclesiology has often been called through the centuries the Spirituality of the Church (hence, SOTC).[27] It is the doctrine that 'meant that the church was a spiritual institution with a spiritual task and spiritual means for executing that task.'[28] Charles Hodge (1797-1878), who trained over three thousand students for gospel ministry, and who has been called the 'supreme Calvinist theologian of the nineteenth-century America,'[29] expressed it this way:

> It is the doctrine of the Scriptures and of the Presbyterian Church, that the kingdom of Christ is not of this world; that it is not subject as to faith, worship, or discipline, to the authority of the state; and that it has no right to interfere with the state, or give ecclesiastical judgment in matters pertaining to state policy.[30]

This is a good concise definition. Consider the following history as an apt illustration of his convictions. Hodge had such strong convictions about this separation between church and state in the early 1860s that he wrote a response to the so-called Spring Resolutions which were adopted by the General Assembly of the Old School Presbyterian Church 'that not only split the denomination along regional lines but also declared that the Presbyterian Church had an obligation to 'promote and perpetuate' the integrity of the United States and the federal government.'[31] Although Hodge's political sympathies were clearly with the Union, he thought that

---

27. Marcus McArthur, *Render unto Lincoln: Disloyalty and the Clergy in Civil War Missouri* (Unpublished manuscript, 2015), notes that the 'spirituality of the church' doctrine existed long before the Southern Presbyterians used it to defend their view of slavery. He calls it 'apolitical', meaning not that ministers who held to it were free from personal political convictions, but that they tried to steer clear of partisan politics and sectional controversy. This was especially problematic in border-states, where such views bred suspicion about secessionist loyalties.

28. Darryl Hart quoted in Katherine Lynn Tan VanDrunen's unpublished doctoral dissertation, 'The Foothills of the Matterhorn: familial antecedents of J. Gresham Machen,' (Ph.D. dissertation, Loyola University Chicago, 2006), p. 185.

29. Alan D. Strange, *The Doctrine of the Spirituality of the Church in the Ecclesiology of Charles Hodge*, Reformed Academic Dissertations, John J. Hughes ed., (Phillipsburg, NJ: P & R, 2017), p. 132.

30. Ibid., p. 279-80.

31. For a short summary, see the article by D. G. Hart and John R. Muether, 'The Spirituality of the Church,' *Ordained Servant* 7/3 (July 1998): pp. 64-66. For a longer account, see Strange, *The Spirituality of the Church.*

'the state has no authority in matters purely spiritual and that the church [has] no authority in matters secular or civil.'[32] Hodge substantiated his points by quoting from Chapter 31 of the Westminster Confession (WCF) which states that synods and councils must handle material only ecclesiastical as opposed to civil matters. Adding his explanation to demonstrate his understanding of the extent and nature of church power, he said: 'The church can only exercise her power in enforcing the word of God, in approving what it commands, and forbidding what it forbids.'[33] Even so, Hodge did demur from some of the views of his Southern counterparts on the SOTC (on this, more below) and went on to speak of times when he thought that it was incumbent upon the church to address moral matters as a church which might have civil consequences.[34]

Although we will talk chiefly about the primary mission of the church in this book, the SOTC was the language used to talk about the spiritual mission of the church, especially in the nineteenth century. Hodge argued that Christ manifests his kingdom on earth by means of the visible church. Christ's kingdom can coexist with all forms of legitimate civil kingdoms on earth without interference because its nature is spiritual. The duties which Christ has enjoined upon his people in the visible church are as follows:

> Christians are required to associate for public worship, for the admission and exclusion of members, for the administration of the sacraments, for the maintenance and propagation of the truth. They therefore form themselves into churches, and collectively constitute the visible kingdom of Christ on earth, consisting of all who profess the true religion, together with their children.[35]

The external manifestation of the kingdom of Christ in the visible church should not be mistaken, says Hodge, for the inward reality; nevertheless, the outward visible church is necessary to demonstrate the inward reality of Christ's kingdom. Hodge continues to press more closely with his description of the nature of Christ's kingdom, and his definition becomes even more clear in what follows:

32. Quoted in Hart and Muether, 'The Spirituality of the Church,' p. 64.

33. Ibid., p. 65.

34. Strange, *Spirituality of the Church*, pp. 262-63, 281

35. Charles Hodge, *Systematic Theology*, three volumes (Grand Rapids, MI: Eerdmans, 1982), 2.604.

First, it is spiritual. That is, it is not of this world. It is not analogous to the other kingdoms which existed, or do still exist among men. It has a different origin and a different end. Human kingdoms are organized among men, under the providential government of God, for the promotion of the temporal well-being of society. The kingdom of Christ was organized immediately by God, for the promotion of religious objects. It is spiritual, or not of this world, moreover because it has no power over the lives, liberty, or property of its members; and because all secular matters lie beyond its jurisdiction. Its prerogative is simply to declare the truth of God as revealed in his Word and require that the truth should be professed and obeyed by all under its jurisdiction. It can decide no question of politics or science which is not decided in the Bible.[36]

This description of the spiritual nature of Christ's spiritual kingdom has often been forgotten, misunderstood, sometimes abused and sometimes ignored, or just unwittingly neglected. Consequently, many in our modern culture, who are deeply disturbed by some misery, suffering, or distress in the world, desperately desire to hear the corporate church say something publicly and officially and take some action corporately about such injustices. This raises the important question about whether the church has been granted the authority by God to do so. It may have such authority on some issues but not others. For example, in the past, some have made distinctions between purely political acts over which Christians could be divided and therefore the church should not speak upon, and taking moral stands on issues that Christians could agree upon that might have civil consequences.[37] The point is that ministers in their pulpits only have declarative authority, that is they may only be ambassadors of Christ and declare what he has authorized them to say, nothing more and nothing less. We will discuss this more below, both the issue of what the church can say about politics and what ministers should or should not say about political issues.

I will suggest that the primary mission of the church is being challenged today by a resurgence of movements that are seeking to expand the primary mission of the church to include some form of a 'redefined' social gospel. That does not mean that the proclamation of

---

36. Ibid.

37. A distinction that Charles Hodge, for example, adhered to on several issues. See Strange, e.g., *Spirituality of the Church*, p. 246.

the gospel doesn't speak either directly or impliedly to social concerns. It often does. However, I maintain that the social gospel as promoted in the late nineteenth and early twentieth century, which sought to expand the primary mission of the church, has made a resurgence and is alive and well today. In 2011, Kevin DeYoung and Greg Gilbert published *What Is the Mission of the Church? Making Sense of Social Justice, Shalom, and the Great Commission* (Crossway). Subsequently, they received more than a slight bit of pushback in the reviews that followed because they wanted precise definitions for what constituted kingdom work and how (if at all) the church should make efforts to change social structures. Let me quickly outline the history of that social gospel movement.

It was prominent in the second half of the nineteenth century and the beginning of the twentieth century. This movement is often associated with such figures as William Gladden (1836-1918), a pastor of the First Congregational church in Columbus, Ohio, and especially with Walter Rauschenbusch (1861-1918), an American Baptist pastor and Professor of Church History in Rochester Theological Seminary. The social gospel movement was a response to the problems of industrialization and all the ills as well as the wealth that it brought: extreme affluence for some, and severe harsh work conditions for others. My view is that redefining the kingdom of God (KOG) along lines that seek to Christianize a culture (or in this case the United States) actually harm faith. For example, 'by appealing to the second person of the Trinity to justify better conditions of factory workers, Protestant activists were trivializing the much grander and glorious aim of Christianity.'[38] Of course, it does not follow that factory conditions are unimportant or 'unworthy of individual Christians' concerns as individual citizens, employers, or government officials. It did mean that the church had a different and, from a minister's perspective, more profound calling which would be neglected if ecclesiastical bodies began to take on the work of civil authorities.'[39] Each should pay attention to their God-given job description. When they don't, the result is fuzzy boundaries.

Rauschenbusch, in a chapter entitled 'the historical roots of Christianity,' published in his 1907 book, *Christianity and the Social*

---

38. Darryl Hart, *A Secular Faith: Why Christianity Favors the Separation of Church and State* (Chicago, IL: Ivan R. Dee, 2006), p. 119.

39. Ibid.

*Crisis*, argued that the Old Testament prophets 'are an integral part of the thought-life of Christianity …. Modern study has shown that they were the real makers of the unique religious life of Israel.'[40] Moreover, he wrote that 'a study of the prophets is not only an interesting part in the history of social movements but it is indispensable for any full comprehension of the social influence exerted by historical Christianity, and for any true comprehension of the mind of Jesus Christ.'[41] Then he moves into his thesis:

> The fundamental conviction of the prophets, which distinguished them from the ordinary religious life of their day, was the conviction that God demands righteousness and demands nothing but righteousness …. the prophets insisted on a right life as the true worship of God …. Morality to them was not merely a prerequisite of effective ceremonial worship …. This insistence on religious morality as the only thing God cares about is of fundamental importance.[42]

His next logical step is to suggest that the prophets were primarily concerned to apply this to the public sphere. He says, for example:

> The morality which the prophets had in mind in their strenuous insistence on righteousness was not merely the private morality of the home, but the public morality on which national life is founded. They said less about the pure heart for the individual than of just institutions for the nation. We are accustomed to connect piety with the thought of private virtues; the pious man is the quiet, temperate, sober, kindly man. The evils against which we contend in the churches are intemperance, unchastity, the sins of the tongue. The twin-evil against which the prophets launched the condemnation of Jehovah was injustice and oppression.[43]

Rauschenbusch's third substantial book, *A Theology for the Social Gospel* (1917), was his most systematic.[44]

Some of what Rauschenbusch writes, about the prophets in particular, is partially true. The ancient theocracy of the Hebrews was organized

---

40. Walter Rauschenbusch, *Christianity and the Social Crisis* (New York: Hodder & Stoughton, 1907), pp. 2-3.

41. Ibid., p. 3.

42. Ibid., pp. 4-6

43. Ibid., p. 8

44. Hart, *A Secular Faith*, p. 103.

as a nation, and we would expect her prophets to inveigh against social and religious affairs. However, Rauschenbusch, first, mistakenly extends these principles to the church of Christ's present kingdom and in so doing fails to recognize that Christ declared that his kingdom was not of this world. We no longer live in a theocracy. Second, he fails to recognize the real genius of the prophets. The Princeton biblical theologian, Geerhardus Vos (1862-1949), recognized this when he wrote:

> Their [the prophets] rebuke of social sin attaches itself to the distinction between rich and poor, powerful and weak, a distinction that has been at all times the symptom and occasion, though not the cause, of social disease …. The note of divine compassion makes itself distinctly heard in these passages. But against the fact that rich and poor exist together the prophet does not raise his voice; all the prophets would have subscribed to Proverbs 22:2.[45]

How different is Rauschenbusch, who writes about Amos: 'We advance another step in our study when we emphasize that the sympathy of the prophets, even of the most aristocratic among them, was entirely on the side of the poorer classes.'[46] Quoting Professor Kautzsch approvingly, he notes: 'Amos was the alpha and omega of prophetic preaching to insist on right and justice, to warn against the oppression of the poor and helpless.'[47]

Raushenbusch's ideas stayed similar for the next couple of decades. For example, in 1926, he published *Christianizing the Social Order*.[48] There he wrote that 'The hope of the Kingdom of God had been wrought into the tissue of Jewish thought by the Hebrew prophets.'[49] He waxes rhetorically and says: 'These men were so alive to God and felt his righteousness so overpoweringly that they beat their naked hands against jagged injustice and inhumanity. They were centers of religious unrest, creators of a divine dissatisfaction, and the unsparing critics of all who oppressed and corrupted the people.'[50] He continues:

---

45. Geerhardus Vos, *Biblical Theology: Old and New Testaments* (Grand Rapids, MI: Eerdmans, 1948), p. 295.

46. Ibid., p. 11.

47. Ibid.

48. Walter Rauschenbusch, *Christianizing the Social Order* (New York, NY: The Macmillan Company, 1926).

49. Ibid., p. 50.

50. Ibid., p. 51.

The prophets were religious reformers demanding social action. They were not discussing holiness in the abstract, but dealt with concrete, present-day situations in the life of the people which were sometimes due to the faults of the people themselves, but usually to the sins of the ruling classes…. their most persistent and categorical demand was that the men in power should quit their extortion and judicial graft. They were trying to beat back the hand of tyranny from the throat of the people. Since the evil against which they protested was political, their method of redress was political too. Their religion did not displace politics but reinforced it. If any modern preacher had told them to disentangle their religion and their politics and keep them in separate compartments, they would not have known what he meant…. This reign of God for which they hoped was therefore a social hope on fire with religions … they were men and dealt with men, but they focused not souls [sic], but society.[51]

It should be clear from the above examples that the social gospel movement taught that the religious life should never be uncoupled from the social life and its needs. Indeed, it was claimed that the church, in her corporate capacity, had a responsibility to address social issues of the day such as economic inequality, poverty and a host of other topics. As David Torbett says:

The goal of the Social Gospel movement was to realize the Kingdom of God on earth: to bring an end to social injustice through the redemption of individuals and social institutions, to heal systemic evils, especially the evils of unbridled industrial capitalism, that corrupted individuals and society as a whole. In pursuit of this goal, Rauschenbusch and other proponents of the Social Gospel established a pattern of church-based social activism that was to endure for generations.[52]

Of course, the issue of addressing systemic evils and systemic injustice is a complicated one, beside the point of defining what 'systemic injustice' is, something we will comment on further below.

It is often assumed that the social gospel movement has declined since the early twentieth century. My claim is that it merely went into a quiet period.[53] The kinds of questions, ideas, and polity in the church

---

51. Ibid., pp. 51-52.

52. David Torbett, *Theology and Slavery: Charles Hodge and Horace Bushnell* (Macon, GA: Mercer University Press, 2006), pp. 181.

53. Here I am following the recent work of Paul J. DeHart, *The Trial of the Witnesses: The Rise and Decline of Postliberal Theology* (Oxford: Blackwell, 2006), pp. 41-53, although he

that the social gospel was producing did not immediately turn into a rushing cataract. Those concepts were steadily rising for a time, but then became slow moving and some of its ideas even went underground. The extended metaphor of a river delta is helpful here. One should think of a large and powerful river (i.e., the social gospel) that supplies a great area but develops into several smaller branches, and the original fount becomes shallower and indistinct, but nevertheless continues to water and nourish many different places.[54] Indeed, this is a complex and long story; nevertheless, in order to simplify, one can think of many loose and different strands that can be detected.

I am claiming that the social gospel 'river,' which went underground for a time, now has many tributaries that are emerging and becoming manifest above ground in the corporate church of Jesus Christ. Nevertheless, the current rivulets are so similar to the fountainhead, that the very fabric of what we observe in these modern versions of the social gospel are not really different in substance from what their source was in the late nineteenth and early twentieth century. Which is to say, that the church of Jesus Christ is facing pressure again to redefine its mission. Therefore, it behooves the church to examine again the fundamentally spiritual nature of her mission as authorized by the Lord Jesus Christ.

In light of the resurgence, I'm claiming that we need to think freshly about the primary mission of the church, which is spiritual. This will necessarily involve us in thinking about the relation between the church and culture, and between the church and the state. The abuses of the Roman Catholic church and the burdens they laid on the backs of Christians, as attested by many of the magisterial Reformers, gave rise to many theories about the relation between the church and culture. Calvin responded with a two kingdoms theology during the Reformation.[55] These ideas gave precise expression to the same classic Christian distinction between the spiritual and the secular (temporal)

develops the metaphor of a river gone underground and applies it to the dormancy and revival of Yale's postliberalism.

54. Ibid., pp. 45-46.

55. See Matthew J. Tuininga, *Calvin's Political Theology and the Public Engagement of the Church: Christ's Two Kingdoms*, Law and Christianity Series (Cambridge: Cambridge University Press, 2017), pp. 142-43. Also see Strange, *Doctrine of Spirituality*, who argues at numerous points that Hodge was trying to confront the Roman Catholic Church's claim as having authority over the civil government.

realms.[56] This bears repeating: although I am emphasizing the spiritual nature of God's kingdom as manifest in his church, this is *not* to say that Christ's kingdom is immaterial or ethereal.[57] This mistaken view would not cohere with Calvin's great emphasis on the 'spiritual' nature of Christ's kingdom. Rather, in order to specify more clearly, the term 'spiritual' means:

> That 1) the power of the kingdom is that of the Holy Spirit, 2) the kingdom completes creation's eschatological purpose [although in a different manner than originally planned], and 3) the kingdom will be consummated only at Christ's return. Put simply, the kingdom is 1) from the Spirit of God, 2) leads humans upward to God, and 3) leads them forward to eternity.[58]

Therefore, we need to ask the simple question: what does it mean that the kingdom of Christ is spiritual? For Calvin (and for me), this 'means that it is oriented toward the sincere worship of God.'[59] Much more will be said about this frequently misunderstood notion, especially in the chapter below on the nature of the kingdom. As Dave VanDrunen says:

> Christianity was never meant to eliminate distinctions in familial, ethnic, political, or economic association. What Christianity was meant to do was to unite people from different families, different ethnic groups, different political factions, and different socio-economic standings into a single community, 'baptized into one body – Jews or Greeks, slaves or free …' (1 Cor. 12:13).[60]

I am a Professor; primarily I teach Hebrew (and sometimes other Semitic languages), and Biblical Theology, and occasionally Practical Theology. But I am not only a Hebraist and Professor primarily of Old Testament language and literature. I am a churchman, a committed one as well. As I became involved in the courts of our church, I have grown increasingly concerned about the vast confusion over the primary mission of the church and particularly what role the church should play towards the surrounding culture. I began to see the institutional church making

---

56. Tuininga, *Calvin's Political Theology*, p. 23.

57. See Ibid., pp. 119-20 and 123-24.

58. Ibid., pp. 119-20.

59. Ibid., p. 127.

60. David VanDrunen, *Living in God's Two Kingdoms: A Biblical Vision for Christianity and Culture* (Wheaton, IL: Crossway, 2010), p. 148.

pronouncements as the corporate church about which I was very uneasy. I have witnessed the attention of many ministers diverted from their primary duties and callings to matters by which clergy two hundred years ago would have never been distracted.

Of course, as Christians, we should be greatly concerned about all kinds of social ills and injustices we observe in our cities and towns. For example, should we not be concerned about severe poverty in our own communities and neighborhoods, especially during a pandemic? Of course, we should. However, how we address those concerns as individual Christians, or as a group of individual Christians collectively joining together with other Christians, or with concerned citizens of other religions to ameliorate those social ills through compassionate acts of kindness towards our neighbors, is not part of the job description given to the church corporately.

My goal, simply stated, is to give a positive exposition of the primary mission of the church. As mentioned above, that is the language I will use even though the ecclesiology I will be explaining has often been referred to as the 'Spirituality of the Church' (SOTC). Sometimes I will use the language of the SOTC, for example in chapters below dealing with the history of the doctrine (e.g., Chapter 12), since discussions and the literature are so permeated with the phrase. However, that nomenclature has become loaded with volatility, and I desire to bring more light than heat to the present situation (cf. Chapter 12 especially, and then Chapter 13).

However, what has really been an impetus for this discussion are recent movements in the Presbyterian Church in America, especially with their actions that were attempted at the General Assembly of 2015 (the 43rd), but postponed, and then acted upon at the General Assembly in a later session (the 44th), and most particularly a writing by Sean Michael Lucas, an associate professor of Church History at Reformed Theological Seminary. His ideas can be seen embodied in an article entitled 'Owning Our Past: The Spirituality of the Church in History, Failure, and Hope.'[61] Lucas, depending upon another scholar—Jack P.

---

61. See, Sean Lucas, 'Owning Our Past,' in *Reformed Faith and Practice: The Journal of Reformed Theological Seminary* Vol. 1/1 (May, 2016): pp. 25-38. https://journal. rts.edu/article/owning-our-past-the-spirituality-of-the-church-in-history-failure-and-hope/

Maddex—who has been quite critical of the doctrine of the spirituality of the church, says: 'historians have viewed the spirituality of the church doctrine simply as a "protective gesture," mainly used to shield or prevent southerners from acting with justice towards African Americans in the nineteenth and twentieth centuries.'[62] This claim has been proved false, or at least exaggerated; Preston Graham proved that the doctrine stretched back most immediately to the Scottish Reformation, which occurred long before the Civil War.[63] Lucas wrote an article in which he attempted to point out the dangers of the doctrine of the SOTC as understood and put into practice. I disagree with his presentation. That article contained factual errors, in part because of its reliance on the historical work of Maddex.[64] Maddex is correct to note that Presbyterians before the Civil War probably did not teach a doctrine of the SOTC that enjoined a strict separation of church and state.[65] However, he is wrong in his construal of the situation by maintaining that the SOTC doctrine was the invention of Reconstruction Southerners, particularly in border state territories by people like Stuart Robinson (1814-1881),[66] whom he also claims had no influence from James Henley Thornwell (1812-1862), the leading Southern Presbyterian of his time, on these matters.[67] Indeed, he overstated the differences between Thornwell and Robinson.[68] Maddex labels the SOTC as a 'new doctrine' when its seminal ideas

---

62. RTS article.

63. Graham, *A Kingdom Not of this World*, pp. 11-16.

64. See Jack P. Maddex, 'From Theocracy to Spirituality: The Southern Presbyterian Reversal on Church and State,' *Journal of Presbyterian History (1962-1985)*, Vol. 54, No. 4 (Winter, 1976): pp. 438-57.

65. See Strange, *The Doctrine of the Spirituality*, pp. 3-4.

66. For a brief description of Robinson's life and ecclesiology, see Craig Troxel's foreword in Rev. Stuart Robinson, *The Church of God as an Essential Element of the Gospel, and the Idea, Structure, and Function in Four Parts* (Willow Grove, PA: The Committee on Christian Education of the Orthodox Presbyterian Church, 2009), pp. 5-12.

67. Ibid. Thornwell was considered the leading theologian in the South during the nineteenth century. For bibliography, see John Lloyd Vance, 'The ecclesiology of James Henley Thornwell: An Old South Presbyterian theologian' (Ph.D. dissertation, Madison, NJ: Drew University, 1990); Brian T. Wingard, 'As the Lord Put Words in her Mouth:' The Supremacy of Scripture in the Ecclesiology of James Henley Thornwell and Its Influence upon the Presbyterian Churches of the South' (Ph.D. dissertation, Philadelphia, PA: Westminster Theological Seminary, 1992); Morton Howison Smith, *Studies in Southern Presbyterian Theology* (Jackson, MI: Presbyterian Reformation Society, 1962).

68. John Lloyd Vance, 'The ecclesiology of James Henley Thornwell,' pp. 228.

actually stretch all the way back to biblical times.[69] He erred in his claims because he did not take into account the early development of Thornwell's and Robinson's thought, let alone the scriptural foundations of their thinking.[70] As will be established in the next chapter, Thornwell's thinking on ecclesiology was fueled by influences from the Old World of Europe, not from the New World. As a matter of fact, Thornwell deeply influenced Robinson. Troxel summarizes:

> Just as there was mutual learning between periodicals and their editors in the intense dialogue of the church board controversy [discussed below in Chapter 10], Peck [who served at Union Theological Seminary (Virginia) from 1860-1893] and Robinson were profoundly influenced by Thornwell *and* his testimony to the spiritual nature of church power .... Although Robinson held to the spirituality of the church at about the same time as Thornwell and came to the doctrine through a somewhat different biographical path than Thornwell, it cannot be maintained that Robinson held to this important truth in absolute independence of Thornwell.[71]

Nevertheless, the publication of the article by Lucas was roughly at the same time when in 2016, at the General Assembly of the Presbyterian Church in America, the PCA 'repented' of past and present sins tied to race and attempted some kind of racial reconciliation, an act considered by some of her leaders to be of social justice. In this book, I will comment here and there on race relations since this has become a major point of debate and discussion within our cultures at this time. I have painstakingly tried to add to the conversation in ways that might help contribute understanding. In my life since becoming a Christian, I have worked with many African Americans in parachurch and church ministries. I have personally discipled young black Christian men in Santa Barbara, California and in Portland, Oregon. I have worked in parachurch ministries with black prison inmates serving out their terms for first degree murder. Most of those inmates had never travelled more than fifteen to twenty miles outside the inner city before they were locked up for their crimes. I have seen the social injustice firsthand. It is painful.

---

69. Strange, *Spirituality of the Church*, pp. 3-4.

70. Craig Troxel, "Divine Right' Presbyterianism and Church Power' (Dissertation, Philadelphia, PA: Westminster Theological Seminary, 1998), pp. 54-55.

71. Ibid.

Many today have fronted the notion that to remain silent on the issue of race (even as a corporate church) signifies complicity in the injustices—both present and past—and therefore, the church should speak out on this issue since the church should have a 'prophetic' voice. Unfortunately, 'racism' has itself become a confusing term, maddeningly.[72] In my opinion, we owe it to people to talk about the issue; however, the venue and where we speak into the issue needs careful thought, as this book will suggest. I have chosen to write about the topic in certain places in this book because people in the church need help thinking through and understanding the complex and problematic behavior of the past. I have not been motivated to write about it because I think that silence entails complicity: that claim is a nonstarter. There may be other reasons for people's silence, even in the corporate church. Indeed, this book suggests a few in the pages that follow.

Returning to issues surrounding the SOTC, according to Alan Strange, there may be some truth to the claims made by the eminent historian, Jack Maddex, with regard to the SOTC doctrine becoming part of the South's civil religion after the Civil War.[73] Moreover, according to Strange, he may be right about cautioning against too strong claims about an absolute separation of religion from politics.[74] Nevertheless, many historians have pointed out the egregious mistakes made by Maddex because it is clear the SOTC doctrine was affirmed and practiced well before the Civil War broke out. The doctrine of the SOTC is not a novel idea invented by Southerners in the Reconstruction period, as claimed by Maddex.[75] Indeed, Maddex's mistake about the origin of the doctrine led him to assert [quoting Peter Slade] that 'the spirituality of the church is in fact the time tested political strategy of powerful men to perpetuate an unjust *status quo* free from more censure …. [It] is a sophisticated theological resistance to systemic change: it is not an innocent doctrine misused.'[76]

The self-expressed goal of Sean Lucas in his article is best stated in his own words: 'I want to attempt the seemingly impossible: to rehabilitate

---

72. See, e.g., John McWhorter's recent article, 'Words Have Lost Their Common Meaning,' *The Atlantic* (March 31, 2021).

73. See, e.g., the concession made by Graham, *A Kingdom Not of This World*, p. 61.

74. Strange, p. 4.

75. Ibid., p. 4.

76. Ibid.

the idea of the "spirituality of the church" in such a way as to make it a vehicle for the church to speak to social and political issues as part of a full-orbed Gospel mission.[77] He concludes the article by saying that 'one of the reasons that the PCA 43rd General Assembly failed to own the past was its commitment to a flawed understanding of the spirituality of the church doctrine.'[78] That conclusion is open to debate. In my opinion, he is wrong.

Consider another recent example: Jemar Tisby's recent book, *The Color of Compromise: The Truth about the American Church's Complicity in Racism*.[79] In this popular book, Tisby introduces James Henley Thornwell and the 'Spirituality of the Church'.[80] Tisby paints a facile caricature of the issues:

> Faced with growing pressure from their northern coreligionists to demonstrate allegiance to the Union and to the eradication of slavery within its borders, southern Christians rejected the call to take firm stances on the so-called 'political' issue of slavery. In Thornwell's exposition of the spirituality of the church, he asserted that the church's one 'Constitution' is the Bible, and the church has no jurisdiction over political or social matters. 'The power of the Church, accordingly, is only ministerial and declarative.' According to Thornwell, the church can merely assert what the Bible teaches and must remain silent on that which the Bible is silent. Over the issue of slavery, the spirituality of the church meant that Christians could insist on the liberty of conscience to choose to practice or abstain from slaveholding since the Bible nowhere explicitly condemns it.[81]

These statements are a facile representation of very complex issues, and they are historically incorrect. Without justifying a clearly racist practice of slavery, or without justifying a pernicious way of ordering economic production in the South prior to and during the Civil War, attempting to understand what Thornwell was doing and saying with regard to the church and its limits can help us understand the principles of the SOTC as promoted by both pro-slavery and anti-slavery theologians during this time.

77. Ibid.

78. Ibid.

79. Jemar Tisby, *The Color of Compromise: The Truth about the American Church's Complicity in Racism* (Grand Rapids, MI: Zondervan, 2019). The book has received a number of reviews already, some more helpful than others.

80. Ibid., pp. 85-87.

81. Ibid., p. 85.

First, there is a sense in which his representation of Thornwell is almost too generous with regard to the issue of slavery. As I will explain below, a major debate over ecclesiology erupted between Charles Hodge, definitely the most influential Northern Presbyterian theologian of the nineteenth century, and James Henley Thornwell, arguably the most influential Southern Presbyterian theologian of the nineteenth century. They locked horns over numerous issues in the church. Details and nuance will be treated in the chapters to follow with regard to their views on slavery. Hodge remembers in debating with Thornwell that he had gone so far as to say, 'the Church, it was said, is so spiritual that she cannot recommend the colonization of society, and cannot condemn the slave trade.'[82] Strictly speaking, this is hearsay, and this writer has found nothing in the published writings of Thornwell to go so far to this effect; nevertheless, if Thornwell did say it on the floor of General Assembly, then it was wrong even by means of applying his own principles of the declarative power of ministers. For example, 1 Timothy 1:10 clearly delineates 'man-stealing' as a blatant sin for any member in Christ's church. How much more so for any officer in Christ's church! No wonder Hodge responded so passionately with the question, 'Is there nothing in the Bible which proves man-stealing and devastating wars for the sake of procuring slaves to be diabolically wicked?'[83] Thornwell did have a measure of self-interest in resolving the issues of slavery in the manner that he did.[84] Nevertheless, the significant question, which we will deal with in detail below in regard to the primary mission of the church, is whether Thornwell was merely hiding behind the skirts of the doctrine of the SOTC or if there was something more at stake for him: the God-determined limitations on the power and authority of the church—the job description of the corporate church—in short, the primary mission of the church. When she doesn't stick to her job description, fuzzy boundaries are the result.

Aside from the squabble between these two titans, the above lengthy quote by Tisby betrays other caricatures. The fact of the matter is that

---

82. Strange, *Spirituality of the Church*, p. 280.

83. Ibid.

84. Hart, *A Secular Faith*, p. 63.

the power of the church is only ministerial and declarative; however, these terms need to be carefully defined and explained according to their time-honored pedigree in Reformed and Presbyterian literature. Moreover, there may be one or more responsible responses by the church to engage the problem of the South's peculiar institution of slavery since it was race-based. Presbyterians, especially of an Old School stripe, have always been hesitant to engage social and political issues, especially by the church in her corporate capacity.[85] This is for biblical and confessional reasons. Tisby's misunderstanding of these issues is evident as the quote and the pages that follow demonstrate. Besides, if one wants to get rid of the doctrine of the SOTC, with what will he replace it? *This is a crucial question.* Especially if the SOTC is a doctrine taught in the Bible and Reformed Confessions. This point can hardly be overstated. If the Scriptures are sufficient for all of covenantal faith and life of the individual Christian and the life of the church corporately, and if the SOTC is a biblical doctrine, and one that is taught in our Confessions which are binding, then it follows that one is suggesting something against the Bible, against the Confession, and against God by throwing the doctrine of the SOTC under the bus. If God ordained it for the polity of the church, then it deserves a seat on the bus. Now, even if we as twenty-first century Christians vehemently disagree with Thornwell's position on slavery, or with his Southern contemporary, another extremely influential Southern Presbyterian theologian, Robert Lewis Dabney (1820-1898), who held to the infamous 'double curse of Ham' theory (more below) which influenced his views of slavery, it does not follow that we can learn nothing from these men. Quite the contrary. Since we believe that we may learn much from non-believers, how much more so may we confess that we can learn much from Christian brothers with whom we might disagree?

The fact of the matter is that all ministers and theologians have clay feet. Thornwell and Dabney had clay feet. Hodge had clay feet. Machen

---

85. For definitions of 'Old School' and 'New School', see, e.g. George M. Marsden, *Fundamentalism and American Culture: The Shaping of Twentieth-Century Evangelicalism 1870-1925* (Oxford/New York: Oxford University Press, 1980), especially pp. 44-45. This book was later expanded and revised in *Understanding Fundamentalism and Evangelicalism* (Grand Rapids, MI: Eerdmans, 1991).

had clay feet, and every modern minister and theologian mentioned either in the body of the text of this book or in the footnotes has clay feet. That is a fact. Perhaps two hundred years from now, subsequent generations will look back and point out some of the weaknesses of our contemporary generation. But that should not stop us from doing theology, history, or ecclesiology. Rather, it should make us humble in our claims about the past and the present.

In some areas as I write on this subject, I write with expertise since I am primarily a Professor trained in how to interpret the Bible. A professional historian I am not. Even so, I have a deep interest in church history. At the very beginning, therefore, I want to say that I will be writing as a person who is trained generally in the disciplines of divinity, and more narrowly and authoritatively in the languages and literatures of the Bible and the cultures that had the most immediate influence on the biblical writers. Even so, the time has arrived to deal with ecclesiology, and particularly to bring the doctrine of the primary mission of the church off the book shelves, dust it off, and begin to examine its biblical and confessional basis, and its honored historical pedigree within the church once again.

To begin on a positive and substantive note, I simply list the principles stated in the Book of Church Order of the Presbyterian Church in America. This chapter is a terse summary of many of the principles that will be unpacked in this book. It is about the nature and extent of church power. This third chapter is found in the PCA's book of church order, and the principles found here are basic and foundational to the conduct and character of her government, especially on the nature of her power, about which I will comment in more detail in subsequent chapters, especially Chapter 13.

3.1. *The power which Christ has committed to His Church vests in the whole body, the rulers and the ruled, constituting it a spiritual commonwealth. This power, as exercised by the people, extends to the choice of those officers whom He has appointed to His Church.*

3.2. *Ecclesiastical power, which is wholly spiritual, is twofold. The officers exercise it sometimes severally, as in preaching the Gospel, administering the Sacraments, reproving the erring, visiting the sick, and comforting the afflicted, which is the power of order; and they exercise it sometimes jointly in Church courts, after the form of judgment, which is the power of jurisdiction.*[86]

3.3. *The sole functions of the Church, as a kingdom and government distinct from the civil commonwealth, are to proclaim, to administer, and to enforce the law of Christ revealed in the Scriptures.*

3.4. *The power of the church is exclusively spiritual; that of the State includes the exercise of force. The Constitution of the Church derives from divine revelation; the constitution of the State must be determined by human reason and the course of providential events. The Church has no right to construct or modify a government for the State, and the State has no right to frame a creed or polity for the Church. They are as planets moving in concentric orbits: 'Render unto Caesar the things that are Caesar's and to God the things that are God's' (Matt. 22:21).*

3.5. *The Church, with its ordinances, officers and courts, is the agency which Christ has ordained for the edification and government of His people, for the propagation of the faith, and for the evangelization of the world.*

3.6. *The exercise of ecclesiastical power, whether joint or several, has the divine sanction when in conformity with the statutes enacted by Christ, the Lawgiver, and when put forth by courts or by officers appointed thereunto in His Word.*

We will return to these principles later in the book. There may be language here with which the reader is unfamiliar, e.g., power being exercised severally or jointly. We will discuss these things at the appropriate juncture. However, the reader should note as we launch into our study that these principles do not necessarily reduce the church to quietism, to indifference to earthly matters, or to some kind of ghettoizing theology and practice.[87] Nor, should an appeal to these

---

86. For those who may be unfamiliar with this distinction between 'severally' and 'jointly', it merely refers to two kinds of power mentioned in this paragraph: 'The first is the power of order, which may be exercised severally by individuals who have been ordained and appointed to office. The second kind of power is the power of jurisdiction, which is exercised jointly by Church courts' (see Morton Smith, *Commentary of the Book of Church Order* [Greenville, SC: Greenville Seminary Press, 1990], §3-2). Even when an officer exercises this power individually, he is still subject to the church courts and, in this sense, such power is always exercised jointly.

87. D. G. Hart, *The Lost Soul of American Protestantism*, American Intellectual Culture Series (Lanham, MD: Rowman & Littlefield Publishers, 2002), pp. 178-81.

principles or the magisterial Reformers suggest that the teaching of the church should not speak against social evils. To see why this is the case, I invite the reader to pick up and read. Don't skip ahead to your favorite and most controversial subject. Rather, examine the evidence, biblical and historical, and learn from what those who have gone before us have to say. Read the book from cover to cover.

## Outline of the Book

This book has four parts. Part 1 gives the biblical basis for the primary mission of the church. Ideally, we should engage the entire canon of scripture; however, that would be a huge undertaking. Therefore, I have been selective. Chapter 2 covers some foundational material from the early chapters of Genesis. Chapter 3 engages the Joseph narrative and demonstrates its relevance for our topic. Chapter 4 turns to the court narratives from Daniel. Chapter 5 discusses some important passages from the New Testament (NT) that are germane to our discussion.

Part 2 of this book explores what the primary mission of the church *is not*. My experience as a teacher has solidified that comparing an idea with illustrations of what it is not is helpful. Such a process clarifies the right idea. This part has four chapters. Chapter 6 deals with two very influential Dutch thinkers, Dooyeweerd and Kuyper. Both had a profound influence on the church and especially regarding how Christians should think about their involvement in culture. Chapter 7 deals with an important theological movement: liberation theology. I'm assuming that many readers are unfamiliar with the history of this movement and its ideas, so I trace its development and interact with a few of its major personalities. My contention is that a thoughtful reader will hear echoes of this movement in many corners of the modern church even if conservative and Reformed churches have not fully embraced its radical, Marxist, and even sometimes violent agendas. Chapter 8 engages the movement of theonomy. Some have thought that the influence of theonomy is waning in recent years; however, several weighty publications seem to suggest this is not the case. Finally, Chapter 9 discusses the so-called missional movement in the modern church. In this chapter I describe the missional movement, and interact with Leslie Newbigin, one of the foremost missionary statesmen of the last century, and his influence on the church and her mission in modern times.

Part 3 of this book pivots toward a positive definition of what the primary mission of the church is. This part also has four chapters. I consider these chapters to be vital for defining the role and primary mission of the church. Chapter 10 discusses the nature of the kingdom of God (KOG) since this often enters into discussion about the mission of the church. Chapter 11 discusses important Confessional teaching (especially the Westminster Confession) about the church. Not only will I discuss at some length the importance of the teaching about the headship of Christ over his church, but we will also explore the role between the church and the state. Brief mention will be made here about the Disruption Controversy in Scotland since this played such an important role in clarifying principles of church government on the anvil of controversy. In chapter 12, we delve into discussions about the role of the church during the American Civil War, and we will also examine the ecclesiology of Thornwell, Hodge, and Robinson. Stepping into the perilous waters of race relations will be covered in this chapter. How could it not? After all, we will be dealing with events surrounding the Civil War.

Part 4 is where the rubber meets the road, so to speak. In these final three chapters of the book, my goal is to discuss several areas where the Scripture's teaching about ecclesiology, specifically on the primary mission of the church, now assumes practical import for her practice. Therefore, Chapter 13 discusses the nature and limitations of church power. Chapter 14 ventures into the mission of the church and politics, the mission of the church and education. Due to space constraints, we will have to be suggestive and selective; however, the zealous reader who craves more can follow the trails in the footnotes to deeper studies on these topics. Chapter 15 concludes with the famous biblical passage in which Paul addresses Athenian citizens on the Aeropagus. This sublime sermon exemplifies his exquisite evangelism and ably pictures and embodies the positive principles in this book on the primary mission of the church. Throughout the book, I will argue that the mission is spiritual, which means that I will be describing *those things that are properly of and properly belonging to the church.*

# PART ONE

CHAPTER 2

# Old Testament, Genesis Foundations

We start with the beginning. If we are going to understand the role and authority of Christ's church, and individuals within the church and culture, then we must start at the beginning, with creation. This is the proper place to begin. What we will notice, from a study of beginnings, is that there are those who view all of life as 'political' and assert that no sharp bifurcation can be made between the spiritual and the political. Jonathan Leeman, in his well-organized and well-written book, would be a good example of such a view.[1] For example, in the section of his book where he is interacting with the so-called oracles of the nations, he says:

> Politics is always contained *inside* religion. A nation's gods determine its politics. First religion, then politics. The political always involves spiritual realities, and a people's spiritual state plays out in political terms, whether they live in harmony with the divine King's righteousness or in rebellion against him. There is no such thing as political or spiritual reality. Everything *is* political, because all of life is lived beneath the rule of God, incurring either his affirmation or judgment.[2]

In fairness to Leeman, he is making a particular point here in his book about how God judges the nations outside of Israel, which stand under

---

1. Jonathan Leeman, *Political Church: The Local Assembly as Embassy of Christ's Rule* (Downers Grove, IL: IVP Academic, 2016).

2. Ibid., 212 (emphasis his).

47

His rule and judgment, for their hubris even though they derive their authority from Him. However, this quote betrays his views which can simply be described as a 'one-kingdom' view. In other words, his view seems to conflate the spiritual and the civil realms which is not the view that I expounded in the last chapter: Jesus, the Son of God, rules over the kingdom of grace as a mediator who redeems, but He reigns over the civil realm, the kingdom of power, as the Second Person of the Godhead. In contrast to this view is another view which was hinted at in the quote from an ecclesiastical book of order at the end of the last chapter, and which says regarding the church and the state that 'They are planets moving in concentric orbits'.[3]

In this chapter, we will claim that Genesis advocates and teaches the latter view, not the former. It is true that God rules as king over His entire creation; however, He rules over His own chosen people in the Old Testament (OT) and the New Testament (NT) as mediator of the covenant of grace. Over the rest of creation through common grace, He rules as king, as the Second Person of the Godhead, to maintain a stable world in which He can gather His elect, preparing and perfecting them for entry into the world-to-come. Waters, in his book *How Jesus Runs the Church*, teaches basically this very point, although he avoids the term 'two kingdoms'. I'm guessing he does so because it has become a flashpoint regarding the subject of the church's relationship to the civil magistrate, or Christianity and culture. Instead, he invokes a distinction, found in the Westminster Shorter Catechism (WSC), between Jesus' *essential* dominion or reign and His *mediatorial* dominion or reign. Citing Ebenezer Erskine and James Fisher, two eighteenth-century Scottish commentators on the WSC:

Q. 17. How *manifold* is [Jesus'] kingdom?

A.     It is *twofold*; his *essential* and his *mediatorial* kingdom.

Q. 18. What is his *essential* kingdom?

A.     It is that absolute and supreme power, which he hath over all the creatures in heaven and earth, *essentially* and *naturally*, as God equal with the Father, Psal. ciii. 19, 'his kingdom ruleth over all–'

---

3. PCA, *Book of Church Order*, 3.4.

Q 19. What is his *mediatorial* kingdom?

A.    It is that sovereign power and authority in and over the *church*, which is given him as Mediator, Eph. i.22.[4]

This distinction between Jesus' reign over the entire universe as the Second Person of the Godhead and His mediatorial reign as the incarnate Son of God, the God-man, has a longstanding pedigree in the Reformed Christian tradition.[5] Sadly, it has often been merely associated with Lutheran theology; however, it is equally common in Reformed theology. It is the position expressed in the Westminster Confession of Faith.[6] I will discuss this in greater detail in Chapters 5 and 13 below; suffice it to say for now that this has its roots all the way back in Genesis.

Here, I take my cue from the great Princeton biblical scholar, Geerhardus Vos (1862-1949). Descended from the French Huguenots and having trained at Princeton Seminary in the late 1800s, he then went to Europe on a scholarship won at Princeton to study at the University of Berlin and the University of Strasbourg. He received his Doctor of Philosophy at the ripe age of twenty-six. Also worthy of mention is the fact that he had, as one of his privileges, the opportunity to study under one of the greatest Semitic scholars of his day, Theodor Nöldeke.[7] Vos returned to his alma mater (Princeton) to assume a chair in Biblical Theology. He taught there until his retirement thirty-nine years later.

Vos, in his attempts to understand the best way to approach God's unfolding plan of redemption, begins his work in the following manner:

> The main problem will be how to do justice to the individual peculiarities of the agents in revelation. These individual traits subserve the historical plan. Some propose that we discuss each book separately. But this leads to unnecessary repetition, because there is so much that all have in common. A better plan is to apply the collective treatment in the earlier stages of

4.  Guy Prentiss Waters, *How Jesus Runs the Church*, pp. 32-33.

5.  See David VanDrunen, *Natural Law and the Two Kingdoms*: *A Study in the Development of Reformed Social Thought*.

6.  See especially, John Fesko, *The Theology of the Westminster Standards*, pp. 299-314.

7.  For good biographical sketch of Vos, see Ransom Lewis Webster, 'Geerhardus Vos (1862-1949): A Biographical Sketch,' *WTJ* 40 (1978): pp. 304-17. Also see, more recently, *The Letters of Geerhardus Vos* (ed. James T. Dennison Jr.; Phillipsburg, New Jersey: P & R Publishing, 2005), pp. 13-85; and Danny E. Olinger, *Geerhardus Vos: Reformed Biblical Theologian, Confessional Presbyterian* (Philadelphia, PA: Reformed Forum, 2018).

revelation, where the truth is not as yet much differentiated, and then to individualize in the later periods where greater diversity is reached.[8]

Taking Vos' cue, the thesis of this chapter is this: all the foundational elements of a worldview in compliance with God's world and its interim structures, both the 'church' and the 'common kingdom', are provided in the first chapters of the Bible, specifically Genesis 1–15. This revelation applies to the theocratic specific applications found especially in the Mosaic covenant; but more importantly, also to the distinctions brought about by the instituting of common grace after the fall (Gen. 3–4) as a way of providing the soil, so to speak, upon which God will carry out his plan in redemptive history.

## Genesis 1–3: The Creation of the World, the Tale of One City and Its Priest-King

The Scriptures represent God as the Lord of Creation and History.[9] Indeed, the very structure of Genesis teaches a kind of philosophy of history. God operates and manifests His redemptive plan through families and through the covenant community which He institutionalizes and administrates; and, as we will see below, amid the common kingdom He carries out His intentions.

But not only is God king; according to Genesis 1:26, man also is created according to the *Imago Dei* with a royal function. This means that being created in the image of God centers around a royal authority with which God invested human beings.[10] Another aspect also informs our discussion of the doctrine of the primary mission of the church: the creation of the world at the beginning of time, a constructive process, is a reflection, a mirror if you will, of the temple of God and its predecessor, the tabernacle.[11] Indeed, the creation of the

---

8. Geerhardus Vos, *Biblical Theology*, p. 16.

9. See, for example, Charles H. H. Scobie, *The Ways of Our God: An Approach to Biblical Theology* (Grand Rapids: Eerdmans, 2003), pp. 106-08.

10. See part 1 of David VanDrunen's book, *Politics after Christendom: Political Theology in a Fractured World* (Grand Rapids, MI: Zondervan Academic, 2020). Also see pages 200-01 of the same.

11. This point is eloquently discussed by Jon D. Levenson, *Sinai & Zion: An Entry into the Jewish Bible* (San Francisco: Harper & Row, 1985), pp. 137-45.

world and the construction of the temple and the tabernacle stand in a complementary parallel relation to one another.[12] This relationship is not merely at the conceptual level but actually is represented at the linguistic level as well; in other words, a close study of the language of all the passages involved demonstrates that there is more than merely conceptual overlap – it permeates to the very language employed and thus moves beyond mere coincidence. When we turn to our treatment of the Noahic covenant below, we will observe in our description of the biblical theology of the image of God that the royal elements are repeated; however, in 'this context God added no priestly responsibility to promote holiness of the human community [as a whole].'[13]

Why is this important? It is important for several reasons. I will discuss this more in Chapter 14 below; however, for now a few points need to be made. First, it seems that after the fall God did not extend the priestly aspect of the original *imago dei* outside of redeemed communities.[14] It may also explain why it 'is not difficult to imagine why so many human rulers have usurped authority over the worship of the people they rule. It may express a pining for the original integration of royal and priestly functions lost in the fall and also a longing for its restoration.'[15] Second, it is important because it demonstrates that every human being should be treated with dignity. Third, it is important because it indicates that the creation at the beginning of time is a sacred space, just as the tabernacle and the temple were later recognized to be spaces of sacred presence. All the activities conducted by the first couple in the space were royal and holy because the place was holy: it was a prototypical sanctuary as will be discussed below.[16] Furthermore, the original couple not only had a royal mandate; they also had a priestly function to perform, as will be argued below. But this was discontinued after the fall for common humanity and reserved for the redeemed alone (cf., Exod. 19:5-6; 1 Pet. 2:9; Rev. 21:22-27).

---

12. Levenson, *Sinai & Zion*, pp. 141-44.

13. VanDrunen, *Political Theology*, p. 201.

14. Ibid.

15. Ibid.

16. For more detailed argumentation, see the author's *Echoes of Exodus: Tracing a Biblical Motif* (Downers Grove, IL: IVP Academic, 2018), pp. 63-67.

Genesis 1:26-28 becomes important in so many discussions connected with the mission of the church:

> Then God said, 'Let us make man in our image, after our likeness. And let them have dominion over the fish of the sea and over the birds of the heavens and over the livestock and over all the earth and over every creeping thing that creeps on the earth.'
>
> So God created man in his own image, in the image of God he created him; male and female he created them.
>
> And God blessed them. And God said to them, 'Be fruitful and multiply and fill the earth and subdue it and have dominion over the fish of the sea and over the birds of the heavens and over every living thing that moves on the earth' (ESV).

The mandate for the couple was to have royal dominion over the earth and fill the earth with their royal kind.[17] In Genesis 9, the fact that Noah's sinful progeny was to carry forth this mandate (9:1-7), does not mean that it was the same as the original mandate. Genesis 1:28 implies dominion over the plant and animal kingdom; this continues after the fall and other creative endeavors could be included in it.[18] However, the New Testament never repeats this mandate, interestingly.[19] Nevertheless, this is not a political goal after the fall; well it is not in the same way in which it carried weight before the fall.[20] Genesis 1:26-28 has played an important role in discussions about the functional outcome for human beings created in the image of God. Jonathan Leeman expresses it like this:

> In one way or another, that whatever it means to be created in God's image ontologically, the ontological serves the functional purpose of bringing God's dominion to the ends of the earth: as God's images (noun), Adam and Even image (verb) God. The form (image) informs the function (rule). The identify informs the office or vocation.[21]

---

17. Meredith G. Kline, *Kingdom Prologue: Genesis Foundations for a Covenantal Worldview* (Overland Park, KS: Two Age Press, 2000), p. 68.

18. See VanDrunen, *Political Theology*, pp. 216-17.

19. Ibid., p. 219.

20. *Pace* Jonathan Leeman, *Political Church*. Leeman sees the goal of Genesis 1:28 repeated to Abraham. He largely leans on NT Wright, McConville, and Greg Beale for development of this. For his development of the Noahic Covenant, he largely depends on Peter J. Gentry and Stephen J. Wellum, *Kingdom Through Covenant: A Biblical-Theological Understanding of the Covenants* (Wheaton, IL: Crossway, 2012).

21. Leeman, *Political Church*, pp. 158-59.

However, this sweeping generalization begs for further nuance, especially in light of the changing redemptive historical contexts. Leeman recognizes the kingly (i.e., ruling) and priestly function of the first pair, that is true.[22] However, I wish he had made more precise statements. His integration of new ideas from the burgeoning developments in 'new institutionalism' from political theorists and the manner in which he defines 'political' influence his constructions significantly. The priestly aspect of the original mandate was not repeated outside the redemptive community after the fall, as mentioned above. This is very important to maintain (see below, Chapter 14).

The goal initially in the garden was to move from a paradise home to a universal city.[23] Had Adam passed his probation, he would have been confirmed in righteousness, and he and Eve would (presumably) parent godly children, also confirmed in righteousness, children that would have no inclination to go astray because sin would have not entered the world. Their parents would have given them *direction* in the way, but they would not have needed *restraint*.[24] This point will become important when I discuss the role of the state to restrain sin below in this chapter, and in subsequent chapters.[25]

It is of vital importance to realize the changes that would happen to this so-called 'cultural mandate', not only with the advent of sin into the world but also after the flood, for much of the language of these verses are echoed in Genesis 9:1-7, and in later scripture as well, especially with Abraham and his children. This is noted by N. T. Wright, who says that as later tradition would put it [*Genesis Rabbah*], 'Abraham would be God's means of undoing the sin of Adam.'[26]

Wright addresses this very point in his writings about Jesus bringing about a 'new exodus.' In his book, *The Day the Revolution Began: Reconsidering the Meaning of Jesus's Crucifixion*, he writes about this.[27]

---

22. Ibid., p. 168.

23. Kline, *Kingdom Prologue*, p. 70.

24. T. W. Peck, *Notes on Ecclesiology* (Richmond, VA: Presbyterian Committee on Education, 1892), p. 140.

25. See, e.g., Chapter 14 especially.

26. N. T. Wright, *The Climax of the Covenant: Christ and the Law in Pauline Theology* (Minneapolis, MN: Fortress Press, 1991), p. 21.

27. See Wright, *The Day the Revolution Began: Reconsidering the Meaning of Jesus's Crucifixion* (San Francisco: HarperOne, 2016), pp. 263-94.

What he stated seminally in an earlier book (*Surprised by Hope*, 2008), he argues further in this work. He says: 'For Paul, exactly in line with Revelation and other early writings, the result of Jesus's achievement is a *new creation*, a new heaven-and-earth world in which humans can resume their genuinely human vocation as the "kingdom of priests," the "royal priesthood."'[28] But for Wright, this means that a major aspect of redemption is that the original human vocation of stewardship has been reestablished – 'the original project of creation is now at last back on track.'[29] But this generalization lacks precision, putting it lightly.

The way in which Greg Beale construes things is better. One of the greatest differences to note in light of changing historical and covenantal contexts, of course, is that the mandate given to Adam and Eve ('Be fruitful') is turned into a promise for Abraham ('I will make you fruitful'). Beale develops this even further by noting that the mandate before the fall is developed into a promise in which 'a remnant, created by God in his restored image, was to go out and spread God's glorious presence among the rest of darkened [i.e., fallen] humanity.'[30] What was command previously is now promise. God's presence would be with His people in order to help them accomplish this goal. In a real sense, we can speak of Genesis 1:28 as the first '"Great Commission," which was repeatedly applied to humanity' according to Beale.[31] Nevertheless, the new Great Commission is more closely aligned with the mission of the church as opposed to humanity in general. As mentioned above, this distinction is construed much differently in the book by Leeman. He maintains that 'Politics is distinct from religion, but not separate. When we fail to recognize this, we overtly separate these things, and eventually we overly spiritualize salvation and the life of the church.'[32] Leeman argues that 'Abraham inherits the Adamic citizenship mandate, a role that combines political and priestly concepts – a vice-regent who is consecrated to God and so rules by being ruled.'[33] Leeman, like Wright

---

28. Ibid., p. 268.

29. Ibid., p. 89.

30. See G. K. Beale, *A New Testament Biblical Theology: The Unfolding of the Old Testament in the New* (Grand Rapids, MI: 2011), pp. 46-58, but especially at p. 57.

31. Ibid.

32. Leeman, *Political Church*, p. 215.

33. Ibid., p. 216.

and Beale, recognizes the change in Adam to Abraham as a change from commands to promise.[34] Nevertheless, Leeman construes Abraham's obedience along 'political lines.'

The church is a *missions* organization, not in the common and customary way in which it is often construed as 'missional'; rather, it is God's chosen instrument for calling in the elect, making disciples of her members by perfecting them through Word and Sacrament as they prepare to enter the world-to-come. The original mandate given to Adam and Eve was not political *per se*, although Leeman, as just one significant example, prefers to label it a 'citizenship mandate.'[35] So too, the Great Commission (Matt. 28:28-20) is definitely not political, and its mandate more closely aligns with the church, as the church, than any other institution on earth. In short, political does not equal kingly, which was part of Adam's office as prophet, priest, and king.

## Genesis 2–3: The Sanctuary of God

The Garden of Eden was a prototypical sanctuary. As we turn to Genesis 2, we shall see that the garden was a 'localized place that is spatially separated from its outside world'.[36] It is here in Genesis 2 that 'Temple theology, which attests to the sovereign presence of God with his people, takes its rise in Eden.'[37] Adam was not only assigned the role of a vassal ruler in the Garden of Eden; he was also the prototypical priest who was to guard the sanctuary of God, which Eden undoubtedly was.[38] He was oriented toward the future, a climactic Sabbath rest, even in this original theocracy.

---

34. Ibid., p. 217.

35. Ibid., p. 163.

36. William J. Dumbrell, 'A Foreshadowing of the New Creation,' in *Biblical Theology: Retrospect and Prospect* (ed. Scott J. Hafemann; Downers Grove, Illinois: Intervarsity Press, 2002), p. 56.

37. Dumbrell, 'A Foreshadowing,' pp. 64-65.

38. For extensive argumentation and bibliography on this issue, see the author's, 'The Covenant of Works in Moses and Paul,' in *Covenant, Justification, and Pastoral Ministry: Essays by the Faculty of Westminster Seminary California*, ed. Scott Clark (Presbyterian and Reformed, 2006), pp. 89-135. Also see, Gordon J. Wenham, 'Sanctuary Symbolism in the Garden of Eden Story,' in *I Studied Inscriptions from Before the Flood*, ed. Richard S. Hess and David Toshio Tsummra (Winona Lake, IN: Eisenbrauns, 1994), pp. 399-404. Also see G. K. Beale, *The Temple and the Church's Mission: A Biblical Theology of the Dwelling Place of God*, New Studies in Biblical Theology 17; D. A. Carson, ed. (Downers Grove, IL: InterVarsity Press, 2004), pp. 81-99.

I am using theocracy in a manner that needs clarification. Theocracy entails the coalescence of God's rule, reign, and realm. Here the cultic (religious worship along the vertical plane) intersects with culture (mankind's horizontal cultural pursuits, including the political) to form a unique institution that arises at sundry times and in various epochs of redemptive history.

In Genesis 2:15, the text says that Adam was placed within the garden in order to *tend it and guard it*.[39] His primary responsibility as a priestly vassal king was to protect the garden, which was the sanctuary of God, from unholy intruders. Adam was not merely a farmer; he was a priest. This duty, as the story runs, Adam failed to discharge. The consequences were dire for him and Eve and the entire human race.[40] There was judgement and there was a common curse, common in that it fell upon all of Adam's descendants. But God was merciful to the human race. There was also the corollary blessing: common grace.

# Genesis 4–8: The Tale of Two Cities After the Fall

Genesis 4 is important for our understanding of the primary mission of the church. In some respects, the church has more in common with the community of God's people as recorded here and in the patriarchal narratives than in the vast material in the Hebrew Bible which would fall under the Mosaic economy. Furthermore, we see hints in this chapter of what will become even clearer in Genesis 9: God's instituting some of the major functions of what will become the common kingdom, common because it is the realm in which believers in the one true God, and those who are not, have to live together in peaceful harmony. Customarily, writers who take up this subject do not do so until Genesis 9; however, it is fratricide, the

---

39. The translation of these two verbs, especially the latter, is most often lost in English versions. The only other places in the Pentateuch where these two verbs occur together are in contexts where the Levites' duties include guarding and protecting the sanctuary. See Gordon J. Wenham, 'Sanctuary Symbolism in the Garden of Eden Story,' in *I Studied Inscriptions from before the Flood*, pp. 399-404. Wenham draws attention to Numbers 3:7-8; 8:26; 18:5-6.

40. See J. V. Fesko, *The Covenant of Works: The Origins, Development, and Reception of the Doctrine*, OSHT, Richard A. Muller ed. (Oxford, Oxford University Press, 2020); Harrison Perkins, *Catholicity and the Covenant of Works: James Usher and the Reformed Tradition*, OSHT, Richard A. Muller ed. (Oxford, Oxford University Press, 2020).

murder of one brother by another, that provides the context in which God places the element of restraint on vengeance as an element of common grace.

To recall briefly the previous section, the reader should notice that God is full of grace and mercy after the fall because he allows human beings to have a common kingdom even after breaking covenant with God. The story line is simple: Cain kills Abel after his brother offered a sacrifice more acceptable to God (Heb. 11:4). Cain now fears retribution and revenge from the kin of Abel because God declares that he will now be a 'vagrant and wanderer on the earth' (Gen. 4:12). What is the essence of Cain's lament, especially his concern to be hidden from the face of God? To be denied access to the face of God is 'to be abandoned to the mortal perils of a lawless world ... he will be denied God's judicial oversight.'[41] His fear is that he will be *ex lex* [outside law] on earth.[42]

What is God's response to this concern of Cain's? Verse 15 tells us: '"If anyone kills Cain, vengeance shall be taken on him sevenfold." And the LORD put a mark on Cain, lest any who found him should attack him' (ESV). God sets forth a solemn affirmation.

One Jewish scholar sums up well by saying that it:

> ... frequently introduces a solemn declaration, while the formulation of the reassurance derives from the realm of law. The unusually emphatic language is directed first to Cain, in order to allay his mortal fear, and then to the world at large, as a kind of royal proclamation that has the force of law. It states that despite his crime, Cain still remains under God's care.[43]

God is setting up a deterrent against unbridled vengeance. He says that Cain himself shall be avenged 'sevenfold' (*šib'ātayim*) if he is killed. This demonstrates that the stipulated retribution will be perfect, divine in origin and authority.[44] This is not to excuse Cain; however, it does set

---

41. Meredith G. Kline, 'Oracular Origin of the State,' 132-40, in *Biblical and Near Eastern Studies: Essays in Honor of William Sanford LaSor* (ed. Gary A. Tuttle; Grand Rapids, Michigan: Eerdmans, 1978), especially pp. 132-33. For further detail on this, see the author's *Echoes of Exodus*, pp. 70-76.

42. Kline, 'Oracular Origin,' p. 134.

43. Nahum M. Sarna, *The JPS Torah Commentary: Genesis* (Philadelphia, PA: Jewish Publication Society, 1989), p. 35.

44. Kline, 'Oracular Origin,' p. 135. Kenneth Mathews, *Genesis 1–11:26* (The new American Commentary v. 1A; Broadman & Holman Publishers, 2001), p. 278, says that seven is here a 'figure of speech meaning completeness or fullness expresses the certainty and severity of God's vengeance against a vigilante.'

a precedence for the future.[45] Genesis 4, therefore, 'expresses through narrative principles that are of fundamental importance in biblical law.'[46] George Mendenhall has noted the important political and legal overtones of the verbal root used here.[47] Consequently Cain, and the world at large, would not be subjected to lawless chaos, for it would be judicially structured. There would be restraint against evil by God's common grace. And of course that is Paul's charter for the state as well – it is a minister of God for good (Rom. 13:3-4). So what would Cain do when he went forth from the presence of the Lord? He built a city:

> Then Cain went away from the presence of the LORD and settled in the land of Nod, east of Eden. Cain knew his wife, and she conceived and bore Enoch. When he built a city, he called the name of the city after the name of his son, Enoch (Gen. 4:16-17).

Therefore, as Thomas Peck (1822-1893), an American minister, theologian, and recognized ecclesiastical leader in the Southern Prebyterian Church in the nineteenth century, expressed it: 'He and his family, therefore, may be regarded as the founders of the state, and of that complex material and worldly civilization which the state embodies and represents.'[48]

Even so, in Genesis 4, we see Lamech, one of the descendants of Cain, rise to power. Peck summarizes:

> They were the sons of *men*, acknowledging nothing higher than *human* wisdom and *human* power, and bending all their energies to the one end of concentrating the forces of humanity, and of securing in this way a worldly *summum bonum*, an all-comprehending good, which might compensate for the loss of the favor and communion of God, which they had deliberately

---

45. Calvin, *Commentaries on the First Book of Moses Called Genesis* (Grand Rapids, Michigan: Eerdmans, 1948), comments: 'The order of nature had been awfully violated; what might be expected to happen in future, when the wickedness and audacity of man should increase, unless the fury of others had been restrained by a violent hand? ... Therefore, the Lord declares, if any will imitate Cain, not only shall they have no excuse in this example, but shall be more grievously tormented; because they ought, in his person, to perceive how detestable is their wickedness in the sight of God.'

46. Gordon Wenham, *Genesis 1–15*, WBC 1 (Waco, Texas: Word Books, 1987), p. 117.

47. Quoted in Kline, 'Oracular Origin,' p. 136.

48. T. E. Peck, *Notes on Ecclesiology*, p. 121. Biographical information on Thomas E. Peck may be found in Morton Howison Smith, *Studies in Southern Presbyterian Theology* (Jackson, MS: Presbyterian Reformation Society, 1962), pp. 268-74.

repudiated. They thus prepared the way for the Babel-builders and for heathenism, which is a worship of nature and its forces, and particularly of the wisdom and power of the highest part of nature, *man*.[49]

Through an act of severe self aggrandizement on the part of Lamech, and with evil avarice and hubris, he tramples over the institution of marriage by taking unto himself two wives (v. 19). Then, he despises the good gifts of civil restraint by boasting of a life for a bruise (v. 23)!

But more important than this is the rise of the community of faith in the midst of that waxing evil generation. God raises—not from the line of Cain—but from Seth, the third son of Adam and Eve, a godly seed who 'call on the name of the LORD' (4:26). This common biblical idiom has to do with making the faith of the heart known in an external expression of worship, or even making known the name of the Lord among hostile peoples. Peck notes this significant development in contrast to the other line of men:

> It is worthy of note that over against this organization of society, and continuation of its forces in the line of the apostate Cain (the sons of men), occurs the record of something like the organization of the true worshippers of God …. But the time had not yet fully come for the organization of the church visible in correspondence with the state.[50]

Here, before the flood, we have an introduction to the common grace situation in ancient days, by which I mean the covenant community of God who bear God's name in the midst of the city of man. This is a crucial passage well-placed just before Genesis 5, a genealogical account leading up to Noah. The distinctive feature of these people in Genesis 5 is that they are God's people, for here are the Sethites. This section of Scripture reveals an analogous passage whose characteristics are similar to the covenant people of God in the present age of the church. Here in the pre-flood age, God had a plan to craft a people for himself. The very structure of the genealogy in Genesis 5 advertises the family structure of this cultic community, this altar-oriented people who call on the name of the Lord. In short you have a covenant community living and pilgrimaging in the midst of the common grace city of man. These earth dwellers, who are also looking for the city to come, whose builder and maker is in heaven

---

49. Ibid., p. 121-22 [emphasis original].
50. Ibid.

above, must live a hyphenated existence.[51] They are citizens of heaven by faith and pilgrim citizens in a world structured by common grace. What is the stance of the covenant community to be during this time of the common grace city of man? There are striking parallels between the situation of the Sethite community represented in Genesis 4:25–5:32 and our own age now. People, all people, are citizens of the world in which they find themselves. As such they are subject to that nation's laws or order.[52] Meredith G. Kline sums up well what the proper posture was:

> They should not then fix any false hopes on the future of the city of man. God's prophetic word heard in the midst of his prediluvian people became indeed an increasingly urgent warning of the imminent doom of that city. While, therefore, they were to have a breadth of *world-view* [emphasis mine] informed by the programmatic purposes of the common grace cultural mandate, it was important that they also possess a depth of historical insight into the mystery of iniquity developing within the city of man and that they keep alive an eschatological vision of the realization of creation's cultural goal in the distant coming of an eternal city as the final fruitage of the mystery of redemptive grace, revealed to them and working in them. Accordingly, though they must not neglect their part in building the common city, they were also to fulfill with eager hope their distinctive covenantal mission. *Though full citizens in the city of man, they were faithfully to maintain within it their altar to the name of Yahweh and remember that they were also citizens of his yet unseen heavenly city.*[53]

What is recorded here in redemptive history has so much instructive importance for later generations of God's people in non-theocratic political commonwealths. I vehemently disagree with the caricatures and misinformation about such a 'two-kingdoms' view that allegedly causes indifference to cultural engagement, e.g., 'This two-terrain doctrine is

---

51. I am indebted to Darryl Hart for this coined term, put to good effect. See Darryl Hart, *The Lost Soul of American Protestantism*, pp. 169-85; and idem, *A Secular Faith*, pp. 256.

52. This is not to deny that some Reformed theologians have seen a place for legitimate resistance and defying earthly rulers if they judged the behavior of a given ruler as violating biblical precepts. See, for example, Richard L. Greaves, *Theology and Revolution in the Scottish Reformation: Studies in the Thought of John Knox* (Grand Rapids, MI: Christian University Press, 1980), pp. 169-82; David VanDrunen, 'Power to the People: Revisiting Civil Resistance in Romans 13:1-7 in Light of the Noahic Covenant,' *JLR* 31, no. 1 (March 2016): pp. 4-18.

53. M. G. Kline, *Kingdom Prologue*, pp. 199-200. [emphasis mine]

not only contrary to the teachings of the Word, but it is actually also very dangerous in practice, since it leads to a tolerant neutralism and makes men indifferent to the demands of Christian warfare.'[54]

On the contrary, this altar-oriented people of God, whether they find themselves pilgrims in the pre-flood era, the time of the patriarchs, at the height of Roman civilization, or in the twenty-first century, always must recognize the general Lordship of God over every area of their lives. Even so, God can and does at certain points in history constitute holy kingdom institutions coexisting side by side with non-holy institutions, which will be discussed further below.

## Genesis 8:20–9:17: The Tale of Two Cities Retold

Genesis 8:20–9:17 recapitulates, in much greater detail, some of the same principles enunciated in Genesis 4, at least regarding civil restraint. Even so, much more is added to demonstrate God's concern for a stable world order, a platform on which He can work out His unfolding redemption. The covenant established here is a covenant of common grace, not redemptive grace, as I have argued elsewhere.[55] In other words, it is made with the common world, believers and unbelievers alike.

Although some theologians in the past have argued for the covenant in Genesis 9 being a common grace covenant,[56] it is the work of David VanDrunen that has advanced this goal more extensively than any in

---

54. See Henry R. Van Til, *The Calvinist Concept of Culture* (Grand Rapids, MI: Baker, 1959), p. 238.

55. See the author's *Echoes of Exodus*, pp. 83-85.

56. This is in distinction from the Covenant of Grace revealed elsewhere in which God promised salvation to his distinctive, chosen people through the atoning work of Jesus Christ. Some examples of significant Reformed theologians who interpret the Noahic covenant as a covenant of common grace include Herman Witsius, *The Economy of the Covenants between God and Man: Comprehending a Complete Body of Divinity*, 2 vols., trans. William Crookshank (1822; reprint, Phillipsburg: P&R, 1990), 2.239 (originally published in 1677); Wilhelmus à Brakel, *The Christian's Reasonable Service*, 4 vols., trans. Bartel Elshout (Ligonier, PA: Soli Deo Gloria, 1992-95), 4.384 (originally published in 1700); A. Kuyper, *De Gemeene Gratie* (Kampen: J. H. Kok, 1945), pp. 11-100 (originally published in 1902-04); Herman Bavinck, *Reformed Dogmatics*, vol. 3, *Sin and Salvation in Christ*, trans. John Vriend (Grand Rapids: Baker, 2006), pp. 218-19 (originally published in 1895-1901); and Meredith G. Kline, *Kingdom Prologue: Genesis Foundations for a Covenantal Worldview* (Overland Park, KS: Two Age Press, 2000), pp. 164, 244-46.

recent years.[57] In his book *Politics After Christendom* he has shown just how crucial the Noahic covenant is for a political theology, especially in the first six chapters.[58] Just to be clear, VanDrunen does not argue that the covenant with Noah (which he sees as beginning in 8:21 and extending through 9:17) gives a detailed blueprint for a Christian legal and political theory or even some concrete Christian policy agenda; rather, the Noahic covenant provides merely a framework for legal and political thinking. Since God had destroyed the world, there was a need to reestablish and reassert the structures of the world previously founded. Such an understanding is crucial for public policy, so to speak, in a fallen world from a Reformed perspective.[59] Its primary purpose is for the stability of the world while God advances His kingdom enterprise.[60]

VanDrunen identifies three basic characteristics of this covenant: it is universal, preservative, and temporary.[61] It is universal in that its purview is the whole world. It is preservative in that the purpose is to preserve the world in spite of residual evil, especially in the regulation of seasons (8:22) and the prevention (generally) of animals harming humans (9:2-4). Additionally, the Noahic covenant provides for human survival by reproduction (9:1, 7); regulations for eating (9:3-4); and perhaps, most importantly, the administration of justice (9:6). Notice that there is no blood transaction in this covenant unlike the redemptive covenant God made with Abraham. There is no promise to redeem anyone or anything. This is a more helpful, and I would claim more precise, way of stating things than other recent treatments. For example, Leeman suggests—due to his broadening of the term 'political', and God's covenantal rule over all of life—that this means for him that all

---

57. See especially, VanDrunen, *Divine Covenants and Moral Order: A Biblical Theology of Natural Law*, Emory University Studies in Law and Religion (Grand Rapids: Eerdmans, 2014), pp. 95-132; and idem, *Politics after Christendom*.

58. VanDrunen, *Politics After Christendom*, pp. 15-176.

59. See David VanDrunen, 'The Importance of the Penultimate: Reformed Social Thought and the Contemporary Critiques of the Liberal Society,' *Journal of Markets and Morality* 9, No. 2 (Fall, 2006): pp. 219-49.

60. In *Divine Covenants and Moral Order*, VanDrunen had argued for the Noahic covenant presented in Scripture as 8:20–9:17 (which is my view); however, in his new work, *Political Theology and Natural Law*, he suggests a switch to 8:21 since he thinks it provides a better starting point in hindsight.

61. VanDrunen, *Politics after Christendom*, pp. 61-65.

of life is political. Furthermore, he maintains that biblical covenants can be divided between common covenants (the Adamic and Noahic) and special covenants (Abrahamic, Mosaic, Davidic, and new covenants). He maintains that the common covenants *command* whereas the special covenants *give*. This is an oversimplification and causes distortion, I maintain, not only in the description of the covenantal system of the Bible but consequently also in the application of biblical teaching respecting the relationship of God's people to culture.[62] Although Leeman shows great appreciation for the nuanced position of those advocating a 'two kingdom' or 'two kinds of rule' approach, he stops short of grasping the biblical evidence. This becomes especially clear in his recent work:

> The God of creation is the King of the nations, and the King of the nations is the Redeemer of his people. It is one piece. He alone is God. He alone has rule. Surely he adopts different postures toward different people. Kings always do. But that is not to speak of two different kingdoms. Furthermore, the two-kingdoms division between God's 'creation rule' and his 'redemptive rule' does not adequately account for God's activity of judgment, and judgment goes to the heart of government and politics, as we observed above. Judgment is the flip side of redemption. And the two often occur in the same act …. The fact that God rules all things means there is no division, strictly speaking, between some so-called spiritual or religious domain and an alternative political domain.[63]

This is what I would call a failure to make precise a cult [religious]/ culture [political] distinction.

Notice that even the sign of this covenant (the rainbow) is vastly different from other covenantal signs, like circumcision, the Passover, baptism, or the Lord's supper. As VanDrunen says: 'The rainbow hangs bloodless in the sky (9:12,17). The Noahic covenant highlights the value of lifeblood (9:4-6), but it provides only for retribution when someone sheds it (9:6), not atonement. In short, the Noahic covenant does not promise to rescue anyone from final judgment. It simply promises to postpone it.'[64]

That last point segues nicely into VanDrunen's third point: the Noahic covenant is temporary. Note that the promise for the existence of this covenant only extends as long as the earth remains (8:22). At the

62. Leeman, *Political Church*, p. 180-88 [emphasis his].

63. Ibid., p. 211.

64. VanDrunen, *Politics after Christendom*, p. 64.

second advent of Christ, this covenant will cease and common grace, the common kingdom, will come to an end. Therefore, this covenant cannot be the one where we look for the origination of the church, let alone principles that specify its authority and its primary mission. The Noahic covenant says nothing about redemption, the Messiah to come, or salvation. However, after the fall and, more conspicuously yet, in the days of the patriarchs we have an explanation of such a promise of a redemptive kingdom. The language of Genesis 9:1-7 demonstrates that this is not 'a simple reinstituting of the creation ordinances but a revision of them in the common grace mode.'[65] Both Leeman and VanDrunen are careful to maintain that Genesis 9 does not establish a government, *per se*; however both see the principles for government established here, and Leeman goes so far as to claim 'that he [God] gives human beings (1) an *obligation* that will best be fulfilled in society by forming or supporting a government and (2) the *authority* to do this.'[66]

We will have much more to say about the Noahic covenant as we proceed; however, for now, note the following important principle: the redemptive community are citizens looking forward to the world-to-come, a city-reality not yet revealed in its entirety, while at the same time remaining full citizens in the present world, striving to live peaceably with those that are not citizens of the world-to-come. Indeed, as citizens of faith looking forward, they still have to walk and sleep with one eye open to the city of man, ever potentially inclining towards a more bestial nature. After the genealogies described in Genesis 10, we see just such a thing arise:

> The spirit of the beastly serpent shows itself in the builders of 'Babel' (a name which, from that time forward, becomes a symbol of the power of *man* in opposition to the power of God, and, therefore, of man as abdicating the dignity of his nature and becoming a 'beast'), who renew the experiment of their forerunners, the posterity of Cain, the experiment of living without God by combining the individual forces of man (see Genesis xi. 1, 4). They built a city and a tower, to make themselves a *name*. They become worshippers of men instead of God; not man as an individual, weak and mortal, but *associated* man.[67]

65. Kline, *Kingdom Prologue*, p. 251.
66. Leeman, *Political Church*, p. 189 [emphasis original].
67. Peck, *Notes on Ecclesiology*, p. 122. [emphasis original].

Therefore, we can see in narrative form, the conflict of the ages playing out.

## The Covenant of Grace after the Fall, rooted in the Pactum Salutis: Genesis 3:15 and following

The church cannot be born out of a covenant that was intended to be common. Therefore, the church did not spring forth out of the Noahic covenant; rather, it was born out of heaven itself. Such is the portrayal of Stuart Robinson, a nineteenth century Presbyterian, when he argued that this was the essence of a true biblical ecclesiology, perhaps a subject that he grappled with from a young age as well as in his mature years, and who, according to no-one less than Thomas Peck, succeeded with as 'much success as has been allotted to many other great men'.[68] For Robinson, the covenant of redemption is the proper starting point for ecclesiology.[69] What is the covenant of redemption? John Fesko offers the following definition:

> The covenant of redemption is the pre-temporal, intra-trinitarian agreement among Father, Son, and Holy Spirit to plan and execute the redemption of the elect. The covenant entails the appointment of the Son as surety of the covenant of grace who accomplishes the redemption of the elect through His incarnation, perfect obedience, suffering, resurrection, and ascension. The covenant of redemption is also the root of the Spirit's role to anoint and equip the Son for His mission as surety and to apply His finished work to the elect.[70]

In the history of the church, there have been two approaches or models in discussing the doctrine – one Trinitarian and the other Christological.[71] While I will not enter into that discussion in any detail here, the reader will note that some of the writers I quote below are following the Christological approach, whereas a robust thicker formulation of the

---

68. Thomas E. Peck, 'A Memorial of the Life and Labors of the Rev. Stuart Robinson,' reprinted in *The Church of God as an Essential Element of the Gospel, and the Idea, Structure, and Function in Four Parts* (Willow Grove, PA: The Committee on Christian Education of the Orthodox Presbyterian Church, 2009), pp. 201-23, especially at p. 204.

69. Stuart Robinson, *The Church of God*, pp. 34-37.

70. For a treatment of historical origins, the primary exegetical passages, and dogmatic construction of the doctrine, see J. V. Fesko, *The Trinity and the Covenant of Redemption* (Fearn, Ross-shire: Mentor, 2016), pp. 131-32.

71. Ibid., p. 3.

doctrine would make space to include the Spirit's role within the *pactum* itself.[72] For example, if the proper starting point for our understanding of the church is the covenant of redemption, as Robinson suggests, then we should note the Father's role to 'Reward the Son by enabling Him to send out the Holy Spirit for the gathering of His body, the church, and for the church's instruction, guidance, and protection (John 14:26; 15:26; 16:13-14; Acts 2:33).'[73]

In this covenant, the Father entered into covenantal arrangement with the Son with reference to the salvation of mankind. The covenant of grace in history was founded upon the covenant made between the Father and the Son. As Berkhof says: 'The counsel of redemption (i.e., the *pactum salutis* or eternal covenant of redemption) is the eternal prototype of the historical covenant of grace.'[74]

Some would affirm this covenant by means of prooftexts. Others, like Charles Hodge, would proceed by means of defining a covenant first so that when 'one person assigns a stipulated work to another person with the promise of a reward upon the condition of the performance of that work, there is a covenant.'[75] If you take this view of a covenant, then nothing could be plainer than that the tasks, together with the rewards promised by God the Father to the Son, is clearly nothing less than a covenant: (a) God gives the Son a work to do, (b) He sends Him into the world to do it, and (c) He promises a great reward if He will indeed accomplish the work (on behalf of the elect). The only means that can bring sinners into communion with God is through union with Christ, and union with Christ, as Fesko claims, begins not in the application of redemption but in the *pactum salutis*.[76]

Important and necessary distinctions arise at just this juncture. Many theologians could be cited here; however, perhaps none is

---

72. Ibid., e.g., pp. 135-36.

73. Ibid., 137-38. See also, pp. 173-180, where the Spirit's role in the fulfillment of the *pactum* is also discussed in terms of mission and procession (along with pp. 319-334), which is rooted and grounded in love (pp. 181-93).

74. Berkhof, *Systematic Theology*, p. 270. For a short essay on the doctrine, see David VanDrunen and R. Scott Clark, 'The Covenant before the Covenants,' in *Covenant, Justification, and Pastoral Ministry: Essays by the Faculty of Westminster Seminary California*, edited by R. Scott Clark (Phillipsburg, NJ: P & R, 2007), pp. 167-96.

75. Hodge, *Systematic Theology*, Vol. 2.360.

76. Fesko, *The Trinity and the Covenant of Redemption*, p. 23.

clearer on the subtleties at this point than Meredith G. Kline. After his discussion of the failed covenant of works, Kline takes pains to discuss the Redemptive Covenant in the Old World (before the flood) and makes a programmatic statement for Redemptive Covenants in the Old World and the New (after the flood). He begins by speaking of the covenant between the persons of the divine being, which has been variously called *Pactum Salutis*, the counsel of peace, or the covenant of redemption. It is simply the intra-trinitarian pact of salvation. Kline summarizes it in the following manner:[77]

### a. eternal covenant

(1) In the eternal covenant [the covenant of redemption, or *pactum salutis*], the Son is assigned the role of covenant servant.

(2) The second party is the Son in His status as 2nd Adam [Christ], included along with Him then, are the elect, whom He represents and them exclusively.

(3) *The operative principle here is works.*

Although this arrangement construes the covenant of redemption in terms of the Father and the Son, other passages could be invoked to demonstrate the Spirit's role in the *pactum* as well but are beyond the purview of this introduction.[78] Such an arrangement seems clearly set forth in our Lord's prayer: 'I glorified you on earth, having accomplished the work that you gave me to do. And now, Father, glorify me in your own presence with the glory that I had with you before the world existed' (John 17:4-5). Here, Jesus, the second Adam, could stand after His probation, having passed the most severe trials, and ask that the grant of glory be given which was promised beforehand. But the covenant of redemption is integrally related to the historical administrations of the covenant of grace. This eternal covenant of God forms a vital link to how He executes its design in time.[79] The *pactum* is the foundation of the covenant of grace in history, in which the voluntary obedience of

---

77. Adapted from Kline, *Kingdom Prologue*, p. 138.

78. See, for example, Fesko's discussion in *The Trinity and the Covenant of Redemption*, pp. 104-05.

79. Herman Bavinck, *Reformed Dogmatics: Sin and Salvation in Christ* (Grand Rapids, MI: Baker Academic, 2006), 3.215.

the Son would secure everlasting life for the elect.[80] So how should we construe its parties and its operating principles? [81]

> *b. historical administrations: the temporal, the gospel administration*
>
> (1) The messianic Son is Lord and Mediator of the covenant.
>
> (2) The second party is the Church, the community of confessors of the faith, their children and even those besides the elect.
>
> (3) *The operative principle is grace.*

Against this backdrop, we are now postured to speak about the covenant of grace after the fall. For this we begin in Genesis 3:15-21, where we read of the Gospel of Redemptive Judgment. God promises that Satan would be punished (reprobated) in this section of Scripture, but there would be enmity between the seed of the woman and the seed of the Serpent throughout history. Moreover, the pangs of childbirth and the toil of the earth would fall upon humans from now on in history. Nevertheless, Eve would become the 'mother of all living'. The Messiah would eventually come and crush the head of Satan:

> By his obedience in the earthly probation phase of his eternal covenant of works the champion [the Messiah] of the woman's seed would open the way for the Covenant of Grace, whose proper purpose is to bring salvation to the rest of the woman's seed and to bestow on them the kingdom of the Glory-Spirit won by their kinsman-redeemer. Indeed, in suffering the bruising of his heel the messianic seed would ratify this new covenant.[82]

Before the fall there was only a works arrangement. Notice the sharp contrast between the covenantal arrangement before the fall and the covenantal arrangement after the fall. This is no small distinction. It is crucial. The Westminster Confession of Faith (chap. 7.1-3) says it like this:

> The distance between God and the creature is so great, that although reasonable creatures do owe obedience unto him as their Creator, yet they could never have any fruition of him as their blessedness and reward, but by

---

80. Fesko, *The Trinity and the Covenant of Redemption*, p. 241.

81. Also adapted from Kline, *Kingdom Prologue*, p. 138.

82. Kline, *Kingdom Prologue*, p. 145.

some voluntary condescension on God's part, which he hath been pleased to express by way of covenant.

The first covenant made with man was a covenant of works, wherein life was promised to Adam; and in him to his posterity, upon condition of perfect and personal obedience.

Man, by his fall, having made himself incapable of life by that covenant, the Lord was pleased to make a second, commonly called the covenant of grace; wherein he freely offereth unto sinners life and salvation by Jesus Christ; requiring of them faith in him, that they may be saved, and promising to give unto all those that are ordained unto eternal life his Holy Spirit, to make them willing, and able to believe.

Deliverance in this Covenant of Grace occurs at two levels now: people are saved from the hostility of Satan, and they will receive redemption. They will be saved from the wrath of God because of the penalty paying substitution of the Messiah and by grace through faith.

The third aspect taught here is the one that Robinson wanted to foreground as the foundation for the church: election. Kline points out that Adam gave his confessional 'Amen' to the Lord's provision of a future Messiah.[83] But it was the future Messiah who would be the surety, the guarantor of the blessings of the covenant of grace for them. Here is the doctrine of sovereign redemptive grace in the Garden of Eden. The Second Adam would in no ways lose any of those for whom He was willing to suffer the bruising on the heel. All those who were given to Him, for whom He not only endured the passion of the cross but for those whom He won by virtue of His fulfilling the works performed in His own probation, they must be given to Him, and none of them, no none of them, will slip away. It was this act of election 'defined at once the design of the Son's work of atonement and his corresponding just reward from the Father. Implicitly included too was an assurance of the sovereign operation of the Spirit, infallibly effecting what the Father promised the Son in their eternal covenant.'[84]

## The Covenant of Grace Retold

All historical administrations of this covenant inaugurated in Genesis 3 onwards are based on a principle of grace, even though they are

---

83. M. G. Kline, 'Abram's Amen,' *WTJ* 31 (1968/69): pp. 1-11.

84. Kline, *Kingdom Prologue*, p. 149.

administered through a series of distinct covenants.[85] This covenant is redemptive. Just as we laid out characteristics of the Noahic covenant above, it is helpful to demonstrate that this covenant has set characteristics as well. VanDrunen identifies four, and interestingly they are opposite of the Noahic covenant: 'it concerns religious faith and worship (rather than ordinary cultural activities), it embraces a holy people that is distinguished from the rest of the human race …, it bestows the benefits of salvation …, and it is established forever and ever.'[86]

The Abrahamic covenant is announced in Genesis 12:1-3:

> Now the LORD said to Abram, 'Go from your country and your kindred and your father's house to the land that I will show you. And I will make of you a great nation, and I will bless you and make your name great, so that you will be a blessing. I will bless those who bless you, and him who dishonors you I will curse, and in you all the families of the earth shall be blessed' (ESV).

This covenant is first and foremost about Abraham's faith, not his common cultural activities. It is not about Abraham's covenant fidelity or faithfulness; rather, it is about Abraham believing in an alien righteousness, not his own righteousness as evidenced in its ratification in Genesis 15.[87] God does not only promise to give him offspring through his own son (15:4). God is not only gracious to give him this promise through words; God also accommodates to give him assurance of this promise through a visible sign: just as the heavens are numerous with stars, so shall his offspring be (15:5). Then, in one of the most significant verses for the Protestant doctrine of justification,

---

85. In my view, the Mosaic covenant is part of the administration of the covenant of grace (cf. WCF 7:5-6); however, the Mosaic economy had a typological works principle embedded in it. This can be evidenced in the manner that the Westminster Divines referred to the Mosaic economy. They use the term *law* to refer to the Sinai covenant-administration by way of synecdoche (in which a part is taken for the whole), probably because they recognized the frequency with which the law was referenced when speaking of the Mosaic covenant and the rigor and fullness with which it was applied (e.g., OT saints were bound to the whole law whereas NT saints are bound only to the Moral). See Westminster Confession of Faith 25.2, 7:5-6 and WSC 27. Also nuanced and helpful is *The Commentary of Dr Zacharias Ursinus on the Heidelberg Catechism* (Phillipsburg, NJ: Presbyterian and Reformed, n.d.), pp. 98-100.

86. David VanDrunen, *Living in God's Two Kingdoms*, pp. 82-88.

87. See John Fesko's helpful discussion in *Death in Adam, Life in Christ: The Doctrine of Imputation* (Fearn, Ross-shire: Christian Focus, 2016), pp. 161-63.

Scripture records: 'And he believed the Lord, and he counted it to him as righteousness' (15:6).

This covenant was unilateral in character. God will make good on his oath, symbolized by the smoking firepot passing through the cleft animal. This physical gesture was self-imprecatory in its substance. Is this covenant as unstable as the covenant of works? By no means! As Bavinck says, 'No, this covenant does not falter; *people* may become unfaithful, but *God does not* forget his promise.'[88] This does not mean that this covenant does not impose obligations on the receiving party. Not 'as conditions for entering into the covenant (for the covenant was made and based only on God's compassion), but as the way the people who had been incorporated into the covenant had to conduct themselves.'[89]

Second, this Abrahamic covenant is about God crafting a people for Himself in distinction from the rest of the human race.[90] As Deuteronomy 7:6 said: 'For you are a people holy to the Lord your God. The Lord your God has chosen you to be a people for his treasured possession (*segullah*), out of all the peoples who are on the face of the earth' (see also Deut. 14:2; 26:18; Ps. 135:4; Mal. 3:17). This term, *segullah*, was a term pregnant with meaning since we now understand it more due to its Akkadian cognates.[91] It signified a cherished treasure.

Third, this covenant, in contrast to the Noahic covenant, bestows salvation upon Abraham and all those who believe in God's promise by faith. More particularly, Genesis 15:6 becomes the cornerstone of Paul's doctrine of the imputed righteousness of Christ to the one who exercises the gift of faith.[92]

Fourth, and finally, this covenant is meant to last forever vis-à-vis the Noahic covenant, which as we observed previously, is only temporary.[93] This covenant is indissoluble.[94]

---

88. Bavinck, *Reformed Dogmatics*, 3.204.

89. Ibid.

90. VanDrunen, *Living in God's Two Kingdoms*, p. 83.

91. See Moshe Held, 'A Faithful Lover in an Old Babylonian Dialogue,' *Journal of Cuneiform Studies* 15 (1961), pp. 11-12 and Moshe Greenberg, 'Hebrew *segullah* and Akkadian *sikiltu*,' *Journal of the American Oriental Society* 71 (1951), pp. 172-74.

92. Fesko, *Death in Adam*, pp. 198-207.

93. VanDrunen, *Living in God's Two Kingdoms*, p. 84.

94. Bavinck, *Reformed Dogmatics*, 3. pp. 204-05.

## Conclusion

In this chapter I have laid the foundations for the biblical teaching on the primary mission of the church. Ultimately the bedrock of this church finds its origins in the intratrinitarian pact of salvation in eternity past. However, in the gospel administration of this covenant in history, God deigns for His people to be citizens participating in both a redemptive covenant and a non-redemptive covenant: the so-called covenant of grace and the Noahic covenant. Therefore, they have a dual citizenship, one sacred and one secular. This is very similar to Calvin's two kingdoms theology, which arose from his view of creation, the fall, and the restoration of the world. Matt Tuininga summarizes:

> All of life falls under the lordship of the ascended Christ and is subject to his law, but Christ exercises his lordship in two different ways, one preservative (the political order), and the other restorative (the spiritual kingdom). In the latter kingdom, which Calvin identifies with the church, human beings are regenerated by the word and Spirit such that they voluntarily submit themselves to the love and justice of God. In hope, they begin to experience the perfect liberty, equality, and peace that characterize Christ's kingdom. At the same time, they continue to serve God in a fallen, temporal world, whose institutions and cultural phenomena, though destined by Christ's providence and law, are destined to pass away.[95]

This great charter for the two cities has continued through the ages, albeit sometimes obscured by the less pristine plans of men. It does not follow that the member's faith of the redemptive community has no bearing on their involvement in the earthly kingdom, as if a Christian could keep his faith out of certain spheres of life. What is necessary, however, are precise distinctions about *how* individual Christians, let alone the corporate church, should conduct themselves in the secular sphere. However, this discussion remains for future chapters.

---

95. Tuininga, *Calvin's Political Theology and the Public Engagement of the Church: Christ's Two Kingdoms*, Cambridge Studies in Law and Christianity, John Witte, Jr. Series editor (Cambridge: Cambridge University Press, 2017), p. 140.

# CHAPTER 3

# Joseph in the Court of a Foreign King

In the last chapter I argued that understanding the primary mission of the church should begin by exploring the origination of the plan for God's church in eternity. Then history began, so to speak, even though technically eternity is outside of time. Adam and Eve failed in their probation. Since the fall, I argued from Genesis 4 and 8:20–9:17 that God had established interim world structures in such a way that God's redeemed people find themselves in a situation of dual citizenship based upon the fact that they are members of the covenant of grace and the Noahic covenant, one sacred and one secular. They live a hyphenated existence.

Of course it is not as though one has nothing to do with the other. Rather, each covenant demands certain obligations and conduct. Each has certain God-given authority structures. In this chapter, we fast forward to two examples of how Jews in the OT conducted themselves in empires other than their own: Joseph in this chapter and Daniel in the next. These examples have similarities and dissimilarities to our own situation as Christians in the new covenant church. We must always respect what Vos called the 'principle of periodicity when we interpret the Scriptures'.[1] By this he meant we should interpret each portion of Scripture in accordance with the covenantal age and historical situation in which it is embedded.

---

1. Geerhardus Vos, *Biblical Theology*, pp. 16.

What these narratives have in common is that they occur in the court of a foreign king. Joseph finds himself in the court of Pharaoh after the ruse of his cruel brothers. Daniel as a Jew in the Babylonian exile must deal with various rulers under whom he serves as a godly Jew. Both are away from the land of promise. Joseph's history is before the conquest and establishment of the theocracy (even though its narrative is largely preparing us for the theocracy). Daniel is after the monarchy.

Of course, that generalizing comment should not overshadow the realities of the differences in their experience and covenantal situation and ours. For example, the Joseph narrative in many respects occurs in Scripture in order to prepare us for the paradigmatic event of salvation in the OT: the exodus, which includes the liberation from Egypt all the way into the entrance and conquest of the promised land.

Additionally, books which discuss life in the exile, which would include Daniel, do not resolve the issues that the prophets introduced into the Scripture during the monarchy, that is the kind of excess of promises and a desire for resolution that is embedded in the Hebrew Bible: the Sinaitic covenant, the theocracy, even the restoration — beggarly as it was—cannot accomplish the Abrahamic and prophetic promises on their own. There awaits a greater fulfillment, which must come with the Messiah.[2]

Even so, in comparison to the theocracy of Israel, there are many more similarities to the church age as far as the situation of the pilgrim people of God having to live a hyphenated existence in this common grace world than the condition of the Israelites in Canaan, dispossessing the Canaanites and setting up a 'body politic.'[3]

It may seem surprising, however, that the lives of those saints before the theocracy (Joseph) and monarchy and in exile outside the promised land (Daniel) have more grist for the mill on principles for the ecclesiology of the New Testament church than many narratives throughout the Hebrew Bible, which speak to the situation of the theocracy.

---

2. See the author's, *Echoes of the Exodus*, p. 242.

3. The language is taken from Chad Van Dixhoorn's, *Confessing the Faith: A Reader's Guide to the Westminster Confession of Faith* (Carlisle, PA: Banner of Truth, 2014), p. 243. Van Dixhoorn's book has the most reliable text historically to date.

## Establishing the Genre

Genre classification helps us understand how to read literature. It gives us a 'reading strategy' and cues us into the intentions of an author or narrator of a book. Genre also helps us not to misread books. Although there was no handbook on genre identification in the ancient Near East (like what survives of Aristotle's *Poetics*, for example), OT scholars recognize that it is important to make observations about similarities between texts in order to generate categories that orient us as readers. Both of the narratives I've selected have significant overlapping similarities. The *high* court setting of Daniel and Genesis 37–50 have led to an identification of these stories as falling into the genre of 'court legend'.[4] We need not follow Will's definition of legend who follows in the wake of Gunkel and folklorists in demurring from the historicity of the accounts.[5] Nevertheless, the definition of 'court' is more helpful for 'In Asia Minor, Mesopotamia, and Israel, the power of the centralized court evidently captured the imagination of the masses in a way that is not true, for example, in mainland Greece.'[6]

A mass of material is available illustrating the elaborate royal court etiquette that was employed in the great empires of the Ancient Near East, especially in Persia. This historical evidence shows that a certain protocol was required on entering the king's presence. Another aspect that is common to these narratives, but that has been disputed and controversial, is that both of these characters—Joseph and Daniel—exhibit a degree of wisdom. Pharaoh, for example, claims that that 'there is no one so discerning and wise' as Joseph in Genesis 41:39 (וְחָכָם כָּמֹךָ אֵין־נָבוֹן). However, the probable correct nuanced interpretation of this is not a quality that Joseph possessed before the dream interpretation

---

4. See Lawrence M. Wills, *The Jew in the Court of the Foreign King: Ancient Jewish Court Legends*, Harvard Dissertations in Religion 26 (Minneapolis, MN: Fortress, 1990). Another important court narrative is included in this group: the tale of Ahiqar. Ahiqar was a wise counselor to Assyrian monarchs; the tale was one of the most renowned stories in the ancient world. The figure of Ahiqar is known from many different sources as the chief counselor to the Assyrian kings Sennacherib and Esarhaddon. We will not embark on a discussion of this important text. The authoritative study of this work and its influence on Scripture is by Michael Weigl, *Die amaräischen Achikar-Sprüche aus Elephantine und die alttestamentliche Weisheitsliteratur*, BZAW 399 (Berlin: de Gruyter, 2010).

5. Ibid., pp. 14-15.

6. Ibid., p. 19.

but the fact that God had uniquely enabled him to interpret the dream, and because of that he is uniquely fitted to the task of government.[7] Daniel is repeatedly compared to the wise men of Babylon (Dan. 1:20; 4:15 MT; and 5:11-16).

Although there has been a long-standing debate among biblical scholars with respect to the influence of wisdom literature and categories on these narratives, it is not immediately germane to my argument here, so we will not touch on the debate. Rather, in the next two chapters we will begin to explore these court narratives. First, we will deal with the Joseph story in this chapter, then proceed with Daniel in the next.

## The Joseph Narrative[8]

Joseph is a type of Christ. Summing up Stephen's speech in Acts 7, Nils A. Dahl writes, 'In Stephen's speech Moses and, to some extent, Joseph are seen as types of Christ, but the typology is subordinated to the recurring pattern of prophecy and fulfillment.'[9] Joseph may also be an antitype of Adam, something beyond what can be developed here.[10] That's a good summary of the importance of the Joseph narrative; however, our immediate interest is considering principles of ecclesiology as we continue to reflect upon the primary mission of the church.

Although the patriarchs were distinctive in many respects compared with Christians in the NT age, reading the patriarchs should find much resonance with Christians because they too were to be 'patient pilgrims in this world' and it was not a time to dispossess the Canaanites.[11] During this era, the Hebrews could enter into economic relations, covenantal contracts and even military confederations (e.g., Gen. 14:13, 24; 21:22ff.; 23:3-18: 26:26ff.) with surrounding nations. Unlike the time

---

7. See the excellent chapter by Stuart Weeks, *Early Israelite Wisdom* (Oxford: Oxford University Press, 1994), pp. 92-109, especially at p. 104.

8. Some of the ideas expressed in this section originally appeared in the author's article, 'Motifs and Old Testament Theology,' *Unio Cum Christi: Studies in Old Testament Biblical Theology* Vol. 5, No. 1 (April 2019): pp. 27-44.

9. Nils Alstrup Dahl, *Jesus in the Memory of the Early Church* (Minneapolis, MN: Augsburg, 1976), p. 73.

10. Lindsay Wilson, *Joseph Wise and Otherwise: An Interaction of Wisdom and Covenant in Genesis 37-50* (Carlisle: Paternoster, 2004), pp. 231-32.

11. Meredith G. Kline, *Genesis: A New Commentary* (Peabody, Mass: Hendrickson, 2016), p. 56.

of the theocracy in Canaan, this epoch was an age of common grace, a time of pilgrim politics.[12] For four centuries there was a postponement of the conquest. The people of God were placed in the schoolhouse of discipleship, they were to be 'cultivating common grace relationships' and learning how to be good neighbors.[13] Fast forwarding the time clock to Joseph, M. G. Kline sums it up this way:

> Outstanding in this regard was the career of Joseph in Egypt (Gen. 40:14ff.; cf. 47:7, 10). The appropriate attitude towards the world realm in which they found themselves was to be one of prayerful solicitude for its peace and prosperity, such as Jeremiah recommended to the Israelites in Babylonian exile (Jer. 29:7) and Paul to the Christians in the Roman world of his day (1 Tim. 2:2). Agreeably, Abraham prayed for king Abimelek (Gen. 20:7, 17) and Jacob blessed the pharaoh (Gen. 47: 7, 10).[14]

Therefore, there are indeed many lessons and applications that can be learned by the Christian during the new covenant church age despite the obvious differences between these pilgrims in Egypt and our own common grace situation. Even so, the believing Hebrews, plopped down in a common grace empire not their own, provide much grist for the way of discipleship for NT Christians. For example, in 'proposing measures for the relief of Egypt, Joseph showed the kind of concern God's people are to have for the general welfare of humanity in the common grace world.'[15] This is a carefully restrained claim: not claiming that Joseph is set forth as an idealized character, a wise model to emulate because of the didactic design of the text.[16]

One thing is clear when reading Genesis and arriving at chapter 37: 'the story appears to reflect a different world, in which interest and delight in the foreign court of Egypt is evident.'[17] Another feature which jumps out is the fact that direct intervention from God is virtually absent from the Joseph story. So who is this narrative about

---

12. Ibid., p. 83.

13. Meredith G. Kline, *God, Heaven, and Har Magedon: A Covenantal Tale of Cosmos and Telos* (Eugene, OR: Wipf and Stock, 2006), p. 104.

14. Ibid.

15. Kline, *Genesis: A New Commentary*, p. 126.

16. See Weeks, *Early Israelite Wisdom*, p. 96 for a critique of views like this to illustrate such 'a jejune truism.'

17. Wilson, *Joseph Wise and Otherwise*, pp. 45-46.

that extends from 37:2 up through chapter 50? If 37:2 is one of our primary indicators, as the beginning of this long section, then it appears that the narrator wants us to focus on Jacob and Joseph, the only two people mentioned here. In fact, a plausible argument can be made that the communicative focus is on Joseph since the narrative opens with Joseph's position in Jacob's family (37:2-4) and the narrative concludes with his death (50:26), which is a very neat way to conclude a story and quite a common one when it comes to biblical literature.[18] He will spend thirteen long years in Egypt before his rise to the highest levels of power and authority in Egypt.

An immediate question presents itself at this point: is Joseph a kind of tattletale on his brothers, which would not be in keeping with the kind of wisdom that Proverbs enjoins? Probably his bad report about his brothers, including Dan, Naphtali, Gad, and Asher, was motivated by his desire to be more a purveyor of truth and revealing his first loyalty to his father.[19] However, the narrator is somewhat coy here and doesn't reveal whether Joseph's character should be read in either a positive or negative manner; he only encourages the reader to read on. Joseph is marked out as Jacob's favorite with the gift of the multi-colored coat; meanwhile his brothers hate him. When Joseph has a dream and he tells it to his brothers, the brothers hate him even more. You can almost hear their speech dripping with sarcasm as they see him approaching from a distance and say, 'Here comes the master of dreams (בַּעַל הַחֲלֹמוֹת).' Almost all of the characterization focus in this opening chapter is on the brothers (consistently negative), not Joseph. His character development will have to wait for the narrator to disclose in later chapters.[20]

Often Genesis 38 is not considered as part of the Joseph narrative (37, 39-50), since Joseph does not appear nor is he even mentioned.[21] However, the narrative effect of placing the story of Judah and Tamar here may be to build suspense by slowing down the plot.[22] Wilson

18. Ibid.

19. Ibid., p. 55.

20. Ibid., p. 72.

21. For a good summary of how narrative critics have shaken up the propensity to reposition this apparently disjunctive story, see Iain Provan, *The Reformation and the Right Reading of Scripture* (Waco, TX: Baylor, 2017), pp. 549-53, 574-75.

22. Wilson, *Joseph Wise and Otherwise*, p. 86.

contends, however, that if the story is read within its context of the Joseph narrative, then it is pregnant with meaning.[23]

Moreover, the very structure of chapter 38 may reflect the whole Joseph narrative as demonstrated in the following table:[24]

| The Joseph Story | Judah/Tamar | Description |
| --- | --- | --- |
| Chapter 37 | 38:1-11 | The wider family picture |
| Chapters 39–47 | 38:12-26 | The human initiatives of the main character (God behind the scenes) to right a wrong through the use of a shrewd plan |
| 46:8-27 and 38:27-30 | | A genealogical summary of subsequent descendants |
| Chapters 48–50 | | [amplified in Joseph's case to include the future destiny of his brothers] |

Tamar has acted shrewdly in such a way that she ensures that her husband's line will continue and that of Judah as well.

Chapter 39 resumes with Joseph being a slave (39:1). However, by the time we reach 41:57, he has become second in power and all the world is coming to Joseph and Egypt in order to be saved. The rise in power and influence within the court was not due to his rhetorical savvy, as von Rad had suggested, but was 'the result of a unique set of circumstances, summoned from prison to interpret the Pharaoh's dreams.'[25] These chapters clearly communicate the rise of Joseph, but in 39:2-6 we learn how Joseph prospers because 'the LORD was with Joseph' (39:2a). Notice the extent of Potiphar's trust in Joseph. Notice also the emphasis on the fact that Yahweh was with Joseph. This shouldn't be understood from a psychological perspective with regard to Joseph, as if he needed to know that Yahweh was present with him at this time. The implied reader is the one the narrator is informing at this point and therefore 'Yahweh is introduced into the story to link Joseph's rise with

---

23. Ibid., 93. His more elaborate argument that Genesis 38 is a microcosm of the fuller Joseph narrative is given on pp. 285-92.

24. Reproduced from Ibid., p. 88.

25. Weeks, *Early Israelite Wisdom*, pp. 94-95.

Yahweh's behind-the-scenes care, but without distracting our attention from the person of Joseph.'[26]

The next section of the plot, when Mrs. Potiphar makes repeated sexual overtures to Joseph, is where the true character of Joseph emerges, and his true wisdom (cf. Prov. 6:26; 5:21-22). The contrast between how Joseph uses privilege and power and how Mrs. Potiphar does could not be starker. The story continues in 39:13-18 with a deception about the garment. Mrs Potiphar serves as a foil to Joseph's integrity as she shrewdly misrepresents the facts since Joseph's garment was left beside her (אצלי) instead of in her hand in verse 12 (בידה). Furthermore, she claims that Joseph's alleged indiscretions have become a threat against all Egyptians. In both Joseph's integrity with regard to Mrs. Potiphar's advances and in his administration of Potiphar's affairs (vv. 2-6), there seem to be indications of wisdom-like elements, which can be defined as 'an element (idea, theme etc.) which is prominent in the canonical wisdom books without necessarily asserting that it has come from a wisdom setting.'[27] That is not to say that this narrative is directly influenced by wisdom passages like Proverbs. In this regard, von Rad definitely made a stretch and perhaps even Lindsay Wilson, who is more nuanced and restrained, did as well.[28]

When we come to Joseph's rise in prison in chapters 39–40, it is important to note that the text does not register this elevation as a result of Joseph's strength of character; rather, it is because Yahweh was with him (e.g. 39:21). In fact, in the subsequent verses, the implication seems to be that the prospering is due to the Lord's hand and that might even be implied (though not mentioned) with regards to Joseph's earlier prospering as well (39:4).[29]

In chapter 40, Pharaoh's two officials are introduced into the narrative, probably to provide a literary foil in order to demonstrate what Joseph's mettle actually is. Joseph seemed to have gained the confidence of such a high-ranking Egyptian official that he is actually considered trustworthy.[30] Perhaps this is more grist for the mill with regards to

---

26. Ibid., p. 101.

27. Wilson, *Joseph Wise and Otherwise*, pp. 299-300.

28. Ibid., pp. 96-97.

29. See the discussion in Ibid., p. 111.

30. Ibid., p. 115.

salutary principles for Christian conduct in a common grace situation. Throughout this material, the narrative silences (e.g., no response from the officials) have the effect of focusing attention on Joseph's character.[31] Joseph as an interpreter of dreams proves reliable, although not because of his own wisdom but because he relies on God (cf. 40:8). This coheres with the next chapter in which Joseph's ability to interpret dreams is credited to the activity of God (41:14-16).

The dreams that Joseph interprets for Pharaoh are severe since they influence both livestock and agriculture. Moreover, this is made more severe yet by the fact that the hot east wind is mentioned in 41:6. The sirocco was a hot east wind well-known in the middle east (Arabic = *kamsin*). Although the hot east wind is often represented as a storm theophany of God's judgment in Scripture, that is not the case here. The famine here is seen as 'merely a future event that requires planning and forethought.'[32] The discourse that ensues in 41:33-36 is not part of the dream but a reflection of Joseph's capacity to demonstrate 'wisdom-like' character to articulate a plan that will help ameliorate the threat. Joseph models courtly deferential behavior in these verses by not addressing Pharaoh directly and changing imperative verbs to jussives.[33] In the subsequent verses, Joseph's plan commends itself to Pharaoh and his servants: the 'economic czar' is appointed and rises to power (vv. 37-45).[34] Joseph is given a signet ring, he is clothed in fine garments, and a gold chain is put around his neck. All these items are loaded with symbolic value: they demonstrate his newly appointed royal power and authority.[35] Joseph's renaming and marriage should not be viewed as a compromise; rather, he is becoming Egyptianized and integrated into the highest ranks of society.[36] The point here is not how to rise to power

---

31. Ibid., p. 118.

32. Ibid., pp. 129.

33. Robert E. Longacre, *Joseph: A Story of Divine Providence: A Text Theoretical and Textlinguistic Analysis of Genesis 37 and 39-48* (Winona Lake, IN: Eisenbrauns, 1989), pp. 132-35. For more on how deferential language worked in the ancient world, see the author's, 'The Use of Deferential Language in the Arsames Correspondence and Biblical Aramaic Compared' (*Maarav* 13.1 [January 2007], pp. 43-74).

34. Longacre, *Joseph*, p. 135.

35. See Wilson, *Joseph Wise and Otherwise*, p. 133.

36. Ibid., p. 134.

but how to use power once one arrives at that station.[37] The Christian in today's context, especially the one who is called to a vocation in the civic sphere, should take note. The next section (vv. 54-57) describes the severity of the famine. This segues nicely into the following chapters (42-43), which describes the encounters with his brothers.

Chapter 42 begins a new section. Jacob is reintroduced, Joseph's brothers are reintroduced, but attention on Pharaoh now recedes. Clearly the focus is on Joseph and his family. Commentators are divided as to whether Joseph is portrayed positively or negatively here in relation to his treatment of his brothers (cf. 42:7). Perhaps he is just playing the part of an Egyptian official here.[38] His treatment, however one interprets it, under the good hand of God, as Bruce Waltke notes, 'mark an important transformation in the brothers' characters from being untrustworthy to trustworthy and in their interrelationships from dysfunctional to functional.'[39] Although at first glance some of Joseph's actions may seem to be marked by revenge, his episodes of crying later reflect his true feelings, 'Neither the narrator nor the protagonists at any time suggest that Joseph is angry with them or motivated by revenge.'[40] These facts should probably inform how we interpret Joseph commanding that each one's money be returned into the bags as well. God continues to act behind the scenes however, for when the brothers discover their money in the grain, they declare, (מַה־זֹּאת עָשָׂה אֱלֹהִים לָנוּ) 'What is this that God has done for us?' (ESV). Of course the reader knows that Joseph commanded it, but once again God is acting behind-the-scenes and Joseph is the secondary means through which He is working. When Joseph offers a way out for the brothers if only they will leave the guilty one behind (Benjamin), the test reaches to the very core of what is at stake. Now Judah speaks (vv. 18-34), the longest speech in the Joseph narrative.

Chapter 45:1-15 contains one of the most beautiful denouements in all of world literature. Joseph finally reveals his true identity. God, active behind-the-scenes, remains a primary focus of the narrative (cf. vv. 5, 7, 8). Because of these delightful circumstances of providence, Joseph's

---

37. Ibid., p. 135.

38. Ibid., p. 145.

39. Bruce K. Waltke with Cathi J. Fredricks, *Genesis: A Commentary* (Grand Rapids, MI: Zondervan, 2001), p. 543.

40. Ibid., p. 544.

family may find refuge in Egypt now, a land and culture in which Joseph has learned to delight in the midst of his honor (cf. vv. 9 and 13). Egypt generally, and this Pharaoh more particularly, are pictured favorably in the subsequent verses (vv. 16-28). Some have questioned whether Joseph should have used his power to uphold a country with a pagan religious establishment, or more poignantly asking the question, 'Was it legitimate for Joseph to cooperate with policies that supported idolatry?'[41] Calvin's commitment to a two kingdoms distinction guides his thinking here, by taking refuge in the law, since Joseph 'was not altogether to dispense with the king's corn at his own pleasure. If the king wished that food should be gratuitously supplied to the priests, he was no more at liberty to deny it to them than to the nobles at court.'[42] Joseph, and Daniel as a matter of fact, had to take a more nuanced posture with regards to false religion and pagan rulers since they had civic obligations to their superior leaders and the rule of law.[43]

In the remaining chapters (46–50), the Abrahamic promises spoken of in the previous chapter of this book come to the fore again. Not only is Joseph's wise administration discussed (cf. 47:13-26), but the resolution with his brothers leaves no uncertainty about cordial fraternal relations. We are prepared for the next books of the Scripture. Some moderns have difficulty with Joseph's accepting self-sale into slavery of some of the Egyptians as recorded in this chapter; however, such a practice in order to save one's life or settle a debt was not unusual in the ancient world.[44] Moreover, their attitude seems grateful, as the text narrates (47:25).

In 46:2-4, God speaks to Jacob, who verse 1 says was offering sacrifices, and the Lord speaks in the midst of visions which is surprising since this is the only time in the entire Joseph narrative that God speaks to anyone directly. He is explicitly directed to go down to Egypt. Thus, as we saw in Chapter 1 of this book, an altar-oriented people is settled in the midst of a common grace situation, in a foreign culture even. Joseph

---

41. See Matthew J. Tuininga, *Calvin's Political Theology*, p. 315.
42. Ibid.
43. Ibid., p. 360.
44. See S. S. Bartchy, 'Slavery' in *The International Standard Bible Encyclopedia*, four vols., edited by Geoffrey W. Bromiley (et al.), (Grand Rapids, MI: Eerdmans, 1988), 4.539-46.

tells his brothers how to answer Pharaoh when they are asked about their occupation (cf. 46:33-34), probably anticipating Pharaoh's question (47:3) as well as acknowledging that shepherds are an abomination to Egyptians (46:34). Indeed, Pharaoh speaks directly to Joseph in order to give him instructions about settling his family in Goshen, which not only reveals the influence Joseph has obtained in the foreign land but his shrewd and careful strategic planning.

## Conclusion

The final chapters of Genesis not only demonstrate assurance of the Abrahamic promises coming to fruition, but they prepare us for the Exodus. More specifically, they tell us of the death of Joseph and Jacob, and the ultimate reconciliation of all the brothers (50: 15-21). Years ago, Sir Francis Bacon wrote: 'Certainly, in taking revenge, a man is but even with his enemy; but in passing it over, he is superior; for it is a prince's part to pardon.'[45] Joseph seems to have played the 'prince's part' to a tee (cf. 50:19, and Deut. 33:16). In 50:24, the Abrahamic promised land is referred to in Joseph's parting words, and the anticipation of the Exodus event comes to the fore.

The Joseph narrative has highlighted his ability not only to end family strife through shrewd planning but also his administrative gifts in bringing relief from the famine, not just for his family but for many others as well (cf. 41:57). Joseph's unique circumstances would make it hard for anyone analogously to emulate today; nevertheless, 'he clearly shows the right way to use power once in a position of authority.'[46] He was a man of faith, looking to the future at the end of his life, making provisions for his own bones to be brought out of this temporary residence as he looked toward another homeland (cf. Heb. 11, especially v. 22). Although Darryl Hart applies the following quote to Daniel, what he says could equally be applied to Joseph:

> Just as he [Daniel] lived a hyphenated life, so Christians—exiles and strangers, as the New Testament refers to them—may be so called to live lives in which they negotiate competing sets of loyalties and responsibilities.

45. Sir Francis Bacon, 'Of Revenge,' in *The Oxford Book of Essays: Chosen and Edited by John Gross* (Oxford: Oxford University Press, 1991), p. 3.
46. Wilson, *Joseph Wise and Otherwise*, p. 240.

Christ himself appears to have been pointing in the direction of this hyphenated existence when he told his disciples to render some things to Caesar and some things to God. The split duties inherent in Christ's teaching, some belonging to Christians as citizens and others to them as church members, run directly counter to the current quest for individual wholeness that fuels the politics of identity and invites Christians to enter the public square as believers rather than as religious citizens. But Christ's instruction, along with Christianity's historic distinction between the realms of church and state, suggest that the politics of integration are not necessary for followers of Christ. Because Christians are pilgrims and exiles in this world, and long for their true spiritual home, a hyphenated existence is essential to Christian identity.[47]

We now turn from our discussion of one Jew in the court of a foreign king to another: Daniel.

---

47. Hart, *A Secular Faith*, p. 256.

# CHAPTER 4

# The Book of Daniel

The first seven chapters of Daniel re-introduce us to a subject that we have touched upon previously, the 'state' or 'the city of man'(see Chapter 2 especially). We cannot understand church power apart from state power and the relationship between them. However, here in Daniel 'we have the state in colossal form, and from the circumstances of its origin we can expect nothing but an identification of the civil and spiritual relations of mankind.'[1] We will interact with the first six chapters since they set forth clearly 'the contest between the supremacy of God in man and the supremacy of man without God and against God.'[2]

## Special Introduction Issues

Other scholars have written on the applicability of the book of Daniel to how Christians should conduct themselves in public life and the civic sphere. As mentioned in the previous chapter, for example, Darryl Hart suggests that Daniel, 'the assimilated and devout prophet, may be the best model for American Christians wanting to know how to participate meaningfully in public life.'[3] David VanDrunen, in an extended discussion, argues that Daniel gives further corroboration to his evidence drawn from the prophets Amos and Isaiah, that 'These chapters [2–6] treat the Babylonian and Persian monarchs not as those

---

1. Thomas Peck, *Notes on Ecclesiology,* pp. 123.

2. Ibid.

3. Darryl Hart, *A Secular Faith,* p. 256.

in redemptive covenantal relationship with God and obligated to Him under the Mosaic law, but as those commissioned to rule nations under God's sovereign authority as established under the covenant with Noah. Their chief sins concern injustice and especially pride, and the chief thing they need to learn is to exercise just rule with humility, found upon a general fear of God.[4] Nevertheless, more can and should be said along these lines and so the remainder of this chapter will deal primarily with the court tales of Daniel. However, before we delve into those areas, some comments on special introduction are in order. The book of Daniel has undergone lots of abuse from higher critical scholars and so the first thing we need to do is establish some introductory matters that will also help us understand the chapters under consideration and the special contribution they make to our topic.

## Authorship and Date

The goal here is not to delve into a detailed analysis about introductory issues surrounding the biblical book of Daniel. I do not follow the mainstream academic community in dating the book of Daniel, so my views need some explaining. However, Daniel, especially, needs some extended comment.

Whenever biblical scholars are discussing ancient texts (biblical or otherwise), identifying who wrote a document and the time in which they wrote can be of tremendous importance if it can be determined. The 'modern higher-critical view,' if we may call it so, is that the book of Daniel was composed in the second century B.C., not during the Babylonian exile. So much in this view, frankly, is based upon what we call *prophecy ex vaticanum*, i.e., 'prophecy after the fact.' The reasons for this, from a modern 'critical view', are as follows.

The argument suggests that there is much too precise a knowledge in the book of Daniel about the history of the second century B.C. for the book to have been written in the sixth century B.C. Critics assume that this type of accuracy (with respect to centuries beforehand) cannot exist. For example, in chapter eleven, the focus of Daniel's discussion becomes the history of the Seleucids, who are in Syria, and the Ptolemies, who are in Egypt, and their various successive campaigns, intermarriages,

---

4. David VanDrunen, *Divine Covenants and Moral Order*, pp. 196 207, especially at p. 197.

and governance. In a remarkably detailed manner, all these empires are discussed. The author of Daniel, it seems, is too well informed about the events of the second century B.C.[5] This becomes problematic, so to speak, because the author seems too 'ill-informed' of the issues in the sixth-century B.C. (the purported time of writing from a traditional, conservative viewpoint) vis-à-vis the second century, about which he seems quite well informed.

More serious yet is the allegation that Daniel's understanding of the succession of the kingdoms (as described in chapters 2 and 7 especially) would have been the following as opposed to the traditional, and if I may say 'conservative', view of the kingdoms. The seriousness lies in the fact that if Daniel didn't have in mind Rome as the last kingdom described in these chapters, then his prophecies really cannot apply to Christ.

| *'Higher Critical' View of the Kingdoms* | *Daniel's View of Kingdoms* |
| --- | --- |
| 1) Babylonian | 1) Babylonian |
| 2) Medes: Darius the Mede | 2) Medo-Persian |
| 3) Persia (Cyrus) | 3) Greece |
| 4) Greece | 4) Rome |

The conservative approach to the book has been that it was written by Daniel in the sixth century B.C., and in Babylon, not in Palestine (after the return from exile). The main arguments have been as follows. Many parts of the book are written in the first person, assuming Daniel is the author. The last chapter of the book, where you get the first person, assumes that Daniel is commanded to preserve the book. In Matthew 24:15, our Lord Jesus attributes the fall of Jerusalem to a passage from Daniel. 'Critical scholars' are happy to assign the book to a figure in the second century B.C., who is interacting with the Maccabean revolt. This then would radically influence the 'messianic passages.' Are we dealing with a Messiah figure or a 'liberator' like Judas Maccabeus in the Maccabean revolt? Therefore, in this view, another ruler is created based on the ostensible reading of the text: Darius, the Mede. So, for example, we read in Daniel 5:30-31: 'That very night Belshazzar the Chaldean king was killed. And Darius the Mede received the kingdom,

5. See D. J. Wiseman, 'Some Historical Problems in the Book of Daniel,' in *Notes on some problems in The Book of Daniel* (London, Tyndale Press, 1965), pp. 9-18.

being about sixty-two years old' (ESV).[6] This would seem to suggest that there were two kingdoms, one of the Medes and one of the Persians.

However, Professor Wiseman has proposed another solution to this issue.[7] When we turn to Daniel 6:28, we read: 'So this Daniel prospered during the reign of Darius *and* the reign of Cyrus the Persian' (ESV). Wiseman's view is that Darius the Mede is to be identified as Cyrus the Persian. This theory, he called the 'Cyrus hypothesis,' and he suggested that the conjunction ('waw') between the two rulers should be read as explanatory and not merely a coordinating conjunction. Therefore, the verse would read in this view, 'so this Daniel prospered in the reign of Darius, *that is*, in the reign of Cyrus the Persian.' Consequently, Darius and Cyrus are one and the same person.

The question that immediately follows this claim is whether such a grammatical feature occurs elsewhere in the Hebrew Bible? Indeed, in 1 Chronicles 5:26, we read 'so the God of Israel stirred up the spirit of Pul king of Israel, *that is* ("conjunctive" "waw"), the spirit of Tiglath-pileser king of Assyria, and he took him into exile' (author's translation). Assyrian texts outside the Bible confirm this identification.[8] Therefore, this occasion is very similar in its use of a 'explanatory' conjunction.

Furthermore, Cyrus very well could have been called a Mede by the Babylonians. Wiseman says:

> Cyrus as much as Gubaru could have been called a 'Mede' by the Babylonians. By 550 B.C. Cyrus had taken over Media and joined it to the 'Persian' federation. When Nabonidus in 546 B.C. declared that the 'King of the Medes' welcomed his proposed return from exile he could at this time refer to no other than to Cyrus, and presumably this title was known as far as Tema' even though it has not been found yet in other inscriptions. Although Cyrus only uses 'King of Anshan', 'King of Persia', 'King of Babylonia' or 'King of the lands' in his inscriptions, it cannot be denied that he might also have incorporated the title 'King of Media' but that, if of Median stock, he did not stress it in view of the unity of the Aryan Medo-Persian coalition under his rule. It is noteworthy that nowhere does the writer of Daniel claim that Darius was '*King* of Media'.[9]

---

6. Cf., 6:1-3, 9, and 28.

7. See Wiseman, 'Some Historical Problems in the Book of Daniel,' pp. 12-16.

8. Ibid., p. 13.

9. Ibid. Also see Bullman, 'The Identification of Darius the Mede,' *WTJ* 35/3 (Spring, 1973): pp. 247-67.

Additional phrases in Daniel, 'according to the Medes and Persians,' seem to confirm that we are not speaking of two different kingdoms, but one (cf. 5:28, 6:8, 6:12, 8:3, 20).

## The Structure of the Book

The book of Daniel is constructed on the basis of a number of distinct but interlocking or superimposed articulations. The most obvious is the ABA pattern of the languages since we have Hebrew (1:1-2:4a) followed by Aramaic (2:4b-7:28) followed by Hebrew (8:1-12:13). I will briefly discuss the language issue below, especially as it relates to dating the book, but first I will discuss the structure of the book.

The book divides into two halves: a cycle of six court tales told in the third person (chaps. 1–6) and a cycle of four visions told in the first person (7:1–12:13).[10] Then, the division of the book corresponds to a dating scheme that repeats the same basic sequencing in both halves of the book as well. There seems to be a succession of (1) the Babylonian kingdom and (2) the reign of Darius the Mede, who is Cyrus (in my view). This succession is repeated in both halves of the book. As mentioned above, this division of the book by language is superimposed onto and cuts across the most basic division between chapters 1–6 and 7–12. As A. Lenglet demonstrated, this forms a most remarkable chiastic pattern.[11] If we were to lay it out in very simple form, it could be pictured in the following manner:[12]

Prologue, **Chapter 1**

  **A: Chapter 2**: Nebuchadnezzar's dream of a colossal statue representing four successive world kingdoms.

    **B: Chapter 3**: The would-be martyrdom of Shadrach, Meshach, and Abednego in the fiery furnace and their rescue by an angel.

---

10. Although 7:1 and the first three words of 7:2 in the MT are still in the third person narrative frame.

11. A. Lenglet, 'La structure littéraire de Daniel 2-7,' *Biblica* 53 (1972), pp. 169-70.

12. For the form of chapters 2 through 7, I am indebted to the influential article by A. Lenglet, 'La structure littéraire de Daniel 2-7,' pp. 169-70. For the rest, I have slightly adapted what has been suggested by Peter J. Gentry and Stephen J. Wellum, *Kingdom through Covenant: A Biblical-Theological Understanding of the Covenants* (Wheaton, IL: Crossway, 2012), pp. 532-33.

C: **Chapter 4**: Nebuchadnezzar's presumption and abasement into madness.

C': **Chapter 5**: Belshazzar's presumption and demise.

B': **Chapter 6**: The would-be martyrdom of Daniel in the lion's den and his rescue by an angel.

A': **Chapter 7**: Daniel's dream of four wild animals representing four successive world kingdoms, final judgment of the world, judgment of four world kingdoms, corresponding to Chapter 12.

A: **Chapter 8**: Vision of future history

B: **Chapter 9**: Daniel's prayer and God's response

B': **Chapter 10**: Daniel's grief and God's response

A': **Chapter 11:1–12:4**: Vision of future history

Epilogue, **Chapter 12: 5-13**

What's the significance of this structure ask Gentry and Wellum?[13] The whole thing produces a unity. In short, what does this double interlocking chiasm represent? It amounts to a description of the kingdom of God established in the midst of world kingdoms and in the midst of the power and wisdom of the world.

Next, I will mainly address the issues concerning language in what follows and will not discuss the complex historical questions that the book raises.

## *The Languages of the Book*

It was S. R. Driver, a very influential higher-critical biblical scholar, whose famous words are often quoted as a starting point for appraisals of the dating of the book: 'The Greek words demand, the Hebrew supports, and the Aramaic permits, a date [for the book of Daniel] after the conquest of Palestine by Alexander the Great.'[14] This dictum is now no longer tenable or even plausible. Let's just take up two of the languages that Driver cites. First Greek, then Aramaic.

---

13. Gentry and Wellum, *Kingdom through Covenant*, p. 533.

14. S. R. Driver, *An Introduction the Literature of the Old Testament* (Edinburgh: T & T Clark, 1961), p. 508.

Even the higher-critical commentator, James A. Montgomery, saw the Achilles heel in Driver's argument years ago. He said, almost one hundred years ago now, that 'the rebuttal of this evidence for a low date [of Daniel, that is in the Maccabean period] lies in stressing the potentialities of Greek influence in the Orient [the ancient Near East] from the sixth century onward.'[15] We have evidence from the Aramaic documents from Elephantine (found in Egypt dating to the fifth century B.C.) that demonstrate that the Greek language and influence was indeed felt earlier than expected. For example, Rabinowitz has shown that the phrase in Greek for 'silver of Greece' along with three other words, very possibly Greek in the Elephantine papyri, show that Greek influence was happening much earlier than Driver maintains.[16] Moreover, Edwin Yamauchi has also demonstrated that the musical terms that were thought to be much later can, in fact, be shown to be earlier than previously thought. He writes:

> It has been asserted that two of the Greek words in question, *psaltērion* and *sumphōnia*, are attested only in the fourth-century Greek works. The verbal root of the first word, however, occurs in the fifth century. (A derived form from a similar root 'to pluck' occurs in Mycenaean Greek.) Upon reexamination of the lexicons it has also been found that the latter word in its basic sense of 'harmony' is attested in the sixth century. It is no longer tenable to maintain that *sumphōnia* means 'bagpipe' – a meaning attested only in the second century B.C. In its use in Daniel it may mean 'concerted music' or it may be an adjective modifying the preceding instrument.[17]

Indeed, Yamauchi goes on to demonstrate some fourteen different points of contact between the Aegean (i.e., Greece) and Mesopotamia during the Assyrian period. Obviously, there was much more contact between Greece and the ancient Near East than Driver supposed. Yamauchi concludes:

> In the light of the many contacts of Greeks with the near East before the fifth century, it should not be surprising to find Greek words in an Aramaic

---

15.  J. A. Montgomery, *A Critical and Exegetical Commentary on the Book of Daniel* (New York: Charles Scribner's and Sons, 1927), p. 22.

16.  Jacob Rabinowitz, 'Grecians and Greek terms in the Aramaic Papyri,' *Biblica* 39 (1958): pp. 76-82.

17.  Edwin Yamauchi, *Greece and Babylon: Early Contacts Between the Aegean and the Near East* (Grand Rapids, MI: Baker, 1967), pp. 91-92.

document of that date [he is talking about the Elephantine documents]. The only element of surprise to this writer is that there are not more Greek words in such documents.[18]

The issue of the language of Aramaic cited by Driver above ('the Aramaic permits') has been a point of contention as well with respect to dating. Aramaic became the international trade language in the ancient Near East in about 925 B.C. Most scholars then divide the 'phases' of Aramaic into purely chronological schemes such as Old Aramaic (925-700 B.C.), Official Aramaic (700-200 B.C.), Middle Aramaic (200 B.C-A.D. 200), Late Aramaic (A.D. 200-A.D. 700), and finally Modern Aramaic, which is still spoken today in North Syria, Iran and Iraq.

A better method, proposed by Douglas Gropp, is to use designations that characterize the language itself.[19] This is the best approach, one which begins with the 'ideal standard language' used by the courtly scribes themselves during the Persian period (522-330 B.C.) when they would draft official documents. We will call this Official Aramaic (OfA). The OfA from this period is amazingly homogeneous especially when drawn from three different sources: the Elephantine legal papyri (fifth century B.C.), the Arsames correspondence (also the fifth century B.C.), and finally the Samaria papyri from Wadi ed-Daliyeh (fourth century B.C.). For Gropp, we must measure changes in the development of the language according to the first stage, the official

---

18. Ibid., p. 94.

19. See Douglas M. Gropp, 'The Language of the Samaria Papyri: A Preliminary Study,' *Maarav* 5-6 (1990): pp. 169-87. Gropp defines Official Aramaic as 'the ideal standard dialect of the Persian period to which Aramaic scribes evidently aspired to conform when drafting documents of an official nature. Any given Aramaic text of the Persian period may adhere more or less to this standard dialect. It is noteworthy that genre is a considerably more significant factor in differentiating between those texts which deviate from the standard, than either geographical, chronological, or ethnic provenience. Thus the Aramaic of private letters deviates somewhat from the OfA of the legal and administrative documents. In my view, then, the Aramaic of the private letters from Hermopolis is a complex product of the interference between the standard OfA and the local vernacular. The deviations from the standard give us the best clue as to the character of this vernacular. In fact, a systematic grammatical description of the Elephantine legal papyri, the Samaria papyri, and the Arsames correspondence (with due respect to the variation between these groups of texts) could constitute the nucleus for a more comprehensive grammar of OfA,' p. 170. See also the more recent article by Gropp, 'Imperial Aramaic,' in *The Oxford Encyclopedia of Archaeology in the Near East* (ed. Eric M. Meyers; 5 vols.; Oxford: Oxford University Press, 1997), 3.144-146.

correspondence of the chancellery, the official place where courtly business took place and scribes composed their letters in OfA. In the second stage, this homogenous 'standard' language is broken up and reconsolidated. The coming of Alexander the Great during this time is a watershed in the development of the language. The book of Daniel has Aramaic in it that is closer to the texts exemplified from Qumran, which would seem to suggest a difficulty for the conservative position: that the book was composed in the sixth century by Daniel. The final stage of development would be exemplified, according to Gropp, in the Aramaic of Targums Onkelos and Jonathan, as well as the Bar Kokhba letters and the Megillat Ta'anit.

Some conservative evangelical OT scholars have argued for the Aramaic of Daniel as representing sixth century Aramaic; however, this position is no longer tenable. The fact remains that the Aramaic of Daniel, although it shares in the hallmarks of Aramaic from the Persian period,[20] is closer to Qumran than to the sixth century. So what are we to make of this and its ramifications for dating the book?

One answer to the problem has been to argue for modernization of the language during the transmission of the manuscript. It was Kenneth Kitchen who picked up on this suggestion and argued that the Aramaic of Daniel may have gone through similar orthographic changes as was customary for texts throughout the ancient Near East. After citing numerous examples, he concludes:

> Therefore, in the abstract (so to speak), there is no reason to deny possible orthographic change during the textual transmission of Daniel … at least … [he concludes] …. In light of the comparative evidence briefly sampled above, it should be obvious that orthographic change (sometimes 'revision', sometimes more gradual) is normal – and the onus of proof lies on those who would maintain that the Aramaic text of Daniel or Ezra could not or did not fare similarly in similar circumstances …. What, then, is the significance of all this? Simply that we have no inherent right to assume that the present orthography of the Aramaic of Daniel requires a second-century date for the original composition of the Aramaic text.[21]

---

20. M. L. Folmer, *The Aramaic Language in the Achaemenid Period: A Study in Linguistic Variation*, OLA 68 (Leuven: Peeters, 1995), pp. 753-57.

21. K. A. Kitchen, 'The Aramaic of Daniel,' pp. 31-79, especially pp. 61-67, in Wiseman, *Notes on some problems in the Book of Daniel*.

This seems to have been E.J. Young's view as well.[22] Moreover, Kitchen's study was endorsed by the famous Jewish Aramaic scholar and linguist, E.Y. Kutscher, praising Kitchen's work as 'well done.'[23] A more important and weighty endorsement can hardly be imagined from such an erudite Aramaic scholar. Therefore, the study of Kitchen, endorsed by Kutscher, effectively dispensed of all arguments against an early date for Daniel, from the perspective of the Aramaic language alone.

With these important introductory matters out of the way, at this point in my treatment of Daniel, I will discuss the court narratives of the book in order to observe a prime example of how Daniel conducted himself in a common grace situation. He shows resolve to maintain his status as a faithful saint even while under pressure in a foreign land, under a foreign tyrant in the court of a foreign king.

# The Jew in the Court of a Foreign King
## Daniel 1

One of the first major points to acknowledge and to deal with is the fact (alluded to above) that two languages are employed to describe Daniel's interactions in the foreign court (i.e., Aramaic in 2:4–7:28 and everything else is Hebrew). This bilingualism has generated much discussion in the scholarly literature. My argument will be that looking at the change in languages together with certain puns made in the language can help us understand Daniel's posture and the other Hebrew lads as well: *because of their faith in the sovereign God who controls all circumstances inside and outside of Israel, they can 'manage' the situation and boldly exercise their 'higher' kingdom status even though they have found themselves in a situation of being in a foreign land and foreign court.* Even so, they attempt to do good to their neighbor and serve the authority under whom they have been placed, despite this oppressive situation. Daniel especially, but also his fellow Hebrews, are given sufficient knowledge to lead God's people and to stay faithful even in the midst of this pressure to accommodate to the culture and especially the idolatry that surrounds them as the faithful people of God. However,

---

22. E. J. Young, *A Prophecy of Daniel: A Commentary* (Grand Rapids, MI: Eerdmans, 1949), p. 23.

23. E. Y. Kutscher, *Current Trends in Linguistics*, 6 (1970), pp. 399-403.

to understand the evidence for this claim, we have to turn to the details of bilingualism in order to understand the argument.

What is the reason for the division between Hebrew and Aramaic? Basically, a debate has raged from the point of view of history and composition of the book whether the materials are all made up of the same period, i.e., between the time of the persecution of Antiochus IV Epiphanes and between synchronic approaches, which generally speaking are less concerned about historical problems. Let me explain the diachronic perspective first.

There have been two main representative views: Rowley and Ginsberg. These well respected and learned scholars argued in favor of a basic heterogeneity between the court tales (which were regarded as pre-Antiochene, third century B.C.) and the visions, which Rowley argued were Antiochene. Rowley has been the ablest defender of the view that there is a unity and homogeneity to the book, in spite of his views about the lateness of certain sections of the book.[24]

H. L. Ginsberg argued strongly in favor of a basic heterogeneity between the court tales (he thought pre-Antiochene – third century B.C.) and the visions, which he regarded as Antiochene. Ginsberg's view has been followed by a number of scholars, but it is premature to speak of a 'consensus.' Ginsberg has proposed that 1–6 and 7–12 were originally composed in Aramaic. Then, Daniel 1 and 8–12 were translated into Hebrew, which he thought was inferior. He thinks this was done for two reasons: 1) to achieve the status of Holy Scripture, and 2) to achieve cohesion in the book. The conclusion may be expressed by saying that attempts to explain the enigma of bilingualism in the book have generally been diachronic in approach or they have assumed some kind of translational history.[25]

Another possibility yet, from a synchronic point of view, is that of B. T. Arnold.[26] His view can be considered an important contribution

24. You may find his defense represented in H. H. Rowley, 'The Unity of the Book of Daniel,' in *The Servant of the Lord and Other Essays on the Old Testament* (London: Lutterworth, 1952), pp. 237-68.

25. See, for example, H. L. Ginsberg, 'Composition of the Book of Daniel,' *VT* 4 (1954): pp. 246-75.

26. B. T. Arnold, 'The Use of Aramaic in the Hebrew Bible: Another Look at Bilingualism in Ezra and Daniel,' *JNSL* 22/2 (1996): pp. 1-16.

from the perspective of 'narratology' and studies on 'point of view' for expressing characterization. Taking this perspective, together with the issue of bilingualism in the book of Daniel, Arnold has come up with some helpful suggestions germane to the topics and issues being studied here: how believers should function in a pluralistic society in which they may not be the majority yet must remain faithful to their religious convictions and still love their neighbor. Arnold's approach has sought to explain the reasons behind the subtle shift from Hebrew to Aramaic and back to Hebrew again.[27] His contention is that these methodologies (translational and diachronic) really don't explain the retention of Aramaic in the canonical Bible. He thinks that his approach (taking into consideration insights from narratology) explains the retention of Aramaic in the traditions and clarifies the use of both languages in the original composition. For this approach, he is relying heavily on Boris Upenski, who studied and wrote on 'point of view.'[28] This is used very broadly in literary criticism. Usually 'point of view' merely means the perspective from which the story is told. Upenski, however, delineated four different levels of point of view: ideological, phraseological, spatial and temporal. Entering into a detailed description of his theory would not serve our immediate purposes at this point. The payoff, rather, is in noticing what the narrator does with the story in Daniel 1 and 2, especially factoring in the issue of bilingualism (i.e., the shift from Hebrew in Daniel 1 to Aramaic in Daniel 2).

As mentioned previously, the main approaches to bilingualism in Daniel have been diachronic in nature. Some authors have argued

---

27. Ibid.

28. Boris Upenski has devoted his work on narration and 'point of view' by his application to Russia epic literature/Russian novels. He has laid the main theoretical ground-work in this area. Since we are going to be talking about characterization shortly, we need to talk about this as well. For it is impossible to talk about characterization without talking about narration since the reader of a text really doesn't experience the character directly. Every time we experience a character in a text he/she is mediated through the telling of the author (implied or otherwise), the narrator or another character even. Upenski has illustrated the use in Russian epic literature. However, this approach is very applicable to biblical literature as well. Earlier I used the analogy of film. T. Longan refers to this in his little book. He gets it from A. Berlin, who contrasts it with drama, or play and it is really quite helpful for getting at the issue. In a film everything is filtered through the eye of the camera. It constantly shifts the perspective showing the action from different points of view, different angles. Biblical narratives behave like film in this respect.

that Aramaic is used for the same reasons as in Ezra (i.e., to 'strive for authenticity in reporting the speech of foreigners'). Arnold's approach argues that the book of Daniel is not a composite, but an intentionally constructed book. Furthermore, literary conventions played a major role.[29] He argues that Ezra uses Aramaic for 'authenticating purposes' whereas Daniel uses Aramaic for rhetorical purposes/literary purposes and conventions. The introductory formulations of the first two chapters are crucial to our understanding of how the literary conventions work. Both signal a shift in *point of view.* Knowing whether an author is working from an external position or an internal position, with regards to point of view, is crucial for applying the argument of Arnold. The Hebrew unit up to 2:4b introduces all the main characters. These characterizations provide clues and a backdrop to the conflicts of world views which will ensure very shortly. Cultural clash comes in two ways: Judean versus Babylonian, pious versus pagan. In short, it is reflected in the use of Hebrew versus Aramaic, obvious in the fall of Jerusalem in 1:1-2, but also in the capture and deportation of the Hebrew lads, and their change of names (an obvious switch). Daniel refuses to capitulate. Notice the conflict portrayed from the point of view of the author in the continued use of the Hebrew names in Daniel 1:19. The author's *point of view comes on two levels* (Upenski discusses the combination of points of view). Phraseologically – the author is internal in position. Upenski would say that is because the narration concentrates on the essence of speech instead of the particularities of speech position, e.g. verse 10 – chief eunuch's speech is in Hebrew, not Aramaic. Note the consistent use of Hebrew names for Daniel's three friends. Then, there is the ideological plane – the author's point of view is clearly on this as well. In Daniel 1:8, the narrator gives us an assessment of Daniel's determination: 'But Daniel resolved that he would not defile himself with the king's food, or with the wine he drank' (ESV). In Daniel 1:17 we see God's blessing: 'As for these four youths, God gave them learning and skill in all literature and wisdom, and Daniel had understanding in all visions and dreams' (ESV). Here's a Jew writing with an interest in the religious significance of the events. Hebrew is the language of choice since the internal position is

---

29. Cf., Bill T. Arnold, 'The Use of Aramaic in the Hebrew Bible,' pp. 1-16, and see also Arnold, 'Wordplay and Narrative Techniques in Daniel 5 and 6,' *JBL* 112/3 (1993): pp. 479-85.

expressed on both the phraseological and ideological planes. The stage is set for a switch to Aramaic in chapter 2. *Now the point of view is expressed on a new level. Now phraseological becomes primary from the standpoint of external.* Now the narrator becomes more detached, now the distance between the speaking character and the describing observer is stressed. There are two reasons the author used Aramaic at 2:4b. Daniel 2:1-4a is a transitional paragraph like that in Ezra. This opening paragraph makes a complete scene shift. Chapter 1:8-20 was internal and 2:1-4 makes a gradually-building transition to this new perspective. Second, the opening of the Aramaic section, 'O King live forever,' is the climax of the shift. From this point forward (chapters 2–7), the emphasis is on the external phraseological plane. Use of this phrase makes complete the distance. The narrator is now on the 'external' plane.

The conclusion of these observations is that biblical authors have all kinds of techniques at their disposal to express point of view: naming, descriptions of the inner life of characters, circumstantial clauses, and direct discourse. Authors who were bilingual (at least) had another tool. They may use this subtlety and rhetorically to describe the relationship between a narrator, character and event. Adele Berlin will go so far as to say: 'Recognizing the multiple points of view is the first step in discovering the point of view of the implied author; and this is the first step in discovering the meaning and purpose of the story.'[30] For the author of Daniel, these techniques may have played a larger compositional role than in Ezra (which also contains sections written in Aramaic and where the thrust is 'authentication'). Word play and puns can also be an effective tool in the hands of a skilled writer. The reader will remember, as I said at the beginning of the chapter, that Daniel demonstrates the tension between the supremacy of man and men without God versus the supremacy of God. These significations of rhetorical point of view in Daniel 1 undergird this plot and structure.

But there is another device used by the author and frequently used by authors in the ancient Near East: word punning.[31]

---

30. Adele Berlin, *Poetics and Interpretation of Biblical Narrative* (Sheffield, Almond Press, 1983), p. 82.

31. See *Puns and Pundits: Word Play in The Hebrew Bible and Ancient Near Eastern Literature*, Scott B. Noegel (ed.) (Bethesda, MD: CDL Press, 2000).

Some literary puns have been frequently discussed by biblical scholars in the past. However, some might be so finely woven into the text that they are hard to perceive on the surface level. Arnold has written another article on the beginning of Daniel in which he argues that diachronic approaches have often underappreciated the way in which word puns prepare the reader theologically and rhetorically for what follows. He does this by noting some significant details of the word play on *wayyāśem* ('and he set') in Daniel 1:7 and 1:8.

Daniel 1:1-2 begins with locating the events in the reign of Jehoiakim, but quickly this fades into the background and the focus comes forward to the dreaded Nebuchadnezzar. This sets the tone for the rest of the book. He may have been the Babylonian king who came, but it was God who gave Jehoiakim into his hand. Verse 2 gives the reader the narrator's central point: 'Adonai *gave* Jehoiakim into Nebuchadnezzar's hand.' Use of the verb *ntn* ('he gave') is important for reading the chapter as a whole. This sentence governs the next phrase as well and therefore should be translated with the 'waw of accompaniment,' and should be translated *'along with* some of the vessels of the house of God.' These opening verses serve as an *orientation*, a term known from sociolinguistic studies which places the ensuing study in time and place, but in this case 'also establishes Nebuchadnezzar's character and God's sovereignty over the events.'[32] Now the narrator turns to a characterization, a characterization make by a third party, a Babylonian official: chosen from the Israelites, chosen from the royal seed, chosen from the nobility, young men without physical defect, and handsome, versed in every branch of wisdom, endowed with knowledge and insight, capable to serve at the royal palace (1:3-4).

This is unusual in several ways as far as characterizations go in the Hebrew Bible. First, and strikingly, these youths and Daniel in particular 'assimilated the ways, culture, and customs of a nation whose religion was false from the perspective of the Jewish people.' Moreover, 'Daniel and the Jews were in captivity to the Babylonian Empire and had been removed from their sacred land and from the sites of their religious worship. Daniel was in a situation of defeat – his faith disestablished, the empire's religion dominant. Yet he submitted to the ways and ideas

---

32. See Bill Arnold, 'Word Play & Characterization in Daniel 1,' pp. 231-50 in *Puns and Pundits: Word Play in the Hebrew Bible and Ancient Near Eastern Literature*, especially p. 235.

of his captors and even excelled at their foreign and pagan culture.'[33] Consequently, with the aid of his God, he rose to a position of power and influence. A better characterization of a hyphenated life can hardly be imagined.[34]

Secondly, usually the Bible prefers techniques of characterization which employ inner life, speech, and contrast.[35] Here, blatantly, the Hebrew youths are given characterization and the narrator seems to approve of the Babylonian's appraisal. This leads us to the key use of 'word play', specifically *antanaclastic paronomasia* (where the same word, when repeated, sometimes requires different renditions). Arnold now drives home his point about *wayyāśem* ('and he set') in verses 7-8: 'I believe the narrator uses this word play to dramatize Daniel's surpassing faithfulness in the face of unprecedented oppression. The irony is that he uses the same verb, albeit in different phrasal idioms, to denote both Daniel's faith and Nebuchadnezzar's persecution.'[36] *Śîm* used here as the verb is not the normal way of expressing 'name.' Usually it is *qārā* in combination with *shem*. So the narrator anticipates a word play in verse 8 by an irregular use, heightened by dramatic tensions since he uses it twice. In verse 8, instead of the chief eunuch, now it is Daniel who is the subject of the verb *wayyāśem*. Here, the term 'heart' is not the direct object of the verb, 'set, place,' but is instead the object of the preposition followed by the relative noun clause introduced by the relativizer, *asher*. Nowhere else in the Hebrew Bible is the direct object of *śîm* a noun clause introduced by the relative pronoun.

Therefore, the real issue here becomes defilement. The idiom used, 'to place/set something upon one's heart,' connotes a subject that cares deeply enough about the object (implied or marked) so as to be compelled to take some action concerning it. Notice the contrast with verse 9. The most important verb of the chapter again occurs there – *natan*. God is again the subject. He is not only in control of sovereign international relations and politics; he is in control of the minutiae of Daniel's life

33. Hart, *A Sacred Faith*, p. 255.

34. Ibid., p. 256.

35. See for customary characterization techniques in the Bible, Adele Berlin, *Poetics and the Interpretation of Biblical Narrative* (Sheffield: Almond Press, 1983), chap. 2. Or see Robert Alter, *The Art of Biblical Narrative* (New York: Basic Books, 1981), pp. 114-30.

36. Arnold, ibid., p. 236.

as well. The narrator has moved from characterization of Daniel by the Babylonians in verses 3-4 to a more overt and subtle technique in which the narrator reveals the inner life of Daniel and his motives (through word pun) and then characterizes him by dramatic, immediate action in 8b: 'Daniel resolved that he would not defile himself with the king's food, or with the wine that he drank' (ESV). Interpreters have differed as to what the motive for this abstaining was, oscillating between some kind of ritual concern and some contrary statement by Daniel to Nebuchadnezzar's claim to absolute lordship. Michael Seufert has recently demonstrated that such a bifurcation is unnecessary and that Daniel's motivation, especially due to the possible allusions to Exodus 15–16 in the chapter, show that Daniel was concerned to demonstrate that the Lord, Yahweh, is the only provider for the exiled Jews vis-à-vis Nebuchadnezzar's implied dominance by prescribing their dietary restrictions.[37] Once again, we see the drama in the details: the alleged sovereignty and supremacy of mankind over and against God and the true sovereignty of God.

## *Daniel 2*

Daniel 2 is our introduction to Nebuchadnezzar, the first of three stories in this book. In this topic the main plot line is developed concerning the interpretation of the king's dreams. When none of the wise men in Nebuchadnezzar's court can make known the king's dream and its interpretation, the king issues a decree that all the wise men of Babylon should be killed, a decree that will reach Daniel and his friends if God does not intervene. Although VanDrunen says that Daniel 2 'does not condemn Nebuchadnezzar for any sin or present him in a particularly negative light at all,'[38] he does come across in the narrative as a raging tyrant who suffers no incompetence and is willing to exterminate not only the immediate courtiers who cannot tell and interpret his dream, but others that have had nothing to do with interpreting his dreams up to the issuing of the decree! Daniel alerts his friends and they all beseech God to make known to them the dream and its interpretation, which God does.

---

37. Michael Seufert, 'Refusing the King's portion: A reexamination of Daniel's dietary reaction in Daniel 1,' *JSOT* 43/4 (2019): pp. 644-60.

38. VanDrunen, *Divine Covenants and Moral Order*, p. 197.

It is not because Daniel excelled more at learning that he was able to interpret the king's dreams, for he himself demurs from such a posture (cf. 2:30).[39] Rather, it is the case that God has revealed it to him. Daniel tells the dream of the colossal statue to Nebuchadnezzar. He tells the king directly from whence the king's power comes; it is derivative: 'You O King, king of kings, to whom the God of heaven has given a kingdom, strength, power and honor' (2:36, author's translation) and that God has given Nebuchadnezzar this power to rule, for he is the head of gold (2:38). As discussed above, three subsequent kingdoms will come to power according to this dream. Nevertheless, Daniel also tells King Nebuchadnezzar that a stone (not hewn from human hands) will ultimately destroy these kingdoms and God will set up an everlasting kingdom (2:45). Many interpreters at this point overreach in their analysis of the last part of the chapter and assume that Nebuchadnezzar converts to the one true God, i.e., Yahweh. This claim goes beyond what the text itself claims, as VanDrunen notes.[40]

Paul makes it perfectly clear in Romans 13:1-7 that all authority among civil magistrates is derived from God. However, here in Daniel 2:37-38, Daniel makes the same point with equal clarity to Nebuchadnezzar that 'God has given a kingdom, strength, power, and honor and wherever the sons of men dwell, the beast of the field and the birds of the heavens, he has given [them] into your hand and caused you to rule over all of them; you are it – the head of gold!' (author's translation). What is particularly striking in this chapter are the correspondences between the early chapters of Genesis and the Daniel stories. It seems that we have an allusion to Genesis 1:26, 28 corroborated by Daniel 2:37-38 since the text states explicitly that the God of heaven had given Nebuchadnezzar dominion 'over the beast of the field and the birds of the heavens.' We will discuss this more in Daniel 4. However, suffice it to say for now that Daniel, without compromise to his convictions, distinguishes himself among Nebuchadnezzar's courtiers such that he ends up in a position of the highest esteem and honor as a godly, faith-filled Jew in the court of a foreign king. He has learned the high art of a hyphenated existence in this sin-cursed exile.

---

39. *Pace* Hart, *A Secular Faith*, pp. 255.

40. VanDrunen, *Divine Covenants and Moral Order*, p. 198.

## Daniel 3

One of my goals in these discussions of Daniel will be to explain how these chapters (stories) hang together. How are they integrated with the previous chapters that go before them and how are they connected with the chapters that follow? Daniel 1 and 2 are linked with dreams. Daniel 2 and 3 are linked with the colossal image that Nebuchadnezzar erects in which the gold head represents him. One clue to unlock the answer to this question comes from observing how the repetitions work.

Learned treatments of 'repetition' in the Hebrew Bible can be found in the secondary literature (e.g., Robert Alter and Adele Berlin), but my favorite author dealing with this is Herbert Chanan Brichto.[41] A key question when analyzing literary repetition is to ask why a particular author uses simple terms with sometimes striking ranges of meaning when his dictionary offered him quite a few alternatives? For Brichto, for example, the little book of Jonah is a masterpiece test case of exquisite use of repetition.[42] This chapter now before us in Daniel is another masterpiece.

Think of the many repetitions used in this chapter. There is the list of officials (3:4, 7, 29). There is the refrain of 'peoples, nations, and languages' in 3:4, 7, and 29 ('*ammayy*', '*ummayy*', *w(e)lišš'ayy*'). Notice the list of musical instruments (3:5, 7, 10, 15). Then, there is the constant refrain of the three young Hebrew youths, 'Shadrach, Meshach, and Abednego' (3:12, 14, 16, 19, 20, 23, 36, 28, 29, 30). And there is the list of garments (cf. 3:21 and 3:27). These elements do not exhaust the recurrent elements in the narrative. There are also recurrent phrases like 'the image of gold that King Nebuchadnezzar had set up,' and 'the furnace of burning fire/blazing fiery furnace,' and 'bow down and worship.' Dana Fewell understands the function of this repetition in the following way:

> The narrator's tone ridicules Nebuchadnezzar's misunderstanding of the dream and this attempt to reassure himself of his powerful control. The tedious repetitions (of which we have not heard the last) undermine

---

41. Hebert Chanan Brichto, *Toward a Grammar of Biblical Poetics: Tales of the Prophets* (New York: Oxford University Press, 1992) and idem, *The Names of God: Poetic Readings in Biblical Beginnings* (New York: Oxford University Press, 1998).

42. See Brichto, *Toward a Grammar*, pp. 67-87.

the solemnity of the occasion and leave the reader wondering about the hierarchy of significance in the story world. Rather than explaining what the image represents, the narrator spends time repeatedly listing officials and musical instruments. The pomp of the event is given more emphasis than the meaning of the event. The narrator constantly reminds us, as if we could forget at any moment, the image is something 'Nebuchadnezzar the king has erected (vv. 2,3,5,6) and thereby mocks the king's attempt to be remembered as the head of gold.[43]

Fewell then asks if these are merely verbose repetitions without any significance and comes to the conclusion that the Chaldeans are 'spin doctors.' Indeed, 'the Chaldeans implicitly contrast themselves to the three Jews.'[44] When the narrator introduces them into the story, they are characterized as slanderers. In 3:8 they 'maliciously accused' the Jews, more literally, they were 'eaters of their flesh' (interesting calque from the Akkadian language that made its influence felt obviously upon Aramaic, for the Hebrew equivalent, see Psalm 27:2).[45] This is a deliberate variation of the original. They expand and reorganize in order to move the king to action. Although they portray themselves as dutiful subjects, the narrator exposes and makes quite clear what their intentions are. This deliberate variation is no accident.

Notice the contrast between the three Jewish youths and the Chaldeans. What are we doing as we read and note characterization in the art of narration? Brichto reminds us that everything depends on the distinction between showing and telling.[46] The art of narration lies largely in the author suppressing his own voice. 'Showing' is the narrator telling you something about a character, and developing characterization through actions and direct discourse is the art of doing just that. Brichto quotes Mark Twain to good effect here: 'As Mark Twain communicated once, there is no art in conveying the image of a bore by letting him run on for page after page of dreary dialogue; the art is in showing him (that is, allowing the bore to show himself as such) in as few words as possible.'[47]

---

43. Dana Fewell, *Circle of Sovereignty: A Story of Stories in Daniel 1-6*, Biblical and Literature Series 6 (Sheffield: Almond Press, 988), pp. 67-68.

44. Ibid., p. 71.

45. Basically, they were 'back biters.'

46. Brichto, *Toward a Grammar*, pp. 10-11.

47. Ibid., p. 12.

For example, when we come to the speech of the three Jewish youths, is there any extensive repetition of musical instruments, asks Fewell? No. There is no self-defense on the part of the Jewish youths. There is no attempt to 'buy time.' The king asks the question (probably meant to be rhetorical by him but they refuse to let it be), 'What kind of god [literally, 'who is a god who'] can deliver you out of my hand?' (3:15, author's translation). Here is the first climactic part of the story.

The Jewish youths affirm their loyalty, not to Nebuchadnezzar, but to their own God (cf. vv. 17-18). An interesting contrast between them and certain Chaldeans who slander them. Both parties are standing before the king. The Chaldeans adopt their strategy, ostensibly, to advance themselves. Their loyalties are to the king. Shadrach, Meshach, and Abednego refuse to adopt the king's religious practices; they don't seek to advance themselves but risk not only losing their political station, but possibly life itself. At great risk to themselves, they follow their hyphenated existence without compromising their allegiance to God.

As we saw from Daniel 1, being aware of certain allusions can also illumine the story for us. There seems to be a satirizing pun employed by the narrator here as well. In 2:31, Daniel says: 'You O king, were seeing [dreaming] and behold a great image (Aramaic צְלֵם): this image was mighty and its brightness was surpassing, [it] was standing before you, and its appearance was frightful' (author's translation). The narrator has used the same Aramaic word that was used for the colossal statue of gold in Daniel 2 to refer to the image of Nebuchadnezzar's face in Daniel 3, especially verse 19: 'Then Nebuchadnezzar was filled with anger, and the image (Aramaic צְלֵם) of his face was changed with regard to Shadrach, Meshach, and Abednego. He answered and ordered that the furnace be heated seven times beyond what was appropriate [to heat it]' (author's translation). The narrator, it would seem, has satirized Nebuchadnezzar's audacity. In comparison with Genesis 1 where God creates human beings in his own image, here Nebuchadnezzar has created in his own 'image' the colossal so that he might be worshiped! Here, we see an example of the state turning bestial against the people of God, conflating the spiritual and the civil in a stupendous act of self-aggrandizement.[48]

---

48. Peck, *Notes on Ecclesiology*, p. 243.

Verse 15 sets us up for other allusions and puns, primarily drawn from 2 Kings 18 and 19. Second Kings describes King Hezekiah's reign. It also describes the fall of the Northern Kingdom of Israel. As is well known, Aramaic by this time had become a major language of diplomacy. As Jerusalem is besieged, they are taunted from outside the walls with the following intimidating questions:

> Has any of the gods of the nation ever delivered his land out of the hand of the king of Assyria? Who among all the gods of the lands have delivered their land from my hand, that Yahweh should deliver Jerusalem from my hand?

But notice Hezekiah's promise: 'Yahweh will surely save us and not hand over ...' Now we are ready. Everything is in place. But notice that the various loyalties talked about before seem to complicate a simple retribution statement.

Returning to Daniel, the reader should notice the loyal, allegedly dutiful courtiers (the Chaldeans) now suffer. We build to a pause. We try and take in what has happened. Now our thoughts turn to the three men. We look, and behold there are four! We have expected, or hoped for, deliverance from the fire, but instead deliverance comes from within. Now the shift occurs, but only from the perspective of Nebuchadnezzar and the onlookers. It is interesting that theophanies often happen in association with fire in the Hebrew Bible (Exod. 3:13, 21-22; Num. 16:35). And so we see that the repetition, 'blazing, fiery furnace', has all along been foreshadowing what would be central in the upcoming focus. So now, one backtracks to the furnace, and Shadrach, Meshach, and Abednego shine forth with the mysterious fourth figure as well. Verse 26 now shifts the reader's perspective to that of Nebuchadnezzar.

Notice the irony in Nebuchadnezzar's response. We know now of God, through Nebuchadnezzar's eyes, so to speak. We know nothing of Shadrach's, Meshach's, and Abednego's feelings at this point. In fact, one could say that their individual characterization is downplayed here and they are put forth in a kind of 'collective characterization.'

In conclusion, we see in Daniel 3 that the state turned its power into a bestial provocation of the principles laid out earlier in the book, 'Who is a God who can deliver you from my hand?' (Dan. 3:15, author's translation). This same spirit of power will surface when we look at the church age as it begins under the emperor Domitian (A.D. 81–96).[49] Although the state is legitimate, as we saw early on in this book, there is a constant tilt towards abuse of power, and the state can turn bestial in a moment. Even so, in the next chapter of Daniel, we will observe Nebuchadnezzar changed into a beast.

## Daniel 4

In Daniel 4, there are further allusions made to Genesis 1. For example, in Genesis 1:30 we see that God gives 'the beasts of the earth and the birds of the heavens, and green plants are given for food.' However, in Daniel 4, when Nebuchadnezzar is punished (cf., 4:13), his portion becomes living off the 'grass of the earth'; furthermore, his human heart (= mind) is to be changed into 'the heart of a beast' (4:13-17). This is his punishment for rebellion against the Creator.

Daniel 4 has lots of tree imagery. In Scripture, sometimes tree imagery is positive and sometimes it is negative. Positively, it is often used to communicate Messianic ideas (cf., Isa. 11:1-3, 10). Sometimes it is used to communicate God's salvation and continuing protection (cf., Hosea 14:5-7). Sometimes the tree imagery is used to communicate negative images, as is the case in Isaiah 10:33-34. Another example can be seen in Ezekiel 31 from which I quote below. Here Ezekiel's imagery is used to describe the reign and fall of the Pharaoh of Egypt:

> Behold, I will liken you to a cedar in Lebanon, with fair branches and forest shade, and of great height, its tip among the clouds .... All the birds of the air made their nests in its boughs; under its branches all the beasts of the field brought forth their young; and under its shadow dwelt all the great nations .... No tree in the garden of God was like it in beauty. I made it beautiful in the mass of its branches, and all the trees of Eden envied it that were in the garden of God.
>
> Therefore, thus says the Lord God: Because it towered in height and set its top among the clouds, and its heart was proud of its height, I will give it into the hand of a mighty one of the nations; he shall surely deal with it as its wickedness deserves. I have cast it out. Foreigners, the most terrible of the nations, will cut it down and leave it. On the mountains and in all the valleys its branches will fall, and its boughs will be broken in all the

---

49. T. E. Peck, *Notes on Ecclesiology*, p. 129.

watercourses of the land; and all the people of the earth will go from its shadow and leave it (Ezek. 31:3, 6, 8b-9, 10-12).

Other scholars have noted more allusions and there are many extra-biblical parallels to this kind of imagery being invoked in classical authors, such as in Greek literature with Herodotus.

As mentioned in our discussion of Daniel 2, Nebuchadnezzar's swelling pride is to be punished. The theme of dominion, with its allusion to the creation narrative here, is ironically employed to speak of his downfall. Dana Fewell is spot on when she comments: 'This theme of dominion—the grasping of it and the loss of it—plays ironically on the theme of the Genesis 1 creation story. There, humanity is given dominion over all the birds, fish and beasts. Here in Dan 4, the one who has seized dominion is the one who now must become like a bird-beast over which other humans have dominion.'[50] Just as we have seen here that there are strong allusions to Genesis 1, there are also strong allusions to the Tower of Babel scene in Genesis 10–11 as well. Just as the focus was on human pride there, so also here in Daniel 4 the focus is on Nebuchadnezzar's swelling pride.

Given the chiastic structure that we have noticed in the overall structure of the book, William Shea asks the further question if we should expect chiastic structures on a smaller scale as well. Indeed, he identifies it in Daniel 4:[51]

*Prologue* vv. 1-3

   *A* vv. 4-7 Dream reception

      *X* vv. 8-9 Dialogue I – King to Daniel

        *B* vv. 10-17 – Dream recital
        vv. 18-19a – King to Daniel

      *Y* vv. 19:b Dialogue II – Daniel to King

        *B'* vv. 20-26 Dream interpretation

      *Z* v. 27 Dialogue III – Daniel to King

   *A'* vv. 28-33 Dream fulfillment

*Epilogue* vv. 34-38

---

50. Endnote 32, of Fewell's book, *Circle of Sovereignty*, p. 182.

51. William Shea, 'Further Literary Structures in Daniel 2-7: An Analysis of Daniel 4,' *AUSS* 23 (1985): pp. 29-52.

This suggestion for a structure seems to have commended itself to other scholars, like Fewell; however, she complains that Shea's representation of the structure doesn't guide the reader into uncovering its significance for the story's meaning.[52] She suggests that the effect of having an implied narrator unveiled here seems to reinforce the exclusivity of Daniel's knowledge and wisdom. In other words, by having the speech of Daniel stand on its own, the implied narrator allows Daniel's variation of the dream (B') to stand in stark relief over and against Nebuchadnezzar's recitation (B). This provides a 'control on Nebuchadnezzar's limited point of view. Daniel's urging Nebuchadnezzar to repent (Z) represents Nebuchadnezzar's situation differently than the king represents it (X).[53] What's the payoff?

In short, Nebuchadnezzar has no accurate self-perception, she claims; he actually has a problem seeing rightly, understanding correctly. The issue is one of reliability on the part of Nebuchadnezzar. The noetic effects of his profound hubris have influenced his interpretation of the world and himself! Nebuchadnezzar may think he is the sovereign of the whole world but in reality he is not even the sovereign of his own story.

When Nebuchadnezzar does regain his reason, he is allowed to resume telling his story. He lifts his eyes to the heavens and his reason returns to him. He recounts his story and launches into doxology. All this fits very well with what we saw in the garden with regards to the juridical function of the tree. The Word must have the last word. Human beings are not interpreters unto themselves. Daniel, with painstaking tact, calls the king to repentance:[54]

> However, O king, may my counsel be acceptable to you and remove your sins by [doing] righteousness and your misdeeds by compassion to the poor, in case there may be a prolonging of your prosperity (MT = 4:24, author's translation. [ET = 4:27])

This passage is especially interesting for several reasons. Notice that 'Human authority structures and systems of justice, even when riddled with serious flaws, should not be despised.'[55] This passage also raises the question of whether Christians are to have a 'prophetic' voice in similar

---

52. Fewell, *Circle of Sovereignty*, p. 103.

53. Ibid., p. 104.

54. See the author's, 'The Use of Deferential Language in the Arsames Correspondence and Biblical Aramaic Compared,' *MAARAV* 13.1 (2006): pp. 43-74, especially at p. 67.

55. VanDrunen, *Divine Covenants and Moral Order*, p. 206.

situations. Moreover, it raises interesting questions about how believers ought to address secular kings (or magistrates) in their official capacity?

Let's be clear that the Scriptures have scant evidence to guide us in such situations. However, one line of reasoning that may be helpful is for us to make proper deductions from broader theological considerations in the Scriptures. The Lord God himself is constantly portrayed as a King; indeed, the supreme King, who cares for the widow, the orphan and the alien when they are in need. God, the Great Father-King, constantly provides for the destitute. Consider, for example, Psalm 68:5-6:

> A Father of the fatherless and a judge for the widows,
> is God in his holy habitation.
> God makes a home for the lonely;
> He leads out the prisoners into prosperity,
> but the rebellious dwell in a parched land.

Would God, who so characterizes himself in his own inspired Word, leave the institutions that he designed to be in place in the world as common grace institutions bereft of any compassionate concern for these destitute of paternal support, for example? This is not a blueprint for a socialist agenda. Such a claim would not cohere with other parts of Scripture. Therefore, the civil state is merely supplementary to the care of the family for the outcasts and the compassion of the faithful towards their own (e.g., in and through the diaconate). In all this, it is remarkable how God has put an overall network of care in the world. But the role of the state in all this is merely supplementary, and thus must remain so. Even so, Daniel gives no quarter to a secular king who will not fulfill these obligations.

## Daniel 5

In Daniel 4 we observed a proud king (Nebuchadnezzar) abased and subsequently restored. Now we will see his son (Belshazzar) abased and not restored: rather, he was killed. The poet George Gordon, or Lord Byron (1788-1824), whom the French critic, Hippolyte Taine said was 'the greatest and most English of these artists [Coleridge, Shelley, and Keats]; he is so great and so English that from him alone we shall learn more truths of his country and of his age than from all the rest together.'[56] Byron said many years ago:

---

56. *The Norton Anthology of English Literature Fourth Edition*, Vol. 2, M. H. Adams (general editor), (New York, NY: Norton & Company, 1979), p. 505.

Belshazzar's grave is made,
His kingdom pass'd away,
He, in the balance weigh'd,
Is light and worthless clay;
The shroud his robe of state,
His canopy the stone;
The Mede is at the gate!
The Persian on his throne!

We have been noting that chiasms (inverted literary structures) abound in the biblical book of Daniel. It's important at this point to note that chiasms can be represented in different ways. For example, a narrator may represent his material in an A:B:C::C:B:A fashion. That is what we observed in Daniel 4. However, a chiasm may be represented in an A:B:C:B:A fashion. That is what we see in Daniel 5. Moreover, it is the center of the chiasm in this case that communicates the most important material and meaning. To contrast Daniel 4 and 5 in another way yet is to say that Daniel 4 tells the fulfillment of a dream prophecy. There the interpretation came in the last major block, which was followed by a short epilogue. In Daniel 5, by contrast, the dream and interpretation are given in the first and last (fourth) major blocks in the chapter. It's in the center of the chiasm of Daniel 5 that we see an important link between the speeches of Belshazzar (Nebuchadnezzar's son) and Daniel. Visually, we may represent it in the following manner:

**A.** verse 16b – [Belshazzar] 'Now if you are able to read the writing and show me its interpretation,

> **B.** verse 16c – with purple you shall be clothed and a necklace of gold shall be upon your neck, as the Triumvir in the kingdom you shall rule' (author's translation)

> **B'** verse 17a – Then Daniel answered and spoke to the king, 'Let your gifts be to yourself and your favors to others;

**A'** verse 17b – nevertheless, the writing I will read *to the king*, and the interpretation, I shall make *him* know.'

At first glance, this may appear as if Daniel has set aside the respect and honor due to the king and forgotten his manners. The narrator, however, has used (in 17b) the third-person term to add greater perceived distance than would have seemed by speaking to the king in second person forms or directly. Moreover, the object suffix ('him') on the end of the verb depends on a reference to 'the king'; therefore, although it may appear as an impolite response, there actually is a high level of deference in the reported speech of Daniel.[57] The point of demonstrating these chiasms is to show the height from which the secular king shall fall. This is especially brought out in the key speech of 5:13b-16a, which 'may be a forceful way to portray the pinnacle on which he [the king] had placed himself and to emphasize the dramatic manner in which he would fall from that pinnacle.'[58]

In Daniel 1, we observed that the issue of defilement was front and center. It is central in this Daniel 5 as well. For now this arrogant son of Nebuchadnezzar will drink wine at his banquet out of the very vessels captured from the Hebrews when they were taken into exile. In a very subtle shift of words, the narrator portrays Daniel as the prophet who speaks in the name of God Most High about events even before they happen.

In Daniel 5:3-4, we read: 'Then they brought the vessels of gold which had been brought from the temple of the house of God that was in Jerusalem, and out of them the king, his noblemen, his wives and concubines drank. They drank wine and they praised the gods *of gold and silver*, copper, iron, wood and stone' (author's translation). Later in the chapter, however, when we read the narrator's description of the events, notice the subtle but important shift that takes place in 5:23:

> But against the Lord of heaven you have lifted up yourself, and the vessels of his house have been brought before you, and you, and your noblemen, your wives and your concubines have drunk wine in them, and the gods of *silver and gold*, brass, iron, wood and stone, which see not, and hear not, and know not, you have praised, but the God in whose hand is your breath and to whom are all your ways, you have not glorified! (author's translation).

Notice the reversal of gold and silver. This is significant because, in Daniel 2, we saw that the gold represented Nebuchadnezzar's Neo-Babylonian kingdom and the silver represented the Medo-Persian

---

57. See Estelle, 'Deferential Language,' pp. 58-59.

58. William Shea, 'Further Literary Structures in Daniel 2-7: An Analysis of Daniel 5, and the Broader Relationships within Chapters 2–7,' *AUSS* 23 (1985): pp. 277-95, but especially at p. 294.

kingdom. Therefore, here we have a narrative that is representing the eve on which the Babylonian kingdom is coming to an end and the Medo-Persian empire is emerging. This is represented—subtly, but importantly—in the materials described just before the actual historical occurrence of the change of kingdoms.

One last and very important matter deserves mention: the interpretation of the mysterious writing on the wall: MENE, MENE, TEKEL, UPHARSIN. First, we need to discuss Belshazzar's reaction when he sees the handwriting on the wall and then we need to discuss the actual writing on the wall, what it means.

For my interpretation of Belshazzar's reaction to the mysterious writing on the wall I follow an important and humorous article written by Al Wolters.[59] Many different translations have been offered for the enigmatic language used in Daniel 5:6 (*weqitre harseh mishtarayin*) to capture the king's reaction:

KJV = 'The joints of his loins were loosened.'

Keil = 'The bands or ligaments of his thighs were loosed.'

RSV = 'his limbs gave way.'

JB = 'his thigh-joints went slack.'

Berkeley = 'The muscles of his loins loosened.'

NASB = 'his hip joints went slack.'

ESV = 'his limbs gave way.'

Wolter's translation is different. His claim is 'that verse five [sic] refers to the panic-stricken loss of sphincter control and that verses twelve and sixteen are a mocking and ironic allusion to this ignominious incontinence on the king's part.'[60] In other words, as Germans would say, '*die Hosen voll haben*' or, he filled his trousers. In other words, he became so frightened, he soiled himself and succumbed to involuntary defecation.

Wolter's lexical evidence for this interpretation is as follows. This interpretation first goes well with the usual meaning of the Aramaic word *haras* ('loins') which is often associated in the Bible with the

---

59. A. L. Wolters, 'Untying the King's Knots: Physiology and Wordplay in Daniel 5,' *JBL* 110 (1991): pp. 117-122.

60. Ibid., p. 118.

reproductive organs, and not typically meaning 'hip' or 'thigh.' Moreover, the Aramaic word *qetar* is the exact etymological parallel to 'sphincter', being derived from verbs meaning, 'to tie up' or 'bind tight.' The idea is to constrict, which is the exact action of the sphincter muscles which constrict the bladder or anus. Moreover, Akkadian cognates further strengthen the argument. Additionally, this interpretation respects the normal meaning of the Aramaic lexemes in the troublesome phrase, *qitre harseh*, an anatomical reference and a well-known response to fear. Rarely does the Aramaic word *qitren* mean 'knots' as it is usually translated in verses 12 and 16. Therefore, the meaning is unknown to the characters in the story; however, we as readers are privy to the narrator's intentions and the dramatic irony involving double entendre.

When viewed from the perspective of the Aramaic-speaking Jews who had suffered very much at the hands of the Babylonians, the queen who enters and suggests that Daniel can 'untie the knots' and then when Daniel enters and the king says, 'I understand you can untie my knots for me,' would have been comedic: the audience would have been rollicking with derisive laughter. The narrator has posed the 'powerful' and arrogant king as a buffoon in the eyes of the audience.

Our final observations on this chapter will engage the mysterious writing on the wall that left the king 'undone' when it appeared. For our interpretation of the writing itself, I will follow another article by Wolters.[61] His thesis for this section of the chapter is that the original Aramaic text would have been written with nine letters (*mn' tqlprs*), which can be divided up differently and vocalized differently. So the difficulty had to do with the writing being continuous (without word division). The wise men were asked to read the consonants and interpret: this could only take place by dividing the consonants and vocalization. Daniel shows his true mettle here.

Wolters suggests three different readings, all having to do with judgment. Daniel reads each of the three words with three different meanings, all under the rubric of 'scales' that weigh, all representing God's judgment. As Wolter's claims:

> It is a *tour de force* which in one stroke fully justifies Daniel's reputation as someone who could 'explain riddles and untie knots' (vs. 12). Daniel divides

---

61. A. L. Wolters, 'The Riddle of the Scales in Daniel 5,' *HUCA* (1991): pp. 155-77.

the nine consonants into three units of three letters each, and then proceeds to give an interpretation based on three levels of meaning for each unit.[62]

Daniel shows himself to be a wise, tactful courtier, an excellent example of what it means to live a hyphenated existence as a God-fearing believer in a common grace situation. He is a citizen of two kingdoms: one civil and one spiritual. What is evident from Daniel 5 is that God does not countenance hubris on the part of secular kings: 'God does not—*in terms of his temporal governance and temporal judgments*—require relinquishment of idols, specific rituals of worship, or any kind of conversion to the Mosaic covenant. Rather, he requires kings to recognize humbly his ultimate sovereignty over the course of history and to keep their hands off his holy things and those who worship him.'[63]

## Daniel 6

As argued previously, when we come to Daniel 6, Daniel finds himself in the court of King Darius, who is Cyrus. Interestingly, in comparison with the previous two kings (Nebuchadnezzar and his son Belshazzar), Darius is the most challenging of the three kings to interpret. He comes across as a 'generally good man, albeit one who falls prey to flattery in a moment of weakness.'[64]

Although it is true that at the end of the day Darius prevents people from worshiping the one true God, his virtues as outlined by the text are manifold: he recognizes Daniel as advisor (6:3), he is immediately distressed when he learns the unintended consequences of his ill-formed decree (6:16), he fasts all night long while Daniel is in the lions' den (6:18), he rejoices when Daniel is finally delivered (6:23), and then he executes justice against Daniel's enemies (6:24).[65]

This is undoubtedly one of the most beloved stories among Christian families. However, the message seems not to be 'Dare to be a Daniel'; rather, the message is how to live a hyphenated existence as a faithful God-fearer in a common grace situation of exile. Just as the prediluvian, altar-oriented people of God must obey him as citizens of two kingdoms

---

62. Ibid., p. 160.
63. VanDrunen, *Divine Covenants and Moral Order*, pp. 203-04.
64. Ibid., p. 201.
65. Ibid., p. 202.

(cf., Chapter 2 of this book), so also now that they are exiled from their homeland:

> For the covenantal people to participate in the common political enterprise with non-covenantal people was entirely in keeping with the genius of the city of man as a common grace arrangement for the pragmatic cooperation of all mankind in cultural endeavor. God's prediluvian people must adopt towards the political order where they resided, even when Cainite dominated, the same stance that was advocated by the apostle Paul for the New Testament saints in the Gentile world (1 Tim. 2:2) and, earlier, by the prophet Jeremiah in his instructions to the Israelites in their exile existence in the world-wilderness (Jer. 29:4ff.). They were to be cooperatively constructive and exhibit towards the city of man an attitude of prayerful solicitude for its peace.[66]

## Conclusion

We are now ready to ask what the preceding detailed treatment of Daniel 1–6 teaches us about the Christian's role in a secular society, and by way of implications for the primary mission of the church.

First, it seems that this more detailed study corroborates the findings of David VanDrunen that 'Daniel 2-6 ... take special interest in kings and hold them liable particularly for hubris toward God and breaches of justice toward weaker human beings.'[67] From Daniel 1 onwards, a major concern of these texts has been to teach that the one true God is sovereign and in control of international politics and the smallest minutiae of the lives of his saints. I have shown how this claim is substantiated through the literary artistry with which Daniel presents his case: point of view studies and word puns in Daniel 1, and the constant exaltation and abasement motifs of kings in these chapters, not only in their content but in the very chiastic forms with which they are organized.

Secondly, the narrator has 'shown' the message through the drama and artistry of narrative: the author is a master storyteller. The rising and falling cadences of the chiasms are matched by the rise and fall from grace of 'great' kings and potentates. Indeed, we saw how even comedy is used to show them to be buffoons sometimes before the

---

66. Meredith G. Kline, *Kingdom Prologue*, p. 199. See similar comments in David VanDrunen, *Living in God's Two Kingdoms*, pp. 92-96.

67. VanDrunen, *Divine Covenants and Moral Order*, pp. 204-05.

power of the supreme sovereign: God Himself. The faithful, Daniel and his companions, remain steady and God vindicates them time and again although they themselves must endure trials. Not only do they remain faithful, but they also actually excel in their vocations since their identity is one of a hyphenated existence.

As VanDrunen puts it, 'Daniel 2 does put the Noahic covenant in eschatological perspective: this covenant will come to an end in the kingdom of God's ultimate triumph. But Daniel 3-6 encourages submission to its structures while it remains in force.'[68] Or, we might say that learning to live gracefully in an assimilated and devout way in a secular nation without accommodating and compromising one's faith is supremely modeled in and through the example of Daniel and his friends. This double-sided character of Christian existence is a crucial lesson to grasp if we are to remain apolitical in the church. Secular society was—ultimately—not a threat to orthodoxy for these Jews.[69]

---

68. Ibid., p. 206

69. Hart, *A Secular Faith*, p. 257.

# The Primary Mission of the Church, New Testament

## Introduction

We have been looking at the biblical foundations for the primary mission of the church. In Chapter 1, we examined foundations for this from Genesis. In Chapter 2, we looked at a number of important OT passages, especially from the time of the Patriarchs as well as the Jews who had been exiled. In this chapter, we want to look at some of the NT teaching on the Kingdom of God in order to see that there has been advancement and change since the OT time period; however, there is also much continuity.[1]

In what follows, I will give emphasis to several texts that focus on the role of the state vis-à-vis the church. This may seem strange to the reader since our subject is the primary mission of the church; however, it is the ongoing argument of this book that the church and state remain two divinely ordained institutions, independent and separate, with very different functions. Therefore, to clarify the role of the state and the roles and responsibilities of Christians individually and as a

---

1. Although Charles Hodge, 'Relation of the Church and State,' pp. 106-118, especially p. 117 in *Discussion in Church Polity* (New York, NY: Charles Scribner's Son, 1878) will argue that we have no authority to argue from the Old Testament economy since it was temporary and has been abolished. No doubt Hodge had the theocracy of the monarchy in view but fails to consider the relevance of the Patriarchs and the Jews in exile for the important topic under discussion here.

church corporately towards the civil magistrate can greatly improve our understanding of the primary mission of the church.

First, I will make an important point about the Bible's claims with respect to Christ as Ruler over all creation. This is a point often misunderstood by many. Second, we will examine some of the classic texts that clearly demonstrate that the church is a distinctively redemptive kingdom. At the same time, some of these passages affirm the legitimacy of the state as a civil kingdom but they do not give any specific outlines regarding the historical origins or detailed instructions about the specific functions of the state. The reader will immediately notice that we are continuing to build an argument that the Scriptures teach a two kingdoms doctrine. That is because it is very difficult, if not impossible, to fully appreciate the Bible's teaching about the primary mission of the church without a biblical two-kingdom's doctrine.

## Two Important Preliminary Claims

The first thing to say before discussing the meaning of these NT passages is that Christ is ruler of all creation. This is assumed throughout this book and in this chapter. However, that does not mean that there are not important distinctions to make about *how* God rules over His creation during this age. Thomas Peck wrote years ago:

> Christians are all agreed that Jesus, their Saviour, is King of kings and Lord of lords, not only in the sense that He is the greatest of kings, but in the sense that all earthly kings and lords are subject to His authority. But the question is, whether civil rulers derive their authority from Him, as Mediator, or whether they derive their authority from God, as moral governor of mankind. Christ says that, 'His kingdom is not of this world.' This is His solemn testimony before a civil magistrate whose authority He recognises. (See John 19:10,11; Rom. 13:1, etc.).[2]

Notice that while there is no denial of Christ's sovereignty or Lordship over all creation, mere distinctions are claimed. The state derives its authority from God as Moral Governor. Its authority is legitimate, but limited. It does not have authority over the meaning or interpretation of the Scriptures; that function falls to the church and her officers. Peck, in another context writes:

---

2. Thomas E. Peck, 'Church and State,' *SPR* 16:2 (Oct. 1863): pp. 121-144, especially p. 135.

> As the state is the ordinance of God, as creator and moral governor, and is designed for man as man, it has nothing to do with any principles of religion but those which belong to man as man: to wit, the being of God and a moral government. To give it any power over the truths of revealed religion, and over the records which contain those truths [the Scriptures], is to confound it with the church, or what is practically the same thing, to abolish the church, except as an auxiliary of the state, in preserving order.[3]

The second thing to make clear is that the church has been given power, although that power is very specifically delineated in the Bible. Moreover, it bears repeating, the primary mission of the church is spiritual, which is to say that its primary mission is related to spiritual functions and matters: rightly interpreting and teaching the Bible, which is her constitution and charter, administering the sacraments (Baptism and the Lord's Supper), caring for and shepherding the elect, and finally disciplining her members when necessary, whose disciplinary goal is good order and the restoration of errant sinners, and maintaining the good name of God to those outside the church. These duties do not imply that the church is anti-material or anti-physical. Meditate on some of these spiritual activities and it will become immediately apparent that the church is concerned with matters material and concrete. For example, she administers bread and wine in the sacrament; visible signs and seals. She engages in preaching through known languages and congregations sing (usually to accompaniment) in real music most often printed on paper. The list could go on and on. Even so, one constantly hears the drumbeat today at all levels in the culture that we must be busy with having a prophetic voice against unjust social structures; however, what do the Scriptures declare as the church's primary mission?

## Matthew 16:18-19; 18:18; John 20:22, 23: 'the Power of the Keys'

The notion of 'power' in modernity in many cases has taken on a negative connotation. However, our minds should be shaped by what the Bible says, and the fact of the matter is that the church has been granted power, properly defined and delineated. As Herman Bavinck (1854-1921) says: 'When Jesus, coming to his own home, was not received by his own people,

---

3. Thomas E. Peck, 'Notes on Ecclesiology,' p. 147.

he organized his disciples into an ἐκκλησια … that, hoping and suffering, had to await his second coming and the victory over all his enemies.[4] He continues: 'There can be no doubt that Christ founded such a church community and entrusted to it a certain power.'[5] We will have much more to say about the exact nature of this power below (see Chapter 13); however, suffice it to say for now that this power is limited to the spiritual.

When we talk about our Lord giving the power of the 'keys' to the church, this has a very special character. Keys are a symbol of control or mastery (Isa. 22:22; Luke 11:52; Rev. 1:18; 3:7; 9:1; 20:1). Here in Matthew, they 'denote the power of Peter to "open" and to "close" the kingdom of heaven, that is, to determine what will or will not be in effect.'[6] What power does Peter receive from Jesus? What will, or rather who will, and who will not be allowed in the kingdom of heaven. Although it is often considered outlandish in our day and age, nevertheless remarkably Jesus grants power to the apostles (and by extension, to officers in His church) 'the right to judge persons.'[7] To be perfectly clear, that is to say that on the basis of the gift of the Holy Spirit, the apostles (and by extension the officers of the church) 'receive the power to forgive or retain the sins of people in terms of whether they accept or reject the gospel.'[8] This is power spiritually defined:

> Accordingly, it is indeed a power, a real and comprehensive power, consisting in the ministry of Word and sacrament (Matt. 28:19); in the determination of what will be the rule in the kingdom of heaven (16:19); in the forgiveness or retention of sins (John 20:23); in the exercise of discipline over the members of the church (Matt. 16:19); Rom. 16:17; 1 Cor. 5:4; 2 Thess. 3:6; Titus 3:10; Heb. 12:15:1-17; 2 John 10; 2 Tim. 2:17; Rev. 2:14); in the discernment of all things (1 Cor. 2:15); in teaching, consoling, and admonishing (and so forth) the members of the church (Col. 3:16); in the use of gifts for the benefits of others (Rom. 12:4-8; 1 Cor. 12:12ff.); and in performing miracles (Mark 16:17-18 and so forth [although this has ceased after the Apostles]).[9]

---

4. Herman Bavinck, *Reformed Dogmatics* Vol. 4, John Bolt ed. (Grand Rapids, MI: Baker Academic, 2008), 4.393.

5. Ibid.

6. Ibid., 4.394.

7. Ibid.

8. Ibid.

9. Ibid.

Consequently, our Lord has invested his church with power to be a missionary society. Matthew 16:18-19 is the first New Testament reference to 'the church' and here we see, in short, that the church 'is to be the gateway for entering the kingdom, and its servants are to go "to the main roads and invite to the wedding feast as many as you find ... both bad and good ..."' (Matt. 22:9-10).[10] Political institutions, states, or countries are not among the things that Christ redeems through His church. This is because the Scriptures ordinarily speak of redeeming *individuals* and the only institution which Scripture applies this language to is *the church*.[11]

The Roman Catholic church takes this concept of power, the authority to open and shut the kingdom through the binding and loosing of sinners and the remitting and retaining of sins, to be judicial and effective. However, in the Reformed tradition, this is taken to be declarative and ministerial in power only.[12] The power associated with the 'Keys' is only 'declarative' and this distinction can hardly be overemphasized, especially in a day in which there is so much confusion. William Cunningham, the Free Church of Scotland theologian of such ability, expressed it this way:

> Ministers can open and shut the kingdom of heaven by the word, only by explaining the statements of Scripture, and by making known to men what are God's decisions and arrangements in regard to the salvation of sinners. Their binding or loosing is valid and effectual only in so far as their expositions of doctrine and duty correspond with the infallible standard and written word. If they state the real truth of God, they may in this way become the instruments of promoting men's eternal welfare; if they misstate or misrepresent it, they will mislead and injure those who may listen to them; but they do not themselves, by any power or authority vested in them, exert any efficiency in producing the result. And as no minister or body of ministers is infallible, so none is to be implicitly followed.[13]

# Matthew 22:15-22 (Mark 12:13-17; Luke 20:20-26)

These passages are where we observe Jesus' classic statement, 'Render to Caesar the things that are Caesar's, and to God the things that are

---

10. VanDrunen, *Living in God's Two Kingdoms*, p. 144.

11. VanDrunen, *Politics after Christendom*, p. 118, emphasis his.

12. A. Craig Troxel, 'Divine Right' Presbyterianism, p. 125.

13. William Cunningham, *Discussions on Church Principles: Popish, Erastian, and Presbyterian* (Edinburgh: T and T Clark, 1863), p. 243.

God's.' The Pharisees come plotting to entrap Jesus; specifically they plan to entangle him on the horns of a false dilemma: shall he recognize and affirm the authority of Rome or shall he speak against giving tribute to Rome and supposedly win the approval of the mob? Jesus' reply demonstrates that this is a false dilemma and in the process sets forth one of the clearest presentations of the two kingdoms distinction, according to Calvin:

> Christ's reply ... lays down a clear distinction between spiritual and civil government [*spiritual et politicum regimen*], in order to inform us that outward subjection does not prevent us from having within us a conscience free in the sight of God. For Christ intended us to refute the error of those who did not think that they would be the people of God unless they were free from every yoke of human authority .... In short, Christ declares that it is no violation of the authority of God or any injury done to his service if, in respect of outward polity, the Jews obey the Romans.[14]

So just as Christ submitted freely to earthly authorities during His incarnation, so also His people are subjected to civil authorities without any compromise of their citizenship in Christ's spiritual kingdom. Rome's authority derives from what Scripture reveals about creation and God's sovereign design: God is satisfied to have His people subjected to earthly authorities, to come under their laws and pay them taxes. Of course, as long as the state doesn't command Christians to do something that would be contrary to His revealed will, this is the case. State authority is a manifestation of common grace at least for the purpose of stability in society and the restraint of evil. Calvin's comments, quoted at length below, make this clear:

> We might be apt to think, no doubt, that the distinction does not apply, for, strictly speaking, when we perform our duty towards men we thereby render obedience to God. But Christ, accommodating his discourse to the common people, reckoned it enough to draw a distinction between the spiritual kingdom of God [*spirituale Dei regnum*], on the one hand, and political order and the condition of the present life [*ordine politico et praesentis vitae statu*], on the other. We must therefore attend to this distinction, that, while the Lord wishes to be the only lawgiver for governing souls, the rule for worshiping him must not be sought from any other source than from

---

14. Quoted in Tuininga, *Calvin's Political Theology*, pp. 169-70. Calvin's Commentary on Matthew 21:21 [sic] [1555]; CO [*Calvini Opera*] 45:601-602.

his own word, and that we ought to abide by the only and pure worship which is there enjoined; but that the power of the sword, the laws, and the decisions of tribunals do not hinder the worship of God from remaining entire among us. But this doctrine extends still farther, that every man, according to his calling, ought to perform the duty which he owes to men; that children ought willingly to submit to their parents and servants to their masters; that they ought to be courteous and obliging towards each other according to the law of charity, provided that God always retains the highest authority, to which everything that can be due to men is, as we say, subordinate. The amount of it therefore is that those who destroy political order [*politicum ordinem*] are rebellious against God, and therefore that obedience to princes and magistrates is always joined to the worship and fear of God; but that, on the other hand, if princes claim any part of the authority of God we ought not to obey them any farther than can be done without offending God.[15]

The next passage of significance with which we will deal is not from the Synoptic Gospels; rather, it is from Paul.

## Ephesians 1:22-23

'And he put all things under his feet and gave him as head over all things to the church' (ESV). It may not be immediately apparent why this test is being emphasized at this point. The fact of the matter is that this is one of the primary neglected doctrines of the church: the headship of Christ. Many of the previous and subsequent passages have been self-evidently cited in support of teaching for the primary mission of the church; however, this one deserves pride of place as well, even if the application of this passage to the primary mission of the church remains hidden in a basically obscure place.[16] I will discuss much more about this below in Chapter 11; however, Ephesians 1:22-23 has much to teach us meanwhile on this important topic which will lay the groundwork for our more detailed discussions later in the book.

Craig Troxel has written a fine article for a volume commemorating seventy-five years of the Orthodox Presbyterian Church referred to at the very beginning of this book. This article, it seems to this author, is

---

15. Calvin's Commentary on Matthew 21:21 [sic] [1555]; CO [*Calvini Opera*] 45:602, quoted in ibid., p. 170.

16. A. Craig Troxel, 'The World Is Not Enough,' pp. 337-65.

the mature reflection over many years on the subject of the headship of Christ and its application to the mission of the church of Jesus Christ. Professor Troxel begins by noting that the Apostle Paul seemingly had exhausted all his strength praising the majesty of Christ in Ephesians 1:15-23; nevertheless, he can't stop himself from speaking further on the topic.

Therefore, he launches into the freighted terminology of Christ as 'head' in Ephesians 1:22. Troxel's point, simply stated, is: '*The* fundamental theological point of Christ's being exalted to the "right hand" of God in majesty is, from beginning to end, about authority. This is true whether it pertains to his headship over "all things," or his headship over the church.'[17] At God's 'right hand', as Troxel correctly notes, is a symbol in the OT of 'his sovereignty.'[18] Knowing that the headship of Christ has been a sadly neglected doctrine in ecclesiology, Troxel rightly notes that the NT never uses the phrase metaphorically to describe Christ's humiliation, only His exaltation.[19] Furthermore, he notes that this is no mere title—as if that would be unimportant in and of itself—but it is used by Paul to teach that 'Christ has obtained a position of power.'[20] He summarizes: 'There is only one kind of "mere and absolute power" and it belongs to Christ the head, which he has reserved for himself, and he will not transfer to any other.'[21]

Troxel's next step is to explore the ramifications of this with regard to scope. Paul seems to be communicating that it is universal: over all creation, visible and invisible, including Christ's enemies, all rulers and authorities, including spiritual forces of evil in heavenly places. Next, Troxel segues into the ramifications of this truth: Paul is taking pains to demonstrate the entailments of Christ's cosmic rule for the church. After some detailed exegetical argumentation, Troxel argues that Paul is drilling down to emphasize the 'priority of the church in Christ's headship.'[22] The pastoral application of this is clear: 'Paul's words were meant to encourage believers, as they looked in faith to

---

17. Ibid., p. 339 [emphasis his].
18. Ibid.
19. Ibid.
20. Ibid., p. 341.
21. Referencing the Second Helvetic Confession, p. 18 at this point.
22. Ibid., p. 345.

the head of the church.'[23] He continues: 'With confidence they could know that his transcendent authority over every power and authority was focused supremely on his glorious purposes in and for the church.'[24] Dovetailing with Stuart Robinson's brilliant notion that the primary mission of the church is to be located in the *Pactum Salutis*, he concludes: 'Contemplated from eternity in the mind of God as the object of his all-wise plan, the church is uniquely "the *very means* by which her glorious head accomplishes His purposes in the world."'[25] Indeed, 'She is the medium of Christ's presence and rule in the cosmos, and she is the community in which the consummation of Christ's rule is anticipated.'[26]

This doctrine—the headship of Christ—was a key doctrine for the Reformers in their development of their teaching on ecclesiology.[27] Troxel recognizes that one way to illustrate the priority of Christ with respect to the world is under the rubric of redemption (in this section, he is dealing with terminology for 'world' [κόσμος, αἰῶν]).[28] Troxel acknowledges that there are appropriate ways to speak of the Kingdom of God as oriented towards the redemption of individuals *as well as* all of Christ's works; nevertheless, 'there are several problems with applying the soteric vocabulary of "redemption" to the world,' he maintains.[29] For example, he claims that the Bible does not speak in categories that are in the process of redemption, nor is the renewal of creation something that will occur through human efforts to 'save the planet'; rather, it is only through the mighty work of God. Therefore, we must be guarded against rhetorical excesses.[30] Building on Vos' insights into the 'two-age' structure of Paul's eschatology, Troxel says:

> A contemporary reader of Scripture must resist imputing too much *spatial*, and not enough *temporal*, thought into the terminology of 'world.' Nowhere else in Paul's thought is this explicitly expressed with greater clarity than it is in Ephesians 1:21, where he says 'not only in this age but also in the one to come.'[31]

---

23. Ibid., p. 347.
24. Ibid., p. 348.
25. Ibid. He is quoting Thornwell here, to good effect.
26. Ibid., p. 348.
27. Ibid., p. 349.
28. Ibid., p. 352.
29. Ibid., p. 354.
30. Ibid., p. 355.
31. Ibid., p. 357 [emphasis his].

Applying this to our manner of thinking means that this world in its 'moral complexion, that is, fallen and in opposition to God, ought to be viewed as something that will pass away and simply cannot be redeemed. It is evil and transitory.'[32] Therefore, it is enslaved sinners that need to be rescued from their plight and redeemed from sin. This important claim sets upright the church's constant inclination to tilt and get off course. It incentivizes the great commission: 'This message is the noble priority of the head of the church and the Great Commission of his body.'[33] It is true that God loves the world and shows care for it in light of common grace; however, the priority is clear for the church.

The danger here is reading one's own view of mission back into the church's identity (a topic that will receive more detailed treatment in Chapter 9). Let me explain. The liability evident here is the potential to jettison the priority the Scriptures place on the church to preach a message about sin, conversion, Christ's divinity, atoning death, and resurrection, and 'replace it with giving attention to medicine, agriculture, education, engineering, human suffering and social justice – drawing inspiration for these from the ethics of Christ.'[34] Troxel continues:

> But if the church begins to define herself in terms of her tasks and mission, this will significantly distort her self-understanding, and potentially displace her primary function, the worship of God .... In our day the ontology of the church is similarly in danger of becoming eclipsed by the mission of the church. And despite the encouraging signs of a renewed interest in ecclesiology in these past few decades, the spate of this movement's volumes reveals shaky ontological foundations, which are warped by presupposed trajectories of mission.[35]

This, therefore, means that there it is not an either-or matter. It's not a matter of the church not showing love to the world; it is a matter of priority. Indeed, it is a matter of the church following her charter and keeping to the priorities of her job-description, so to speak. Keeping this in mind helps the church stay focused on what kind of transformation she

---

32. Ibid. Troxel is paraphrasing Vos at this point from *Redemptive History and Biblical Interpretation: The Shorter Writings of Geerhardus Vos*, ed. Richard Gaffin, Jr. (Phillipsburg, NJ: Presbyterian and Reformed, 1980), p. 28.

33. Ibid., p. 358.

34. Ibid., p. 359.

35. Ibid., p. 360.

is to be occupied with: 'The transformation and renewal that the church is principally called to, is the reformation of herself (Rom. 12:1-2).'[36]

In light of this sublime exegesis of the headship of Christ, what should the response of the church be to the increasing pressure put upon her in her corporate capacity to address concerns for peace and justice, social malaise and injustices? Of course Christians should be concerned about such issues; however, 'The church's greatest expression of compassion for the world is to preach the good news of Jesus Christ. *Individual* Christians must not lose sight of their responsibility to show compassion for their neighbors and to be salt and light in the world, especially in times of crisis and natural disasters.'[37] As D. G. Hart says: 'This is not to say that the members of confessional Protestant churches are inherently indifferent to social and political affairs. As citizens, confessional Protestants may participate in a variety of reform and welfare endeavors according to the dictates of their consciences.'[38] As a matter of fact, sometimes people outside the church who are trained in medicine, law, or construction are better equipped than folks inside the church to perform difficult tasks in society.[39] Therein is the key: not losing the distinction between what the church's corporate responsibility is in the world and what is the duty of individual Christians in their compassion and the manifestation of that in a world filled with pain, hurt, and injustice. She must not lose sight of the priority. She must not fear the charge of 'ghettoizing the gospel' or neglecting a 'holistic gospel.'[40]

## John 18:36, 37… John 19:10-11

These passages in which Christ claims before Pilate that His kingdom is not of this world are germane and foundational to our discussion about the primary mission of the church. Moreover, there are several enlightening nuances about the mission of Jesus (and impliedly His church) taught in this passage that are fundamental to any right construal of a doctrine of the primary mission of the church. The familiar text of John 18:33-40 reads as follows:

---

36. Ibid., p. 362.
37. Ibid., p. 363.
38. D. G. Hart, *The Lost Soul of American Protestantism*, p. 180.
39. VanDrunen, *Living in God's Two Kingdoms*, p. 159.
40. Troxel, 'The World is not Enough,' p. 364.

131

So Pilate entered his headquarters again and called Jesus and said to him, 'Are you the King of the Jews?' Jesus answered, 'Do you say this of your own accord, or did others say it to you about me?' Pilate answered, 'Am I a Jew? Your own nation and the chief priests have delivered you over to me. What have you done?' Jesus answered, 'My kingdom is not of this world. If my kingdom were of this world, my servants would have been fighting, that I might not be delivered over to the Jews. But my kingdom is not from the world.' Then Pilate said to him, 'So you are a king?' Jesus answered, 'You say that I am a king. For this purpose I was born and for this purpose I have come into the world – to bear witness to the truth. Everyone who is of the truth listens to my voice.' Pilate said to him, 'What is truth?' After he had said this, he went back outside to the Jews and told them, 'I find no guilt in him. But you have a custom that I should release one man for you at the Passover. So do you want me to release to you the King of the Jews?' They cried out again, 'Not this man, but Barabbas!' Now Barabbas was a robber [ESV].

The first thing to notice from this passage is that Jesus claims that His kingdom is not of this world. This coheres with what He says in the Beatitudes of Matthew's gospel – His kingdom is 'the kingdom of heaven.' Its origin and source is not from the common soil of this world; it comes from above, it is heavenly. Secondly, this kingdom is not one of coercion with the sword, or, as Jesus states, His disciples might have justifiably defended Him with arms; rather, His kingdom is one of persuasion based on the truth. Just as Jesus recognized the legitimacy of the Roman kingdom, that is Caesar's kingdom as demonstrated in the last passage treated above, here we see that Pilate actually recognizes the distinction of Christ's kingdom as a totally different kind of thing than Caesar's:

> The ideas of 'the truth' and 'the sword' are set over against each other. A kingdom of force is not a kingdom of truth, and *vice versa*. This is the very point of the contrast between the two kingdoms, as Christ presents it. And the question of Pilate, 'What is truth?' taken in connection with the following declaration to the Jews, 'I find no fault in him,' shows that he understood this much, that Christ's kingdom was a totally different thing from that of Caesar. He understood the difference better than many Christian kings, and even Christian churches, have understood it in later times.[41]

---

41. Peck, 'Notes on Ecclesiology,' p. 149.

Even regarding the state's authority to exercise the sword, Christ affirms that this derives from God. In the next chapter of John, when Pilate asks Jesus, who was remaining silent, "'You will not speak to me? Do you not know that I have authority to release you and authority to crucify you?' Jesus answered him, "You would have no authority over me at all unless it had been given you from above. Therefore he who delivered me over to you has the greater sin'" (John 19:10-11 ESV).

## Matthew 28

In the passage from Ephesians 1, discussed above, we observed that Jesus reigns in glory over His church in the present age. This is no temporary reign, for Christ proclaims that He is with His people until the end of the age (Matt. 28:20).

Some in recent times have greatly misunderstood the so-called cultural mandate of Genesis 1:26-28 (cf., Chapter 2 above) by saying it should be extended into the new covenant institution of the church in the application of the great commission (Matt. 28:18-20) to culture more broadly. This is one of the fundamental errors of the recent aberration in theology of Theonomy (cf., Chapter 8 below). These misapplications of Scripture are an extension of the creation/cultural mandate and are a fundamental confusion of the covenantal patterns I have laid out above. At this point in the book, I will cite only one example. Gary North writes:

> The Bible affirms the legitimacy of power. It places all power in the hands of Jesus Christ (Matt. 28:18). Then it directs Christians to go forth, preaching the gospel and discipling nations, teaching them to observe 'all things whatsoever' Christ has commanded (Matt. 28:20). 'All things,' as Greg Bahnsen's study, *Theonomy in Christian Ethics* (1977) demonstrates so forcefully, includes the whole of biblical law. What we call the Great Commission of Christ to His church (Matt. 28:18-20) is in fact another reaffirmation of the covenant of dominion [read Gen. 1:26-28], taking into account the progress of redemptive history.[42]

The question here is whether he really has taken into account the progress of redemptive history.

---

42. See Gary North, *The Dominion Covenant* (Tyler, TX: Institute for Christian Economics, 1987), p. 31.

This passage was given especially to the apostles; however, since there are no present-day apostles, God has given the authority of administering the sacrament of baptism (and the sacrament of the Lord's supper, cf., Matt. 26) to ministers alone in our present place in redemptive history. Nowhere in Scripture is there an example of a ruling elder administering either sacrament; it is the prerogative of ministers of the Word alone.

## Romans 13:1-7

This passage has arguably one of the most extensive discussions in the NT on the legitimacy of the civil government. My discussion of this passage is largely indebted to the work of my colleague David VanDrunen.[43] He has marshalled persuasive evidence to demonstrate that Paul's thinking in Romans 13 is rooted in the so-called Noahide commandments:

> Let every person be subject to the governing authorities. For there is no authority except from God, and those that exist have been instituted by God. Therefore whoever resists the authorities resists what God has appointed, and those who resist will incur judgment. For rulers are not a terror to good conduct, but to bad. Would you have no fear of the one who is in authority? Then do what is good, and you will receive his approval, for he is God's servant for your good. But if you do wrong, be afraid, for he does not bear the sword in vain. For he is the servant of God, an avenger who carries out God's wrath on the wrongdoer. Therefore one must be in subjection, not only to avoid God's wrath but also for the sake of conscience. For because of this you also pay taxes, for the authorities are ministers of God, attending to this very thing. Pay to all what is owed to them: taxes to whom taxes are owed, revenue to whom revenue is owed, respect to whom respect is owed, honor to whom honor is owed (Rom. 13:1-7 ESV).

VanDrunen has claimed that it is probable that Paul is alluding to the so-called Noahide Laws from Genesis 8–9. It is clear in this passage that governments derive their authority from God. Moreover, he has instituted civil authorities for a particular purpose: to administer justice. This corresponds to the notion in one of the Noahide laws: God expect Gentiles to enforce just laws.

These laws are binding on Gentiles since, according to Jewish tradition, the laws of Sinai bind Jews alone. These Noahide laws, according to Jewish tradition, 'prohibit six things—worship of idols, taking God's

---

43. VanDrunen, *Politics after Christendom*, pp. 106-13.

name in vain, murder, sexual immorality, theft, and eating flesh torn from a living animal—and require one thing, the enforcement of just laws through a legal system.[44] These laws don't all come from Genesis 8–9; however, that text does touch on several of them. Finally, they are named after Noah because, according to Jewish tradition, Noah was the righteous man who was designated the father of the human race after the flood. Could it be that Paul actually had this tradition in mind when he penned Romans 13:1-7? It is likely.

Paul received a good Gentile education and the very best Jewish education of his day. He memorized huge portions (including entire books) of the Hebrew Bible. He was raised in Tarsus and brought up at the feet of Gamaliel, one of the leading rabbis of the day. Therefore it is entirely plausible that Paul was exposed to the notion of Jewish teachers associating Noah with passing along universally binding laws upon Gentiles, not only in Paul's day but even before Paul's time.[45] Therefore, it seems not only plausible but likely that Paul had the Noahic laws in mind. Consider some of the following similarities between Romans 13:1-7 and Genesis 8:21–9:17, especially 9:5-6.

First, both passages speak of judicial authority as derived from God.[46] Second, both passages speak of coercion as the means by which justice is maintained.[47] In Romans 13:4 it is explicitly by the sword, whereas in Genesis 9:6, it is by bloodshed. Thirdly, the purpose of judicial authority in both passages is for retributive justice, the notion of a deeds-consequence nexus in which the wicked get their comeuppance for their deeds as do the righteous.[48] In Romans 13:4, which alludes back to Romans 12 (especially 12:17 and 12:19), Paul declares that the civil magistrate is 'an avenger who carries out God's wrath on the wrongdoer' (ESV). In Genesis 9:6, human beings are also enjoined to perform retributive justice; however, in both passages it appears that this task is entrusted to the civil authorities, not to individuals.

Fourthly, both passages portray God as delegating this authority for protectionist ends, not perfectionist ends. VanDrunen uses these terms,

44. Ibid.
45. See Ibid for evidence.
46. Ibid., p. 107.
47. Ibid., p. 108.
48. Ibid.

which are borrowed from political theory, to make a distinction between the state's goal of protecting citizens from being wronged as opposed to working virtue in her citizens.[49] The fifth point is that both texts embed their injunctions 'about judicial authority in the context of a general, sparse moral structure.'[50] In other words, although Paul has robust moral injunctions that are laid upon the Christians in Romans 12:1-21 and 13:8-14, the statements in Romans 13:1-7 show a striking sparseness with regards to specificity in moral injunctions. Therefore, commentators recognize Romans 13:1-7 as a kind of remarkable parenthesis. Genesis 8:21–9:17 also describes judicial authority in a similarly general and sparse moral structure which lacks specificity.[51]

A sixth similarity between the two texts is their universal character—as opposed to being particularistic or parochial—since both texts seem to have the broader human race in view.[52] Notice that Paul begins Romans 13 appealing to every person. As discussed previously with respect to the Noahic covenant, that arrangement appeals not only to God's particularly chosen people but to the whole human race. The covenant established here is a covenant of common grace and not redemptive grace, as I have argued previously. In other words, it is made with the common world, believers and unbelievers alike. There is no blood transaction in the Noahic covenant, unlike the covenant God made with Abraham.

The seventh and final similarity between these two passages is that both lack redemptive elements.[53] God is portrayed in both passages as moral governor and sustainer, but not as redeemer. VanDrunen goes on to make further claims about how Genesis 8:21–9:17 bears a closer resemblance and similarity to Romans 13:1-7 than any other passage in the NT. That discussion would take us too far away from our main point here; nevertheless, VanDrunen has made a very good case that the Noahic covenant is a substantive and important part of Paul's teaching about the role of the state, albeit often under-appreciated. Again, the importance of focusing on the civil magistrate at this point is that such an emphasis helps us delineate the primary mission of the church.

---

49. Ibid., pp. 108-09.

50. Ibid., chapter 4 (p. 13).

51. As VanDrunen points out, that doesn't mean the texts are vacuous or relativistic.

52. Ibid., p. 110.

53. Ibid., pp. 110-11.

## 1 Peter 2:9-17

Often it is the case that a focus is placed upon 1 Peter 2:13-17 when examining NT passages that touch upon the legitimacy and function of the state. However, I suggest that it is helpful in our present discussion to more broadly focus our gaze on the surrounding context in order to reinforce what I have been suggesting in this chapter, and in the previous ones as well: God's people bear a dual citizenship, which includes the fact that they are a 'peculiar people,' but also includes that as citizens of nations in this age, it is their duty to show obedience to worldly institutions which in no ways necessarily compromises their allegiance to Christ, their true Head.

Notice the first part of the selected section, which reads:

> But you are a chosen race, a royal priesthood, a holy nation, a people for his own possession, that you may proclaim the excellencies of him who called you out of darkness into his marvelous light. Once you were not a people, but now you are God's people; once you had not received mercy, but now you have received mercy. Beloved, I urge you as sojourners and exiles to abstain from the passions of the flesh, which wage war against your soul. Keep your conduct among the Gentiles honorable, so that when they speak against you as evildoers, they may see your good deeds and glorify God on the day of visitation (1 Pet. 2:9-12 ESV).

This passage is laden with OT allusions, including Hosea 2:23 and Exodus 19:5-6, and even Isaiah 43:20-21.[54] What is especially significant is the way in which the apostle is emphasizing in the text, together with its subtle allusive meanings, that the audience he is addressing is the new Israel. The Jews were that 'peculiar people' but they were a type of the Christian church, whom Peter is addressing. Peter has transferred attributes, privileges, and nomenclature belonging to Israel to the Christian church in Asia Minor. They are therefore the true spiritual citizens, with reframed identities cast in the language stock of images taken from the 'treasured possession' language, the 'royal priesthood' language of the participants of a new exodus community, the church.

However, in the next breath, without skipping a single beat, the apostle continues to exhort them along an entirely different line. Although they are citizens of a kingdom that is 'not of this world',

---

54. See the author's *Echoes of Exodus,* pp. 294-96.

137

nevertheless, at one and the same time, they have duties and obligations to obey the civil authorities in the common, earthly kingdom (instituted by God) in which they also find themselves at home:

> Be subject for the Lord's sake to every human institution, whether it be to the emperor as supreme, or to governors as sent by him to punish those who do evil and to praise those who do good. For this is the will of God, that by doing good you should put to silence the ignorance of foolish people. Live as people who are free, not using your freedom as a cover-up for evil, but living as servants of God. Honor everyone. Love the brotherhood. Fear God. Honor the emperor (1 Pet. 2:13-17 ESV).

The dual citizenship here could hardly be more clearly expressed in such a short space. Of course, the passage says nothing about the origin of the state, nor does it describe any particular functions of the civil magistrate; but it does describe the legitimacy of the magistrates and commands Christians to honor them and to submit to them. Therefore, part of our obligation as Christians and the church is to honor and to esteem the rulers that God has placed us under, and especially to pray for them (1 Tim. 2:1-2).

## The Eschatological Role of the Kingdom

One of the main and most important points to be gained from the above discussion is the particular nature of the kingdom of God as reflected in so many of these passages: it is eschatological. What do I mean by this? My former colleague Steven M. Baugh has stated it simply and lucidly in the following manner:

> The New Testament writers were unanimous that the period of time between Christ's first and second coming is thoroughly eschatological. The term 'eschatology' refers simply to the study of the last things of this age and of things that pertain to the eternal era that immediately follows it, the new creation. The resurrection of Christ, his ascent to the Father's right hand, his rule from heaven over all things, the giving of the Holy Spirit at Pentecost, are all eschatological events—final, climactic events—which have intruded into this age. Hence, this whole age is the 'last days' (Acts 2:17; 2 Tim. 3:1; Heb. 1:2; James 5:3; 2 Pet. 3:3), the 'end of the ages' (1 Cor. 10:11; Heb. 9:26), and even 'the last hour' (1 John 2:18).[55]

---

55. S.M. Baugh, *The Majesty on High: Introduction to the Kingdom of God in the New Testament* (self-published, 2017), p. 5.

This is a point that can hardly be emphasized enough. We will comment more upon this in a subsequent chapter dealing with the nature of the kingdom of God (cf., Chapter 10 below). However, it is sufficient for the time being to make the claim and briefly explain it with further development below. In more recent times, it is the natural trajectory of the work of Geerhardus Vos, who thought that this eschatological aspect of Paul's theology was the essential key in order to understand his corpus.[56]

The back story lies in Calvin's understanding of the kingdom of God. In Calvin's theology, 'the Kingdom of Christ is the consummation of God's purposes for creation and for human beings.'[57] This is a fundamental distinction in Calvin's two kingdom doctrine, the contrast between the eternal and the present: 'The fundamental distinction underlying Calvin's two kingdoms doctrine is the contrast between the present age, marked by corruption and temporality, and the future eternal kingdom of Christ.'[58]

If one fails to 'get' the two kingdom's distinction, one fails to understand Calvin:

> The key to properly interpreting [sic] Calvin's kingdom theology—and hence his theology of two kingdoms—is recognizing its fundamentally eschatological character, for underlying much of the terminology that allegedly betrays Neoplatonic influence is Calvin's Pauline commitment to the eschatological distinction between creation corrupted and creation restored, the present age and the age to come. Although in Christ the kingdom has already been consummated, and it is the resulting eschatological tension, between the 'already' and the 'not-yet' that characterizes the kingdom in the present age.[59]

## The Diaconate (Acts 6:1-6 and 1 Timothy 3:8-12)

I conclude this chapter on the NT evidence for the primary mission of the church with a brief discussion of the role of deacons. At the

---

56. See, e.g., Geerhardus Vos, *The Pauline Eschatology* (Princeton University Press, 1930), pp. 11, 27-29, 62, 315-16. The book was later published by Presbyterian and Reformed, with a foreword by Richard B. Gaffin, Jr. (Phillipsburg, NJ: Presbyterian and Reformed, 1979).

57. Tuininga, *Calvin's Political Theology*, p. 92.

58. Ibid., p. 151.

59. Ibid., pp. 93-94.

beginning of the book, I said I was not going to comment much on the offices of the church, nor on the diaconate. In part this is due to the fact that there is already so much good material on the offices of the church that anything I would have to add would be a mere rehash. Without looking at all the details of these or other passages that could be invoked, some important matters stand out. The fact of the matter is that this is a timely topic because, as alluded to above, there is so much pressure on the church of Jesus Christ to expand her God-given job description. Fuzzy boundaries are evident all over because the corporate church has not been sticking to her job description. The diaconate is one place where that pressure is currently being felt.

The diaconate is to fulfill a similar supplementary role, but for the household of faith! Here, the church, like the state, merely supplements the family. Here, we can notice God's overall compassionate concern is in place for the people of the earth. In this whole pattern, there is no room for utopian visions and flattening out of all wealth for some kind of Marxist or socialist plan. Indeed, such a supposition would actually undercut the very reasons for which God instituted the state. For the state, by God's common grace design was put in force for the sake of protecting the rights of its citizens. Of course, apostate mankind is constantly trying to transgress the boundaries that God has instituted. But that must never be.

The church should consider Calvin's emphasis on the office of deacon, something he took very seriously in the life of the church in Geneva:

> Calvin's emphasis on the enduring prescription of ecclesiastical offices devoted to poor relief and discipline is significant because, arising out of his unique two kingdoms theology, it became the focal point for early Reformed struggles over the appropriate relationship between the church and civil government.[60]

For Calvin, the diaconate is not immediately connected with or tantamount to the ministry of the Word; nevertheless, as Tuininga summarizes, 'Calvin was explicit and adamant that the diaconate is part of Christ's spiritual government of his church, and that, in contrast to civil government, it is spiritual, not secular.'[61]

---

60. Ibid., pp. 68-69.
61. Ibid., p. 225.

Thomas Peck, whose greatest literary achievement was probably his work on ecclesiology, sets forth a foundational principle about the office of deacon that is often completely neglected or ignored in modern discussions: 'The communion of saints is implied in the very notion of an organized church having its polity and its ordinances of the church.'[62] He begins his discussion of the deacon's office with the insight that the 'communion of saints is implied in the very notion of an organized church having its polity and its ordinances of worship.' Then he continues: 'This communion (κοινωνια) is most impressively exhibited in two ordinances, both of which are emphatically denominated by the word *communion*, to wit: the Lord's supper and contributions in money, or its equivalent (Acts ii. 42-45; 1 Cor. x. 16; 2 Cor. viii. 4; Heb. xiii. 16; Rom. xv. 26, 27).'[63]

For Peck, these financial contributions to the saints demonstrate profoundly the communion of the saints. There is a principle active in the hearts of God's people that has its origin in heaven. This manifested itself even more dramatically in the NT when Gentile Christians alleviated the suffering of the Jews in Jerusalem with their effusive offering (Acts 11:29, 30; Rom. 15:25-28; 1 Cor. 14: 1-4; 2 Cor. 8 and 9). This was not a gift given out of the bond of blood (from Jews to Jews); this was a gift given out of the 'bitter prejudice of race.'[64] Rarely is this noted in the current crisis of race relations. However, it should be. That this is a reflection of the reality of the communion of the saints is confirmed by our confession, 'in relieving each other in outward things, according to their several needs and necessities.'[65] This radical expression of the communion of the saints was first demonstrated in the early church with the erection of the diaconate (Acts 6:1-6).

Acts 6 is the chair passage that is usually referenced first and foremost for the foundation of this office (together with 1 Timothy 3:8-12 for qualifications). There we learn that deacons were to be servants of tables, to free up the apostles as servants of the Word and prayer. Therefore, as Peck rightly says, 'The prime aspect, then, of the office of deacon is

---

62. Thomas E. Peck, *Notes on Ecclesiology*, p. 197.

63. Ibid.

64. Ibid., p. 198.

65. WCF, XXVI.2.

that of a representative of the communion of saints.'[66] Moreover, the institution of this office imbues it with great dignity and spirituality.[67] Why? Because 'it is not a little remarkable that a deacon should have been chosen rather than an apostle to see that it was God's plan to abolish the Mosaic form of the true religion, and to establish one which should be spiritual and universal.'[68] Moreover, James the apostle, the brother of John, when martyred is given merely one verse describing his death by Doctor Luke whereas a deacon's death (Stephen) is given in great detail two full chapters (Acts 6 and 7). These facts, and others, demonstrate the honor, dignity and importance of the office of deacon and the role of the diaconate.

First Timothy shows us that the diaconate is a spiritual office with spiritual tasks. Moreover, the Scriptural data (together with evidence from 1 Timothy 5 about serving widows) seems to suggest that 'the proper object of diaconal ministry is the membership of the visible church.'[69] This is related to the ministerial and declarative authority of the church, which was discussed in the opening chapter. That means that the diaconal ministry should only be conducted in ways that the Scripture authorizes. As VanDrunen asks, 'Should the church start a soup kitchen or medical clinic in a poor neighborhood? Should it pursue community economic development as well as preaching the gospel in third-world mission fields?'[70] VanDrunen's answer is no: 'The New Testament ... never commands the church's diaconal work to assist people outside the church.'[71] Even so, Reformed Churches have debated this issue.

My own denomination, for example, the Orthodox Presbyterian Church, has adopted statements in her General Assembly to suggest that the objects of diaconal aid may include those outside the church, i.e., the world. Much of the debate has centered around the interpretation of Galatians 6:10, which we will not deal with at this

---

66. Ibid., p. 198.

67. Ibid.

68. Ibid., p. 199.

69. Guy Prentiss Waters, *How Jesus Runs the Church* (Phillipsburg, PA: P & R, 2011), p. 102.

70. David VanDrunen, *Living in God's Two Kingdoms*, p. 157.

71. Ibid., p. 158.

point.[72] Other examples of thoughtful contributions, even if incorrect in the opinion of this author, could be cited as well among Reformed writers. For example, Steve Corbett and Brian Fikkert's book, *When Helping Hurts: How to Alleviate Poverty without Hurting the Poor ... and Yourself*, makes a long and thoughtful argument for the local church and individual Christians being a part of poverty alleviation in the world and especially in communities where a particular church is located.[73] The book is sophisticated in its analysis, peppered with many anecdotal examples, and suggestive; however, I would still maintain that it is not the responsibility of the corporate church, nor is it within her purview, to address issues of economic development or possible social upward mobility of those outside the church. This results in unnecessary fuzzy boundaries. Likewise, Harvie M. Conn's manifesto for a more 'holistic' gospel that does word and deed evangelism, and especially in answering many questions surrounding social injustice, remains also unconvincing and under-argued.[74] Although Conn is to be commended for his wide reading and holding conversation partners outside customary conservative conversation partners, he has remained unconvincing to this author that the restricted job description given to the corporate church of Jesus Christ needs to be expanded to include objects of the corporate church's aid outside those of the church's membership. As has been and will be mentioned numerous times in this book, addressing the issue of 'systemic injustice' is more often than not extremely complex. Examples of 'systemic injustice' abound, especially when unjust laws are legislatively passed and may even incentivize malicious and sinful persons to treat others in a way that demonstrates injustice. In my opinion, the practices of Apartheid in South Africa and Jim Crow laws in the southern United States are clear examples. However, there are a host of extralegal 'systems' and policies that are often decried as unjust but as a matter of fact are almost impossible to

---

72. See, e.g., Leonard J. Coppes, 'The Discussion of the Theology of the Diaconate,' pp. 427-34 in *Between the Times: The Orthodox Presbyterian Church in Transition, 1945-1990* (Willow Grove, PA: The Committee for the Historian of the Orthodox Presbyterian Church, 2011).

73. Steve Corbett and Brian Fikkert, *When Helping Hurts: How to Alleviate Poverty without Hurting the Poor ... and Yourself* (Chicago, IL: Moody, 2009).

74. Harvie M. Conn, *Doing Justice and Preaching Grace* (Grand Rapids, MI: Zondervan, 1982).

prove. Moreover, has God deigned that the corporate church, as the church, should prophetically denounce such issues of social injustice as part of her primary mission? Herein lies the rub.

Of course none of these critical comments are intended to suggest that the diaconate of the church may not offer counsel and advice to the poor outside the church. Nor am I suggesting that *individual* Christians should not offer relief to those outside the members of the church. Nor am I even suggesting that the proper objects of diaconal aid cannot include occasionally and extraordinarily those outside the church, especially in our local communities. However, the proper and normal customary objects of diaconal aid should be poor church members in need of assistance since the diaconal ministry is a reflection of participation in κοινωνια (koinonia) participation with the members of the church and a reflection of the communion of the saints of Jesus Christ.[75] More will be said below (in the final chapter) about how such aid and assistance might be organized by individual Christians (even collectively) joining together in order to alleviate the plight of the poor, or through education helping those who are bereft of common grace benefits; nevertheless, at this point we must move on in the book to further illustrations of what the primary mission of the church is and is not.

## Conclusions

In the past few chapters I have been laying some theoretical foundations for understating the primary mission of the church. We have traced several key institutions that have been part of God's overall plan for the world. In many respects, primary focus has been on the church, the state, and the family. If we pause to reflect, we will note God's overall care for the world, both inside and outside the church. I have, at this point in the argument, merely been suggestive in noting how comprehensive God's care is for the world he sovereignly rules, both inside and outside the church. More will be said about this below.[76] In this chapter we have looked at a number of NT passages that reinforced the notion of the Bible's teaching a two kingdoms theology.

---

75. See, e.g., the balanced discussion by Waters, *How Jesus Runs the Church*, pp. 103-03.

76. See, e.g., the insightful comments about comprehensive care by M. G. Kline, *Kingdom Prologue*, pp. 174-79.

As we have been building our argument, I have made the claim that some covenants are redemptive and some are not. The NT clearly teaches that Christ is ruler of the Universe; however, how He rules in creation and civil society as moral governor of the world is different from how He rules His church as mediator of the covenant of grace. As we continue to examine the primary mission of the church, we will observe that God has set up one, and only one, institution to be the instrument by which He will accomplish the goals of the covenant of grace: the church. The church is 'the *only* institution and community in this world that can be identified with the redemptive kingdom and the covenant of grace.'[77]

---

77. David VanDrunen, *Living in God's Two Kingdoms*, p. 102.

# PART TWO

# CHAPTER 6

# Kuyper, Dooyeweerd, and North American Neo-Calvinism

This chapter will begin with examples distinguishing what the primary mission of the church *is not*, or what it should not do. It should be self-evident that the church should not be just described in negative terms such as it is not the state. Rather, the church should also be described in positive and constructive categories.[1] Even so, nothing becomes clearer than when it is compared with what it is not. Moreover, both here and later (Chapter 14), looking at how the state and the church differ can help us to understand the distinct mission of the church. Therefore, these next four chapters will give examples of what the primary mission of the church is not. Sometimes, we will discuss what other institutions are and how they function in order to clarify the role of the church. Then, in Chapter 10, I will begin to discuss what the nature of the church is in positive and constructive categories. I have chosen two modern reformed theologians to begin this section, or, more precisely one theologian and one philosopher. These men were amazing figures in their own right. In many respects, it is not so much what they did with the mission of the church, but how their followers radicalized their ideas. This then will help us to see that many today have not lived up to God's designed description for the church.

---

1. A. Craig Troxel, 'Divine Right' Presbyterianism, pp. 66.

## Abraham Kuyper

In order to understand A. Kuyper (1837-1920), and H. Dooyeweerd (1894-1977), one first needs to discuss Guillaume Groen van Prinsterer (1801-1876), Kuyper's predecessor as leader in the nineteenth century of the Christian political movement. Without his work, Kuyper's projects would not have been possible.

G. van Prinsterer was part of the Dutch aristocracy, born to a family of privilege. He at first held to a very vague and moralistic, deistic Christianity. Then, however, he became influenced by the orthodox and embraced Calvinism. He served in parliament three times. He was the founder of the Anti-revolutionary political party in the Netherlands. He agreed basically with Edmund Burke's conservative analysis of the French revolution. He thought that it was an attempt of unbelieving men to promote their autonomous ideas of man's laws through revolution.[2] He stated: 'This lecture and the following one are accordingly devoted to the argument that when it is free to run its natural course in religion and politics unbelief leads to the most radical doctrines.'[3] He further stated: 'The defining feature of the Revolution [the French Revolution] is its hatred of the Gospel, its anti-Christian nature. This feature marks the Revolution, not, mind you, when it "deviates from its course" and "lapses into excesses," but, on the contrary, precisely when it holds to its course and reaches the conclusion of its system, the true end of its logical development.'[4] G. van Prinsterer held, however, that God was the source of all authority. He was known as a general without an army and the people that followed him were called the 'little people.'

Abraham Kuyper was born to a minister in the state church. He studied for six years at the gymnasium (a classical school) which laid a foundation for a very thorough education for him. He was known as a great student of languages and for his voracious appetite for study, enduring long hours from the morning until late in the evening. He is a figure of huge proportions, having established a church, a newspaper, a major university, a political party, and even becoming the Prime Minister of the Netherlands between 1901 and 1905.

2. See G. Groen van Prinsterer, *Unbelief and Revolution: Lectures VIII & IX*, edited and translated by Harry Van Dyke (Amsterdam, The Groen Van Prinsterer Fund, 1975), p. 29.

3. Ibid., p. 5.

4. Ibid., p. 29.

Kuyper entered the university at Leiden in 1855. He had rejected the orthodox faith when he was a student and had embraced the starkest intellectual rationalism of the time. In 1858 he entered the Seminary at Leiden. One of the leading teachers there was J.H. Scholten, who had a profound impact upon Kuyper and who was, according to James Bratt, 'the best systematic theologian in the country and the foremost Modernist.'[5] It was here that the seeds of liberalism influenced Kuyper. For Scholten had at first accepted the authority of the Scriptures but he rejected the Gospel of John as unauthoritative later. These ideas influenced his preaching and his theology. Kuyper became concerned about so-called 'malcontents' in his church. After being told to ignore them, he actually began visiting them and found that they were maintaining their orthodoxy by reading giants like John Owen. Their influence became profound on him.

He was called to serve as a minister at Utrecht, a church with approximately 35,000 members and eleven ministers. It was while he was serving at Utrecht, that he gained fame. The influence of G. van Prinsterer, whom Kuyper took as a mentor during these years at Utrecht, can be vividly seen in his rhetoric. Kuyper writes:

> Unlike the revolution [French] which it opposes, it [Christianity] lives not by hollow ideas but by real power; it does not conjure up castles in the air but builds a solid home on the *given* foundation from the materials at hand. Revolution demolishes and destroys, willfully overturning all existing structures to rave about a better world, a world that appears in its dreams and disappears along with them. It is—to quote Isaiah—like one 'who flees upon horses and has no confidence in quietness' [Isa. 30:15-16]. Restlessly, ever onward, it trots up its highway in the sky until the world sinks away at its feet, leaving not a whisper of compassion for that broken creation down below. Thus it finds conservatism repugnant; both the false type and the true fall under its judgment. Not so Christianity.[6]

A very important issue during this time, one which has direct bearing on our topic of the primary purpose of the church, had to do with the

---

5. James D. Bratt, *Abraham Kuyper: A Centennial Reader* (Grand Rapids, MI: Eerdmans, 1998), p. 7.

6. See Jonathan Chaplin, *Herman Dooyeweerd: Christian Philosopher of State and Civil Society* (Notre Dame, IN: University of Notre Dame Press, 2011), pp. 70-71. Chaplin's book is arguably the most detailed and authoritative work on Dooyeweerd to date. He also shows some important influence from Kuyper upon Dooyeweerd.

issue of how much the government should be involved in Christian education.

Then, in 1870, Kuyper was called to be a minister in a church in Amsterdam. During this period, he also became the associate editor of *The Herald*. This was the christening of his journalistic career. By this point in his career, he was indeed orthodox. However, he wanted also to be more progressive. He wanted to reform the state church. He developed a slogan, 'For a free school, a free church, and the free land.' In 1874, he was elected to parliament. It was here that he took on emeritus status from the ministry; however, he did retain a seat as an elder in the consistory at Amsterdam.[7] He wanted to produce a reformed society, even reformed labor unions. In a word, he wanted a Christianized culture, although even this does not precisely represent his political thought (more below).

Next, Kuyper resigned from the parliament to pursue a journalistic career. During this time, the new liberal government passed a new education bill that increased the excellence and standards of the schools. In 1879, he organized the first national meeting of the so-called 'Anti-Revolutionary' party. In 1880, he founded the Free University of Amsterdam with the emphasis being on 'free from' government control. The University opened with five professors and merely five students. Kuyper himself taught many of the topics there, including Hebrew and Aesthetics. His opening address became one of his most celebrated messages, 'Sovereignty in the Individual Spheres of Life.'

Kuyper was interested in exploring how 'sovereignty' didn't rest in either the state or the individual. Rather, it rests in God and He alone gives it to the institutions that He has set up in society. So, Kuyper was interested in the state, the church, the family, and 'voluntary associations' (e.g., universities). Each of these institutions, according to Kuyper, have their own sovereignty. Each of these institutions have their own 'sphere' sovereignty. Each of these institutions is responsible to God alone. This is not to say that they are hermetically sealed from one another; rather, he wanted to say that there is an irreducible sovereignty that each holds on to. For example, the church has the sole right over doctrine. The state has no right to transgress this boundary. The family has the right to

---

7. Ibid., p. 11.

raise its own children. Therefore, the school is delegated responsibility from the family. Kuyper would argue that because the state has a vested interest in the education of its children, then it is appropriate for the state to provide funds for the education of its citizens.

In the 1880s, Kuyper's attention turned towards the church. In 1883, a new form of subscription to the creeds of the church emerged, which required ministers to promote the cause of the state church and in their view the kingdom of God more generally. Changes in the church constitution brought about changes in the requirements of church membership. It seems that members were asked questions at the doctrinal level, without any reference to personal piety and whether they believed the doctrines or were practicing holiness. Now certificates were given to catechumens transferring from one church to another. The whole process made the consistory very uneasy and so they refused transfers. Consequently, the catechumens appealed to the synod level, and synods that had a very liberal influence ordered the consistory to issue them and controversy broke out. In December of 1886, the synod deposed the consistory in which Kuyper was involved. About 7000 members of the church of Amsterdam followed Kuyper and formed the churches of the 'Doleantie', which is Latin from 'grieving.' This appellation was chosen because they did not desire to leave, but felt that they had to. The movement gathered about 10,000 members. Many still stayed in the liberal state church, believing they had the freedom to preach what they wanted.

Then in 1892, the Doliente and the Afscheiding churches were united which led to the formation of the Gereformeerde church. The Christian Reformed Church of the United States derived from the Afscheiding Church before the union. The state church was the Hervormde. Two primary Seminaries were formed: the Afscheiding one in Kampen and the other being located at the Free University of Amsterdam.

During this period, Kuyper believed that for the anti-revolutionary party to function well, it needed to cooperate with the Reformed Church party. In 1891, Kuyper organized the first Christian Social congress, a convention of the Antirevolutionary Party at Utrecht. Kuyper's address at the opening of this congress captures the tone and essence of his politics.[8] In 1893 and 1894, he produced his three-volume encyclopedia

---

8. '*Maranatha,*' Republished in James D. Bratt, *Abraham Kuyper: A Centennial Reader* (Grand Rapids, MI: Eerdmans, 1998), pp. 206-28.

of sacred theology. In 1894, he was re-elected to Parliament. In 1898, he came to America and presented the famous six lectures on Calvinism delivered at Princeton Seminary, under the auspices of the L.P. Stone Foundation and often referred to simply as the Stone Lectures.[9]

In order to understand Kuyper's lectures it is crucial to understand the fundamentals of his thinking. First, he believed in a distinction between what is normal and abnormal. Christians have a duty to declare what people experience presently as abnormal vis-à-vis the world's message which is that what we experience here and now is normal. The 'antithesis' and common grace are foundational to all his thought. It is no understatement to claim that for Kuyper, to meditate on common grace is to engage God's grand masterpiece, and not to think in a reductionistic way about church life.

He maintained that there is a fundamental antithesis between the thinking of the regenerate and the unregenerate. This is foundational to his model. Even so, because of God's common grace, believers and unbelievers can participate together in similar things. For Kuyper, 'Common Grace was thus a theology of public responsibility, of Christians' shared humanity with the rest of the world.'[10] This is a result of God's mercy. Kuyper thought that Roman Catholics do not address this antithesis seriously enough, since the pillars of their system are built upon a dualism of nature and grace. You can hear this in his essay on common grace: 'For if we set *nature* and *grace* against each other as two mutually exclusive concepts, we get the impression that nature now persists *apart from* all grace and that grace is and has been extended exclusively to God's elect.'[11]

For Kuyper, the antithesis was crucial, which can be described as 'the antagonism that must obtain between Christian and non-Christian views of the world owing to the contrary commitments that inspired them.'[12] For Kuyper, the key distinctions between people were religious ones. After the final judgment this antithesis becomes absolute. Even so, the distinction is not absolute in this life because the unregenerate

---

9. Abraham Kuyper, *Lectures on Calvinism: Six Lectures Delivered at Princeton University Under Auspices of the L.P. Stone Foundation* (Grand Rapids, MI: Eerdmans, 1931).

10. Bratt's editorial comment, *Kuyper Reader*, p. 165.

11. Ibid., p. 173 (emphasis original).

12. Bratt, *Kuyper Reader*, p. 15.

are not as wicked as they can be due to common grace, especially in the area of civic righteousness. This raises the timeless and big question: how does one account for unbelievers' accomplishments, given the antithesis? For Kuyper the answer is in common grace:

> Now I proceed to consider the dogma of '*common grace*,' that natural outcome of the general principle, just presented to you, but in its special application to *sin*, understood as corruption of our nature. Sin places before us a riddle, which in itself is insoluble. If you view sin as a deadly poison, as enmity against God, as leading to everlasting condemnation, and if you represent a sinner as being 'wholly incapable of doing any good, and prone to all evil,' and on this account salvable only if God by regeneration changes his heart, then it seems as if of necessity all unbelievers and unregenerate persons ought to be wicked and repulsive men. But this is far from being our experience in actual life. On the contrary the unbelieving world excels in many things. Precious treasures have come down to us from the old heathen civilization.[13]

God has restrained the full outworking of corruption in the life of both the regenerate and the unregenerate. However, if we emphasize common grace too much then we are in danger of slipping into Thomism. In other words, if we stress the antithesis too much, we run the risk of becoming sectarian. Indeed, according to Kuyper, there are things which the unregenerate can learn truly and pass on, even to the regenerate. The unregenerate can know true things. Kuyper's genius, perhaps, was to hold these two great truths in tension.

Thus, it is true that Kuyper's goal has been described the 'rechristianization' of Dutch culture.[14] However, Jonathan Chaplin gives a more nuanced and precise description:

> Insofar as he worked tirelessly to restore Christian influence in Dutch public life, he sought to move toward this goal not by claiming a privileged political status for the church or its confessions, as had his early Calvinist and Puritan forebears, but rather by instituting a constitutional and legal framework that recognized the equal rights of all existing confessional or ideological groups—Calvinist, Catholic, Liberal, Socialist—to participate in the shaping of public life.[15]

---

13. Abraham Kuyper, *Lectures on Calvinism*, p. 121.

14. See Jonathan Chaplin, *Herman Dooyeweerd,* p. 21.

15. Ibid., p. 21.

Indeed, both in his capacity as Prime Minister (1901-1905), and even later in his writings on statecraft, he offered a plan in which he hoped that people could live within a peaceful pluralistic society.[16] His model came to be known as a 'pillarisation' or 'vertical pluralism' [*Verzuiling*] which was a result of Kuyper's notions of sphere sovereignty.[17] Therefore, the goal in Dutch society was to have a Roman Catholic bloc, a Calvinistic bloc, a Socialistic bloc etc. The result of this 'pillarisation' was that each bloc would produce its own institutions.

A major question that has occurred in today's international debates about Kuyper is whether he had direct influence on South Africa's apartheid policies. In short, was Kuyper a racist and/or did his ideas have direct racist consequences, in South Africa?

## Excursus on Kuyper, 'The Father of Apartheid'?

It's not difficult today to find those circulating the widespread belief that Kuyper was an outright racist. This is so in popular material (blogs and such) as well as academic tomes and peer-reviewed journals.[18] By many, he has been considered the ideological father of apartheid. In fact, this has sparked an international debate. That there were shameful and horrible acts and deeds committed by white Christians, in the name of Reformed Christianity no less, is undeniable, as first-hand accounts testify.[19] Even so, whether Kuyper and his theology was *directly* responsible for such racist attitudes and actions is another issue.

Nevertheless, perhaps it is best to sit lightly on such notions until at least we have examined the issue from those who are competent and who might actually read the languages of the texts in play. As often is the case, the issue may be more gray than merely black and light. Patrick Baskwell, in the article cited above, traces the development of apartheid while relying heavily on Tracy Kuyperus' work, *State, Civil*

---

16.  Patrick Baskwell, 'Kuyper and Apartheid: A Revisiting,' *HTR* 62/4 (2006): pp. 1269-90.

17.  Ibid., p. 1278.

18.  https://medium.com/@timothyisaiahcho/how-learning-about-abraham-kuypers-influence-on-apartheid-changed-me-661304895466; https://hierstaanek.files.wordpress.com/2012/02/kuyper.pdf; cf. James D. Bratt's introduction to Kuyper's famous essay, 'The Crisis in South Africa' (published in 1900), in *Abraham Kuyper: A Centenniel Reader* (Grand Rapids, MI: Eerdmans, 1998), pp. 323-24.

19.  See, e.g., Allan Boesak, *Black and Reformed: Apartheid, Liberation, and the Calvinist Tradition*, edited by Leonard Sweetman (Maryknoll, NY: Orbis Books, 1984).

*Society and Apartheid in South Africa* (1995). She notes a dramatic shift from 'horizontal segregation' to 'positive apartheid.' She writes:

> While *Verzuiling* in the Netherlands was the result in society of Kuyper's theological concept of 'sphere sovereignty,' in a South African context 'sphere sovereignty provided for a significant variant: Apartheid' .... While Kuyper's ideas were prominent in Apartheid's structure, they were not pure Kuyper. Kuyper's concepts were received by enthusiasts of his thought and transformed into something, which I believe, Kuyper, had he lived to see it, would have abhorred.[20]
>
> White domination and control continued through Verwoed's [prime minister in South Africa between 1958-1966] 'restructured' apartheid vision which assumed a more 'vertical' apartheid but in reality encompassed 'political' separation superimposed upon economic and social inequality in an integrated society [Kuyperus, 1995: 95].[21]

It was during this period that theological categories began to be applied to the social situation. For example, the idea of 'election' was applied to South Africans, and not just along soteriological lines. Now 'this fertile soil of theological exclusivity and its justification for racial inequality and, thus, separation, provided a ready medium for the reception [of] Abraham Kuyper's concept of "sphere sovereignty."'[22] Kuyper, as discussed previously, wanted to emphasize the grand religious antithesis and demur from any notion of 'secular' disciplines, strictly speaking. But with this emphasis on sphere sovereignty, we 'now have the notion of antithesis writ large.'[23] Nevertheless, when Kuyper became Prime Minister in 1901, he was seeking in this capacity and in his later writings on statecraft to create a model in which people could exist peaceably in a pluralistic society. This model, as mentioned above, became known as 'pillarization' or 'vertical pluralism' [*Verzuiling*]. Therefore, in Dutch society at this time, you could have Calvinistic blocs, socialist blocs, Roman Catholic blocs, etc. But the result of this *Verzuiling* was that each bloc produced their own institutions, and this naturally flowed from Kuyper's notion of sphere sovereignty. But the real basis for this,

---

20. Ibid., pp. 1278-79.

21. Quoted in Baskwell, 'Kuyper and Apartheid,' p. 1270.

22. Baskwell, 'Kuyper and Apartheid,' p. 1275.

23. Ibid., p. 1277.

in Kuyper's program, was common grace.[24] However, in a South African context, this generated a different variant.

So what happened? How is it that Kuyper is often associated as the father of apartheid? Are there some missing links in these assertions? The answer is yes, according to Baskwell.

First, he claims that there were several Professors of note from Potchefstroom University in South Africa that were the point of contact between the Netherlands and South Africa. Tracy Kuyperus refers to these players as the 'Neo-Kuyperians,' and 'Calvinists within the NGK and GK[25] (who) adopted Kuyper's ideas of diversity and separate structural spheres in their explanation of racial and ethnic separation.'[26] First, there was Professor Potgieter, whom Kuyperus argues was 'one of the many prominent NGK clergymen who devised the … neo-Calvinist framework of separation using neo-Kuyperian logic applied to the South African situation.'[27] Second, and worse yet, Professor du Toit at Potchefstroom University demonstrated that he was even a more enthusiastic supporter of Apartheid. He actually claimed that racial integration was sinful and against the ordinances of creation. Segregation represents the Divine Will, according to du Toit.[28] Yet, Baskwell ardently demurs and says, 'Nowhere in any of Kuyper's writings, at least to my knowledge, can one find prescriptions for racial segregation based upon tradition, Divine mandate or anything else for that matter.'[29]

Professor Stoker, also of Potchefstroom University, exasperated these principles even more and distinguished between 'individual, social, or cultural spheres,' all under the rubric of sphere sovereignty.[30] The upshot of this movement was the view that culture:

> … is thus the handiwork of God, working through man. Cultural spheres exist apart from social relationships and have their own structural principles

---

24. Ibid., p. 1278.

25. NGK in Afrikaans is *Nedervitse Gereformeerde Kirk* (The Dutch Reformed Church in South Africa) and GK is *Gervormeede Kerk* (Reformed Church).

26. Ibid., pp. 1279-80, quoting Kuyperus 1999: 67.

27. Ibid., p. 1280.

28. Ibid.

29. Ibid., p. 1281.

30. Ibid.

defined by their unique destinies .... (Therefore) the People (*volk*) was a separate social sphere with its own structure and purpose.[31]

This introduces another important concept, namely, that the Afrikaners as a *People* or *Volk* also becomes integral to the notion of separate development, i.e., apartheid.

The political victory of the National Party in 1948 became pivotal. Now Afrikaner nationalism was 'enshrined with a vengeance in a series of laws, that, collectively, came to be known as Apartheid.'[32] Unfortunately, religion became mixed in with politics, and the rest is history for the National Party leader was formerly a Dutch Reformed minister prior to entering politics: Dr Daniel Francois Malan. He was the architect of Apartheid.[33] At this point in the political party, most of the people believed that the native races were 'both inferior and unassimilable.'[34] Under Verwoerd, these ideas were put into action to the full extent. For example, Allan Boesak opines from first-hand experience: 'The basic dictum underlying black education in South Africa, as maintained by Dr Verwoerd in the 1950s, is still true: black children must not get the kind of education that will give them the idea that they can have the same position as white children in South African Society.'[35] As Baskwell summarizes, citing Paul Johnson's apropos comparison with the rise of Zionism, what had started out as a defense of the underdog during the Boers—the white poor—advanced and evolved into systemic evil that supported the overdog and with a vengeance![36] As I stated in the first chapter, addressing the issue of 'systemic injustice' is complicated, let alone defining such a concept. Surely legislatively passed law, to which Christians must seriously consider whether they are bound to submit, is a profound question (cf., Rom. 13). Once apartheid became civil law, this is a clear example of 'systemic injustice' by almost any definition of the term.

In Kuyper's original design, the state was supposed to keep separate spheres from encroaching on one another, but with apartheid in full

---

31. Ibid., p. 1281.
32. Ibid., p. 1282.
33. Ibid.
34. Ibid., p. 1283.
35. Boesak, *Black and Reformed*, p. 44.
36. Baskwell, 'Kuyper and Apartheid,' p. 1284.

bloom, this healthy distrust of the state was lost. Rather, with apartheid, it was implemented at gunpoint.[37]

In short, was Kuyper a racist? The word 'racist' has been used in so many different contexts, and in so many different ways in our modern context, that it has become very imprecise.[38] In this book, 'racist' refers 'to the belief that the black race was inherently inferior to the white.'[39] In Chapter 12 of this book, we will discuss race and racist ideas to a greater extent. However, for now, we will not drift too far from Kuyper.

In 1901, when he became Prime Minister, he made statements which would seem to deny this. In the introduction to the so-called 'ethical policy', the reader should consider the following statement from George Harinck, the Director of the Archives and Documentation Center of the Reformed Churches, Kampen:[40]

> The Netherlands were not allowed to abuse their superiority over the Dutch East Indies. I do not deny the paternalistic character of this view, but this policy marked a major advance over the nineteenth-century Dutch colonial policy of exploitation, and it shows that Kuyper was not guided by the culture racism of his day, but by his Calvinistic creed of human equality.[41]

It seems that Bratt would agree, putting this under the rubric of 'common European racism of the time.'[42] While Kuyper was not a racist, *per se*; nevertheless, there is a certain racial arrogance or pride in some of his statements. Baskwell agrees, but with a qualification.

He describes, as an historian, how the dynamic of 'political correctness' works.[43] Referring to an article written by South African Professor, Gerald Pillay, 'Church, State, and Christian Pluralism in South Africa – A Historical Perspective,' he notes how Pillay urges people to take the long view in analyzing the relationship between the church and the state in apartheid South Africa. And why is this? Because

---

37. Ibid.

38. Thomas Virgil Peterson, *Ham and Japheth: The Mythic World of Whites in the Ante-bellum South* (Metuchen, NJ: The Scarecrow Press, 1978), p. 65.

39. Ibid.

40. https://hierstaanek.files.wordpress.com/2012/02/kuyper.pdf

41. Ibid.

42. See Bratt, *Abraham Kuyper: A Centennial Reader*, p. 323.

43. And most remarkably, he published in the peer-reviewed *Harvard Theological Review*!

an attitude of 'political correctness' often follows in the wake of unjust systems that are blatantly oppressive and inhibit sober reflection on serious social problems. Baskwell thinks that political correctness, which he considers a very real phenomena, is akin to cultural mythology in how it functions.[44] In referring favorably to Professor Pillay's article, he says that he helpfully reminds us that the political correctness of our time inhibits our sober reassessment of previous times. Likewise, what is considered politically correct now, in the present for us, would have horrified any right-minded person in the Victorian era. Baskwell says with regard to Kuyper's paternalistic comments:

> In this respect, it is difficult to see how Kuyper himself could have helped but been influenced, to some degree anyway, by this same political correctness. So then, was Abraham Kuyper a racist in the way in which we use the term today? I leave that to you, dear reader, to decide.[45]

Therefore, to the question—Was A. Kuyper the father of apartheid?—the answer is neither a simple 'yes' or 'no.'

It seems that his model of sphere sovereignty provided form and structure for some academics to twist into the misshapen monster which apartheid was to become. Kuyper, in this respect, was not the father but perhaps the 'grandfather' of such misshapen ideas.[46] Professors Stoker and du Toit not only reworked many of Kuyper's ideas, but they added quite a bit of theoretical baggage of their own.[47] Furthermore, Kuyper loathed coercion.

In short, Baskwell finally notes that Kuyper's '*Verzuiling*' was 'of a purely voluntary nature of those involved. It was not saturated with government and was not coercive in nature. This is a far cry from apartheid which was coercive in the extreme.'[48] Consequently, Baskwell claims, in his opinion, that Kuyper because of the extreme coercive nature of apartheid, would not have supported it had he lived to see it. Perhaps, in short, we may observe some notes of racial

---

44. See my extensive discussion on the role and function of 'myth' under the topic of the Ham myth in Chapter 12.

45. Baskwell, 'Kuyper and Apartheid,' p. 1288.

46. Ibid.

47. Ibid.

48. Ibid., p. 1289.

superiority in his extant writings which were characteristic of much of the Victorian era. Nevertheless, the conclusion that Baskwell comes to is that Kuyper's very own actions show that he was more interested in equality than segregation at the end of the day, and Kuyper would have eschewed apartheid from the beginning because of its coercive separation in the extreme.[49]

## End of excursus

Returning to our main topic, where our interests lie with Kuyper is his influence on the topic of the primary mission of the church. As will become clear throughout this book, one cannot separate this issue from the proper role, function, and limitations of the state. This entails, therefore, that we will be constantly addressing the relationship between the state and the church.

Kuyper can be credited with making a sharp break with the Christendom mindset that preceded him.[50] Moreover, he affirmed religious liberty in a manner that went beyond some of his Reformed predecessors.[51] Nevertheless, there are certain tensions in Kuyper's thought that opened the door to subsequent thinkers misconstruing his balanced approach which in turn led to muddying the waters with regard to the primary mission of the church. Let me explain.

David VanDrunen has made the case that 'Kuyper defended the awkward notion of a non-redemptive yet "Christianized" common grace realm by an appeal to the doctrine that Christ is mediator of both creation and redemption, of both common grace and special grace.'[52] This muddies the distinction, however, between Jesus' reign over the entire universe as the second person of the Godhead and His mediatorial reign as the incarnate Son of God, the God-man in the covenant of grace over His redeemed people. As I have been asserting throughout this book, this position has a long-standing pedigree in the Reformed Christian tradition.

This raises an important question: can one maintain a theological position of trying to develop a 'Christianized' culture while maintaining

---

49. Ibid.

50. David VanDrunen, *Natural Law and the Two Kingdoms*, p. 306.

51. Ibid.

52. Ibid., p. 313.

a distinct two-kingdom dual ruling of the Son in the universe generally as Second Person of the Godhead, and over the church specifically as the mediator of the covenant of grace? The answer suggested here is no. Kuyper, complex figure that he was, 'articulated an approach to cultural and political issues grounded largely in the creation order, like his Reformed predecessors, yet opened the door for an approach grounded in soteriological Christology and/or eschatology.'[53] Although he articulated a view of common grace and an approach to political and cultural issues which was largely grounded in the creation order; nevertheless, his practical rhetoric on the Christianization of culture and his political views were very influential for the Reformed church in the West, especially in the Netherlands and in North America as we shall see below. This had profound ramifications for considering the primary mission of the church, especially in its relation to the Kingdom of God.

## Herman Dooyeweerd

Although Kuyper is better known (at least in North America), in part because of his influence as a churchman, journalist, political leader, and educator, than Herman Dooyeweerd, nevertheless Dooyeweerd is probably the most influential Dutch Philosopher/Theologian after Kuyper.[54] Without a doubt, it can be said that Dooyeweerd is one of the most original philosophers that Holland ever produced, even more so than Spinoza. Dooyeweerd is no less important than Kuyper, especially for the topic of this book.[55]Most of his reflections were on statecraft; nevertheless, a constant refrain in this book is that one's thinking about the role of the state is integrally related to one's thinking about the role of the church in human society.

Herman Dooyeweerd was born in Amsterdam on October 7, 1894. He was born to Calvinist parents, who had been deeply influenced by

53. Ibid., p. 314.

54. J. V. Fesko, *Reformed Apologetics: Retrieving the Classic Reformed Approach to Defending the Faith* (Grand Rapids, MI: Baker Academic, 2019), p. 173.

55. See James W. Skillen, '*The Pluralist Philosophy of Herman Dooyeweerd*,' in Jeanne Heffernan Schindler, ed., *Christianity and Civil Society: Catholic and Neo-Calvinist Perspectives* (Lanham: Lexington Books, 2008), pp. 97-114, especially at p. 97. See also *The Amsterdam Philosophy: A Preliminary Critique, Papers by John Frame and Leonard Coppes* (Phillipsburg, NJ: Harmony Press, n.d.) and Robert A. Morey, *The Dooyeweerdian Concept of the Word of God* (Phillipsburg, NJ: Presbyterian and Reformed, 1974).

Abraham Kuyper. Almost all admit that Dooyeweerd is a very difficult thinker to understand.[56] This fact may contribute to his being less well-known than Kuyper.[57] Moreover, like Kuyper, anything said about Dooyeweerd needs to be situated against his intellectual context.[58] Additionally, there is the problem of translation. What is translated into English of Dooyeweerd's work may not precisely reflect the nuances of the Dutch language.[59] Even so, much can be said about him and his work that touches on the topic of this book.

After attending law school, Dooyeweerd held various practical positions. In 1922, he was appointed the assistant director of the Kuyper Institute in The Hague. This position was in the newly established research center of the Antirevolutionary party, described above in the discussion about G. van Prinsterer and Kuyper. This opportunity 'gave Dooyeweerd the opportunity to engage in some systematic reflection on the nature of Christian politics.'[60]

The central thought of all of Dooyeweerd's philosophy and system (obviously influenced by Kuyper) is that 'all philosophy has nontheoretical, religious presuppositions which it cannot do without, and that philosophy fails as soon as it desires to be "autonomous" and thus is itself not aware of this presupposition.'[61] For Dooyeweerd, the 'ground idea' becomes central for all theoretical abstraction, by which he means 'the idea of reality as a whole with which a thinker starts when abstracting a particular field or mode for special examination.'[62] This move was an attempt to offer an alternative to Thomist constructs.[63] His

---

56. See Chaplin, *Herman Dooyeweerd*, p. 187.

57. Ibid., p. 2.

58. For biographical details and Dooyeweerd's intellectual background, see Jonathan Chaplin, *Herman Dooyeweerd*, pp. 24-25. Also helpful is Skillen, 'The Pluralist Philosophy of Herman Dooyeweerd,' p. 97.

59. Ibid., pp. 187-88. This author neither speaks nor reads Dutch, so in this regard I am relying on scholars like Chaplin.

60. Bernard Zylstra's introduction in L. Kalsbeek, *Contours of a Christian Philosophy: An Introduction to Herman Dooyeweerd's Thought*, Bernard and Josina Zylstra, editors (Toronto: Wedge, 1975), pp. 14-15.

61. G.E. Langemeijer, 'An Assessment of Herman Dooyeweerd,' in Kalsbeek, *Contours of a Christian Philosophy*, p. 11.

62. Skillen, 'Pluralist Philosophy,' p. 97.

63. Chaplin, *Herman Dooyeweerd*, p. 74.

project was an ambitious one: to critique every attempt at theorizing apart from a true religious ground motive [read Christianity].[64] Chaplin writes:

> Dooyeweerd's major project was a hugely ambitious attempt to reconstruct the entire foundations of Western philosophy on the basis of what he called a 'transcendental critique' of theorizing. Radically recasting Kant's transcendental method, this sought to demonstrate, from an analysis of the nature of theorizing itself, that theoretical activity in every discipline presupposed particular, contestable philosophical frameworks, which in turn depended upon pre-theoretical assumptions of an essential religious character.[65]

This ambitious project was set forth in encyclopedic project, *De Wijsbegeerte der Wetsidee*, which is literally translated, according to Chaplin as '"The Philosophy of the Law-Idea" but has generally, and awkwardly, been rendered into English as "The Philosophy of the Cosmonomic Idea."'[66] Better known now in the English speaking world as *A New Critique of Theoretical Thought* (hence, *NC*), this book represents the 'considerably revised and extended English translation, and it contains the most detailed articulation of his mature social and political theory.'[67]

For Dooyeweerd, the only ground motive for a truly Christian Philosophy was the biblical ground motive, the spiritual motive: creation, fall, and redemption in Jesus Christ.[68] For Dooyeweerd, in the big picture, 'there are two primary ground motives: biblical and apostate.'[69] He writes:

> Thus the central theme of the Holy Scriptures, namely, that of creation, fall into sin, and redemption by Jesus Christ in the communion of the Holy

---

64. For a contrast with Greek form-matter and scholastic nature-grace ground motives, vis-à-vis Dooyeweerd's allegedly Christian ground-motive, see John Fesko, *Reforming Apologetics*, pp. 168-69.

65. Chaplin, Ibid., pp. 73

66. Ibid., p. 30. In English, Dooyeweerd's *magnum opus* was *A New Critique of Theoretical Thought: The Necessary Presuppositions of Philosophy*. 4 volumes; trans. David H. Freeman and William S. Young (Philadelphia, PA: Presbyterian and Reformed, 1953-1958).

67. Ibid.

68. Herman Dooyeweerd, *In the Twilight of Western Thought: Studies in the Pretended Autonomy of Philosophical Thought* (Nutley, NJ: The Craig Press, 1972), pp. 41-43.

69. Fesko, *Reforming Apologetics*, p. 167.

Spirit, has a radical meaning, which is related to the central unity of our human existence. It effects the true knowledge of God and ourselves, if our heart is fully opened by the Holy Spirit so that it finds itself in the grip of God's Word and has become the captive of Jesus Christ.[70]

If ideas have legs, this is what puts feet to North American Christian education movements in the work of Henry Stob (Calvin College), Cornelius Plantinga (Calvin Seminary), Albert Wolters (Redeemer University College in Ontario), and finally Craig Bartholomew and Michael Goheen (more below). In Dooyeweerd's work, an antipathy runs deep against any notion of a division between the secular and the sacred. At this point, it seems that Dooyeweerd is not merely eschewing secularism in the wake of the 'secular' as defined in the wake of the French Revolution, but anything not having as its ground motive a reference first and foremost to the Bible, to the religious. At this point, a more precise delineation between secular in an Augustinian sense and secular in the sense of 'secularism' coming out of the French Revolution, i.e., an antipathy towards the Bible and God, would have been helpful.

What is needed, Dooyeweerd came to realize, was an account of 'the *internal structure of theorizing itself*, one capable of embracing any particular conception of the philosophical task,' and his aim was to show that 'the most basic of these conditions is the inescapable dependence of all theorizing upon a commitment of a *religious* nature.'[71] He is constantly concerned for the influence of 'dualism' in nonchristian thought. In other words, any view of reality which grows 'out of an idolatrous, dualistic ground motive which posits two origins of reality and thus splits it into two opposing parts.'[72] Again, for Dooyeweerd, 'the proper starting point is the biblical ground motive of creation-fall-redemption. Hence, Dooyeweerd rejected any view that did not

---

70. Dooyeweerd, *In the Twilight*, p. 86, quoted in Fesko, *Reforming Apologetics*, pp. 169-70.

71. Chaplin, *Herman Dooyeweerd*, p. 41. [emphasis original]

72. Herman Dooyeweerd, *Roots of Western Culture: Pagan, Secular, and Christian Options*. Trans. by John Kraay; Mark Vander Vennen and Bernard Zylstra, editors (Toronto: Wedge, 1979), p. 31. This theme rises frequently in Dooyeweerd. Cf., pp. 35, 36, 43, 112-13 etc.. This book is more accessible than *NC*. This comprises a set of articles from a journal that Dooyeweerd himself edited. It's important when reading the book to realize that the mood in the Netherlands at the time was that sharp differences between the Reformed, Roman Catholics, and Humanists could be set aside in order to try and build a national consensus.

embrace the biblical ground motive. Anything less inevitably led to antithetical dualism because of the idolization of the temporal realm and the inability to account for supratemporal realities.'[73]

In order to clarify, let's delve briefly into Dooyeweerd's system. One must grasp his idea of 'modality.' Skillen is helpful here:

> By 'modalities' (or 'modal aspects' or 'modal spheres') of reality, Dooyeweerd means that which answers the question of *how* things exist, in contrast to *what* exists. Every creature and every concrete thing and institutions is subject to laws and/or norms of both a *modal* character and an *individual-identity* character.[74]

Dooyeweerd established fifteen of these modal aspects in his major work (NC). These aspects are interdependent and yet cannot ultimately be 'split up.' For Dooyeweerd, time 'splits up' the fullness of meaning to which each of these modal aspects contributes independently; however, just as light is refracted in a prism into seven colors, so cosmic time is like a prism in which each of these resulting modal aspects reflects the fullness of meaning but is yet irreducible and 'sovereign in its own sphere.'[75] Moreover, each of these aspects has a law-side and a subject-side, so Dooyeweerd will use the language of 'law-spheres.'[76] When using this language of sphere sovereignty, there is a danger of confusion because Dooyeweerd has retained this nomenclature from Kuyper, where Kuyper intended it to refer to the distinctions and autonomy between societal structures. Yet, Dooyeweerd means more than Kuyper by this terminology. Dooyeweerd understands sovereignty to refer not to universality of scope but to the *'originality of source.'*[77] His view is more sophisticated than Kuyper's was, rendering his system as having more potential for Christian pluralism.[78]

Another important fundamental feature of Dooyeweerd's system is the claim that these modal aspects exist in sequence, they are not arbitrarily juxtaposed.[79] This means, according to Dooyeweerd, that

---

73. Fesko, *Reforming Apologetics*, p. 172.

74. Skillen, 'Pluralist Philosophy,' p. 102.

75. Dooyeweerd quoted in Chaplin, *Herman Dooyeweerd*, p. 56.

76. Ibid., p. 57.

77. Ibid., p. 209.

78. Ibid., pp. 13-18.

79. Ibid., p. 57.

each 'builds on the foundation of the preceding ones, and is in turn the foundation for the following ones.'[80] However, Dooyeweerd's system becomes even more complex here. These aspects are not hermetically sealed from one another; rather, they interact. But this does not occur externally. It occurs internally. As Chaplin says, 'The coherence among them [the modal aspects] is not an ordered juxtaposition but a mutual interpenetration.'[81] The aspects are listed in the following column, on the left. These aspects may be viewed from the bottom up or the top down. In other words, in spite of their sovereignty, they have internal coherence, and they can be viewed in a transcendental direction (beginning with the faith aspect). From this perspective then, we are 'directed towards the religious root of our cosmos.'[82] However, in the chart that follows, the fifteen aspects according to their proper succession are as follows with the 'meaning nuclei' in the column on the right:[83]

| Aspects | Meaning-nuclei |
| --- | --- |
| Numerical aspect | discrete quantity (number) |
| Spatial aspect | continuous extension |
| Kinematic aspect | motion |
| Physical aspect | energy |
| Biotic aspect | vitality |
| Psychic aspect | feeling |
| Logical aspect | distinction |
| Historical aspect | formative power |
| Lingual aspect | symbolic meaning |
| Social aspect | social intercourse |
| Economic aspect | frugality in managing scarce goods |
| Aesthetic aspect | harmony |
| Juridical aspect | retribution (recompensing) |
| Ethical aspect | love in temporal relationships |
| Faith aspect | faith, firm assurance |

80. Ibid.

81. Ibid., p. 58.

82. Dooyeweerd, quoted in Ibid., p. 58.

83. See L. Kalsbeek, *Contours of a Christian Philosophy: An Introduction to Herman Dooyeweerd's thought*, Bernard and Josina Zylstra, editors (Toronto: Wedge, 1975), p. 100.

Dooyeweerd's integration of time in his system is crucial to understand what he is trying to do. For him, 'modal rather than individual (typical) phenomena' describe the reciprocal and interconnected coherence of these diverse aspects of the cosmic order.[84] At the intersection of one modal aspect with another are analogical moments, which do not 'exist' as such; rather they are '*aspects* of existence.'[85] These meaning-nuclei always indicate a 'how' or 'function', not a concrete something.[86] More could be said about the complex nature of this interconnectivity; however, that would take us too far afield from the main argument at this time.

The important point to grasp at this turn is that Dooyeweerd is concerned about any kind of reductionism, and he applies his analysis of theoretical thought with 'powerful critical effect' at this point to many academic disciplines. Reductionism for Dooyeweerd appears in any discipline when there is 'a conflation of the original meaning of a concept with one of its analogical meanings.'[87] An example from the discipline of social science is illustrative. Consider the efforts of sociobiologists to explain social behavior primarily in terms of evolutionary biological factors. For example, consider the postwar efforts of systems theory proponents working within cybernetics that tried to explain political developments (perhaps in a deterministic way) as a living organism in which the fittest political bodies adapt and survive. For Dooyeweerd, this would be a reductionism in explanatory power because complex and large-scale networks of political interactions are attempted by isolating one aspect (primarily the biotic), and hence the results are skewed.[88] Thus, effectively, one modal aspect has been absolutized to the neglect of others appropriate to the subject matter. This is not to say that Dooyeweerd didn't think that such enterprises are worthless and that nothing can be learned from them; rather, he was concerned to demonstrate what kind of reductionisms are involved.[89]

More germane to our topic of the primary mission of the church and a Christian's responsibility within this task, is that this means that

---

84. Chaplin, *Herman Dooyeweerd*, p. 58.

85. Ibid., p. 59 [emphasis original].

86. Kalsbeek, *Contours*, p. 100.

87. Chaplin, *Herman Dooyeweerd*, p. 61.

88. Ibid.

89. Ibid.

there could be no absolutization of individual freedom, for example, or a skewed view of the role of the state results, and potential damage is done to other non-political spheres. Dooyeweerd spent more time analyzing the state than any other institution, although as mentioned previously, this has profound ramifications for a person's understanding of the church as well.[90] According to Dooyeweerd, the state should have limits and not be absolutized. Indeed, his concept of *rechtsstaat* was chosen to prevent just such an absolutizing of the state. The genuine law-state is one in which 'the limits to its lawmaking competence are acknowledge as intrinsic to its very nature: "in the true idea of the law-state [according to Dooyeweerd], the divine structural principle of the body politic limits the peculiar universality of the internal public law to a universality and sovereignty within its own sphere of competence."'[91]

So with regards to administering *public justice*, this is where the state is aptly suited when she functions in a healthy, God-given manner. Other structures in society may attempt to perform *public justice* (e.g., families, churches, etc. ....); however, as Chaplin says, 'they do so very badly, and the progressive thrust of history pushes state builders toward acknowledging the norm of differentiation in which the state comes into its own as *the* institution fitted precisely to administer public justice.'[92]

Dooyeweerd himself summarized his views in this way:

Special grace, however, is concerned with the renewal of the religious root of the creation in Christ Jesus as the Head of the regenerated human race and must not be considered in an individualistic soteriological sense. From this it follows that particular grace is the real root and foundation of common grace. It is therefore absolutely contrary to the Biblical standpoint when a distinction is made between two independent realms or spheres of grace.[93] As the Redeemer, Christ is the Regenerator of the entire fallen cosmos. As the Mediator of the Covenant of grace in its religious fullness, He is the Root of common grace, the King whose kingship embraces the whole of temporal life. The *civitas terrena*, as the world in apostasy, cannot claim any sphere of life as its own in opposition to Christ. A State divorced from the new root of life does not owe its

90. Ibid., p. 35.

91. Ibid., pp. 208-09, quoting Dooyeweerd.

92. Ibid., p. 99.

93. Again, you can hear the concern against any kind of dualism here.

manifestation of apostasy to Christ but to the *civitas terrena*. In such a State the structure office is maintained and thereby God bestows his temporal blessings on mankind. Both this office and its blessings belong to the Kingdom of Christ, who is the king of common grace, because He is the Head of regenerated mankind. We must therefore undertake the struggle for the Christian State.[94]

Thus, for Dooyeweerd, his philosophy of societal pluralism implies that Christians strive to redeem God's fallen creation with 'creative, history-making stewardship.'[95] In addition to the complexity and nuance of Dooyeweerd's system is the fact that his followers often exaggerated or misunderstood his views and the proper application of them. Just as there are neo-Kuyperians who skewed Kuyper's ideas (even resulting in systemic racism, as noted above), so also there are neo-Dooyeweerdians, who have skewed his ideas, especially in the realm of education. We could focus on critical engagement with Dooyeweerd and his followers at numerous levels, especially the view of Scripture that many in the Amsterdam movement have held. John Frame, for example, has written critically that the philosophical premises of the Amsterdam movement are extremely problematic and probably undermined the authority of Scripture.[96] I will focus my critical comments on what I judge to be one of Dooyeweerd's principal problems: his polemics against 'dualism.'

John Fesko has already criticized Dooyeweerd's rejection of 'so-called' dualistic thought with four major points: he does not base his dualism on exegesis of Scripture, he actually criticized Reformed confessions (particularly the WCF for its allegedly dualistic Thomistic-Aristotelian conception of body and soul), he eschewed a tradition approach to the relationship between philosophy and theology, and finally his dualistic methodology has been the most influential on Reformed thinking since Kuyper.[97] I'll not rehearse the evidence explaining those points here since Fesko's criticisms are easily obtainable elsewhere. My point will be rather a simple biblical one.

---

94. Dooyeweerd quoted in Kalsbeek, *Contours*, pp. 236-37.

95. Skillen, pp. 110-111.

96. See, for example, *The Amsterdam Philosophy: A Preliminary Critique, Papers by John Frame and Leonard Coppes* and Robert A. Morey, *The Dooyeweerdian Concept of the Word of God.*

97. See Fesko, *Reforming Apologetics*, pp. 172-73.

Over and against Dooyeweerd and his followers, why can't God, after the fall, set up a structural dualism in the world, with holy kingdom institution and non-holy institutions coexisting side by side, as I have suggested earlier in the book (see Chapter 2)? Take, for example, the subject of hell. Does God rule over hell? Yes. However, the fact that God rules over hell does not mean that hell is holy as a realm, or should be (cf., Rev. 21:8 and 22:14-15). Quite the contrary. Hell is outside the gates of the holy city, that is, the Jerusalem above where the saints worship God forever and ever. Nevertheless, hell is under King Jesus' reign, but it is outside of God's kingdom realm. Therefore, at least in the creation of the cosmos, *God has instituted a dualism in which He reigns over both realms, albeit in different ways.* Moreover, if God has been pleased to create this dualism in the cosmic realm, how much more is God free to do likewise in the created mundane realm also!

Meredith Kline, merely trying to mediate a Christian world and life view (i.e., meaning that we should align our thinking with God's design of the world in which we live), wrote:

> If we listen to what the Word of God says specifically about the institutions in question [he has been talking about the institution of the state], we discover that with the emergence of the religious antithesis, the Lord God, in the interests of his redemptive purposes, sovereignly revised the original structure of things, bringing into being within the arena of earthly history an interim world which involved the holy/common distinction as one of its fundamental features. In particular, he established the institution of the state as a nonholy structure under the principle of common grace. The sphere of the state, though not exempt from God's rule and not devoid of the divine presence (indeed, though it is the scene of God's presence in a measure of common blessing) is, nevertheless, not to be identified as belonging to the kingdom of God or sharing in its holiness.[98]

The question now before us is this: *are we willing to listen to God's Word on this matter?* In other words, shall we listen to God and His Word not only on issues of sin and salvation, but also on His design of the world in which we live and its interim world structures? Kline continues: 'We may

---

98. Meredith G. Kline, *Kingdom Prologue,* p. 171.

not deny to the Creator his sovereign prerogative of creative structuring and restructuring and authoritative defining and redefining. And least of all should venture to do so in the name of honoring the universality of his kingly rule.'[99]

The point here is that everything is under the reign of God (even hell); however, He rules over these realms in different ways. Kline concludes:

> Summing up then, the meaning or essential identity of the postlapsarian city [i.e., the state] is not found in identification either with the kingdom of Satan or with the kingdom of God. Nor is it to be explained in terms of a dialectical seesawing between the demonic and the divine. This divinely appointed institution [the state] exists within the sphere of common grace, which is the corollary, the counterpoise, of the common curse. The fundamental shape of the city is the resultant of the interplay of these two correlative principles of divine action, a divine wrath and a divine grace that restrains that wrath according to the measure of sovereign purpose. Such is the biblical conceptual framework for defining the basic meaning of the city [i.e., the state].[100]

Dooyeweerd's polemic against 'dualistic' categories was contrary to Scriptural teaching as Kline rightly recognized. Dooyeweerd was positing a *one* kingdom model; and, in so doing, he was 'setting forth a program for Christian participation in culture with fundamental theological differences from the earlier Reformed natural law and two kingdoms traditions.'[101] In setting forth these arguments and others, Kline did not explicitly refer to his Reformed predecessors and confessional tradition in articulating a distinct two-kingdoms doctrine with Jesus' dual mediatorial role as sovereign over the entire universe and simultaneously ruling over the realm of his church as mediator of the covenant of grace; nevertheless, Kline does fall within this tradition by expressing God's design in 'two kingdom categories in describing the church and the common grace city as two God-ordained, legitimate realities structuring life in the present world.'[102] Now, we are prepared to look at what occurred in the wake of this teaching.

---

99. Ibid.

100. Ibid., p. 172.

101. VanDrunen, *Natural Law and the Two Kingdoms*, p. 349.

102. Ibid., p. 413.

## The Neo-Kuyperian/Neo-Dooyeweerdian Legacy. Is There Such a Thing as Christian Scholarship or a Unique Christian View of Various Academic Disciplines?

How did these two thinkers primarily influence developments within the church in the West? The church has long had an uneasy affair with learning, interacting with culture, and what is distinctively 'Christian' about certain disciplines. I will argue the influence was most often felt within the Christian education endeavors of the church (especially Christian schools sponsored by the church, and universities/colleges that have sought to do likewise). Much could be said about the importance of education. Much could be said addressing the question of who is responsible for education? Indeed, many Christians have spent countless hours home-schooling their children, sending them to Christian day schools and even some churches have sponsored, started, and supported Christian schools and colleges/universities. My wife and I sent our kids to Christian schools and spent many thousands of dollars to educate them in such institutions. Moreover, I have served many hours on the Board of Trustees of a Christian school. Obviously these are important areas in which Christians often invest large personal resources and time. In hindsight, overall, it was a good investment.[103]

In other words, in Christian colleges and universities, the notion was planted, germinated, and grew that Christians think in fundamentally different ways than those who are not. Of course in some limited ways this is true; however, the calculus in math is the calculus and it matters not whether a person learns it at Cornell or Wheaton, as long as they learn it well, especially if they plan on being a civil engineer.

Of course, ironically, that means that it also influenced the pulpit since so many of the sons and daughters of the church were influenced not only in the Sunday schools and catechism classes of the modern church, but also many were trained at colleges and seminaries that perpetuated such influence before they returned to serve their mother: i.e., the church. Let me be clear, I am not arguing that Christians don't have an obligation to renew their minds and think biblically about a

---

103. The reader should consult David VanDrunen's carefully phrased comments, *Living in God's Two Kingdoms*, pp. 172-87.

number of significant issues with which they are confronted as they grow older and mature in faith. But there are many things that the Scriptures do not touch upon. So when N. Wolterstorff talks about 'Christian' agriculture, or farming, it sounds like a loose use of the adjective at best. When members of a CSI[104] school stand up and argue at a society meeting for the need of developing a 'Christian' wood shop at the local Christian high school, based allegedly on the model of God raising up Bezaliel and Aholiab as God-inspired artisans to build the tabernacle, this is sheer foolishness.

There can be no doubt that our Christian faith has recognized that the natural world is beautiful and the good gift of the Creator. Moreover, to a greater or lesser extent, the church throughout history has recognized secular learning and the highest measure of intellectual, literary, and artistic gifts with which those outside of Christ and the church are sometimes endowed. Nevertheless, the church's posture towards secular learning and achievements has been unsure and uneasy. Uneasy in the sense that the church has lacked confidence to leave 'secular' learning to its own nature and thus there have been postures of eschewing nature and secular reasoning on the one hand, and on the other hand, the church has tried to 'Christianize' culture for its own ends. In speaking of classical culture, for example, with its great achievement in creativity, beauty and literature, Quirinus Breen expresses it like this:

> To read poets, the dramatists, the philosophers of Greece is to leave one wishing for ourselves their strong sense of truth and beauty. We cannot enough admire their wonder about what is that walk which is worthy of a human being. This wonderful manifestation of man's rational nature, we urge, must be maintained in its freedom to be what it is, to act in accordance with its own potential. And as this natural, this secular, this Greek life of reason unfolds in our history, our criterion of the reception it gets is whether or not the receivers (notably the church) left to this life of reason a place for the hollow of its foot. The argument of these lectures cannot be understood unless it is clearly grasped that the life of reason, the secular learning, must be free to be what it is by its nature.[105]

---

104. Christian Schools International.

105. See Quirinus Breen, *Christianity and Humanism: Studies in the History of Ideas* (Grand Rapids, MI: Eerdmans, 1968), p. 213.

With lucidity often absent in discussions about 'the Christian mind,' Breen continues to discuss the church's main object: the redemption of man. He says, 'Thus man, the object of redemption, must be known.'[106] In a long paragraph he explains that man is part of the natural order, that he is free in the sense of 'his right to be an individual who finds his fulfillment in good part through being unique.'[107] Moreover, he asserts that man finds his individuality through being unique, pursuing excellence and finally he claims man is a social being, who makes states, communities and the like. Then Breen returns to the mission of the church: the redemption of man. He says:

> What is redemption? Surely, not to be saved from the natural order, from rationality; nor from individuality; nor from excellence; nor from making political societies. There can be no redemption if there is no man to save; we must know him as he has existed actually and historically.[108]

Finally, distinctions with precision!

This brings the problem of the Kuyperian and especially the Dooyeweerdian legacy, with its one-kingdom emphasis and antipathy towards any 'dualisms,' into sharp contrast with these sharply expressed ideas since the complaint against dualistic thought is common among neo-Calvinist writers and thinkers. This group of people has often offered critiques of the older two-kingdoms and natural law approach described in this book.[109] We will call them 'neo-Calvinists,' a common appellation that accurately groups the folks we are talking about into a recognizable taxonomic category. Let me explain.

The term is not applied with pejorative intentions.[110] Rather, the term has often been applied to followers of Kuyper, who—through the mediation of Dooyeweerd, whether inside or outside of conscious awareness—apply their ideas about the relationship between Christianity and culture.[111] A number of figures would appropriately fit here. I will only engage a few and let the reader follow up on other

---

106. Ibid.

107. Ibid.

108. Ibid.

109. VanDrunen, *Natural Law and the Two Kingdoms*, pp. 3-4.

110. Ibid. p. 368.

111. Ibid., p. 368.

published works in order to examine whether this author's claims fit the description.

What is held in common (though not exactly) among these authors, are the 'givens' of 'anti-dualistic' categories together with an 'eschatological' thrust. What I mean by the latter point is the following. In creation, Adam and Eve were given dominion or cultural mandates (cf., Chapter 2) which were radically transformed because of their failed mission and the fall of humanity into a condition of sin and misery. This group of authors will often express themselves in terms of a 'renewed cultural mandate' in which 'transformed' culture is allegedly redeemed and ushered into the world to come. This becomes, for Dooyeweerd and neo-Calvinistic followers, the biblical ground motive of creation-fall-redemption ground motive. Such ideas are trafficked to thousands of students at Christian colleges and universities every year. The influence is profound.[112] The influence is particularly felt in a 'one kingdom worldview' vis-à-vis a more historic two kingdom view as expressed in this book throughout. Ironically, the argument of this book is that the church, even at church-sponsored Christian day schools, colleges, and universities, has been responsible for the inculcation—either wittingly or unwittingly—of the one kingdom thinking of Dooyeweerd among her sons and daughters.

The complaint is often made that the church has succumbed to a faulty epistemology of 'dualistic' thinking, often attributed to Roman Catholic influence. Consider, for example, Henry Van Til, formerly a Professor of Bible at Calvin College, who also studied at Westminster Theological Seminary and the Free University of Amsterdam:

> Thus Rome, which claims for itself the appellation 'Catholic,' has changed New Testament catholicity, which purifies and sanctifies as its proper domain the whole of life, and has substituted in its place a *dualism*, which separates the supernatural from the natural. Salvation always remains above the natural, but does not enter it to transform it; creation and recreation remain two independent entities. Thus a compromise is made between nature and the supernatural, between body and soul, world and church, knowing and believing, mortality and religion.[113]

---

112. Ibid., p. 369.

113. Henry R. Van Til, *The Calvinistic Concept of Culture* (Grand Rapids, MI: Baker, 1959), pp. 18-19.

After demonstrating the influence of Kuyper, Dooyeweerd and others, the author's true colors come out in the latter part of his book: 'Due to the influence of the Enlightenment and Rationalism, the consciousness of this basic, irreconcilable antithesis has been practically erased from the mind of the church.'[114] Of course, he doesn't fail to demonize all who don't hold his views: 'Now it ought to be observed that one of the most subtle tactics in the arsenal of Satan is the attempt to soft pedal the antithesis, to lull the people of God to sleep so that they become at ease in Zion and are complacent with respect to the world.'[115]

Previously, I argued that at times Kuyper reasoned in such a manner that demonstrated an adherence to the two types of rule that Christ exercises over the world. However, I agreed with VanDrunen that he was a transitional figure who had certain tensions in his thought, and that his followers often neglected his nuance, seized on his rhetoric, and ran with one strain, especially in North America. Again, Henry Van Til demonstrates this:

> In the spirit of Groen van Prinsterer, the general without an army of Dutch politics, Kuyper began to call the people of the Reformed persuasion to spiritual separation (*geestelyk isolement*). Under the tutelage of Kuyper, who became the titular head of the Anti-revolutionary Party after the death of Groen, the Calvinists of the Netherlands increasingly realized that if Christianity is to exert and influence upon the life of the world it must live out of its own distinctive principles. Men began again to see that not by might, nor by power, but through the Spirit of God the cause of God shall prevail; they believed that faith is the victory that overcometh the world .... Kuyper draws the conclusion that there are two kinds of people, hence also two kinds of science, art, politics – witness the organization in The Netherlands of the Anti-Revolutionary Party, on the foundation of the Word of God versus the principle of Revolution which cries 'No God, no master!' ... On the other hand, that part of fallen humanity which was not restored through Christ, continues its existence in apostasy from the living God .... And since this antithesis roots in the heart, it does not merely affect the periphery, but the whole of man's life under the sun. Not a single aspect of life, even the seemingly most neutral, lies outside this antithesis of godliness versus godlessness. For God is sovereign over his creation and

---

114. Ibid., p. 180.
115. Ibid., p. 181.

Christ's kingship extends to the whole of this creation of God .... This hatred not only expresses itself religiously but also culturally. For the hatred of the world need not be expressed in persecution and burnings at the stake; it can be effectively expressed by negation and the ignoring of Christ's claims in so-called 'neutral' culture.[116]

So the real question that emerges from these currents in the wake of Kuyper's and Dooyeweerd's thought is: is there such a thing as 'Christian' scholarship or a 'Christian' approach to culture?

As an undergraduate, whose intellectual light had just turned on, I remember first bumping up against this important question in an address given by Charles Malik at the dedication of the Billy Graham center at Wheaton College in 1980. Malik was Eastern Orthodox, a scholar, and a Lebanese diplomat. He did not pull his punches. He claimed that if the church wanted to evangelize the West, let alone the world, then she would have to get over her anti-intellectual tendencies and take back thought in the university. It was a powerful message and struck a nerve, especially among evangelicals.

Among those in the audience was Mark A. Noll, a Professor of Christian Thought and history at Wheaton College. His influential book, *The Scandal of the Evangelical Mind*, by the author's own admission, became a 'historical footnote in support of Malik's sage words.'[117] Additionally, I can remember my Arabic Professor (a Roman Catholic) putting a copy of George Marsden's work (Professor of History at Calvin College and then later at the University of Notre Dame) in my hands (he knew I was a confessional and Reformed Christian, like Marsden), which also follows similar trajectories, advocating for a distinctively Christian scholarship.[118] In this significant book, Marsden argues for a place for faith-informed Christian scholarship in the secular academy. These two evangelical historical titans would become what I call the 'Noll-Marsden' approach to religious scholarship. If the reader wanted

---

116. Ibid., pp. 182-83.

117. Mark A. Noll, *The Scandal of the Evangelical Mind* (Grand Rapids, MI: Eerdmans, 1994), p. 27.

118. See, for example, George M. Marsden, *The Outrageous Idea of Christian Scholarship* (Oxford/New York, Oxford University Press, 1997). For reviews and a rejoinder by Marsden, see the Review Symposium on the book in *The Council of Societies for the Study of Religion Bulletin*, Vol. 27/3 (September 1998): pp. 59-65.

a quick way to enter the differences among arguments for so-called 'Christian scholarship' then one could see the debate that ensued among historian Darryl Hart (now at Hillsdale College) and Christian college professor and philosopher Bill Davis (Covenant College).[119]

Bill Davis takes a more Noll-Marsden approach to religious scholarship. He argues that a Christian scholar will produce more works which reflect upon an appreciation for and love of those in need. He reflects a more Kuyperian approach to education and scholarship. Hart, on the other hand, takes a 'Lutheran' two-kingdom view: distinguishing between the Kingdom of God, which is spiritual and eternal and the Kingdom of Man which is temporal and worldly. Hart argues that the Christian must participate in the Kingdom of Man as a citizen of the world and heaven at the same time. Elsewhere, Hart calls this a 'hyphenated' existence (as mentioned previously), which allowed Americans to produce confessional Protestantism to escape the dangers of the balkanization and tribalization of American society.[120] Moreover, Hart believes that such a hyphenated existence is essential to Christian identity.[121] These differences should not be ignored. The response by Davis to Hart demonstrates a real fundamental difference with regard to the Christian's calling and his or her role as a citizen of the Kingdom of God and the Kingdom of Man simultaneously. Disagreement can be a great achievement and need not be eschewed if it brings clarity.

My take is that Hart's critique has some seeds of truth to it since sometimes Christians speak in exaggerated terms about the antithesis. Basically, Hart's point is that the difference between Christian scholarship and non-Christian scholarship, is not, strictly speaking, epistemological. Do Marsden and Noll really believe that there is a religious approach to scholarship whose key to understanding is the difference that regeneration of the soul makes in the mind of a believer? No wonder Hart asks if believers and non-believers really know differently? Just because a person is a Christian does not give him or her the epistemological high ground, necessarily. Perhaps a careful read of Marsden's work would leave the

---

119. See Darryl Hart, 'Christian Scholars, Secular Universities, and the Problem with the "Antithesis,"' *CSR* 30 (2001): pp. 383-402; Bill Davis, 'Contra Hart: Christian Scholars Should Not Throw in the Towel,' *CSR* 34 (2005): pp. 187-200.

120. Hart, *The Lost Soul of American Protestantism*, pp. 169-86.

121. Hart, *A Secular Faith*, pp. 244-57.

impression that he is not suggesting a different epistemology as much as a different perspective and approach. Faith may very well influence and make a difference in the kinds of questions one asks, let alone the kinds of evaluations one gives to the answers gleaned from those questions. My opinion, after many years of reflection on these issues, is that the subject of Christian scholarship becomes more complex and difficult the deeper one goes in the humanities. In other words, there may be very little, if any difference between how a Christian thinks about the calculus vis-à-vis a non-Christian. However, how they engage and analyze World War 1 poetry may be profoundly different as will their thinking on numerous weighty ethical issues where world views and presuppositions emerge about humanity, discussions about God, ethics, where we came from and where we are going as human beings.

Although Davis' argument is that a Christian scholar will produce works of scholarship that reflect an appreciation and love for those in need, does this not seriously do injury to a robust view of common grace? Davis' argument can sound like it denies common grace. Although Mozart largely rejected God, yet that same God distributed gifts, skill and creativity to produce some of the most sublime music ever created. Likewise, God can grant skill, wisdom, and knowledge to whomever He pleases—Christian or not—to create, make manifest, and bring about good among human beings in all areas of culture: art, medicine, engineering, the humanities, producing vaccinations, etc.

I suspect that many demur from a two kingdoms approach, as represented by Hart, because they hear—rightly or wrongly—the notion that one should keep his or her faith out of cultural endeavors. But what does this mean? Remember, as we distinguished earlier, all our efforts are religious in the sense that they flow from our person, which is whole; however, it does not follow that the work of a Christian and a non-Christian will always be distinguishable, let alone transform whatever cultural project we happen to be working on. In other words, while we may concede that all our thoughts and actions must be an expression of and tribute to our Lord Christ, whom we love and serve, it does not follow that the act of a Christian will always be different from that of unbelievers.

Part of the problem with the cry for the church to give more attention to social injustice is our own cultural context in the West and the decline in biblical literacy, familiarity with Greek and Roman literature, and knowledge of ancient history.[122] This curriculum, which was the foundation of so much education until recently, has sometimes been called 'general education' which was steeped in the classics and great books, especially of Greek and Roman literature. Let me explain.

There has been a turn in institutions of higher learning away from a classical curriculum and programs focusing on the great books. In those decades, especially following World War II, an increasing emphasis has been placed on practical disciplines, such as science and politics. This is not bad in and of itself; however, it has occurred with a concurrent de-emphasis on the humanities.[123] In his profound and suggestive book, Legaspi cites C. P. Snow, who captures the mood of the 'The Two Cultures,' in his 1959 lecture. There, Snow criticized the insularity of the 'literary intellectuals' when he set out a clarion call to bridge the gap between science and the humanities. He also claimed that education should be oriented towards improving the material conditions of all people.[124]

Legaspi continues to describe this malaise and cites Max Horkheimer as unmasking the 'traditional' approaches as 'descriptive, conceptual, and abstract,' pointing back to the Greeks and refracted through the Enlightenment. This, Horkheimer maintained, was a 'Bourgeois cultural activity arising from and suited to capitalistic systems.' Like Snow, he argued for a 'critical' mode of theoretical engagement with cultural phenomena that was sensitive to historical context, existentially engaged, and *fundamentally oriented toward social justice.* Horkheimer thus reinforced Marx's famous maxim concerning philosophy, that its purpose is not to interpret the world but to change it.[125]

So much of neo-Kuyperian and neo-Dooyeweerdian transformation-alism has not really helped the church understand the role of secular

---

122. See, for example, the excellent essay by Jeffrey S. McDonald, 'J. Gresham Machen and the Culture of Classical Studies,' *WTJ* 82 (2020): pp. 95-119. McDonald's article convincingly argues that Machen's education in humanistic and classical studies contributed to his view of culture and Christianity.

123. See, e.g., Michael C. Legaspi, *Wisdom in Classical and Biblical Tradition* (Oxford/ New York: Oxford University Press, 2018), p. 245.

124. Ibid.

125. Ibid., p. 246 [Emphasis mine].

learning. This is perhaps nowhere summed up better than in the essays of historian Quirinus Breen, even though he did not have Kuyper in mind, to the best of my knowledge.[126] In his chapter on 'The church as a mother of learning' he writes of the many ways in which the church has been a stepmother to secular learning: either by shunning it, by desiring it for the sake of prestige and worldly security, and even to use it as a handmaid to the faith.[127] He notes that this latter category, i.e., as a 'handmaid to faith', has been the most generally accepted of the stepmotherly ways of treating learning.[128] He acknowledges that there has often been a desire to honor learning, even secular learning, from the church in this regard; nevertheless, he deems this approach is mistaken because it often lapses into the desire to Christianize everything.[129] I quote him below at length due to the clarity of what he says:

> I know some mean in this way to honor secular learning, but I believe they are mistaken. They do want learning in the church, but what often happens is that learning is there on the church's terms, and thus has a servant status. The assumption is that learning has no good reason for existence in its own right. E.g., the desire to Christianize everything is very common, as if something acquires true goodness if done in a Christian way: the student working a problem in mathematics, the professor lecturing on Milton, the banker managing the money of other people, and so on. The source of this is a piety that is as sincere as it is mistaken. There are students, professors, and bankers who are Christians, and the equation can be reversed. But what does a man *qua* Christian add to the quality of his mathematical work? Does he add even a feather to the integrity of a problem's solution? What being a Christian does for *him*, or the quality of his reason for doing his problems, is another matter. But it is a mistake to think that by being a Christian, a grocer, a bricklayer, fireman, plumber, or politician is improved in the grocery business or in bricklaying, and so on. Nor is secular learning improved by it. Let nature, the world and its fullness be what they are; for God made them good, and his providence maintains them impartially, as the rain that falls on the just and the unjust unlike.[130]

---

126. See Breen, *Christianity and Humanism.*
127. Ibid., pp. 201-66.
128. Ibid., p. 231.
129. Ibid.
130. Ibid.

We must ever be wary of the loose use of the adjective 'Christian.' Of course, this does not mean that we are unconcerned to use the very best of secular learning to aid religion, as Breen points out. After all, the best Old Testament commentaries, as he says, are written by those with a grasp of Semitic languages and literatures and the best of New Testament commentaries are written by those whose knowledge of Greek goes beyond *koiné* and extends to classical Greek and Latin literature.[131] This is what I have tried to inculcate into the very DNA of my students through the years. The religion of a calculus teacher makes no difference to the calculus itself. I suppose a teacher of calculus who recognizes the beauty of the order deriving ultimately from a God of order and math may communicate to her students the wonder and awe of such a thing; however, she will not 'change' the objective nature of calculus. If the reader will indulge me in another illustration, I think it makes the point.

When my wife and I moved from one side of town to another side years ago, the house from which we had to move and sell in order to buy the newer one was on cesspool instead of sewer. Anyone who has been in a similar situation knows that in order to close escrow, one must have the cesspool tank exposed to the lid so that an inspection can be made and the prospective buyers reassured that the system they are buying as part of their house deal is in good working order. Well, being Scottish on my mother's side, I was not nearly prepared to pay someone forty dollars an hour for something I could do myself: namely, grab a shovel and dig a hole down to the lid of the cesspool tank so that it may be inspected?

Now I ask you, when the workers from 'Honey Bee' cesspool services showed up in order to inspect the tank, did they jump out of their truck and declare, 'Well, that is the best dug hole I have ever seen!' Did they reason, 'A Christian must have dug that hole!' Or, perhaps being even more impressed with the size, shape, and dimensions of the hole that was dug in preparation for their arrival, did they say, 'Wow, that is such an exquisitely dug hole, a Pastor must have dug this hole, or perhaps a Seminary Professor, a Pastor to Pastors!' No, they did not reason thus. Such reasoning sounds ludicrous to us and our common sensibilities. So also does the constant desire to 'Christianize' everything under the sun.

---

131. Ibid., p. 232.

## Conclusion

We have been looking at contemporary examples of what the primary mission *is not*, or maybe more precisely, what kinds of negative influences we should be alert to upon the church. In this chapter, I traced the lives and thinking of Abraham Kuyper and Herman Dooyeweerd. I also argued that their followers, whom we dubbed 'neo-Calvinists', had a profound influence on Christian education endeavors in North America, and consequently in the ministry and work of the church especially though Christian education day schools, colleges and universities, and in the thinking and ministry of pastors trained at such institutions.

In the next chapter, I turn to further examples of what the primary mission of the church is not. I trace the history and influence of Liberation Theology. This may be a new area for some readers; however, so much of the current pressures upon the church to broaden her mission and attend more to issues of social justice are related to many of the influences we see in the rise of Liberation Theology. Becoming more educated about this significant theological movement can help us avoid the pitfalls inherent in such a turn. It can also cause us, hopefully with a spirit of humility, to look directly at areas where the church may have fallen short at times. For the rise of liberation theologies may be directly related to some of the unpaid bills of the church.

# CHAPTER 7

# Liberation Theology

*'Philosophers have only interpreted the world, in various
ways; the point, however, is to change it.'*

KARL MARX

In the last chapter, I began the first portion of defining what the primary
mission of the church is not. In order to illustrate this, I explored
the thought and influence of H. Dooyeweerd and A. Kuyper. As an
extension of further exploration into what the primary mission of the
church is not, I am leading the reader into another area that has been
very influential on the modern church: liberation theology. The import
of what this movement has to do with the primary mission of the
church may not be immediately apparent. However, I can remember
my Seminary professor stating in a beginning class that if one did not
adopt the interim world structures outlines in God's Word as they
are, and conflated the 'upper line' of God's dealings with his covenant
family and community with the 'lower line' of God's dealing with the
common world, then it could entail one long slippery slope leading
directly into liberation theology.

My goal in this chapter is to introduce the reader to the history of
liberation theology and its hermeneutic. J. Andrew Kirk has declared:
'It is not an exaggeration to declare that the theology of liberation
marks a watershed for the continuing theological task of the Universal
Church.'[1] To immerse oneself in the issues surrounding the theology

---

1. J. Andrew Kirk, *Liberation Theology* (Atlanta: John Knox Press, 1979), p. 204.

of liberation is to plunge into the depths of many major questions as they make contact with ecclesiastical topics: the classic problem of the relationship between the church and state; the relationship between profane history and salvation history; the significance of the prophets' preaching regarding justice towards the poor; the association between presuppositions, hermeneutics and, perhaps most significantly, the very nature and mission of the church itself. Although the theology of liberation encompasses large geographic boundaries, and in very broad strokes may include feminist theologies and black theologies of North America, this chapter will only concern itself primarily with the movement in Latin America.

## Historical Antecedents: the Importance Blondel and Moltmann

Theology in Latin America did not evolve out of a vacuum. Hector Borrat sees fundamentally two sources: the theoretical sources of liberation theology he says are mainly European political theology and J. Moltmann's theology of hope.[2] First, I will address the issue of the influence of European political theology, or more specifically the influential philosophy of Maurice Blondel (1861-1949).[3] Gustavo Gutiérrez studied in Europe for a couple of years before he returned to Peru. Blondel died before Gutiérrez arrived in Europe; however, he was a major influence on some of Gutiérrez's professors.

Gutiérrez regarded Blondel's influence on his own thought as 'crucial to the development of his Liberation Theology.'[4] Indeed, Gutiérrez claimed that Blondel, a lay philosopher, is 'one of the most important thinkers of contemporary theology, including the most recent trends.'[5] At this point, I will sketch briefly his philosophy of action and political philosophy.[6]

---

2. Hector Borrat quoted by Harvie M. Conn, 'Theologies of Liberation: An Overview' in *Tensions in Contemporary Theology* (ed. Stanley N. Gundry and Alan F. Johnson; Grand Rapids, Michigan: Baker, 1976), p. 349.

3. I am indebted to my former student, Tyler Moser, for drawing my attention to Blondel as an extremely influential figure for the theology of Gutiérrez. See Moser, 'To Speak Well in Two Languages: The Book of Job in the Theology of Gustavo Gutiérrez' (MAHT thesis, Westminster Seminary California, 2020).

4. Moser, 'To Speak Well,' p. 13.

5. Quoted in Ibid., p. 22.

6. I am indebted to Moser in the following description.

Blondel's project was working to improve on the traditional neo-Thomistic notion that God is *actus purus*, or 'pure act', and the notion that human beings can only simply act, which he considered as sterile. He envisioned his project as a way to open up contemporary reflection to the necessity of the supernatural. Moser explains:

> He did his philosophy from the bottom up, so to speak, beginning with human beings in the world. Blondel argued that action is the link between thought and being, and as such there is always a discrepancy between the 'willed will' and the 'willing will.' The 'willing will' is the aspiration of a being for the infinite, and the 'willed will' is the action undertaken to achieve it .... Philosophy begins with the reality of human action in the world, so it necessarily takes note of the interconnectedness of human life .... Thus, Blondel's philosophy advances a certain 'social-realism' in that it considers interrelated human beings in history as a fundamental starting point.[7]

Blondel's claims that Christ's coming was as important or more important than his words have been noted in recent works on ecclesiology.[8] Blondel was also known for promoting a 'pan-Christian' universalism that is akin to that of Teilhard de Chardin, also a point of concern.[9] It is not hard to imagine how these notions had ramifications for his political philosophy. Although he never systematized his thought here, importantly, he did actually criticize Marxism for 'reducing the notion of liberation to material and economic freedom.'[10] Moser argues that this is important since many scholars assume that Gutiérrez adopted a Marxist ideology outright.[11] But if it can be demonstrated that Gutiérrez used Karl Marx critically and that Gutiérrez attributed his thinking to something more along Blondel's train of thought, then the notion that

---

7. Ibid., p. 15.

8. Edmund Clowney, *The Church*, Contours of Christian Theology, Gerald Bray (ed.) (Leicester, Intervarsity, 1995), p. 21.

9. Ibid. p. 94.

10. Moser, 'To Speak Well in Two Languages,' p. 17.

11. Ibid. See pp. 20-24 for a critique of the traditional position. Moser notes that Gutiérrez critiques Marx's system, and that he also made fundamental changes to the second edition of *Liberation* in order to rebut the charge that he was solely indebted to Mark. Moser also notes that Gutiérrez received strong criticisms from Marxists. Moser maintains that Gutiérrez used Marx with 'critical qualification' and that Marx was a stimulus to 'Gutiérrez's reflection and creativity, but they do not form the substance of it' (p. 23).

Gutiérrez might be solely indebted to Marx methodologically might be suspect.[12] Gutiérrez did register in his writings that Marxism can be used as a tool of analysis without going 'all in' since prominent theorists in the social sciences have done so without considering themselves Marxists.[13]

Blondel profoundly influenced at least two of Gutiérrez's instructors: Yves Congar (1904-1995) and Henri de Lubac (1896-1991). I will not specify further how Blondel influenced these two significant Roman Catholic theologians; however, both of them in their own specific ways reflected the influence of Blondel's epistemology since Blondel thought that the church 'can be an effective witness in apologetics only when it acts in one accord, responding to concrete situations with solidarity.'[14]

Others, besides Blondel, such as Marxist spokesman Ernst Bloch and Catholic representative of European political theology, J.B. Metz, could be named, but in my opinion it is Jurgen Moltmann whose work has probably been most seminal in the development of liberation theology.[15] Moltmann's work was esteemed by Gutiérrez as 'undoubtedly one of the most important in contemporary theology.'[16]

For Moltmann, hope and eschatological promise of the future are the central categories of theology. He says, for example: 'On the ground of the promised future of the truth, the world can be experienced as history. The eschatological sense of the event of promise in the resurrection of Christ awakes in remembrance and expectation, our sense for history.'[17]

Moltmann was aware of the dangers of theology remaining cerebral, disconnected from the present world and its many needs, a concern echoed by the liberation theologians and a possible liability when expositing the Exodus motif. He writes, for example, 'If God is not

---

12. Ibid.

13. See, e.g., 'Toward a New Method,' in *Gustavo Gutiérrez Essential Writings*, edited by James B. Nickoloff (Minneapolis, MN: Fortress Press, 1996), p. 45.

14. Ibid., p. 19.

15. Metz and Bloch are referred to frequently in Gutiérrez's revised *A Theology of Liberation: 15th Anniversary Edition with a new introduction by the Author*, translated and edited by Sister Caridad Inda and John Eagleson (Maryknoll, NY: Orbis, 1988); however, it is Moltmann that receives 'pride of place.'

16. Ibid., p. 125.

17. Jurgen Moltmann, *Theology of Hope: On the Ground and the Implications of a Christian Eschatology* (trans. James W. Leitch; New York: Harper and Row, 1967), p. 92.

spoken of in relation to man's experience of himself and his world, then theology withdraws into a ghetto.'[18]

Nevertheless, many of the liberation theologians saw his theology as unable to transcend the problem of the historical present – his ideas were swallowed and enveloped in the promised future; thus, liberation theologians were critical, placing charges of 'docetism' at his feet and reproaching him for abstractionism.[19] Even more serious was the distaste that Miguez-Bonino felt towards Moltmann's apparent failure to give concrete identification to the oppression of the poor.[20] Based on the brief overview just given, it is apparent that the liberation theologians have not adopted Moltmann completely. Despite all this critical dialogue, it is nonetheless clear that Moltmann's influence on the liberation theologians is significant. In order to see further how liberation theology is a good example of ecclesiology and hermeneutics run amok, we will now briefly survey the rise and historical development of liberation theology in Latin America; then we shall turn our attention to some of its major themes before we offer an overall critique of the movement and especially its shortcomings.

The years between 1961 and 1969 marked a decisive turn for the function and ministry of the Protestant Church in Latin America. This was the period between the Second Evangelical Conference of Latin Americans (II CELA) in Lima, Peru, and the third assembly (III CELA) in Buenos Aires, Argentina. The conference at III CELA signified new political directions according to Miguez-Bonino in at least three areas: '(a) The acknowledgement of the revolutionary situation and of the just demands of the oppressed ... (b) the affirmation that the gospel refers not only to personal life (and through it to the structures) but also in the structures of society themselves ... (c) consequently, the possibility of a revolutionary commitment of Christians.'[21]

---

18. Ibid., p. 89.

19. See, for example, Gustavo Gutiérrez, *A Theology of Liberation* (trans. and edited by Sister Caridad Inda and John Eagleson; Maryknoll, New York: Orbis Books, 1973). Despite the criticism, Gutiérrez has many positive things to say about Moltmann's work. In this chapter, I will cite Gutiérrez' first edition of *Theology of Liberation*, unless noted otherwise.

20. Conn, 'An Overview,' p. 352. Bonino's charges brought a fierce response from Moltmann himself. See his piercing questions and criticisms in Jurgen Moltmann, 'An Open Letter to Jose Miguez-Bonino,' *Christianity and Crisis* 35, no. 5 (March 29, 1976): pp. 57-63.

21. Miguez-Bonino quoted in Conn, 'An Overview,' p. 346.

Closely connected with the movement above was the influential, though now disbanded, ISAL, the Protestant-initiated organization whose origins are in the World Council of Churches stretching all the way back to the Second World War. In 1971, this group had its fourth general assembly in Nana, Peru. It was there that a sea change occurred towards the political left. Orlando Costas wrote: 'Theology cannot be done simply in dialogue with political praxis, but must be done in the midst of political engagement.'[22] Eventually the group was actually disbanded and declared illegal by the Uruguayan government, but the questions raised by the movement and its influence continued.

As stated previously, though Protestants have been involved in liberation theology, it is common knowledge that the movement is more essentially Roman Catholic. For the Roman Catholics, the 1968 Second General Episcopal Conference of Roman Catholic bishops (CELAM) at Medellin, Columbia, in Conn's words, 'marked a new stage in the progress of liberation theology.'[23] Medellin's social significance for the discipline of theology as practiced by many is pithily stated by Juan Luis Segundo:

> Medellin is distinguished, furthermore, because therein the magisterium of the Church shows Christians that they can be sinning—although strictly speaking they may be doing nothing—in a structurally unjust and violent society. In effect, the structures themselves reproduce violence, injustice, and dehumanization without anyone's direct intervention, but with everyone's complicity.[24]

Gutiérrez is in full agreement with Segundo regarding the influence of Medellin, for he states, 'As regards doctrinal authority and impact, the most important text we will mention is, of course, that of the Episcopal Conference at Medellin.'[25] The reader should take note of the idea of 'sinful social structures' that are mentioned here. It is a theme that will occur repeatedly in this book and the concept itself will be treated below.

---

22. Quoted in Conn, 'An Overview,' p. 347.

23. Conn, 'An Overview,' p. 344.

24. Juan Luis Segundo, *Theology and the Church: A Response to Cardinal Ratzinger and a Warning to the Whole Church* (trans. John W. Diercksmeier; San Francisco: Harper and Row, 1970), p. 110.

25. Gutiérrez, *Theology of Liberation*, p. 107.

CELAM III, the third meeting of the bishops of Latin America, was held at Puebla, Mexico on October 12-28, 1978. Many considered it to be a kind of 'standoff' between the traditional party line of the frustrated Vatican and the new directions in which liberation theologians of Latin America were moving.[26] Tensions between the Vatican and the theologians of liberation grew in the 1980s, as evidenced by the dialogue between Cardinal Joseph Ratzinger (later, Pope) and Juan Luis Segundo.[27]

We have only begun to scratch the surface with respect to surveying the developments giving rise to the movement known as liberation theology. Now I will discuss some of the major themes.

## Major Themes

### Theme 1, The Starting Point: Marxist Analysis

Marxist themes are pervasive throughout the writings of liberation theologians. Marxism can be simply defined as the economic and political ideas of Karl Marx and Friedrich Engels and their followers. They basically divided people into two classes: the workers and the rich. Class conflict arises between these classes leading society from bourgeois society under capitalism to socialism and ultimately communism. The use of Marxism as an 'analytic tool' by almost all liberation theologians is undeniable. Bonino says, 'The thought of these men is characterized by a strict scientific-ideological analysis, avowedly Marxist.'[28] Conn, in general terms, nuances the particular kind of cooperation with Marxist analysis :

> That commitment [from many to socialism] and analysis have been articulated increasingly and self-consciously, using Marxist conceptions. The extent to which liberation theologians in particular are truly Marxist

26. Pedro Arrupe, S.J., 'Marxist Analysis by Christians,' *Catholic Mind* (September 1981): pp. 58-64. In 1980, Pedro Arrupe, S.J., Superior General of the Society of Jesus, sent this letter to the Jesuit Provincials in Latin America. It is basically an explication of 'Marxist analysis' as set forth in the Puebla Document and discourages the kinds of efforts in which the liberation theologians are engaged.

27. Joseph Ratzinger, *Instruction On Certain Aspects of the 'Theology of Liberation'* (Printed in the U.S.A. by the Daughters of St. Paul; Boston, MA). The instruction was given on August 6, 1984, at the Sacred Congregation for the Doctrine of the Faith, and its publication was ordered by Pope John Paul II.

28. Jose Miguez-Bonino, *Doing Theology In A Revolutionary Situation* (Philadelphia: Fortress Press, 1975), p. 71.

is subject to vigorous debate. But it cannot be debated that, to borrow Jose Porfirio Miranda's phrase, 'We are all riding on Marx's shoulders.' More particularly, the liberation theologians see Marxism primarily as an instrument of social analysis rather than as a philosophy or a plan of political action.[29]

Can Marxism as a 'social-analytic tool' be separated from the ideological whole? Is Marxism foisted upon the Bible in such a manner that it colors all exegesis? To what extent is the employment of Marxism in this fashion connected indivisibly with the materialistic and atheistic presuppositions which undergird it?[30] Some Protestants have voiced similar concerns, not only with respect to Latin American liberation theologians but with regard to Marxism making forays into more theologically conservative pockets of Evangelicalism as well.[31]

Important for understanding the liberation theologian's use of Marxist analysis are some early writings, representative of Marx's thought, known as 'The Economic and Philosophical Manuscripts of 1844.' The fundamentals of Marx's philosophy of history are found here and, more importantly, the seminal ideas of 'alienation' and 'self-estrangement.' These manuscripts were written by Marx four years before he and Engels published the *Manifesto of the Communist Party*,[32] and they were not published in German until 1932 and only published in English many years later.[33] Once published, they caused a virtual reinterpretation of Marx. Indeed, these and other earlier writings caused a sea change in understanding Marx known as 'Humanistic Marxism.' The dominant theme of 'alienation' was seen to be a continuous thread in the mature writings of Marx. Indeed, some scholars of Marx would

---

29. Conn, 'An Overview,' p. 334.

30. Ratzinger, *Instruction*, VII, p. 6. This is one of the primary concerns of the *Instruction*. For example, Ratzinger writes, 'The ideological principles come prior to the study of the social reality and are presupposed in it. Thus no separation of the parts of this epistemologically unique complex is possible. If one tries to take only one part, say, the analysis, one ends up having to accept the entire ideology.'

31. Ronald H. Nash, *Poverty and Wealth: The Christian Debate Over Capitalism* (Westchester: Crossway Books, 1986), pp. 89-92.

32. See Marx-Engels, *On Religion* (Moscow: Progress Publishers, 1957), pp. 78-80.

33. A readily accessible version may be found republished in Erich Fromm, *Marx's Concept of Man: With a translation from Marx's 'Economic and Philosophical Manuscripts' by P.B. Bottomore* (New York: Frederick Unger Publishing Co., 1961).

go so far as to assert that these early writings needed to assume the role of interpretive glasses for viewing all of Marx's later writings.

Not all students of Marx see these writings as deserving of so much attention. Nash, for example, marshals many arguments against the influence of these earlier writings.[34] Another French Marxist, Louis Althusser, also cannot recognize the continuity of the theme of 'alienation' throughout Marx's works.[35] Even so, whether or not we want to go as far as Robert Tucker in saying that a complete reinterpretation is needed upon discovering the early manuscripts,[36] it is assumed in this chapter that a continuity does exist between the early phases of Marx and his later stages,[37] and it is probably the case that 'the theme of alienation is buried but still there in the later work.'[38]

This new perspective on alienation was profound for Marx. Feuerbach had 'naturalized' Hegelianism. Marx praised him for being a liberator of minds: 'He has delivered the disciples from bondage, shown them the way out of the wilderness of Hegelian idealism to real man in the material world.'[39] Essentially, Marx was to be Feuerbach's follower in all this although he was to extrapolate on Feuerbach's ideas. Therefore, 'Feuerbach was truly the fulcrum of the movement of thought from Hegelianism to Marxism.'[40]

The alienation theme is most prominent in his earlier writings as opposed to his later writings. If it is most prominent here, it is also most difficult. 'Everyone agrees that Marx is a difficult writer, and never more difficult than when he speaks of alienation,' says John Plamenatz.[41] If

---

34. Nash, *Poverty and Wealth*, pp. 97-100.

35. See the discussion in David Lyon, *Karl Marx: A Christian Assessment of His Life and Thought* (Downers Grove: InterVarsity Press, 1979), p. 68.

36. Robert Tucker, *Philosophy and Myth in Karl Marx* (Cambridge: Cambridge University Press, 1961), p. 7.

37. Gary North, *Marx's Religion of Revolution: The Doctrine of Creative Destruction* (Nutley: Craig Press, 1968), pp. 59-60, sees the continuity all the way up through Marx's posthumously published third volume of *Capital*.

38. Leslie Stevenson, *Seven Theories of Human Nature* (New York: Oxford University Press, 1987), p. 57.

39. Quoted in Tucker, *Philosophy and Myth in Karl Marx*, p. 95.

40. Tucker, *Philosophy and Myth in Karl Marx*, p. 97.

41. John Petrov Plamenatz, *Karl Marx's Philosophy of Man* (Oxford: Clarendon Press, 1975), p. 11.

earlier it was his economics and ideas on revolution that captivated people's minds, today this theme of alienation has become the central focus of Marx studies. Even so, his language and expression here is difficult to comprehend.

Ronald Nash has provided four helpful forms to categorize worker alienation that are discussed in Marx's Philosophical Manuscripts of 1844.[42] The first is that 'capitalism causes the worker to become alienated from that which he produces.' Secondly, 'the worker is estranged from the labor process itself.' Marx himself had summed up this in the following way: 'All these consequences are contained in the definition that the worker is related to the product of his labour as to an alien object ... the alienation of the worker in his product means not only that his labour becomes an object, an external existence, but that it exists outside him, independently, as something alien to him.'[43]

The third form of alienation that Nash cites is that the 'worker under capitalism becomes alienated from other men and women.' Marx states: 'The proposition that man's species nature is estranged from him means that one man is estranged from the other, as each of them is from man's essential nature.'[44] The fourth form of alienation according to Nash is that the worker becomes alienated from what he produces, from his work, and from other workers – and he also becomes alienated from himself in the end. Marx comments: 'The alien being, to whom labour and the produce of labour belongs, in whose service labour is done and for whose benefit the produce of labour is provided, can only be man himself .... Not the gods, not nature, but only man himself can be this alien power over man.'[45]

What is the source and origin of this worker alienation? Gary North thinks this is the most important question one can ask of Marx's entire system.[46] In the one and only place in Marx's writings where North has been able to identify some answer to this crucial question, Marx shows the Achilles' heel of his system when he states, 'although private

---

42. Nash, *Poverty and Wealth*, pp. 93-94.

43. Karl Marx, *Economic and Philosophic Manuscripts of 1844*, quoted in Robert C. Tucker, *The Marx-Engels Reader* (New York: W.W. Norton & Company, 1972), p. 58.

44. Quoted in Tucker, *Marx-Engels Reader*, p. 63.

45. Quoted in Tucker, *Marx-Engels Reader*, p. 64.

46. Gary North, *Marx's Religion of Revolution*, p. 53.

property appears to be the basis and cause of alienated labour, it is rather a consequence of the latter.'[47] North marshals one of his most trenchant criticisms at this point:

> Once private property is seen as a result of alienated production, one of the central flaws in Marx's system is revealed. If the original cause is psychological rather than economic, then there is no guarantee that the coming revolution will permanently wipe out alienation merely because it destroys private property.[48]

Marx would have done well to come up with a fifth variety of human alienation – alienation from God, which Nash points out.[49] This fundamental alienation would have brought new perspective to many varieties of alienation that Marx was keenly aware of on both the individual and social level.

One does not have to possess any powers of keen insight to notice that Marx's doctrine of alienation is really a kind of substitution for the Christian doctrine of the fall. Marx believed in a past utopia, which was before the existence of money, and that utopia was free from all alienation. Christianity, however, grounds alienation and subsequent evil in the historical fall of human beings as recorded in the book of Genesis.

Neither should the Christian deny what Marx has pointed out with respect to man being a self-conscious and rational creature as opposed to other creatures. This very fact necessitates social intercourse and is part of man's constituent makeup. What the Christian should deny is 'that man's social environment, continually transformed by his activities, becomes eventually such that frustration and alienation disappear,' says Plamenatz.[50] Such thinking betrays a fool's paradise of wishful thinking, never intended to take place this side of glory.

We can agree with Marx that alienation comes from within man, as North has suggested.[51] This seems to be verified by such passages as James 4:1. Beyond these points, however, the parallels between Christianity

---

47. Karl Marx, 'Alienated [Estranged] Labour,' quoted in North, *Marx's Religion*, p. 54.

48. North, *Marx's Religion*, p. 54.

49. Nash, *Poverty and Wealth*, p. 94.

50. Plamenatz, *Karl Marx's Philosophy*, p. 30.

51. North, *Marx's Religion*, p. 56.

and Marxism cease and the differences become pronounced. Marx has never answered the most crucial question of all; from whence comes this alienation, truly? What is its origin? Marx had proposed a solution to the problem for alienation; he suggested the elimination of private property. But in doing so, he had 'mistaken the symptom for the disease ... and that has even deeper roots.'[52]

## Theme 2: The Historical Situation and 'Praxis'

Concentrating on this theme, which is so pervasive in the liberation theologians, is to concentrate on what is the most important concern among them: the plight of the downtrodden in society. In a word, liberation theologians are concerned with praxis. For example, Miguez-Bonino writes: 'in the last decades, converging lines of human experience and thought and of biblical research have pointed to the realm of history as the proper quarry for theological building material.'[53] From the liberation theologian's perspective, that situation best expresses itself in terms of underdeveloped nations under the domination of the developed nations. Gustavo Gutiérrez writes:

> Therefore, it [underdevelopment] must be studied from a historical perspective, that is, in relationship to the development and expansion of the great capitalist countries. The underdevelopment of the poor countries, as an overall social fact, appears in its true light; as the historical by-product of the development of other countries.[54]

Whether or not Gutiérrez's estimation about the plight of Latin America is correct or not is open to debate.

In Latin America, the primary spokesman—and all agree—is Fr. Gustavo Gutiérrez (b. 1928), the Peruvian Roman Catholic Theologian. Gutiérrez is considered by many to be the founder of Liberation Theology and he is now Professor emeritus at the University of Notre Dame and formerly held the John Cardinal O'Hara chair of theology at the University of Notre Dame. Although Gutiérrez uses a profound amount of Scripture in his theology, his approach, nevertheless, is somewhat unique and innovative; thus, it deserves careful attention.

---

52. Lyon, *Karl Marx, A Christian Assessment*, p. 60.

53. Bonino, *Doing Theology*, p. 78.

54. Gutiérrez, *Theology of Liberation*, p. 84.

In a famous passage, well worth quoting, Gutiérrez makes a clear statement on this new way of doing theology:

> The theology of liberation offers us not so much a new theme for reflection as a new way to do theology. Theology as critical reflection on historical praxis is a liberation theology, a theology of the liberating transformation of the history of mankind and also therefore that part of mankind—gathered in ecclesia—which openly confesses Christ. This is a theology which does not stop with reflecting on the world, but rather tries to be part of the process through which the world is transformed. It is a theology which is open—in the protest against trampled human dignity, in the struggle against the vast majority of people, in liberating love, and in the building of a new, just, and fraternal society—the gift of the Kingdom of God.[55]

What is reflection on historical praxis for Gutiérrez and how does it affect his hermeneutic and his view of Scripture as well?

Regardless of the possible faulty analysis of liberation theologians concerning the cause of the plight of their underdevelopment, the fact of the matter is that the dire situation in many countries in Latin America is one that should move any Christian to pity. This is poignantly summed up by Ratzinger and well worth quoting at length:

> In certain parts of Latin America, the seizure of the vast majority of wealth by an oligarchy of owners bereft of social consciousness, the practical absence or shortcomings of a rule of law, military dictators making a mockery of elementary human rights, the corruption of certain powerful officials, the savage practices of some foreign capital interests constitute factors which nourish a passion for revolt among those who thus consider themselves the powerless victims of a new colonialism in the technological, financial, monetary or economic order ...[56]

This is the context in which the Latin American theologian finds himself pondering. It is in this setting that a new way of doing theology is proposed. 'Theology does not produce pastoral activity; rather it reflects upon it,' says Gutiérrez.[57] This new way of doing theology, claims Gutiérrez, 'tries to be part of the process through which the world is transformed.'[58] Part of Gutiérrez's problem here (as seen below), however,

---

55. Ibid., p. 15.
56. Ratzinger, VII., p. 12.
57. Gutiérrez, *Theology of Liberation*, p. 11.
58. Ibid., p. 15.

is to delimit properly whose responsibility this is. Should this be the responsibility or mission of the church as the corporate church, or is it the better relegated to the vocational concerns of individual Christians, or another group of concerned citizens or Christians joining together in order to bring about justice?

Praxis is more than practice for liberation theology. It is a term borrowed from Marx which 'describes the circular traffic that is always going on between action and reflection – engagement in the world in transforming action.'[59] Moreover, it contains the Marxist sense of participation which has as its goal the transformation of society. Marx's famous dictum echoes throughout the work of liberation theologians. 'Theology has to stop explaining the world and to start transforming it. Orthopraxis, rather than orthodoxy, becomes the criterion for theology,' according to Bonino.[60]

The object of reflection in this dialectic of praxis is the predicament of the poor. One Mexican scholar that has done significant work on the Exodus writes, 'Here we have the explicit definition of what it is to know Yahweh.' According to Jose Miranda, 'To know Yahweh is to achieve justice for the poor.'[61] Of course, this raises the whole issue of addressing 'systemic injustice,' which is complex, as I have mentioned previously. In addition, the only legitimate perspective according to the liberation theologians is the Marxist category of 'class' analysis. 'Only a class analysis will enable us to see what is really involved in the opposition between oppressed countries and dominant peoples,' Gutiérrez asserts.[62] This entails that one may not be a 'fence straddler,' either as an individual or as the church. According to the liberationists, to not recognize class struggle, to not side with the poor, is necessarily to side with the rich.[63]

Consider another major figure in the liberationist movement: Jon Sobrino. *Time* magazine claimed that Sobrino's book, *Christology at the Crossroads*, is the most thorough study on Christ from Latin America's

59. Conn, 'An Overview,' p. 400.

60. Bonino, *Doing Theology*, p. 81.

61. Jose Porfirio Miranda, *Marx and the Bible: A Critique of the Philosophy of Oppression* (trans. John Eagleson; New York: Orbis Books, 1974), p. 44.

62. Gutiérrez, *Theology of Liberation*, p. 87.

63. Ibid., pp. 274-75.

liberation theology perspective to date.[64] This book was seen to fill the gap that Hugo Assman bellowed needed to be closed as early as 1971.[65] It is often asserted that the Exodus motif is reserved the pride of place as the major theme of the liberation theologians; however, this is not the case for Sobrino. Rather, 'In the task of liberation theology, Jesus has always held the ultimate primacy and he cannot be compared to, still less surpassed by, other liberating figures.'[66] Sobrino's point—pitting the Exodus motif over and against Christ as primary—may be moot. Sobrino, the liberation theologian that has written the most on issues of Christology, even predicates this perspective of Jesus himself: 'Jesus clearly had some notion of the situation as a totality, for that is what is suggested in the term "kingdom of God." But he concretizes his morality by immersing himself in the situation on the basis of a class outlook rather than by disregarding or evading the dualism in society.'[67] It is in this context that the need for 'conscientization' arises. This is the name coined by Paulo Freire for the process which essentially is the awakening of the individual to his situation and the commitment on his part to the transformation of his unjust circumstances.

For the liberation theologians, the Old Testament prophets provide an abundant source of ammunition for their 'new way' of doing theology. 'The Prophets condemn every kind of abuse, every form of keeping the poor in poverty or of creating new poor people,' says Gutiérrez, for example.[68] 'They [the O.T. Prophets] are rightly characterized as being severely critical of an escapist approach to religion and worship, particularly as related to sociopolitical duties toward the classic categories of the oppressed: the orphans, the widow, the stranger, the worker, and so on,' writes Segundo in his response to Cardinal Ratzinger.[69] Whether or not the reading that is given to the prophets of old is a fair one will be dealt with in greater detail below.

---

64. 'New Debate over Jesus' Divinity,' *Time*, 27 February, 1978.

65. Hugo Assman quoted in Emilio A. Nunez, *Liberation Theology* (Chicago: Moody Press, 1985), p. 207.

66. Jon Sobrino, *Jesus in Latin America* (New York: Orbis Books, 1987), p. 11.

67. Jon Sobrino, S. J., *Christology At The Crossroads*, (trans. John Drury; New York: Orbis Books, 1978), p. 123.

68. Gutiérrez, *Theology of Liberation*, p. 293.

69. Segundo, *Theology and the Church*, p. 54.

## Theme 3: The Social Structure of Sin, Sacred and Profane History

I'm sure that it has already been clear from the previous discussion that the theologies of liberation wish to see a greater appreciation of sin in the sense of how it manages to work itself out within social structures. Of course, it is no wonder that they would be moved to ask such a question given the context of so many of their own cultural circumstances. 'An unjust situation does not happen by chance; it is not something branded by a fatal destiny; there is human responsibility behind it ... to which the Church itself belongs,' claims Gutiérrez.[70] Juan Luis Segundo writes about similar themes:

> But Christians have been taught to identify sin—disorder in one's relationship with God—as that which directly has evil as its object. And when an action does not follow a straight line from the one who executes it—or avoids it—to the one who receives its effects, but rather is transmitted through traditional social structures, Christians are accustomed to think that God is not involved and that sin does not exist.[71]

Given this background and view of the sinful causes that lay behind social structures, the liberation theologians are led to ask how a remedy is procured by Christians? For them, it is not a matter of what has often been the typical Christian response, that is, that structural change is brought about by the conversion and discipleship of individuals who in turn effect change by virtue of, and consequent to, their own particular changed lives.[72] Rather, it is fair to say that the theologians of liberation more often see a direct and immediate relationship between faith and political action through institutional transformation:

> The phrase 'kingdom of God' is a utopian symbol for a wholly new and definitive way of living and being. It presupposes renewal in many areas: in the heart of the human person, in societal relationships, and in the cosmos at large .... If we take due note of Jesus' demand to bring about the kingdom, and even more of his personal example, then we are forced to conclude that personal conversion must always be associated with social praxis.[73]

---

70. Gutiérrez, *Theology of Liberation*, p. 175.

71. Segundo, *Theology and the Church*, p. 62.

72. See, for example, Kevin DeYoung and Greg Gilbert, *What is the Mission of the Church?: Making Sense of Social Justice, Justice, Shalom, and the Great Commission* (Wheaton, IL: Crossway, 2011), p. 69.

73. Sobrino, *Christology*, pp. 119-21.

What is the result of this manner of thinking? The outcome is often the blurring of the lines which delineate the building of the kingdom of God and the maintenance of the secular city of man. 'All these factors have caused many gradually to substitute working for the kingdom with working for the social revolution – or, more precisely perhaps, the lines between the two have become blurred,' so says Gutiérrez.[74] Thus, there has developed a blurring of the distinctions between the sacred and the profane, the spiritual and the temporal, between that which is ecclesiastical and that which is not. The categories I argued for heretofore in this book have become fuzzy boundaries in this thinking outlined above.

For example, Bonino, who makes the same mistake, remarks: 'There are not histories: one sacred and one profane or secular. The one history in which God acts is the history of men; it is in this history where we find God.'[75] This sounds pious and truly commends itself by the most popular of credentials, surface simplicity. But it ignores a deeply embedded principle in Christianity: God has instituted different structures to exist in parallel and to exist side by side – one is the church (the sacred) and the other is the common society in which the church exists, moves, and has her being (civil society). On the other side of the world, Leslie Newbigin, one of the founders of the World Council of Churches (who will be considered at length below, especially as he has been popularized by Tim Keller), has raised the bar in talking about how sin and demonic powers influence political and institutional structures as well. For Newbigin, the power of the cross, the resurrection, and other ramifications of the gospel should have as one of its goals to 'unmask' how principalities and powers are constantly at work in the social and political structures of the world. Therefore, any robust proclamation of the gospel and the kingdom must address the abuse of power at the structural level, not merely at the individual level.[76] Newbigin would consider this one aspect of the 'central message' of the New Testament.[77]

---

74. Gutiérrez, *Theology of Liberation*, p. 103. For similar comments, see also pp. 45-48, 67-68, 150, 225, and 236.

75. Bonino, *Doing Theology*, pp. 70-71.

76. See Paul Weston ed., *Leslie Newbigin, Missionary Theologian: A Reader* (Grand Rapids, MI: Eerdmans, 2006), especially pp. 38-47. Paul Weston has extracted a number of important primary sources for this book which is representative of Newbigin's thought.

77. Ibid., p. 47.

Unlike so many revolutionaries who have taken liberationist concepts to violent extremes, Newbigin would suggest, rather, that we are to be 'patient revolutionaries who know that the whole creation, with all its given structures, is groaning in the travail of a new birth, and that we share this groaning and travail, this struggling and wrestling, but do so in hope because we have already received, in the Spirit, the firstfruit of the new world' (Rom. 8:19-25).[78] I have raised the issue of the complexity of addressing 'systemic injustice(s)' at many places in this book. The term is now commonplace in our popular culture and in mainstream media in the United States. My view is that malicious sin is perpetuated by individuals, not 'systems' *per se*. Of course, that does not mean that we shouldn't recognize that poverty—or racism—or many other social ills cannot be perpetuated by 'systems' once unjust laws become legislatively passed law. Apartheid, Jim Crow laws in the United States, especially in the Southern states, would be easy examples to cite. Whether one has a right or an obligation to disobey such laws, or to change the status quo through the instrumentality of the corporate church, is another issue altogether.

As mentioned above, praxis is a term adopted from Karl Marx and can best be understood as the 'circular traffic that is always going on between action and reflection-engagement in the world in transforming action.'[79] For Gutiérrez, it seems that praxis is best understood in terms of a dialectic in which 'pastoral' action leads to reflection and reflection leads in turn to action. Negatively, albeit perhaps more accurately, Vree poignantly asserts that 'Praxis is really a euphemism for revolutionary action as prescribed by Marxist categories.'[80] Unfortunately, the precise definition of this term which Gutiérrez borrows from Marx is somewhat vague and elusive. As stated before, Bonino sums up nicely what seems to be a fair representation of Gutiérrez's position, 'Theology has to stop explaining the world and to start transforming it. Orthopraxis, rather orthodoxy, becomes the criterion for theology.'[81]

---

78. Ibid., p. 46.

79. Conn, 'An Overview,' p. 400.

80. Dale Vree, 'Ideology versus Theology: Case Studies of Liberation Theology and the Christian New Right,' in *Christianity Confronts Modernity* (eds., Peter Williamson and Kevin Perrotta; Ann Arbor, Michigan: Servant Books, 1981), p. 62.

81. Bonino, *Doing Theology*, p. 81.

What is the object of reflection in Gutiérrez's praxis-oriented hermeneutic? It is the plight of the poor. Moreover, in sticking with his commitment to Marxist categories, he says, 'Only a class analysis will enable us to see what is really involved in the opposition between oppressed countries and dominant people.'[82] We can see, therefore, that Gutiérrez predicates significant importance to surrounding historical events as one enters into class analysis reflection. What has been the response to such a method? Some have reacted with strong criticism. Kirk's assessment, for example, is to say, 'If the classical way of doing biblical exegesis has been to move from the biblical texts to the writer's theological intentions and then to external referents, then the theology of liberation reverses the order, moving from the external referents to the biblical text.'[83]

In another sense, however, Kirk considers that Gutiérrez has done a great service to the church here; he thinks that Gutiérrez has uncovered an aspect of Marx that is true and should be recovered in sound biblical epistemology as well. 'Knowledge is not gained speculatively but obtained through obedience in concrete historical action.'[84] Perhaps a more nuanced way of putting it would be to say that 'knowledge is not gained *merely* through speculation.' Readers that have some familiarity with the history of philosophy will see why this is so. In classical philosophy, Plato gave detailed attention to the premise that experience alone is not enough for understanding in his *Theaetetus*. David Hume also demonstrated that experience is always limited in its scope. Immanuel Kant, finally, demonstrated that experience is not self-interpreting.

It is important to note, as Kirk has suggested, that Gutiérrez's procedure is analyzed in such a way as to give rise to the epistemological problem of the theory of knowledge and its various difficulties as it relates to hermeneutics. Essentially the problem can be stated in the following manner: on the one hand, the theologian must try and communicate the biblical message that speaks out of the historical past into the historical present, mediating it by means of certain analytical tools; on the other hand, the theologian

---

82. Gutiérrez, *Theology of Liberation*, p. 87.
83. Kirk, *Liberation Theology*, p. 186.
84. Ibid., p. 199.

must attempt to articulate the gospel message in such a way that its own critical and creative task is neither impeded by the analytical tools that he employs, nor restricted by the particular philosophical perspective of either historical context. This is a tall order without a doubt. It is essential to keep this dynamic in mind as we observe how Gutiérrez performs his exegesis. Although Gutiérrez makes abundant use of the Bible, he does not deal much with 'formal' exegesis except in the case of a few passages.

This politically engaged gospel, according to Gutiérrez, finds its locus inherent in the Gospel message itself, not in the historical praxis-oriented situation. Gutiérrez sums up:

> The deep human impact and the social transformation that the Gospel entails is permanent and essential because it transcends the narrow limits of specific historical situations and goes to the very root of human existence: the relationship with God in solidarity with other men. The Gospel does not get its political dimension from one or another particular option, but from the very nucleus of its message.[85]

The best read I can give Gutiérrez at this point is that his claim is still fraught with problems. The first one that I note is the insistence on a certain particularism that leads to a kind of astigmatic monism. Let me explain. Realizing the dangers of oversimplifying the problem, yet, I think that it is fair to say that Gutiérrez is concerned with a single issue: liberation [politically defined] which stems from critical reflection on historical praxis. Too often Gutiérrez speaks in terms that reveal an identity of the Gospel with liberation as he defines it in reductionistic terms and boundaries. Does liberation swallow up any legitimate Gospel norm similar to the way it seems that Moltmann's Theology of Hope swallows it up in the future? Conn asks:

> Does the monistic insistence on the historical situation in liberation theology ultimately make that, through the process of absolutizing, the only normative universal in the hermeneutics at stake here? And in so doing, is not even context flattened out by absolutizing into something other than a concrete?[86]

I question the exegetical criteria used by Gutiérrez. Is there any reconciliation between these two problems here: on the one hand, a

85. Gutiérrez, *Theology of Liberation*, p. 231.
86. Conn, 'An Overview,' p. 412.

kind of particularism that we can label astigmatic monism and, on the other hand, the lack of exegetical criteria? Is Gutiérrez's approach to Scripture symptomatic of basic problems that we all face in the exegetical enterprise no matter where we fall on the exegetical spectrum?

Kirk's work, which I have cited numerous times, proposes that we return to the Reformation principle of 'sola scriptura' for an alternative hermeneutic to the liberationists' approach. However, as he unpacks what he thinks the return to a 'sola scriptura' approach entails, I find elements in his analysis that need clarifying. For example, he says:

> Biblical theology, as a methodology for scriptural interpretation, needs to disengage one or more theological frameworks which appear absolutely central to the Bible. The choices it makes are then open to the scrutiny of the committed community and to the test of time and circumstances. Unfortunately, the choice has often been made uncritically, according to unquestioned ecclesiastical confessions or philosophical systems. There is also the danger of valuing the chosen elements too highly, regarding them as beyond criticism. However, these dangers do not negate the necessary procedure. We have selected the kingdom-theme as central (without, of course, foreclosing the interpretation of its meaning, which is still vigorously debated) for two complementary reasons. In the Bible the theme is both sufficiently universal in its scope to be able to organize coherently other fundamental themes and sufficiently specific to be able to offer a definite *kerygma*; in the contemporary situation it both points to and demands a radical transformation of human relationships.[87]

Although Kirk cautions against the placing of too much value on one's chosen elements, we must exercise caution in making any theological topic as *central*, which in the process may necessarily lead to a kind of reductionism. In fact, it may run the danger of the same kind of astigmatic monism about which I have already accused Gutiérrez. The theme Kirk suggests, kingdom, is indeed a prominent one in the Scriptures but even it cannot dominate everything.

Related to Kirk's suggestion above and possibly also making contact with the concern of Gutiérrez in the area of liberation, we could ask about the need for more work in other areas as well. 'Have evangelical Christians perhaps sacrificed to Marxists and religious humanists what stands at the heart of the Bible, namely, a profound sense of social

---

87. Kirk, *Liberation Theology*, pp. 189-90.

concern for a radically different society?' asks Carl Henry.[88] We may disagree with Henry as to what constitutes 'the heart of the Bible,' not to mention ecclesiological concerns deriving from the doctrine of the primary mission of the church; however, Henry's question does raise a pressing question for the modern church: what is the church's social responsibility, if anything? Should the church, as the corporate church, address extralegal 'systems' or policies in the culture in which she finds herself that someone (perhaps even the pastor or some of the elders) perceives to have produced some kind of social injustice, whether it be racism, poverty, police brutality or a host of other issues? My simple answer at this point is to say that if Scripture clearly and directly addresses the issue, then the answer is yes.

Regardless of all the necessary work still to be done in the above areas, in the domain of 'central messages,' we must remember that, in an ultimate sense, Christ Himself is that message (and the ultimate message of the Exodus motif), as Kevin Vanhoozer has eloquently stated in his discussion on genre:

> Unlike a photograph that shows everything there is to be seen, a map is a symbolic representation of selected aspects of reality .... This is what makes the map such an apt metaphor for postfoundationalist rationality that strives to hold onto the ideal of objective truth while acknowledging the provisional and perspectival nature of human subjectivity .... The diverse literary forms of Scripture [read genres] are like different kinds of maps, maps that have been collected together in a unified atlas: the Bible. As with maps, so with the forms of biblical discourse: each renders reality selectively, according to its own 'scale' and 'key'. The biblical stories, commands, promises, songs, prophecies, and didactic discourse all mediate God's communicative action, but not all in the same way. What they share, however, is the same basic orientation. The canon is a unique compass that points not to the north but the church's North Star: Jesus Christ.[89]

The danger of absolutizing any particular message within the biblical canon must be cautioned against. For the present writer, the correcting influence in delineating the exegetical criteria necessary for resolving

---

88. Carl Henry, *God, Revelation and Authority* (Waco, Texas: Word Books, 1979), vol. IV, *God Who Speaks and Shows*, 4.573.

89. Kevin J. Vanhoozer, *The Drama of Doctrine: A Canonical Linguistic Approach to Christian Theology* (Louisville, KY: Westminster John Knox, 2005), pp. 296-97.

Gutiérrez's approach to hermeneutics as described above seems to be to keep the central message (Christ Jesus and His mission) clear in light of the particular messages that are the subtexts of scripture, albeit important as well. This approach appears to be one way in which to keep our exegesis on an even keel and to maintain the liberty of the text within proper boundaries (canonical boundaries), a liberty that guards against any unwarranted particularism (such as social liberation of the poor from allegedly oppressive power structures).

Finally, a word in closing regarding an appreciation for Gutiérrez's hermeneutic. Gutiérrez, and the liberation theologians in general, have done a service for the church by reminding her of the need to be sensitive to the presuppositions that we bring to the biblical text. Even as our theological-philosophical presuppositions that we bring to bear on Scripture must be dictated by Scripture itself, so our socio-economic presuppositions must be as well.

In conclusion, we have seen how Gutiérrez's use of Scripture illustrates well the dangers we all face in the hermeneutic undertaking. There are dangers in absolutizing the particulars as well as the universal in our encounter with the biblical text. In Gutiérrez's methodology, in this author's estimation, he has set up his own boundaries within the canon and restricted the message of Scripture. The result: this is no robust gospel news; it is a toning down. Gutiérrez, instead of liberating the text, has imprisoned it. This becomes evident in Gutiérrez's treatment of the Exodus, for example.

The Exodus, and the response of human participation in political liberation that is elicited therein, is a leitmotif in virtually all of the liberation theologians, but I single out for discussion here Gutiérrez. The Exodus becomes a paradigm; the liberation of the poor from the midst of the oppressor/oppressed axiom. For Gutiérrez, for example, the Exodus is especially a leitmotif and it is seen primarily as political. 'The liberation of Israel is a political action. It is the breaking away from a situation of despoliation and misery and the beginning of the construction of a just and fraternal society,' he says.[90] Gutiérrez views the Exodus as fulfilled in Christ in some sense. But in what sense? It is with a political agenda, nothing short of a culturally transformational

---

90. Gutiérrez, *Theology of Liberation*, p. 155.

agenda. 'The work of Christ forms a part of this movement and brings it to complete fulfillment.'[91] He also sees the Exodus as paradigmatic, for he declares, 'The Exodus experience is paradigmatic. It remains vital and contemporary due to similar historical experiences which the People of God undergo.'[92] From all this, Gutiérrez draws the following conclusion:

> Consequently, when we assert that man fulfills himself by continuing the work of creation by means of his labor, we are saying that he places himself, by this very fact, within an all-embracing salvific process. To work, to transform the world, is to become a man and to build the human community; it is also to save. Likewise, to struggle against misery and exploitation and to build a just society is already to be part of the saving action, which is moving towards its complete fulfillment. All this means that building the temporal city is not simply a stage of 'humanization' or 'pre-evangelization' as was held in theology up until a few years ago. Rather it is to become part of a saving process which embraces the whole of man and all human history.[93]

It is interesting to note the seminal thoughts of self-regenerative powers which Gutiérrez predicates of man at this point. As mentioned above, these are not uncommon themes in Gutiérrez.[94] Marxist influences are wafting about here. Henry has correctly stated about the liberation theologians at this point: 'Man is viewed as divinely endowed with a creative nature that enables him to shape his own destiny.'[95] Gutiérrez seems to be enjoining man to take up that duty.

Significantly, it seems to this author, that Gutiérrez's interpretation doesn't spring from the text itself. 'The final conclusion does not spring from a direct reading of the text, but from a new interpretation of the Exodus motif based on a new pre-understanding of the meaning of Christ's universal work of salvation in the historical process of man,' says Kirk.[96] Has the freedom of this text to speak been maintained within this analysis? This is a fair and legitimate question. One must ask further if this is an isolated point or a regular hermeneutical habit?

---

91. Ibid., p. 158.

92. Ibid., p. 159.

93. Ibid., pp. 159-60.

94. See Ibid., pp. 32, 36-37, 47, 69, 110, 116, 205 etc.

95. Henry, 'Marxist Exegesis of the Bible,' in *God, Revelation, and Authority* (Waco, Texas: Word Books, 1979), IV. p. 566.

96. Kirk, *Liberation Theology*, p. 63.

The Exodus now becomes the rubric of interpretation under which not only the Israelites of the past, but all those people who are under the oppression of dominating forces may discover a key in order to free themselves. In what sense, however, one may ask? Croatto states:

> The Exodus is an event full of meaning (as the biblical narrative and Israel's experience show) which even now has not been concluded. If our recalling of the biblical kerygma has any relevance, the 'memory' of the Exodus becomes, for us—oppressed peoples of the Third World—an inciting Word, the announcement of liberation. It remains for us to prolong the Exodus, for it was not an event for the Hebrews, but for all peoples. Within a hermeneutical treatment, it is perfectly legitimate to understand ourselves as from the biblical Exodus and above all to understand the latter from within our situation of peoples in economic, political, social and cultural slavery.[97]

In my opinion, within this hermeneutical grid, even categories as simple and profound as conversion take on a completely new meaning. Such a political reading of the Exodus redefines the intended meaning of the Exodus for all peoples, including the Hebrews. Now, the Exodus doesn't mean a Nicodemus type rebirth any longer; rather, it means 'thinking, feeling, and living as Christ-present in exploited and alienated man. To be converted is to commit oneself to the process of the liberation of the poor and oppressed,' writes Gutiérrez.[98] Now instead of receiving grace, man becomes the active agent in procuring that salvation. As Carl Henry pointed out years ago, man now becomes the one who is shaping his own destiny.[99] Conn notes that this theme is due to Freire's studies on the consciousness of man and the responsibility one must take for his own deliverance.[100] Given the identification of conversion with liberation, this self-regenerative theme occurs repeatedly.[101] But Segundo writes as a rejoinder: 'In reality, not one of us—including all the theologians who can be considered liberation theologians whom I know in Latin America— ever hesitated to admit that radical liberation is liberation from sin.'[102] But

---

97. Croatto, quoted in Kirk, *Liberation Theology*, p. 102.

98. Gutiérrez, *Theology of Liberation*, p. 205.

99. Carl F. H. Henry, 'Marxist Exegesis of the Bible,' p. 566.

100. Conn, 'An Overview,' p. 337.

101. See Gutiérrez, *Theology of Liberation*, pp. 32, 36-37, 47, 69, 110, 116, 205 etc.

102. Segundo, *Theology and the Church*, pp. 87.

in response, now the question becomes, sin in what sense; do you mean institutional sin defined and qualified as outlined above? Also, by means of this radical redefinition, Gutiérrez would push this notion even farther yet to include a kind of universalism:

> The conclusion to be drawn from all the above [a lengthy discussion of the Exodus motif and the eschatological pattern of the prophets] is clear: salvation embraces all men and the whole man; the liberating action of Christ ... is at the heart of the historical current of humanity; the struggle for a just society is in its own right very much a part of salvation history.[103]

From the above, it should now be apparent that the Exodus motif is a recurring theme in the theology of liberation and that man is seen as an agent who is endowed with the ability to determine the events of his own salvation.

## Liberation Theology as Segue to Postcolonialism

Postcolonialism is still in its infancy, and it is definitely a child that was conceived in the womb of liberation theology. Therefore, a clear definition and characterization of the movement is still emerging.[104] Even so, the movement has emerged out of liberation theology and therefore there are some major similarities such as a cry against Western, scholarly, and European readings. Some have wondered whether the new movement may even be distinguished from liberation theology.

There do seem to be some major distinctions. For example, the postcolonialists are steeped in Western readings themselves and use Western methods. They have been criticized for being too simplistic, i.e., they make facile predications about rich/poor distinctions, civilized/primitive distinctions, and finally about Christianity and the relationship with paganism. Finally, postcolonialism is concerned about liberation theology's desire to maintain a Christian meta-narrative, something which allegedly caused the dynamics of oppression to begin with. Postcolonialism desires a kind of 'decentering' of the Bible as a privileged text and seeks to give more

---

103. Gutiérrez, *Theology of Liberation*, p. 168. Cf. also pp. 71 and 154.

104. See R. S. Sugirtharajah, *The Postcolonial Biblical Reader* (ed. R. S. Sugirtharajah; Blackwell Publishing, 2006);idem, *The Bible in the Third World: Precolonial, Colonial, and Post-Colonial Encounters* (Cambridge University Press, 2001); Fernando F. Segovio, *Decolonizing Biblical Studies: A View From the Margins* (New York: MaryKnoll, Orbis, 2004).

authority to cultural traditions, texts, and oral studies in order to value the cultures under consideration. Additionally, such readings would apply to all sociological and economic stratums. Furthermore, there is a desire among postcolonialists for indigenous scholars to arise from the cultures under question.

## Summary

One hesitates to assign a negative assessment to the theologies of liberation in such a short chapter. However, even those vehemently opposed to capitalism see the liberationist's attempts to rectify matters as flaccid.[105] This chapter, by its very limitations of space, can neither do justice to the differences among the various theologians, nor be properly nuanced. As Segundo has said, '… the theology of liberation has been accustomed for many years to being attacked in a manner that is almost a caricature.'[106] Nevertheless, as has been demonstrated above, there are common threads that weave throughout the various theologians; both the methods of their theological analysis and the radical implications which are entailed therein require the evaluation of at least some of the points which have been discussed heretofore.

The first question one must raise is with regard to the usefulness of Marxist categories in the analysis of the theologies of liberation. How is it, asks one sociologist, that one who has proven himself to be a discredited economist, an inconsistent philosopher and poor financial manager of his own resources, could hold such a powerful sway over the minds of very intelligent people?[107] Perhaps the reason is that, 'the force of Marxism has its roots in the semi-autonomous psychological needs of man. These needs for a simplified understanding of reality, for a prophetic reassurance as to the future,' says Csikszentmihalyi.

Let us return to the issue of 'Marxist analysis.' As Pedro Arrupe, the Superior General of the Society of Jesus, has stated the concern: 'Can one accept the set of explanations that constitute Marxist analysis without subscribing to Marxist philosophy, Marxist ideology, Marxist

---

105. Daniel M. Bell, Jr., *Liberation After the End of History*: *The Refusal to Cease Suffering* (London and NY: Routledge, 2001).

106. Segundo, *Theology and Church*, p. 8.

107. Mihaly Ciskszentmihalyi, 'Marx: A Social-Psychological Evaluation,' *Modern Age* 2 (1967): pp. 272-82.

politics?'[108] It seems that many, if not most, and even the former Pope (i.e., Ratzinger) in the Roman Catholic Church would answer no to the above question.

This would seem to be the case with conservative Reformed theologians as well. For example, former Westminster professor Harvey Conn thinks that such an attempt at isolating Marxism for mere instrumental use of analysis is doomed from the start and probably reflects, in his opinion, an 'autonomous ideologizing.'[109] But before we pass too hastily over this important subject, let us see what the liberation theologians themselves have to say on this.

Juan Luis Segundo sheds enormous light on this very issue in his response to Ratzinger. His lucid account is worth quoting at length:

> The dilemma is all the more difficult to avoid when the liberation theologians take only elements of that analysis. What is more, as far as I know, they complement and correct those elements with analytical elements from other sources. If it were impossible to separate from the rest of Marxist thought, how is it that well-known non-Marxist and even anti-Marxist thinkers and sociologists—such as Weber or Mannheim—can use those analytical tools without being pushed to the same consequences? The Supreme Pontiff himself makes excellent use of Marxist analysis, such as the category of alienation, to describe the worker who gives up the fruits of his or her labor in exchange for a salary in capitalist (or socialist) systems.[110]

The contention here expressed is that liberation theologians, (to the best of their knowledge), complement and correct those sources they employ for analysis as they take them into service. Whether or not this is possible is one issue; whether the liberation theologians succeed in this enterprise is another. Is it possible to employ the tools and language of Marxism without being pushed to the same consequences as a person who cordially embraces the system of Marxism? A historian could ask similar questions about other tools of analysis. For example, D. G. Hart has recently asked similar questions about the use of Scottish Moral Philosophy by the Princeton theologians. Contrary to the often-stated notion that Scottish Common Sense Realism

---

108. Pedro Arrupe, S. J., 'Marxist Analysis by Christians,' *Catholic Mind* (September 1981), p. 60.

109. Conn, 'An Overview,' pp. 413-416.

110. Segundo, *Theology and the Church*, p. 96.

unduly and in an unhealthy manner influenced the theologians of Old Princeton, Hart argues that they used the philosophical system with discernment and shrewdness.[111]

For example, a question that arises and complicates this whole analysis is whether the societies in which the theologians of liberation are exercising their craft are similar to the traditionalist societies which Marx was criticizing (this is a big 'if' indeed). Is it possible that even some of Marx's insights might be valid in this context? This is not to propose one economic system over another; rather, it is to ask a question about the usefulness of non-Christian knowledge and methods under the rubric of common grace in which we presently find ourselves. In my opinion, Marxism is less amenable as a hermeneutical method that helps us in our exegetical analysis of biblical texts than something like Scottish Common Sense Realism.

Again, whether or not liberation theologians succeed in this endeavor is another issue entirely. Ironically, it is Moltmann that has some very serious charges concerning the Latin American theologians' use of Marxism. Not only does he call into question their depth of explanation regarding Marxist analysis in general, but he also questions their dearth of explanation about the truly dire circumstances of the Latin American people:

> It is one thing to be involved in an incisive analysis of the historical situation of the people and quite another thing to make declamations of seminar-Marxism as a worldview. Whoever assumes that sociology can be a substitute for a deficient contact with the working and suffering people ... practices a sociology about the people but does not tell the history of the people as his/her own history. Marxism and sociology do not yet bring a theologian into the people but, at least at first, only into the company of Marxists and sociologists.[112]

One must ask again if there is not some kind of astigmatism among the liberation theologians in light of the failed history of Marxism throughout the world? Isn't the history of Russia, or all the countries of

---

111. D. G. Hart, 'Princeton and the Law: Enlightened and Reformed,' in *The Law is Not of Faith: Essays On Grace and Works in the Mosaic Covenant* (edited by Bryan D. Estelle, J. V. Fesko, and David VanDrunen; Phillipsburg, New Jersey: P & R, 2008), pp. 44-75.

112. Jurgen Moltmann, 'An Open Letter To Jose Miguez Bonino,' *Christianity and Crisis* (March 29, 1976), p. 60.

Africa that have tried Marxism, enough to make one seriously question the efficacy of it? It would seem that a free-market system works best in a fallen world. 'Capitalism works better than its circumspect ideology; socialism far worse than its romantic hopes,' says Michael Novak.[113] But now I digress and I write outside my area of competence and training. Perhaps we should follow the advice of Clark Pinnock, namely, that we should stick to setting forth biblical principles and leave the development of the economic implications and implementations to those lay people with the requisite knowledge.[114] We should respect the limits of the primary purpose of Scripture, which is not to give us in much detail economic principles and answers to the plight of the poor.

My most serious objection to the liberation theologians is their use of Scripture. For example, although Gutiérrez and others make a liberal use of Scripture, the historical situation and Marxist analysis which they foist upon their reading becomes so controlling for them that the original context and horizon of the speech utterances in the narrative of Scripture is often blurred and becomes opaque. For example, Amos is often quoted as a text which is an attack on the rich in general terms, but this is to separate it from its proper covenantal context and thus to misconstrue its meaning. As Henry notes:

> Yes, the O.T. prophets demanded justice but ... they called also for the personal appropriation and internalization of God's law as an irreducible spiritual goal and moral requirement and they pointed to the coming messianic kingdom as the reality in which violence is done away and universal justice and peace prevail.[115]

Regarding the use of the Exodus motif by the liberation theologians, it seems apparent that they misread the entire event by reading their own theological presuppositions back into the text.[116] Politico-economic liberation is not the central theme of Scripture, nor of the Exodus

---

113. Quoted by Walter W. Benjamin, 'Liberation Theology: European Hopelessness Exposes the Latin Hoax,' *CT* (March 5, 1982), p. 23.

114. Clark Pinnock, 'The Pursuit of Utopia,' in *Freedom, Justice, and Hope* (ed. Marvin Olasky, et al.; Westchester, Illinois: Crossway Books, 1988), p. 82.

115. Henry, 'Marxist Exegesis of the Bible,' pp. 572-73.

116. Kirk, *Liberation Theology*, pp. 147-52. Kirk devotes a whole chapter to this issue although his decisive criticisms come later in the book.

motif.[117] The liberation theologians seem to miss the central message of the Exodus deliverance, 'Let my people go "that they might serve me"' (Exod. 8:1). As O. Palmer Robertson says:

> According to the Pentateuch, the exodus from Egypt did not occur merely as the dramatic deliverance of one more people from the bondage of enslavement. These great events were instead a redemptive action by God himself in which he delivered his chosen people from their sinful pollution through the blood of the Passover lamb.[118]

This seems to go to the core of the liberationists' reading of the Exodus. Indeed, in some of the most current debates, it is Levinson's critique of John Collins.[119] Levinson states that Collins has based his reading of the Exodus upon Pixley, who in Levinson's mind has offered a Marxist critique of Israelite society that goes far beyond the liberationist views of Gutiérrez or Croatto.[120]

Levinson recognizes a run-around when he sees one. He wants to call exegesis just that, and political manifestos another thing:

> Whatever the grounds for that preference in Pixley's case—I believe they lie in his political activism—they do not derive from exegesis or a historical-critical reading of the Bible. This is not to say that one may not have a preference that contradicts the biblical text. The point, rather, is that the statement of the preference should not be disguised as exegesis. And I still find it odd that Pixley applies the term 'evangelical' to a theology that is so at odds with the Bible itself.[121]

Perhaps another one of the most damning criticisms marshaled against the liberation theologians use of Scripture is their confusion

---

117. See the author's, *Echoes of Exodus: Tracing a Biblical Motif*. Also see, DeYoung and Gilbert, *What is the Mission of the Church?*, p. 80.

118. O. Palmer Robertson, *The Christ of the Prophets* (Phillipsburg, New Jersey: P & R, 2004), p. 3.

119. See Levinson, 'Liberation Theology and the Exodus,' and 'The Perils of Engaged Scholarship,' and 'The Exodus and Biblical Theology: A Rejoinder to John J. Collins,' in Alice Ogden Bellis and Joel S. Kaminsky (eds.) *Jews, Christians, and the Theology of the Hebrew Scriptures*, SBLSymS 8 (Atlanta: Society of Biblical Literature, 2000).

120. See George V. Pixley, *On Exodus: A Liberation Perspective* (trans. by Robert R. Barr; Maryknoll, New York: Orbis, 1987); Jorge Pixley, 'Christian Biblical Theology and the Struggle against Oppression,' and 'History and Particularity in Reading the Hebrew Bible: A Response to Jon D. Levenson,' in *The Theology of The Hebrew Scriptures*.

121. Levinson, 'The Peril of Engaged Scholarship,' p. 242.

between special and general revelation. Stephen Knapp notes in his study of Gutiérrez:

> As I have studied *A Theology of Liberation* and compared it with my own perspective, I have concluded that at the most basic level, the differences lie in the different value he and I place on the Bible in comparison to other elements of theological reflection process (i.e., ecclesiastical tradition and practice and the socio-political analysis of our situation). This difference is perhaps rooted in my inability to ascribe revelation value—or better, what traditional Reformed systematic theology called 'special' revelation value—to these other elements.[122]

This raises the issue of the *a-priori* role of Scripture in the interpretation of general revelation.

Lastly, I must question the liberation theologians' view of salvation and its implications for history. As stated before, at least in some of the liberation theologians, salvation is identified with political involvement. As if this is not aberrant enough, there is a heavy stress laid upon the regenerative powers of the individual as mentioned earlier in this chapter; thus, the liberation theologians have been cited by some critics for making a serious stumble into the pit of Pelagianism.[123]

Reading liberation theologians does pose an interesting question. With regard to the mission of the church and ecclesiology, have we focused too exclusively on individual salvation and discipleship of individuals? Should we not also be concerned with the transformation of social structures and the eradication of sin therein? Perhaps too often we have opted for an individualistic discipleship model at the expense of some of the concerns for social involvement which the theologians of Latin America raise. This has been recognized by evangelicals such as Knapp:

> Does our disciple-making approach (or the way we carry it out in practice) lean too heavily on the notion that society can be changed by changing individuals, or that authentic conversions can take place without an antecedent change in political and social structure? Are our appeals to 'conversion' and 'repentance' too individualistic? Do they recognize too

---

122. Stephen C. Knapp, 'A Preliminary Dialogue with Gutiérrez, *A Theology of Liberation*' (ed. Carl E. Armerding; Phillipsburg, New Jersey: P & R, 1979), p. 20.

123. Dale Vree, 'Ideology versus Theology,' pp. 58-78.

little the unlikelihood of radical transformation prior to the formation of a social and community context support of such transformations?[124]

These are interesting questions for theologians and biblical scholars that are especially concerned to address issues connected with the true mission of the church and the vocational calling of individual Christians amid the secular world. A fair question at this point is whether liberationist readings have provided a segue for the postcolonial readings of the Scriptures hermeneutic approach commonly practiced on Christian seminary and college campuses.

Amidst all this negative criticism, we must pause before closing and ask some hard questions of ourselves lest we become guilty of the suspicions which the Latin American theologians are so quick to levy against those in the United States and Europe. In the opinion of this writer, these are important thought-provoking questions. As Harvey Conn has said, 'If liberation theologians can be described as arising because of the "unpaid bills of the church," what bills should we pay first?' The answers that Conn himself later published are not the answers I myself would give.[125] That question actually provides a nice segue for the next part of this book, 'what the primary mission of the church is'; however, first we must deal with two more areas: theonomy and missional creep in the church.

---

124. Knapp, 'A Preliminary Dialogue,' p. 65.

125. Harvie M. Conn, *Evangelism: Doing Justice and Preaching Grace* (Grand Rapids: Zondervan, 1982).

# CHAPTER 8

# Reconstructionism, Theonomy, and the Church's Relationship to Civil Society

We have been looking at the primary mission of the church from the perspective of what it is not. In Chapter 6, we discussed Kuyper, Dooyeweerd and their followers. In Chapter 7, we described liberation theology and some of influential leaders within that movement. We could consider our discussion of liberation as the politics of the left, which gets the primary mission of the church wrong because they focus on 'social sin' and its negative effects. So much of the movement, as we saw, is infused with Marxism, an ideology that is dangerous to society, the state, and the church.

It's probably the case that there are not many Christians in the world today that would identify themselves as theonomists. Nor, would many coming before Presbytery or classis for their ecclesiastical exams identify themselves as theonomists or reconstructionists; however, many in the church *act* or *function* like theonomists when it comes to the way they view society, make their decisions to vote in a certain manner, or even educate their children. Therefore, to describe the movement including its leaders may be helpful to notice the influence.

In this chapter, we will discuss the 'politics' of the right by looking at Christian reconstructionism or theonomy. Whereas liberation theology went awry by focusing on social justice to the exclusion of focusing on the world-to-come, so in this chapter we will note that these movements, which could be called the politics of the right, focus too much on civic transformation to the exclusion of the world-to-come and, thus, they too miss the emphasis of the Gospel. Although these are two distinct but overlapping movements (theonomy and reconstructionism), they are definitely related to one another and we will treat both of them in this chapter. Reconstructionism, or theonomy, denotes a 'theological, social, political and ethical movement calling for the transformation of civil society along biblical lines modelled upon the Mosaic (OT) civil polity.'[1]

Some readers may think that I have made a *faux pas* in discussing reconstructionism and theonomy since it may appear that the influence of these movements is waning. However, two recent books by mainline publishers would seem to contradict this point.[2] Ideas do have legs. Reconstructionism and its cousin, theonomy, is still influential in North America at least especially to be noticed in Tea Party politics and the home-schooling movement. We will focus on the problem of the relationship of the state to the law of God, since that has been a major interest in the reconstruction/theonomy movement and because it touches directly on the subject of this book: the primary mission of the church. As McVicar suggests, Rushdoony wanted to change conventional evangelical thinking in three key areas:

> First, he made it his mission to destroy the hard-won gains made by a generation of wrongheaded evangelical theologians and preachers who mistakenly emphasized pietism and conversion as the answer to all of humanity's problems. Second, conservative Christians must overcome their aversion to taking social responsibility for the nation and instead assert Christ's sovereignty in all spheres of human existence through the application of the Mosaic law. Third, fundamentalist and evangelical Christians needed to abandon their all-too-recent infatuation with premillennial rapture theology and return to the aggressive postmillennial vision of the ultimate triumph of Christ's Kingdom on earth.[3]

---

1. R. S. Clark, 'Reconstructionism,' in *New Dictionary of Christian Apologetics* (eds. Campbell Campbell-Jack, Gavin J. McGrath and C. Stephen Evans; Downers Grove, Illinois: InterVarsity Press, 2006), pp. 601-02.

2. See Julie J. Ingersoll, *Building God's Kingdom: Inside the World of Christian Reconstruction* (Oxford, Oxford University Press, 2015); Michael J. McVicar, *Christian Reconstruction: R. J. Rushdoony and American Religious Conservatism* (Chapel Hill, NC: University of North Carolina Press, 2015).

3. McVicar, *Christian Reconstruction*, p. 109.

In opposition to this Rushdoonian vision, we have been arguing in this book that God has imposed certain limiting factors on the mission and job description of the corporate church. If she doesn't stick to her job description, fuzzy boundaries are the result.

Stated negatively, as we have been arguing, the mission of the church definitely has some limitations imposed on it with regards to its relationship with the state. Stated positively, the church has certain responsibilities towards the state in her mission. In this chapter, we will take up three issues which are central to the topic of the relationship of the church to civil society. First, we will take up the primary purpose of Scripture, or the sufficiency of Scripture for defining the relationship of the church to the civil realm. Secondly, we will engage a NT text that has become an exegetical crux in this debate, i.e., Matthew 5:17. Thirdly and finally, we will discuss how theonomy is essentially a misconstrual of the common grace order and therefore indirectly of the primary mission of the church.

## The Sufficiency of Scripture to Define the Mission of the Church

Without getting too far ahead of ourselves, it is the argument of this book that the mission, government, and polity of the church is prescribed by our Lord in His Word, i.e., the Scriptures. Historically, this has been called *jus divinum*, or divine right Presbyterianism. Usually, in popular parlance, when we speak of the regulative principle it is applied merely to worship. In other words, the church of Jesus Christ is only permitted to include in her worship that which is commanded. However, the sufficiency of Scripture and its attendant doctrine of the regulative principle also applies to church power, i.e., what the church is limited in its power to do. The historic text of WCF 21:1 reads:

> The light of nature shows that there is a God, who has lordship and sovereignty over all, is good, and does good unto all, and is therefore to be feared, loved, praised, called upon, trusted in, and served, with all the heart, and with all the soul, and with all the might. But, the acceptable way of worshipping the true God, is instituted by himself, and so limited by his own revealed will, that he may not be worshipped according to

the imaginations and devices of men, or the suggestions of Satan, under any visible representation, or any other way not prescribed in Scripture.[4]

This same regulative principle which flows from the doctrine of the sufficiency of Scripture, however, not only applies to doctrine and worship but also to church government and polity. Consequently, as Craig Troxel says, 'Therefore, the church is permitted to do only that which she is commanded to do, and whatever is not commanded is forbidden.'[5] James Bannerman (1807-1868), who was one of Scotland's principal leaders in the beginnings of the Free Church of Scotland that moved out of the establishment church in response to the meddling of the state in church affairs, expresses the principles at stake:

> Such, then, is the source of the power of the Church, - using the word power in its most comprehensive sense, to denote not merely a power to act in the way of authority and rule, but also, in addition to this, a power to act in every way in which it is competent for the Church as a Church to act; a power, namely, to act in the way of spiritual jurisdiction, in the way of administering word, and ordinance, and discipline, in the way of dispensing grace to its members. The source of all this power belonging to the Christian society is in the Lord Jesus Christ, as its ever present and ever living Head. This cardinal doctrine lies at the foundation of every other that concerns the Church of Christ, and ought to be guarded from those that would deny or derogate from it, with the utmost jealousy and care. It is so very explicitly and broadly laid down in Scripture, that few are found to controvert it in so many words, or expressly to deny that the Head of the Christian Church is Christ Himself.[6]

However, this definition of the power of the church—with all its limitations and positive competencies—is precisely where theonomy is misguided. For it seeks to extend the power of the church into the civil realm in a manner that was never prescribed by God in His Word.

This is what T. David Gordon, professor of Greek and New Testament at Grove City College, wrote in 2002: 'I am friendlier to theonomy than Calvin was: he thought it was "perilous, seditious, false,

---

4. The most reliable historical rendition quoted from Chad VanDixhoorn, *Confessing the Faith: A Reader's Guide to the Westminster Confession of Faith* (Carlisle, PA: Banner of Truth Trust, 2014), p. 275.

5. Craig Troxel, '"Divine Right" Presbyterianism,' p. 203.

6. Bannerman, *The Church of Christ*, 1.199-200.

and foolish." I think it is perilous, false, and foolish; but I don't consider it seditious.'[7] If Matthew J. Tuininga's argument is accurate, namely, that Calvin should be categorized as a two-kingdom proponent, then Gordon's point is not too sharp.[8]

Professor Gordon had discussed these issues in an academic article in *Westminster Theological Journal* and later in a forum on the topic of the sufficiency of Scripture in *Modern Reformation* magazine. Gordon's real point in his earlier *WTJ* piece, and later written up in more popular form in *Modern Reformation*, is that theonomy is a good illustration of the misunderstanding of the 'primary purpose' of Scripture (and hence the mission of the church).

In the opinion of this reviewer, raising the issue of the correct understanding of the sufficiency of Scripture, or as put in the later published material the 'primary purpose' of Scripture, is not an insignificant or unrelated matter with respect to a biblical evaluation of theonomic ethics; rather, a proper understanding of the primary purpose of Scripture and correctly discriminating the applicability of the theocratic judicial laws to later epochs in the civil sphere is integrally related to the issues raised by theonomy, with respect to a possible over extension of the concept of the sufficiency of Scripture.[9]

Such a restriction on the sufficiency of Scripture has not been respected by leaders in the reconstruction movement or theonomy. Consider, for example, the prolific writer Gary North. North was trained in economics. He was the former intern at R. J. Rushdoony's Center for American Studies and future son-in-law, and a prolific writer and 'movement man' with respect to the reconstruction movement that so profoundly influenced conservative Calvinist circles in the last several decades.[10] North writes:

---

7. T. David Gordon, 'Response' *Modern Reformation* May/June 2002, p. 48. This clarification is to Gordon's original article, 'The Insufficiency of Scripture.' *Modern Reformation* (Jan.-Feb. 2002): pp. 18-23. See also, T. David Gordon, 'Critique of Theonomy: A Taxonomy,' *WTJ* 56 (Spring 1994): pp. 23-43.

8. Tuininga, *Calvin's Political Theology and the Public Engagement of the Church: Christ's Two Kingdoms.*

9. Some of this line of thinking was covered in the author's review article in *Ordained Servant* of Kenneth L. Gentry, *Covenantal Theonomy: A Response to T. David Gordon and Klinean Covenantalism*, 2005, see *Ordained Servant*, Vol. 16, No. 5, 2007.

10. See McVicar, *Christian Reconstruction.*

Power renounced is not power diminished; it is merely power transferred. What is needed is a reassertion of the total sovereignty of God. Then, as a direct consequence, power must be redistributed widely, away from central governments and into the hands of local political bodies, local churches, local voluntary institutions of all kinds. The Bible affirms the legitimacy of power. It places all power in the hands of Jesus Christ (Matt. 28:18). Then it directs Christians to go forth, preaching the gospel and discipling nations, teaching them to observe 'all things whatsoever' Christ has commanded (Matt. 28:20). 'All things,' as Greg Bahnsen's study, *Theonomy in Christian Ethics* (1977) demonstrates so forcefully, includes the whole of biblical law. What we call the Great Commission of Christ to His church (Matt. 28:18-20) is in fact another reaffirmation of the covenant of dominion, taking into account the progress of redemptive history.[11]

Not only is this an example of a wrongly construed so-called 'cultural mandate' (discussed in Chapter 2), it shows no deference for the history of church teaching on the limitations of church power with respect to her primary mission.

The same kind of overextension of the sufficiency of Scripture can be demonstrated from Greg Bahnsen, arguably the most learned and articulate of the leaders in the theonomic movement:

The church and state, though separate from each other, are united *under the authority of God* (emphasis his). The second thing which the present examination has indicated is that the power of the church sword is such that God's word will see worldwide prosperity, the reign of Christ being extended to earth's remotest ends. *All authority* [emphasis his] in heaven and earth is His, and thus all 'authorities' (civil magistrates) are subject to His role [sic]. Since Scripture speaks of Christ establishing justice in the earth we can speak of the Older Testament Theocracy becoming in the new Testament a Christocracy with international boundaries. There is no reason why the 'Theocratic' character of Israel should prevent the application of God's law to the civil magistrate today. If, as Morrison maintains, eschatology and Christology ultimately shape the Christian view of the state, then the same conclusion that has been derived from a study of the scriptural views of moral obligation, law, and civil authority would follow here as well. The magistrate today *ought* [emphasis his] to obey and enforce God's law in society. A nature/grace dichotomy in the area of civil government is totally

---

11. See Gary North, *The Dominion Covenant: Genesis*, Economic Commentary on the Bible, Vol. 1 (Tyler, TX: Institute for Christian Economics, 1982), p. 31.

alien to the scriptural outlook; Christ does not merely rule in His church, leaving the world governments to Satan. Moreover, a further way in which God's word teaches us that magistrates are to obey His direction is the indication that Christ is to rule them Himself. All authorities, whether ecclesiastical or civil, are under His divine rule. Therefore, state leaders are just as obligated to follow Christ's direction *as the church elders* [emphasis his] are required to obey the *Head of the Church* [emphasis his]. The Word has commandments relevant to both church and state.[12]

This is a clear abuse of functional objectives prescribed by God in his Word that belong to the church and should not be applied to the common grace institution of the state. However, one may ask, why is it that such misconstruals occur? In order to answer this question, we need to turn to the exegesis of a crucial passage from the NT.

The problem with the theonomic reading of scripture is that it normativizes the Mosaic period. Let me explain. Most theonomists recognize the temporary nature of Israel but they do not discern how the typology of the Mosaic economy functions. This then is a problem of too much continuity. In other words, they see a continuity between Israel and the church; however, they carry that continuity forward in such a manner that the Mosaic economy remains normative in many respects. This is done, for example, by trying to apply the Mosaic law inappropriately in the church age, with the suggestion that laws and punishments attached to those laws are reinstituted during the church age without proper recognition of change. Hence, the relationship between church and state in the church age is wrongly construed.

## The Crux of the Matter: Matthew 5:17-20

All parties, no matter what side of the table they come down on regarding the role of God's law in civil society during the church age, recognize Matthew 5:17-20 as a crucial passage in understanding the role of biblical law during the New Testament age. At issue here is the understanding of Matthew 5:17 in its larger context and the communicative intention of *abolish* (*katalusai*) and *fulfill* (*plerōsai*). Perhaps one of the best places to observe how theonomists themselves interpret this passage is to note

---

12. Greg Bahnsen, *Theonomy in Christian Ethics* (Phillipsburg, PA: P & R, 1984), pp. 432-33.

Gentry's discussion of it in his book and the incorporation of Greg Bahnsen's exegesis of the passage.[13]

In Gentry's defense of Bahnsen's exegesis of this passage and his position that Jesus is *confirming* the law and the prophets (his take on translating *plerōsai*), he says Hagner's commentary 'goes on to observe that "prophets" is added "in the first instance [to] refer to the further stipulation of the *requirements of righteousness,* i.e., of the will of God."'[14] However, simple research will reveal that Gentry has botched the quotation: the actual quote has been lifted inappropriately from its context since the quote is embedded in a concessive clause, '*Although* [emphasis mine] the "prophets" here may in the first instance refer to the further stipulation of the requirements of righteousness, i.e., of the will of God ... an added dimension with the implication of fulfillment is introduced by these words.'[15] Obviously, this gives the sentence its correct emphasis.

Indeed, Hagner himself, whom Gentry quotes tendentiously, correctly understands that the issues raised by this crux passage cannot be solved by mere word studies alone but must be understood with deference to the larger context, particularly verse 18 and verses 21-48.[16] Hagner continues:

> Since in 5:21-48, Jesus defines righteousness by expounding the true meaning of the law as opposed to wrong or shallow understandings, it is best to understand [*plerōsai*] here as 'fulfill' in the sense of 'bring to its intended meaning' – that is, to present a definitive interpretation of the law, something now possible because of the presence of the Messiah and his kingdom.[17]

In other words, for Hagner (correctly, I might add), 'the way in which the law retains its validity for Matthew is in and through the teaching of Jesus.'[18]

This discussion demonstrates a fundamental astigmatism with respect to a correct reading of Matthew 5:17-20 by theonomists: by insisting on a translation of *plerōsai* as *confirm/ratify,* they simply miss Matthew's point. To the original auditors of Jesus' Sermon on the Mount, the most

---

13. See the author's review *article* of Kenneth L. Gentry, *Covenantal Theonomy: A Response to T. David Gordon and Klinean Covenantalism,* 2005. *Ordained Servant,* Vol. 16, No. 5, 2007.

14. Gentry, *Covenantal Theonomy,* quoting Hagner, p. 57.

15. Hagner, *Matthew 1-13* (WBC 33A; Waco: Word, 1993), p. 105.

16. Ibid., p. 105.

17. Ibid., p. 106.

18. Ibid., p. 107.

jarring message would not necessarily have been the new teachings, although the penetrating read, the demand for perfect obedience, and the application of the law would no doubt have found its mark, but the real surprise is the teacher himself. This fact was driven home to the present reviewer years ago when he was reading a Jewish author, not a Christian interpreter, on the Sermon on the Mount:

> Yes, I would have been astonished. Here is a Torah-teacher [referring to Jesus] who says in his own name what the Torah says in God's name. It is one thing to say on one's own how a basic teaching of the Torah shapes the everyday .... It is quite another to say that the Torah says one thing, but I say ..., then to announce in one's own name what God set forth at Sinai .... For what kind of torah is it that improves upon the teachings of the Torah without acknowledging the source – and it is God who is the source of those teachings? I am troubled not so much by the message, though I might take exception to this or that, as I am by the messenger.[19]

Hagner emphasizes that 'Jesus' words stress [commenting on "not one iota or mark"] that the law is to be preserved not as punctiliously interpreted and observed by the Pharisees (although the language apart from the context could suggest such a perspective) but as definitively interpreted by Jesus the Messiah.'[20]

This directly relates to the application of God's law for the modern Christian in today's society. An appeal to Calvin is timely here. The reader should consider, for example, two brief citations from Calvin (*Institutes* II. 7.15 & I. 7.16). For Christians, no longer under the Old Testament dispensation, according to Calvin, 'the moral law now no longer condemns us, because of Christ. Though it retains the power to condemn, its use is not to condemn, but to point to Christ. So the moral law is not abolished in use, but in effect, or in one of its effects.'[21] On the other hand, according to Calvin, 'the ceremonial laws were indeed abrogated in use, but not in effect.'[22]

Consider now, Paul Helm's summary after a careful discussion of these passages of Calvin:

---

19. Jacob Neusner, *A Rabbi talks with Jesus: An Intermillennial, Interfaith Exchange* (New York: Doubleday, 1993), pp. 30-31.

20. Hagner, *Ibid.*, p. 106.

21. See Paul Helm, *John Calvin's Ideas* (Oxford, 2004), p. 351.

22. Ibid.

What these nuances reveal is that Calvin's approach to ethics, or the part played by the revealed law of God in ethics, is heavily influenced by his understanding of the progress of revelation and of the successive eras of God's unfolding redemptive purposes. This makes a straight comparison between his views and those of the medievals, who understood divine law in a rather more formal and abstract way, somewhat difficult.[23]

Scripture itself, as well as Reformed luminaries such as Calvin, have maintained the importance of recognizing the principle of periodicity (G. Vos' term) for a correct understanding and application of biblical law. In other words, the covenantal context for a proper interpretation of God's law is essential.

Just as Marxism leads liberationists into a kind of hermeneutical astigmatism, so also lack of sensitivity to the unfolding redemptive historical development in Scripture leads theonomists into a kind of hermeneutical astigmatism. But such fuzzy eyesight does not only influence the way one reads Scripture; it also affects the way in which one reads a confession of faith.

## Westminster Confession of Faith: 19.3-4

This theonomic confusion on this point in turn leads to an inadequate understanding of the Westminster Confession, as one would expect (see *WCF* 19.3-4). Many theonomists want to make much of the distinction between the ceremonial laws being 'abrogated' vis-à-vis the judicial laws merely 'expiring' together with the state of that people, i.e. Israel. In keeping with theonomic assumptions, they often desire to soften the latter word in comparison with the former used by the Divines. Although the fact that the qualifying statements in 19.4 are perfectly clear for the purpose of 'freighting' the language of 'expire' correctly, perhaps some further confessional exegesis will clarify since the word 'expire' is used nowhere else in the Westminster Standards.[24]

---

23. Helm, *Calvin's Ideas*, pp. 351-52.

24. I have in mind especially, 'not obliging any other now, further than the general equity thereof may require.' The reader should see A. Craig Troxel and Peter J. Wallace, 'Men in Combat Over The Civil Law: "General Equity" in *WCF* 19.4,' in *WTJ* 64 (2002): pp. 307-18. Also see Sinclair B. Ferguson, 'An Assembly of Theonomists? The Teaching of the Westminster Divines on the Law of God ,' in *Theonomy: A Reformed Critique* (eds. William S. Barker and W. Robert Godfrey; Grand Rapids, MI: Zondervan, 1990), pp. 315-49.

The Oxford English Dictionary (OED) is helpful at this point. The legal connotations of 'expired' seem to be the most apt choice here: 'to cease, come to an end, die out, become extinct.'[25] In other words, the judicial laws of Israel 'ceased, came to an end, died out, became extinct,' with that political body, i.e., Israel, 'not obliging any other now, further than the general equity thereof may require' (*WCF* 19.4). This theonomic understanding of *WCF* 19.3-4 is strained at best, and more probably, in this author's opinion, cuts deeply across the logic of at least Chapter 19 of the Confession.

## Misconstrual of the Common Grace Order?

In the period after the fall, the people of God live in a world that often involves both functioning in a world with holy activities, like prayer, sitting under the preaching of the Word of God, and partaking of the sacraments. As such, they demonstrate that they are citizens of another world, a spiritual one. Furthermore, they are to love their neighbor during their pilgrimage in this life and they are to perform charitable deeds and acts as individual Christians, and they should seek to improve the plight of their neighbor as individual Christians; nevertheless, they should always maintain a realistic balance about what to expect of this world with regards to change for the better.

At the same time in their pilgrim existence, they function as citizens of the country in which they reside. They pay taxes, often work in secular vocations for many hours every week, attend the sports games of their children or attend professional sports games. They fix up their houses and prepare them for sale. All these things, both the sacred/holy activities and the secular ones, should be done with a view to serving the Lord and glorifying Him. As the apostle Paul said in Colossians 3:17-23: 'And whatever you do, in word or deed, do everything in the name of the Lord Jesus, giving thanks to God the Father through him …. Whatever you do, work heartily, as for the Lord and not for men' (ESV).

Christians would do well to remember certain distinctions at this point. Some of the activities we participate in are truly holy: prayer, giving offerings to the Lord on the Lord's Day, singing praises to God in a worship service, etc. These activities are truly redemptive, in that

25. See entry 6c in *The Compact Edition of the Oxford English Dictionary* (Oxford; Oxford University Press, 1971), 'Of an action, state, legal title,' p. 434.

they prepare us on our pilgrimage in this life for the world-to-come. Other activities are not. Those activities are common in the sense that we share them with unbelievers. We perform them as part of our civic duty, like voting or paying taxes. So, even when we perform these 'secular' duties we do them as unto the Lord, with thankfulness; however, this is reflected in our internal disposition and not in an external transformation, whatever cultural object we happened to be engaged with at the time.

This does not mean that we deny the religious orientation of a believer's life in all that she does. It more precisely means that we make distinctions between the holy and the common spheres. This is one of the fundamental problems for theonomists. In its essence, theonomy is a misconstrual of the common grace order with their customary insistence that God's law, all of God's law, is to be applied to today's society. But this is also a mistake of so many today that misunderstand an application not only of the laws of Israel but also the so-called cultural mandate of Genesis 1:26-28.

It is probably more appropriate to apply the commands of the so-called cultural mandate to the church's mission today as the redemptive instrument whereby God calls in all His elect. In other words, in the original covenantal context of Genesis, 1:26-28 was about Adam obeying the command of God so that he would advance eschatologically to a state of *non posse peccare*, not being able to sin. His duty then was to be fruitful and multiply, in the terms of M. G. Kline, to build megapolis, the 'big city' that would be peopled by his godly progeny. This was intended to usher in the world-to-come. The goal now, this side of the fall and this side of the whole world being cast into a condition of sin and misery, is not to return to Eden. Nor is the goal to 'redeem' creation *per se*. As argued in Chapter 2, the goal is actually not to return to Eden; rather, the goal is now to reach the original objective (eschatological advancement) by another means. Now there must be another Adam to achieve what the first Adam failed to achieve or merit. The goal is not, as NT Wright and many others suggest, to get the cultural mandate back on track. The end game is completely different now. In short, theonomists, New Perspective(s) on Paul adherents, and those who succumb to the recent fads of 'missional' movements in the church all make common mistakes in this area.

Something similar at this point could be said of N.T. Wright's elaborate metanarrative of a New Exodus (NE) or Sylvia Keesmaat's interpretation of Paul's use of the Exodus motif. This is especially the case with regard to Wright's view since the destination of the New Exodus is defined along the lines of reclaiming all creation as opposed to heaven.[26]

Wright's view claims to be more robust than traditional western Protestant views, which have been too infected with 'residual Platonism that has infected whole swaths of Christian thinking' with its devaluing of this present world.[27] I have suggested, pace Wright, that the goal of the New Exodus is heaven, not the reclaiming of all creation.[28] Neither does Sylvia Keesmaat, a former student of Wright – with her emphasis on Paul's retelling of the Exodus as a subverting of the original Exodus story for the sake of emphasizing that the newly minted community has a common calling that is supposed to be bent towards 'suffering and compassion towards one another' – ultimately satisfy.[29] Compassion one towards another is important, but rather than a transformation of the present creation, true Christian liberty is far more satisfactory in its pristine simplicity: consisting in 'freedom from the guilt of sin, the condemning wrath of God, the curse of the moral law; and, in their being delivered from this present evil world, bondage to Satan, and dominion of sin; from the evil of afflictions, the sting of death, the victory of the grave, and everlasting damnation; as also, in their free access to God, and their yielding obedience unto him, not out of slavish fear, but of a childlike love and willing mind.'[30]

It's probably closer to the truth to say that the so-called cultural mandate of Genesis 1:26-28 is being carried out in the program of salvation by the church since the covenant of grace is the redemptive program according to God's current strategy for the world. M.G. Kline is worth quoting at length here:

---

26. Wright, *Paul and the Faithfulness of God*, p. 735. This is essentially more of the same that he already claimed in *Surprised by Hope: Rethinking Heaven, the Resurrection, and the Mission of the Church* (New York, NY: Harper One, 2008).

27. Wright, *Surprised by Hope*, p. 19.

28. See the authors, *Echoes of the Exodus* (Downers Grove, IL: 2018).

29. Keesmaat, *Paul and his Story*, pp. 216-37.

30. Westminster Confession of Faith, p. 20.1.

The genealogical and earthly aspects of the original cultural mandate that were to constitute its preconsummation history are not part of the redemptive program *per se*. For example, even though it may be said that Christ, through the Spirit, begets the new mankind, this redemptive work of regeneration sustains a metaphorical, or analogical, not literal relationship to the genealogical function stipulated in the commission assigned to man in the beginning. The treatment of the great commission (Matt. 28:18-20) by theonomic reconstructionists may be cited as a glaring instance of confusion in this fundamental area. Indeed, dominion theology as a whole represents the systematic outworking of their failure to understand the biblical concept of common grace culture. As brought over into the postlapsarian world, the cultural mandate undergoes such refraction that it cannot be identified in a simple, unqualified way with either the holy or common enterprises. Nevertheless, when dealing with postlapsarian functions and institutions, both common and holy-redemptive, it is important to recognize their creational rootage and the kind of continuities that do obtain between them and the terms of the original cultural mandate.[31]

This is a kind of 'immanentizing of the eschaton,' an idealistic dream about the improvement of this world that never was intended to be.

## John Frame's Theonomic Vision for the State

As was mentioned in Chapter 4, John Frame was critical of Dooye-weerdism earlier in his career (he has recently retired from being a Professor at Reformed Theological Seminary). Nevertheless, many of his comments later in his career sound much like the system he set out to criticize early on in his career, at least regarding the civil state.[32] The article which we are engaging here came out of Frame's inaugural lecture at Westminster Seminary in California, when Frame was promoted to full Professor. Here Professor Frame argued that essentially 'the state' is a governance of earthly tribes or clans. States, alleged Frame, are 'family governments.'[33] Although he argues in certain places for a 'two kingdom' or 'two citizen' view, he also argues vigorously for the religious character to be applied to the state similar to how Christians erect Christian schools to educate their children. He says, for example:

---

31. M.G. Kline, *Kingdom Prologue*, p. 157.

32. See J. Frame, '*Towards a Theology of the State*,' WTJ 51 (1989): pp. 199-226.

33. Ibid., p. 218.

Why should government be any different from any other project in which the believer is involved? If we promote Christian schools because Christ is to be Lord of all of life, doesn't the same argument apply to government? And once Christian standards become the norm in such institutions, why should that institution not formally recognize that commitment by confessing Christ?[34]

But then at the end of his article, he enters into many suggestions of what such a 'Christian nation' would look like if it were ever to emerge. It seems to me at this point that his analysis has some helpful distinctions (e.g., nuancing what it means to punish religions, or cults, punishing expressions of false religions in such crimes as theft and murder – i.e., *at this point,* you can't practice your religion, when you murder!). Of course this kind of thing is timely, and comes up in the news at times. This would apply to the state overruling, for example, a Jehovah's Witness refusing blood transfusions for a dying child or fanatical polygamists in Utah wanting to kill off disloyal former members. However, when he begins to travel down the road of what a 'Christian Nation' would look like, then we must part company. He says, for example, that the Christian nation would ultimately have the same membership as church. Moreover, then he says that the legislative and executive branches should be seeking to bring the laws of the land into concord with biblical standards. What does this mean, however? Which biblical laws? He even claims that church leaders would overshadow the state courts? However, in what way? He denies that all religions should be treated on a precisely equal basis, with no favoritism given to any. Why? Because he says that 'it would in effect make a truly Christian state impossible.'[35]

Kline's trenchant summary analysis is spot on here:

> Summing up then, the meaning or essential identity of the postlapsarian city is not found in identification either with the kingdom of Satan or the kingdom of God. Nor is it to be explained in terms of a dialectical seesawing between the demonic and the divine. This divinely appointed institution exists within the sphere of common grace, which is the corollary, the counterpoise, of the common curse. The fundamental shape of the city is the resultant of the interplay of these two correlative principles of divine

---

34. Ibid., p. 217.
35. Ibid., p. 223.

action, a divine wrath and a divine grace that restrains that wrath according to the measure of sovereign divine purpose.[36]

## Conclusion

As we continue to look at modern examples of what the primary mission of the church is not, this chapter has argued that expressions of theonomy make egregious mistakes when it comes to ecclesiology.

Not only do they misconstrue common grace as it is revealed in the Bible, they also do not exegete a fundamental NT passage that deals with Jesus' application of the law in the New Covenant epic. In turn, this leads them to misunderstand Chapter 19 of the Westminster Confession of Faith. My hope is that this chapter has emphasized the importance of general revelation and common grace. God has given us so many blessings in the world that provide for a stable existence: e.g., modern medicine and science (which can even develop vaccines in record time to help with pandemics), ease of travel, stable economies, engineering which has harnessed the laws of nature for the common good, and the list continues. General revelation and common grace are often neglected in theonomic quarters. This leads only to a neglect of God-given gifts and insights which He reveals to Christians and non-Christians alike.

Finally, we observed that even some like John Frame make similar misappropriations in theologizing on the relationship between the church and the state. In this next chapter, we draw upon one more area to illustrate what the primary mission of the church is not. Here, we focus on recent trends in the so-called missional movement.

---

36. Kline, *Kingdom Prologue*, p. 172.

# CHAPTER 9

# Missional Creep, Newbigin, MLK, and Social Justice

What is the relationship between the church and mission? That introduces a huge and important question. There have been major shifts in the way people are thinking of the missional purpose of the church in recent years. It used to be that what came to mind was that the church did have a mission: to reach those lost in sin with the free offer of the gospel and to disciple and train members of the church in their most holy faith to help them to grow in grace as they pilgrimage towards the world-to-come.

## The Missional Movement in the Modern Church

Trending now is a new definition of missional which profoundly influences the way we understand the church. It flows out of the *Missio Dei* movement, or the 'mission of God' movement. Here, the church is subordinated to mission. See, for example, the *Missional Manifesto* (ed., Ed Stetzer, Alan Hirsch, Tim Keller, et. al).[1] For example, it used to be that maturing disciples from infancy to maturity included growth in knowledge of Word and doctrine, growth in holy living, putting off the old nature of sin and the corruption of sin, with the new man marked by the fruits of the Spirit. Now, as the *Manifesto* explains it, such a growth from infancy to maturity (Col. 1:28) includes more:

---

1.  http://www.missionalmanifesto.net/

That this means the church trains its members to be leaders in deeds of justice and ministry to the poor, as well as live out the implications of their faith in business, the arts, in politics, the academy, the home, and in all of life. As the church makes disciples, it equips them to bring their faith to bear on every area of their lives, private and public.[2]

This is a different expression of the kind of transformationalism we examined in an earlier chapter. This seems somewhat different from the old social gospel liberalism of Walter Rauschenbusch in the twentieth century (recounted below in Chapter 10, when I talk about the nature of the kingdom of God). God's mission, according to the new missional movement, encompasses all aspects of life: art, business, helping the poor, and social justice projects. Where and when did the church pivot in its ecclesiology? In what follows, we will examine the life of Newbigin and his influential ideas. We will also look at the life of Martin Luther King, Jr. and what I am calling the 'social justice' movement resurgence in the modern church.

## Lesslie Newbigin

When Lesslie Newbigin died in 1998, the *Times* called him 'One of the foremost missionary statesmen of his generation' and among 'the outstanding figures on the world Christian stage in the second half of the century.'[3] He had a keen and creative intellect. From this author's perspective, he was the kind of writer that challenges readers and is very elegant in his prose.

Newbigin was born in Newcastle, England, in 1909. He was the second of three children. Not insignificantly, his father was a successful businessman, who had founded his own shipping company, but even more importantly was 'actively concerned to apply his faith to politics and business.'[4] Undoubtedly, this would have a profound influence later on Newbigin's thought and life. Even so, by the end of his school days before he headed off for college, Newbigin had abandoned his parents' faith. After finding his joy in outdoor pursuits (including rock climbing), Newbigin came into contact with peers who did embrace

---

2. Ibid.

3. *The Times*, 31 January, 1998.

4. See *Lesslie Newbigin: Missionary Theologian, a Reader*, compiled and introduced by Paul Weston (Grand Rapids, MI: Eerdmans, 2006), p. 1.

Christianity in the Student Christian Movement (SCM). When he returned to his university studies at Cambridge in 1929, Newbigin had become a committed Christian. The three years at Cambridge profoundly influenced and strengthened his Christian faith. He pursued ordination, got married, and was approved in 1935 by the Foreign Mission Committee of the Church of Scotland to become a foreign missionary and was assigned to serve in India. On the mission field, not only did his family grow and prosper, but so also did his career as he took on increasing responsibilities. Later, as a committed Anglican, he became the Bishop at Madurai in 1947. In 1959, he became very involved in the work of the International Missionary Council. He was also involved in the World Council of Churches (WCC) in the proposed Commission of World Mission and Evangelism. It was this organization which embodied so many liberal principles in its own program.[5]

It was this organization, and other ecumenical movements, that emphasized in the 1960s that the church was primarily a 'servant church,' affirming 'that the church does not *have* mission, but *is* mission: that the church exists only in mission.'[6] As Clowney notes, predictably the question became, '"What is the mission of the church'? At the 1966 World Conference on Church and Society in Geneva, it was said that the church's mission was to carry forward the work that God was doing in the world, namely, the liberation of the oppressed.'[7] Undoubtedly the reader will hear echoes of Gustavo Gutiérrez's theology here (discussed previously in Chapter 7).[8] The WCC Assembly in Canberra in 1991, which met after the discrediting of Marxism in Soviet Russia and Eastern Europe, planned its future agenda to feature 'newer concerns, including those of feminists, environmentalists and advocates of other religions.'[9] Much of the current brouhaha in the churches over social justice concerns in our societies and our churches is undoubtedly related to the homecoming of these seeds planted decades ago.

Returning to Newbigin, we note that he had been reluctant to leave India, but the new Commission was near and dear to his heart. In 1965,

---

5. See Edmund Clowney, *The Church.*

6. See Ibid., p. 155.

7. Ibid., p. 156.

8. Ibid.

9. Ibid.

he returned to India to assume his role as the newly elected Bishop of Madras. This entailed ever more responsibilities since in the mid-1960s, Madras, already a sizeable city, was growing at nearly a rate of 100,000 people per year. In this new post, Newbigin not only quickly became involved in evangelistic work; he also became involved in developing new programs for 'social welfare among those who lived in the slums around the city.'[10]

It was in the 1960s that Newbigin's approach to theology and mission underwent a significant change.[11] This was especially the case following the WCC's New Delhi assembly in 1961. Before this, Newbigin thought the primary agent of the 'world mission' of God was the church of Jesus Christ. 'During the New Delhi assembly, however, he came to realize that this approach was inadequate, and that only a "fully trinitarian doctrine" on mission would do justice to what the Bible had to say, setting "the work of Christ in the Church in the context of the overruling providence of the Father in all the life of the world and the sovereign freedom of the Spirit who is Lord and not the auxiliary of the Church."'[12] Newbigin's published work following this turned increasingly to engaging culture as part and parcel of the primary mission of the church.

Newbigin reached retirement age in 1974. He felt that he should do so and make room for an Indian leader. He and his wife decided to return to the UK. There, he taught at Selly Oak Colleges in Birmingham for several years; even more significantly he was invited to serve in a small, struggling, inner-city congregation in Birmingham. It was during this time that Newbigin entered a period of prolific writing. After a very productive retirement, Newbigin died when he was eighty-eight years old, succumbing to heart disease.

During this time, Newbigin wrote about the definition, mission, and purpose of the church. But what Newbigin means at this point is that the church must be recognizable as a different place, a place that is a sign of the world to come. A place that someone could recognize as different than this world. A place that represents justice and peace and the end of sadness and sorrow.

---

10. Newbigin, *Missionary Theologian*, p. 11.

11. See Paul Weston's comments in Leslie Newbigin, *Missionary Theologian*, p. 81.

12. Ibid., p. 81.

But here's the rub: Newbigin thinks that a 'Word'–oriented ministry apart from a deed–oriented ministry will never communicate to the world if the church, *qua* church, is not actively involved in the public life of the community in which it finds itself. I do believe that loving our neighbors as Christians can and should have a profound influence on the integrity of our words on the Lord's Day; however, such claims are pejorative towards a Protestant ministry that focuses on the truth of what is communicated by Word.

He says, for example, in 'On Being the Church for the World' (1988):

> I constantly hear people talking about 'Kingdom issues' versus 'Church issues'. 'Forget about the Church, all this ecclesiastical stuff which has nothing to do with God's will. On the last day, when the sheep and the goats are finally separated, they are all irrelevant questions. The important things are the Kingdom issues: justice, peace, liberation.' This has a certain element of truth in it. But if it's taken by itself, then Church just becomes a crusader for liberation which is a very different thing. The Church cannot fulfill the Kingdom purpose that is entrusted to it – and certainly the Kingdom is the horizon for all our thinking: that God reigns and that the Church is sent into the world as a sign of the Kingdom – if it sees its role in merely functional terms. The Church is sign, instrument and foretaste of God's reign for that 'place', that segment of the total fabric of humanity, for which it is responsible – sign, instruct and foretaste[13] for *that* place with its particular character.

On the next page, he continues, and I quote at length because it is elucidating for his views:

> The first thing, therefore, is that the Church is a foretaste, and that means it will be different from the world. If it isn't, it's no good. Don't let us be afraid of the fact that the Church is different than the world, that the reality which we celebrate, which we share, which we rejoice in our worship is a reality which the world treats as an illusion. We must not evade that, or try to slide over it or make it seem less sharp.
>
> But in so far as it is a foretaste, it can also be an instrument. It can be an instrument through which God's will for justice and peace and freedom is done in the world. That takes the Church out into the secular world with whatever is relevant to the real needs of that secular world. If that is not happening, how is the world going to know that the reality we talk about is true?[14]

---

13. Ibid., p. 138.
14. Ibid., p. 139.

However, this is just the old liberal drum. J. Gresham Machen identified it years ago: 'We preach the gospel, they tell us, by our lives, and do not need to preach it by our words. But they are wrong. Men are not saved by the exhibition of our glorious Christian virtues; they are not saved by the contagion of our experiences.'[15]

Ultimately, from a linguistic perspective, this is a semiotic problem. Let me explain. Semiotics is the science of signs and how they communicate meaning. It is primarily a linguistic discipline. Words do not have meaning in isolation but in relation to one another and to the environment in which they appear. Ferdinand Saussure is considered by many to have initiated the modern discipline of semiotics. The purpose of this special branch of linguistics is to 'investigate the production of the sign constitution of the text of enabled text senses.'[16] Without getting into some very complicated details on this subject, my own view is actually that words (with properly interpreted semantics) in the context of their discourse (hence, syntax) and how they are used in a real discourse event with all its social ramifications (pragmatics), are what communicates meaning to addressees. The linguistic discipline of pragmatics has to do with language use that is context dependent. Particularly, pragmatics seeks to explain intended speaker meaning. A discussion of pragmatics and its interface between human interactions and relations is crucial to any discussion of successful communication. However, what I mean

---

15. J. G. Machen, 'The Importance of Christian Scholarship,' in *Education, Christianity, and the State: Essays by J. Gresham Machen*, edited by John W. Robbins (Jefferson, MD: The Trinity Foundation, 1987), pp. 13-44, especially at 21. Originally an address given at Bible League Meetings in Caxton Hall, Westminster, London on June 17, 1932.

16. See Stefan Alkier, 'Intertextuality and the Semiotics,' pp. 251-52 in Hays, Alkier, and Huizenga, *Reading the Bible Intertextually* (Waco, TX: Baylor University Press, 2009). There are different branches of Semiotics: the Structuralist approach, which depends on Saussure who studied the closed structure between syntactic and semantic relationships in terms of intratextuality; the Poststructuralist approach, which is also dependent on Saussure but because of criticisms of Structuralism and due to Kristeva's work (among others), this second approach inquires about intertextuality that is opened to a wider field of sign/signified relations but is still based on Saussure's binary sign model; and finally, the Categorical Semiotics approach, which is a triadic scheme (a text's sign system is worked out on the basis of syntactic concerns, semantics and pragmatics). This last approach, which seems like the method that will yield the most explanatory power of texts, was first worked out by Charles Sanders Peirce and then made more accessible through Umberto Eco's and Charles Morris' work.

by this and what Newbigin and his epigones mean are two vastly different things.

For Newbigin, the local church must be a 'sign' pointing to the consummated kingdom that non-Christians can recognize and even understand because of our concrete deeds when we work out our faith in the public sphere. The seeds of this notion were undoubtedly planted in Newbigin's mission work among the poor in India. But this raises many questions. For example, if we are not involved *as the church* in rectifying social injustice in our communities, does it really follow that those who come into our midst cannot understand the truth of what is preached on the Lord's Day regarding a kingdom that will come in the future at Christ's second advent? This seems pejorative towards the power of the preached Word and the truth it can communicate. Moreover, it does not seem to square with how language can work either. Additionally, this could lead to a denial of much figurative and metaphorical truth in the Scripture. In short, Scripture can communicate truth in and through metaphorical or even figurative language without someone 'seeing' it enacted or lived out in the life of the preacher or the lives of church members. This, of course, is not to deny the importance of living holy lives before unbelievers so that we do not scandalize the Gospel by an incoherent life not matching our words.

Newbigin is often depended on by those who want their faith to influence their work and transform their culture. Consider two short quotations from his writings and you will see why that is the case:

> The Church cannot accept as its role simply the winning of individuals to a kind of Christian discipleship which concerns only the private and domestic aspects of life. To be faithful to a message which concerns the kingdom of God, his rule over all things and peoples, the Church has to claim the high ground of *public* truth (From the Gospel in a Pluralist Society, 1989).[17]

> Jesus, as I said earlier, did not write a book but formed a community. This community has at its heart the remembering and rehearsing of his word and deeds, and the sacraments given by him through which it is enabled both to engraft new members into its life and to renew this life again and again through sharing in his risen life through the body broken and lifeblood poured out.[18]

---

17. *Newbigin Reader*, p. 148.
18. Ibid., p. 152.

[For the Gospel to challenge public life, he says,] It will only be by movements that begin with the local congregation in which the reality of the new creation is present, known, and experienced, and from which men and women will go into every sector of public life to claim it for Christ, to unmask the illusions which have remained hidden and to expose all areas of public life to the illumination of the gospel. But that will only happen as and when local congregations renounce an introverted concern for their own life, and recognize that they exist for the sake of those who are not members, as sign, instrument, and foretaste of God's redeeming grace for the whole life of society.[19]

Perhaps no-one has done more in modern times to popularize Newbigin's ideas than Tim Keller. He thinks that the cultural responses of the church are one of the most significant questions the church can currently engage in her reflections. Finding the two-kingdom model to be reductionistic, Keller suggests that we take both the good and bad of the various models out there to come up with a balanced synthesis.[20] Indeed, Tim Keller has become one of the chief architects of the missional movement in the last decade or so.[21]

## Martin Luther King, Jr.

Martin Luther King Jr. (hence MLK), the most visible spokesperson of the civil rights movement from 1955 until his assassination in 1968, is a personality whose ideas demand engagement, especially in light of the topic of this book and the recent brouhaha in the past several years of social unrest and a demand to respond to systemized injustice. I find so much of what MLK did and wrote about to be commendable and praiseworthy. For example, he profoundly recognized that racism is unbiblical and eloquently and sacrificially tried to put a stop to it in all its various manifestations in the United States. Additionally, his commitment to non-violence in bringing about social change is admirable.

---

19. Ibid., p. 157.

20. Timothy Keller, *Center Church: doing balanced, Gospel-centered ministry in your city* (Grand Rapids, MI: Zondervan, 2012), especially pp. 194-234.

21. See Lee Irons, www.upper-register.typepad.com/blog/mission. For a helpful critique of Keller's emphasis on evangelistic worship, the reader should consult the paper which Lee Irons has written at http://www.upper-register.com/papers/evangelistic-worship.pdf. Although many have appropriated the work of missionary theologians, perhaps no-one is better known for this popularizing of Newbigin than Tim Keller.

However, I must confess that I am still uneasy that he (especially as an eloquent and charismatic leader) insisted that the corporate church, as the church, join him in his efforts and mission. King's emphasis on the church as an agent of social transformation was integrally related to his being raised in the faith, language, and culture of the black church.[22] Raphael Warnock has convincingly demonstrated that for King, 'the work of social transformation and bearing witness against the social sin of racism is not only appropriate for the church but mandatory if it would truly be the church.'[23]

MLK is a personality of special interest to the topic of this book since he thought the corporate church should be engaged directly as a social change agent in ameliorating racial injustices in the land. In this section, I will take the perilous step of describing and engaging (albeit all too briefly) MLK's life and work (especially in light of his familial influence) and give my own opinions with regard to how we ought to evaluate his work in light of the topic of this book: the primary mission of the church.

I agree with a colleague's simple statement that 'Martin Luther King Jr.'s vision of society in which people are judged not "by the color of their skin but by the content of their character" seems to capture the Noahic vision.'[24] However, much more needs to be said about King's influence on current discussion in light of all the brouhaha in recent years especially on race relations and the church's responsibility to speak up. The life and work of Martin Luther King, Jr. undoubtedly had an influence on the missional movement of the church, especially with regard to the civil rights movement. What has been missing in studies of King's work and influence, however, is the impact of his family, his church, and his cultural experiences, as Mika Edmondson has demonstrated in his excellently written book.[25] But not only was it those influences, it was

---

22. For an excellent and nuanced discussion, see Raphael G. Warnock, *The Divided Mind of the Black Church: Theology, Piety & Public Witness*. Religion, Race, and Ethnicity Series, Peter J. Paris, General Editor (New York, NY: New York University Press, 2014).

23. Ibid., p. 48.

24. See David VanDrunen, *Politics after Christendom*, p. 193. It is important to note that VanDrunen rightly registers the fact in a footnote on the same page that King went on in his 'I Have a Dream' piece to 'portray his dream in terms of the realization of Scripture's eschatological promises, which no present political community is able to achieve.' This is exactly correct in this author's opinion.

25. Mika Edmondson, *The Power of Unearned Suffering: The Roots and Implications of Martin Luther King, Jr.'s Theodicy* (Lanham, MD: Lexington Books, 2017), p. 60 and following.

also his encounter with liberal ideas at Crozer in his education. It was there that he came into contact with the ideas of the social gospel in the works of Rauschenbusch mediated through his professors. He wrote a paper there called, 'Pilgrimage to Nonviolence,' in which he wrote on his contact with the liberal works of the social gospel:

> There [in that paper], King affirmed the helpfulness of Protestant liberal works such as Rauschenbusch's *Christianity and the Social Crisis* for helping him develop his homespun ideas and addressing the social needs of the oppressed.[26]

Indeed, King's years studying at Crozer were filled with intense study, especially with the problem of evil. Edmondson summarizes:

> King's Crozer years mark a period of intense philosophical and theological reflection on the problem of evil. Although he almost never made direct reference to his family and cultural roots during his academic writings on theodicy at Crozer, his basic approach to theodicy and the unique insights he offered reveal a mind fundamentally shaped by the black church and the black experience in America.[27]

What's interesting to note at this point is that King saw the moral factor in education as essential. As King saw it, education without moral development was just plain wrong. Edmondson quotes King:

> 'The most dangerous criminal,' he warned, 'may be the man with gifted reason, but with no morals.' King went on to argue that the goal of critical thought is the development of character and intellect towards the betterment of society.[28]

Throughout this period, what becomes influential for King is the notion of 'redemptive suffering.' What did King mean by this? It is evident even in his early work on the biblical book of Jeremiah during his school days. King wrote a paper on Jeremiah that showed significant influence of the integration of 'the redemptive suffering interpretation of Jeremiah's ministry' on his thought. Applied to the black community, this meant that 'these sources reflect the longstanding belief within the black

---

26. Ibid., p. 64.

27. Ibid., p. 65.

28. Ibid., p. 63. One might want to explore King's own alleged sexual ethics in light of such a claim.

community that God can use the tragedies of life as raw material out of which to forge some redemptive quality to the soul.'[29]

King studied elsewhere also, but though he had been 'set up' to engage liberalism at Morehouse through the influence of George Kelsey and Benjamin Mays, it was really at Crozer that he was confronted with liberalism and the serious engagement of those ideas. Morehouse had introduced him to critical ideas and ideology, to critical methods and concern for 'black suffering.'[30] The questions engaged at Crozer became central. As Edmondson recounts:

> As a frequent houseguest and guest preacher for Re. J. Pius Barbour, a longtime family friend, King remained engaged with the religious outlook and social struggles of his people. Hence, the questions that attended black suffering such as what good can come from it, why would God allow it, and how can it be effectively engaged were often at the forefront of his academic writings.[31]

The trajectories in King's writing themes had already been set:

> For King, the enduring message of Jeremiah is that the religious insights forged through suffering experiences pushes Jeremiah beyond the social status quo of his day. So King drew out an important social implication of his theological assertions. *Indeed, using religion to resist the social status quo would mark King's lifelong efforts to alleviate black suffering.* With this, we see that right from the beginning of his education at Crozer, King synthesized and developed his homespun redemptive suffering ideas with liberal tools in order to apply them to the current social situation.[32]

King's contact with liberal ideas continued to influence his overall ministry, says Edmondson:

> King's higher critical examination of the *Twelve Patriarchs* only helped him develop a homespun value that had already been instilled in him in his formative years. Informed by his family, communal, and religious influences, King already possessed a firm commitment to the centrality of forgiveness as a Christian value and that hatred must be responded to with love. Years earlier, King's paternal grandmother, Delia Lindsay King

---

29. Quoted in Ibid., p. 66.
30. Ibid., p. 59.
31. Ibid., p. 65.
32. Ibid., pp. 66-67 [emphasis mine].

ensured that her son Martin (Michael) 'Daddy' King Sr. embraced the ethics of forgiveness. Tempted to hate white people for the pain they caused her throughout her life, Daddy King was rebuked by his mother on her deathbed, who admonished him that 'Hatred ... makes nothing but more hatred, Michael. Don't you do it.'[33]

This attitude becomes a powerful antidote to the rolling injury that bitterness often encourages. Indeed, for King, this becomes a powerful weapon against social evil:

> In a sermon entitled 'The meaning of Forgiveness,' probably delivered sometime during his days at Crozer, King applied the lessons from his paper directly to the social plight of African Americans. The last point of the sermon asks the question, 'What then is forgiveness [?] ... forgiveness is a process of life *and* [emphasis his] the Christian weapon of social redemption .... Here then, is the Christian weapon against social evil. We are to go out with the spirit of forgiveness, heal the hurts, right the wrongs, and change society with forgiveness .... This is the solution to the race problem.'[34]

One might ask in light of this, as I would if I had been his Professor, *What is social redemption exactly?* Interestingly, much of this emphasis was the result of engagement with higher critical scholarship, especially R. H. Charles' work on the *Testament of the Twelve Patriarchs*. Charles was a top-notch scholar, especially in Syriac and ancient Greek sources. As Edmondson recounts:

> [these writings] helped him nuance the homespun ideas about forgiveness. Through his critical engagement with Charles, King articulated the idea that suffering is not redemptive *per se* .... [the offense and suffering they cause, but they] provide opportunities for creative and redemptive engagement, for grace and forgiveness to be extended.[35]

These notions that originated with Charles' analysis of *The Testament of the Twelve Patriarchs* provided the following insight to King: 'unearned suffering can be non-violently engaged so as to help produce a redemptive outcome.'[36]

---

33. Ibid., p. 67.
34. Ibid., p. 68.
35. Ibid.
36. Ibid., p. 69.

One of the questions that emerges at this point, however, is whether the kind of redemption that MLK enjoins here is something that can *genuinely* happen outside the covenant community, with those empowered by the Spirit of God, in order to sincerely and lastingly bring about such a forgiveness? Many other questions emerge as well after this brief engagement with some of the powerful ideas that MLK suggested.

## A 'Thought experiment' regarding MLK's ideas and actions

In this section, I am taking a perilous step. This I realize. This I embrace. I am used to taking calculated risks in the realm of Alpinism and mountaineering; I guess that is what I am doing here as well. I do think that tracing his early family life and educational influences helps us to develop a kind of *eloquent listening* and understanding. In other words, the more I read (and listen to audio recordings) and study MLK, the more I understand why he took the path he did and why he suggested the agendas for action that he did. I was a very young boy when he was at the forefront of his civil rights movement and his life's vocation. Therefore, I vaguely remember this all taking place; nevertheless, it is only much later in life and following the recent social unrest that we have observed around that world that I have made a concerted effort to understand him in a deeper and more sympathetic manner.

I grew up in Los Angeles and lived through the Watts riots and the period immediately thereafter. Moreover, I used to install and repossess carpets in fire-damaged homes in East Los Angeles during the 1980s. It was a tense environment going into those neighborhoods as a middle-class white teenager and telling a black woman (in Watts, Los Angeles) that we needed to repossess the new carpet we had laid in her home after a fire because she was not making her payments. My boss carried a loaded revolver in his tool box for such occasions. Thankfully, he never used it in my presence, although it would not have been too far beyond him since he himself was a racist who had adopted the same posture which his father had inculcated in him. That woman chased us out of the house and out of her neighborhood with a loaded shotgun. So I experienced those hate-filled tense times.

Dr King wrote a famous letter from the jail in Birmingham that addressed concerns that had been communicated to him from other clergy about his actions of non-violent protest.[37] MLK had been arrested at the height of the Birmingham movement which was organized in 1963 by the Southern Christian Leadership Conference (SCLC) of which Dr King was a prominent leader. Although he did not customarily respond to critics of his social action agenda, in this letter he was responding to certain Southern pastors that considered his recent actions that landed him in the jail in Birmingham as 'unwise and untimely.' What follows in his almost hour-long response is an extremely eloquent rejoinder, filled with charity and forgiveness in its tone; however, it is nevertheless firm and unequivocal in its response. Dr King had a lot of time on his hands during those five days in jail to reflect upon his principles and his own justification for the actions he had inspired among so many thousands of followers.

There are many brilliant and powerful ideas eloquently expressed in his letter. I recommend that the reader listen to the oral reading of the letter by Dr King himself (while he was behind bars). Some of the following ideas in response to his detractors are as follows. MLK expressed that segregation distorts souls. He argued that it is morally wrong, and he argued this very well. He expressed his opinion between what makes the difference between just and unjust laws. For example, he appealed to the fact that malicious laws presently prevented negroes from voting, and this was outlandish. He appealed to the conscience of those listening, that breaking the law is a serious issue for a Christian, but breaking a law because one's conscience tells him it is unjust is justified if one is willing to accept the penalty for such actions. Here, he cited the case of Shadrach, Meshach, and Abednego (referenced earlier in the chapter on Daniel).

Next, he addressed his brothers in Christ, those 'white moderates' with whom he is frustrated. These are the ones devoted to good order rather than this issue of justice. It is at this point that he addressed the 'mythical concept of time.' Let me explain, in so far as I understand it, his description of this notion and his opposition to it.

Dr King was frustrated about the response of the 'white moderates.' By this term (the mythical concept of time), he meant apparently to

---

37. There were over a million copies of this letter of response published and purchased. It is easily accessed online and you can even listen to a reading of it (public domain) by Dr King himself via Stanford University's archives. See 'Letter from Birmingham City Jail,' April 16, 1963.

address the idea he was hearing from white moderates that the black person needed to be patient and wait for change to come in time. Rather, MLK thought that the present tension his and others' actions had created (felt everywhere throughout the civil rights movement) was a necessary condition to precipitate change. He thought that the present 'tension' that was in the Southern states was necessary for true change and transition. He thought that this could be accomplished through non-violent direct action. MLK's letter from jail is eloquent and mesmerizing (for lack of a better word). It is full of love, humility, 'eloquent listening' to opposing positions, and full of empathy and compassion: yet, it is full of firm conviction.

He addressed the 'appalling silence of good people,' which I take to be referencing the 'white moderates' who are Christians, and perhaps even Christian ministers. In his references to the 'myth of time,' he seemed to be polemicizing against the notion that time will cure these ills in the social world, and the imploring of patience vis-à-vis action. He noted the movement of 'radical Nationalist black groups' (Black Panthers?),[38] and wondered if his non-violent approaches might be a much better approach than the answer/resolution of these groups. In fact, he asserted that if our 'moderate white brothers' condemn our efforts, then the frustrated negro, he maintained, will turn to violence and the black nationalist groups. He suggested, that the 'healthy discontent,' that the black man feels, can be channeled more appropriately through non-violent protest.

Here Dr King appealed to a list of Protestant leaders that have allegedly protested likewise: Martin Luther, John Bunyan, Jesus Himself, Amos the prophet, Abraham Lincoln, Thomas Jefferson. At the end of this, he asked, 'What kind of extremists will we be?' This is of course a measured response to the fact that he and his followers had been called 'extremists.' Addressing the issue of 'extremism,' he then wanted to impute definitional authority to the word 'extremist.'

Granting a positive gloss to the notion 'extremist,' he then made an appeal for 'creative extremism.' By this, he meant to say that injustice must be rooted out in society. He even went so far as to suggest that many of his ministerial colleagues in the South have 'found themselves

---

38. One is reminded of Michael Zinzun, who lived in Pasadena, California and dedicated his life to bring change to police brutality, and even was a member of the Black Panther group for two years.

more cautious than courageous.'[39] Dr King was greatly disappointed with the church in Montgomery, Alabama and elsewhere in the Southern states as he described. He then used a powerful metaphor and declared that the 'Church must not merely be a thermometer that records the ideas of popular opinion, it must be a thermostat that transforms the mores of society.' His main concern (I think fairly stated) was that the church needed to become an active agent of social change, and that the 'Church as a whole needs to come to the aid of justice' in the world.

So how should we evaluate these statements and claims in light of our topic? I have placed MLK in this chapter because he has significant overlaps with the other figures discussed here, especially with regard to his views that the church should play a part in social transformation, and publicly, as the church corporate, she should play a part in ameliorating social injustices. My thought experiment is to suggest that much of Dr King's agenda could have been fulfilled by appealing to individual Christians to speak up and act as opposed to invoking the church, as the corporate church, to come to the aid of justice.

In other words, MLK was resolute in the prosecution of his agenda, which was to enact change. Much of what he accomplished was indeed commendable. Who, in this age, would want to go backwards to the days of legalized segregation? But how should we bring about social change? Does the corporate church have as part of her mission and job description a mandate to address these social injustices especially in changing laws, whether just or unjust? My thought experiment is to suggest that alternative approaches to social action and change may cohere better with Scripture's job description for the church. I too want to see all forms of racism eradicated; however, I believe it is up to the individual Christian to achieve this relative to his or her own gifts, callings and opportunities.

What keeps the individual Christian (or even a group of like-minded Christians) from addressing and acting upon the injustices that MLK was so skilled at bringing to everyone's attention? Nothing. If we are to maintain the apolitical nature of the church and its mission, then moving society towards more equitable laws with regard to civil rights

---

39. Ibid., 'Letter from Birmingham Jail.'

seems to be a political goal. Consequently, incentivizing people to real change to ameliorate social inequities and racial injustice is a laudable goal. How one goes about operationalizing this is not first and foremost the primary mission of the church. It should be the task and passion of every person created in the image of God and especially individual Christians. Ending racism is a good goal and an admirable outcome to work for as individual Christians. How one goes about achieving this laudable goal and outcome will manifest itself differently in various parts of the world. How it will look in Israel, the Gaza Strip, and the West Bank will be different from how it looks in Compton, Los Angeles, or the South side of Chicago. I agree that the church must be a change agent in society, not merely a thermometer. However, I am suggesting that addressing what MLK called 'white moderate' ministers who had been more cautious than courageous may not have been the most felicitous words in order to respond to his colleagues.

In Chapter 6, I addressed the issue of whether the church should seek to transform the culture through her educational endeavors. In Chapter 7, in which I addressed the movement known as liberation theology, I raised concerns about the church addressing social injustices. In Chapter 8, I looked at the movement of theonomy, which also tries to transform the culture but does so—I hope I convinced the reader—in ways that God never intended for the present age of the church. In this chapter, I addressed the emphasis of the 'missional movement' as observed in Leslie Newbigin's views (popularized by Tim Keller), and I engaged briefly with MLK's life and vocation as one of the major spokespersons in the civil rights movement. The question I took up in Chapter 7, namely, has the church been too individualized in its view of discipleship and in expressing the true mission of the church was engaged implicitly as well. I have suggested as a 'thought experiment' that Dr King's ideas could have been operationalized through more biblically mandated means such as individual Christians, solely or through collectives, as those Christians could influence legislative change through what I would call 'legitimate' channels as voting citizens. This suggestion is not to concede that everything King said was realistic: his rhetoric often amounted to a portrayal of and desire for eschatological Scriptural promises that are intended for the age to come, not something that can be realized in this sin-stained world by any political commonwealth.

In short, I think that Dr King's work, as helpful as it was in some respects, created what I have called 'fuzzy boundaries' in this book. That is to say, the blurring of what is legitimate work of the church vis-à-vis the duty of individual Christian citizens to influence change within the culture that they find themselves in. Another option would be that Christians called to civil office (locally or nationally) could also bring about social change through constitutionally legitimate mechanisms in order to effect changes such as Americans observed in the historical decade of the 1960s. My point is merely that the church, as the corporate church, should stay apolitical. Individual Christians, at least in most of the countries in which this book will be read, have the opportunity for deliberative change in democratic societies which have institutionalized voting and other mechanisms for substantive legislative change.

The next chapter switches gears, radically. There we will talk about what the primary mission of the church is supposed to be. We will engage this topic first from the standpoint of talking about what the Kingdom of God (KOG) is according to the teaching of Scripture and its relation to the church.

# PART THREE

# CHAPTER 10

# Primary Mission of the Church and the Nature of the Kingdom of God

*'For if, because of one man's trespass, death reigned through that one man, much more will those who receive the abundance of grace and the free gift of righteousness reign in life through the one man Jesus Christ.'*

ROMANS 5:17 ESV

The kingdom of God is vast in scope since its plan originates in eternity past and its ultimate goal and end is realized fully in the world-to-come. As Rev. Tim Keller has stated recently: 'It is evident that one of the main reasons for many of the divergent approaches to cultural engagement—among many aspects of ministry today—is the differing views of the nature of the kingdom.'[1] This is true. However, in service of our main topic, which is the primary mission of the church, we must explore the basic nature of the kingdom of God (KOG) in the simplest terms possible. Before doing that, however, we need to have a little historical background to the Protestant and Reformed notion of the KOG. Therefore, we will discuss some key theologians who laid the foundations for thinking about the KOG. Then we will need to discuss exactly what the KOG is according to the Bible. At this point

---

1. Timothy Keller, *Center Church*, pp. 229.

in the chapter, I will give a brief overview of what the KOG is and then we will discuss its relation to the church. Then I will argue that recent interpreters, including Tim Keller who has been so influential in these areas, have oversimplified some of the best Reformed biblical theologians on these issues, which has led to some of the divergent approaches among Christians to cultural endeavors. In this chapter, I will seek to set forth a biblical and historical position that uprights the picture that has been misrepresented and hopefully return to precise and clear vision for the mission of the church.

## Some Historical Background

Calvin set the pace for thinking on the KOG, when he declared that the essential nature of the KOG is spiritual. This was perhaps Calvin's greatest legacy, namely, the insistence on 'the autonomy and integrity of the spiritual kingdom of Christ, which is to say, the church.'[2] When Calvin maintained that the KOG is spiritual, he essentially meant that it is eschatological.[3] When one takes such a position, the practical outcome is indeed beautiful.[4] In 1541, Calvin was invited back to Geneva; however, the church which he had left was now in disarray, as Tuininga sums it up: 'Calvin was assigned the task of reorganizing the church, and in fact he only returned under the condition that the church would establish discipline along the lines proposed in 1537-1538.'[5] It was in this context that Calvin organized the first non-hierarchical system of church government:

> The synodical or Presbyterian system established by the French, built on the rejection of centralized control by magistrates or bishops, may have been the first thoroughly non-hierarchical system of church government in history.[6]

Ultimately, this plan for the church and the KOG finds its 'back story in the eternal mind and plan' of God as explained so eloquently by Stuart Robinson so many years later. He says, 'in no other system of thought is this power of a central idea so great as in that revealed system which is

---

2. Tuininga, *Calvin's Political Theology*, p. 62.

3. Ibid., p. 21.

4. Ibid., p. 74.

5. Ibid., p. 69.

6. Ibid., p. 85

in itself the evolving of one great idea that lay in the Divine Mind from eternity.'[7] After tracing very clearly the clarification that God brought in such an area of theology, Robinson explains that the American scene is what provided such a clear opportunity for Ecclesiology:

> Do not the providences of God toward the American Church in freeing her from the civil domination which, by violence or seduction, silenced the martyr-voice of her Scotch mother when she would testify for Christ's crown and covenant, and in placing the Church here in a position (for the first time, perhaps since the apostles) to actualize fully and without hindrance her true nature and functions as a spiritual commonwealth, – do not all seem to indicate that the time has fully come for the final development of the visible Church as a governmental power on earth, yet a kingdom not of this world, a people not reckoned among the nations?[8]

As was discussed in Chapter 1 of this book, Robinson located this purpose in the mind of God all the way back in eternity in the covenant of redemption, which is evidenced by what he says: 'this general view of the subject is confirmed by the Scripture account of the mode in which the eternal purpose of God was manifested in time.'[9] In eloquent prose, he summarizes:

> Contemplated as a part of the process of manifesting to men the purpose of God to gather an elect people, the Church is a means through which God makes known his counsel. Contemplated as to its immediate end, the Church is a divinely-appointed institute, by which and through which to accomplish his purpose in the calling and edification of his elect. But both these views, however important and essential, are, logically speaking, secondary and incidental to the idea of the Church actual on earth as the development of the Church ideal, – the 'pattern in the heavens.'[10]

What is the goal for the church in the mind of God? Again, Robinson summarizes:

> For the fundamental idea of the Church as a separate and distinct portion of the human race is found in the peculiar *mode* [emphasis his] of that purpose

---

7. 'Stuart Robinson,' *The Church of God as an Essential Element of the Gospel, and the Idea, Structure, and Function in Four Parts* (Willow Grove, PA: The Committee on Christian Education of the Orthodox Presbyterian Church, 2009), p. 31.

8. Ibid., p. 28.

9. Ibid., p. 45.

10. Ibid., p. 37.

itself. It is set forth as a distinguishing feature of the purpose of redemption, that it is to save not merely myriads of men as *individual men* [emphasis his], but myriads of sinners, as composing a Mediatorial body, of which the Mediator shall be the head; a Mediatorial Kingdom, whose government shall be upon His shoulder forever; a Church, the Lamb's Bride, of which He shall be the Husband; a bride whose beautiful portrait was graven upon the palms of his hands, and whose walls were continually before him, when in the counsels of eternity he undertook her redemption.[11]

This is Robinson's brilliant contribution to the primary mission of the church. Of course, if one does not hold to the 'covenant of redemption,' otherwise known as the *Pactum Salutis*, then, lacking categories for such a position, it might be hard to imagine such a claim. Even so, this raises the question of the relation of ecclesiology to the general scheme of redemption, for as Robinson claims, 'the question of the Church has an intimate relation to the general scheme of Redemption.'[12]

Calvin, like Augustine before him, and like modern scholars, invoked Jeremiah's instructions to seek the welfare of Babylon.[13] Calvin frequently was very content to invoke Jeremiah 29:3-6 to encourage his audience to look to the future kingdom.[14] This is a fundamentally different approach than Rome:

Calvin reminds his readers that one cannot conflate what is legal with what is moral, and he explicitly appeals to the two kingdoms doctrine as underlying the distinction, for 'political and outward order [*politia et externo ordine*] is widely different from spiritual government [*spirituale regimen*].'[15]

This really does exacerbate the problem of Rome, which is in essence, 'unbounded dominion.' As Tuininga says:

The pope deceived the masses by mere masks [larvae]' (45.5) while establishing 'unbridled dominion' [dominationem]. The problem had filtered through the entire clergy. When the papists chose a bishop 'they choose a lawyer who knows how to plead in a court rather than how to preach in a church' (4.5.2), and the bishops simply immersed themselves

---

11. Ibid., pp. 38-39.
12. Ibid., p. 32.
13. Tuininga, *Calvin's Political Theology*, p. 241.
14. Ibid., p. 346.
15. Calvin quoted in Ibid., p. 330.

in the political interests of their benefices (4.5.6). Whereas the task of the presbyter is 'to feed the church, and administer the spiritual Kingdom of Christ' (4.5.9), the Roman clergy 'have cast off as burdens too troublesome the preaching of the word, the care of discipline, and the administration of the sacraments.'[16]

This is not to suggest that Calvin thought Christ's spiritual kingdom had nothing to do with politics. Nothing could be farther from the truth. Calvin thought that Christ's spiritual kingdom was to be involved in politics, humanity and even outward behavior; however, the difference lies in this:

> Its power penetrates further than these phenomena [politics, citizenship] toward spiritual matters, the conscience, the soul, piety, and the inner mind. On the other hand, Calvin's meaning is not that the civil government should have no concern for spiritual realities, the conscience, the soul, piety, and the inner mind, but that the political order is properly limited in its powers to matters of polity, humanity, citizenship, and outward behavior.[17]

Fast forwarding to Charles Hodge, in the nineteenth century, he too emphasized the spiritual kingdom of Christ. Hodge arguably was the most influential Old School theologian of the nineteenth century.[18] Aside from his two years of study in Europe, Hodge settled into a remarkably productive career at Princeton Theological Seminary. He trained more Presbyterian ministers than any Professor of his time. His crowning achievement was his magnum opus, a three-volume *Systematic Theology*. More will be said of Hodge in the chapters below. After surveying the nature of the KOG in the OT, Hodge speaks of the Kingdom in the NT period as something that is very different than the Kingdom in the OT period. He says:

> First, it is spiritual. That is, it is not of this world. It is not analogous to the other kingdoms which existed, or do still exist among men. It has a different origin and a different end. Human kingdoms are organized among men, under the providential government of God, for the promotion of the temporal well-being of society. The kingdom of Christ was organized immediately by God, for the promotion of religious objects. It is spiritual, or not of this world … all secular matters lie beyond its jurisdiction … It

---

16. Ibid., p. 188.

17. Ibid., p. 146.

18. Strange, *The Doctrine of the Spirituality of the Church,* p. xxiii.

can decide no question of politics or science which is not decided in the Bible. The Kingdom of Christ, under the present dispensation, therefore, is not worldly even in the sense in which the ancient theocracy was of this world …. The kingdom of Christ being designed to embrace all other kingdoms, can exist under all forms of civil government without interfering with any. It was especially in this view that Christ declared that his kingdom was not of this world …. He intended to say that his kingdom was of such a nature that it necessitated no collision with the legitimate author of any civil government. It belonged to a different sphere.[19]

For Thornwell as well, this view of the KOG in a fallen society can not only exist, but thrive, in any fallen society.[20] For Calvin, he did not identify the KOG on the one hand with a narrow individualism, nor does he merely make the KOG tantamount to the church (more below in this). Tuininga sums up:

> It is important to stress, though, that Calvin clearly avoids reducing the kingdom to a narrow salvation of individuals, or even of the church despite concerns to the contrary. For while he certainly has an anthropocentric emphasis, it is consistently moderated by his insistence that renewed human beings are the first fruits of a restoration of the entire physical creation.[21]

However, this must be balanced against the fact that Calvin is constantly emphatic throughout his works that the church is God's kingdom. Even so, he doesn't make the two tantamount because he believes in the renewal of the entire creation at the end of the world. Still, 'during the present age, the kingdom is established only where the gospel is proclaimed and humans respond in faith and obedience, which is to say, in the true visible church.'[22] Thus, as Geerhardus Vos would summarize the matter:

> Our Lord looked upon the appearance of this church from a point of view that was peculiarly his own. He was to be its Lord and King. Now to him

---

19. Charles Hodge, *Systematic Theology* (Grand Rapids, MI: Eerdmans, 1982), vol. 2, pp. 605-606.

20. Christopher Cooper, 'Binding Bodies and Liberating Souls: James Henley Thornwell's Vision for a Spiritual Church and a Christian Confederacy,' *The Confessional Presbyterian* 9 (2013): pp. 35-47, especially at p. 41.

21. See Tuininga, *Calvin's Political Theology*, pp. 116-17, especially footnote 120 on p. 117. See Tuininga's subtle critique of Dave VanDrunen's definition of Kingdom in footnote 99, p. 113

22. Ibid., p. 182.

there was not that sharp divisions between the church-kingdom and the final kingdom which is for us who live on earth. For him the consummation of the kingdom in which all is fulfilled began with his resurrection and ascension … it appears that every view which would keep the kingdom and the church separate as two entirely distinct spheres is not in harmony with the trend of our Lord's teaching. The church is a form which the kingdom assumes in result of the new stage upon which the Messiahship of Jesus enters with his death and resurrection. So far as extent of membership is concerned, Jesus plainly leads us to identify the invisible church and the kingdom. It is impossible to be in the one without being in the other.[23]

## What is the precise nature of this KOG?

I have been helped here by many books but especially one authored by S.M. Baugh, *The Majesty on High*.[24] In his accessible book on the kingdom of God, Steve limits his biblical corpus to several key New Testament passages: Revelation 4–5, 1 Corinthians 15, John 3, and Matthew 5. This method of starting at the end (with Revelation), and reading 'backwards' as it were, is tremendously helpful in making a complex subject clear and simple. Moreover, he chooses some key distinctive elements in his discussion about the nature of the kingdom which help clarify matters for the modern reader and slice through the cut and thrust of debates on the nature of the kingdom of God. First, he talks about the role of the king. Next, he helps the reader understand the importance of the ruling power, royal authority, and dominion of the king. Third, he helps us understand the realm of the kingdom and, fourthly, the role of kingdom subjects or citizens. Finally, he argues that covenant is the constitution of the KOG.[25] Since definitions of 'covenant'[26] have been so controversial and confusing, Professor Baugh defines it as 'an oath-bound commitment between two or more parties.'

---

23. Geerhardus Vos, *The Teaching of Jesus Concerning the Kingdom of God and the Church* (Phillipsburg, PA: P & R, 1972 rpt.), pp. 85-86. Let the reader note that this was originally published in 1903.

24. S. M. Baugh, *The Majesty on High: Introduction to the Kingdom of God in the New Testament.*

25. Ibid. First stated on page 11 and then repeated (helpfully) throughout the book (e.g., pp. 46, 59, 66, 137 etc.).

26. Ibid., p. 109. This is a good definition since it is broad enough, and inclusive enough to include virtually all biblical covenants as described in the Bible.

Terminological confusion, or lack of precision in defining terms, almost always retards healthy debate and discussion in theology. This is especially true with discussions about the KOG. Baugh defines the KOG in the following simple manner. Early on in his monograph, he states the important claim that the KOG 'is, to put it simply, the new creation.'[27] For Baugh, the new creation has been inaugurated with the coming of Jesus, but not consummated. This is an important distinction as well, since it avoids some of the confusion that has emanated from using categories like 'already, not yet.' Baugh quotes 2 Corinthians 5:17, in which he says, '"Therefore, if anyone is in Christ, *he is a new creation*, the old has passed away; behold, the new has come" (2 Cor. 5:17; emphasis added; cf. Gal. 6:15).' The language of 'already, not yet,' writes Baugh, 'expresses an important truth, but I think it is more helpful to say that some aspects of the kingdom have been *inaugurated* now but await final *consummation* on the last day.'[28] In his sixth chapter Baugh deals with the beatitudes in Matthew 5. He says, contrary to many popular interpretations, that the beatitudes are 'not exhortations; they are royal pronouncements of God's favor upon kingdom citizens.'[29] Its intended audience are Christ's disciples.

The KOG was a major topic in the early teaching of our Lord's ministry as well as his later teaching. His pronouncements about the KOG in his day would have been shocking. In a general sense, we may say that most of the Jews of Jesus' time had come to expect a kingdom that would manifest itself primarily socially and politically; however, what our Lord did was to elevate the concept to a whole new level. As Vos says:

> What our Lord did was to give to this Jewish mode of representation an infinitely higher content, while formally retaining it. He lifted it out of the political sphere into the spiritual. The conquests to which he refers are those over Satan and the demons, over sin and evil. It is kingdom against kingdom, but both of these opposing kingdoms belong to a higher world than that to which Rome and her empire belong.[30]

---

27. Ibid., p. 34.
28. Ibid., p. 66.
29. Ibid., p. 90.
30. Geerhardus Vos, *The Kingdom of God and the Church*, p. 53.

This principle is stated with even greater clarity in one of Vos' shorter writings: 'Our Lord repeatedly speaks of the kingdom as a state of things lying altogether above the sphere of the earthly and natural life, being so different from the natural conditions that it could not be evolved from the latter by any gradual process (cf. Matt. 8:11; 13:43; Mark 14:25; Luke 13:20, 29; 22:16, 29, 30).'[31]

Baugh deftly notes that the saints have already been made citizens of this new creation; however, it has not been consummated as of yet, as mentioned above. This is because the 'kingdom which Christ inaugurated is not of *this* world (e.g., John 18:36). However, Christ himself does rule *over* this earth as we have seen.'[32] After demonstrating the importance of the resurrection for developing a definition of the KOG, Baugh helpfully supplements his definition:

> Hence we see the main definition of the kingdom of God we've been working with: it is the new creation, the new heavens and the new earth, fit out as a dwelling for Christ's resurrected new human race drawn from the four corners of the earth. And by saying that resurrection was necessary to enter the kingdom of God, Paul understood these things. For him the kingdom of God is the new creation begun at Christ's resurrection as Last Adam and at his exaltation as King. As risen King he rules now throughout this age for the consummate goal of our resurrection.[33]

Baugh also deals with Matthew 5 as one of his primary texts. As noted earlier, he says that 'the Beatitudes are not exhortations; they are royal pronouncements of God's favor upon kingdom citizens.'[34] Continuing to support his notion of the KOG as being inaugurated but not consummated, Baugh states regarding the beatitudes: 'By specifying that six of his beatitudes will not be fulfilled in this life but in the future, Jesus is revealing that the kingdom of heaven will be consummated in the future world, not in this creation.'[35]

---

31. G. Vos, 'The Kingdom of God,' in *Redemptive History and Biblical Interpretation: The Shorter Writings of Geerhardus Vos* (Phillipsburg, NJ: Presbyterian and Reformed, 1980), pp. 304-16, especially at p. 307.

32. Baugh, *Majesty on High*, p. 43.

33. Ibid., p. 58.

34. Ibid., p. 90.

35. Ibid., p. 91.

If this is so, and the emphasis is often on the spiritual nature of the KOG in Jesus' teaching, then the question presents itself: why was so much of the KOG in Jesus' ministry identified with the effects of a power working in the physical sphere? It is important to obtain the right nuanced answer to this question; otherwise one may slide into views of the KOG that have more in common with Rauschenbusch (more below) than with the Bible at this point. Vos answers:

> The answer is that the physical evils which the kingdom-power removes have a moral and spiritual background. Satan reigns not merely in the body, nor merely in the mind pathologically considered, but also in the heart and will of man as the instigator of sin and the source of moral evil. Hence Jesus made his miracles the occasion for suggesting and working the profounder change by which the bonds of sin were loosed and the rule of God set up anew in the entire inner life of men. Because this real connection exists, the physical process can become symbolical of the spiritual.[36]

And thus the goal of kingdom acts and manifestations in this earthly life are not merely to serve the renovation or even the transformation of this earthly existence, not even for the purposes of those renewals entering into the world to come eventually. No, they are but the symbols of something much greater to come. This raises another complex but extremely important question as well and it offers the opportunity for more reflection on exactly how the KOG is made manifest here on earth now.

## What is the relationship of the Church to the KOG?

It would be a mistake to merely equate the KOG with the church. The differences between the church as the people of God and the expression KOG are not insignificant, as Herman Bavinck notes.[37] After all, the KOG includes, as we have seen above, 'an eschatological term for the messianic kingdom with all its benefits.'[38] It is the new creation inaugurated but not consummated as described above, and its spiritual benefits are more than merely the fellowship of the saints in the church.

36. Vos, *Kingdom of God and the Church*, p. 55.

37. Herman Bavinck, *Reformed Dogmatics: Holy Spirit, Church, and New Creation* (Grand Rapids, MI: Baker, 2008), 4. 297.

38. Ibid.

Nevertheless, it is the church which is the means by which Christ 'distributes the benefits of the kingdom of God and lays the groundwork for its completion.'[39] Whereas the KOG is not to be woodenly equated with the church, it is the church which is the community that Jesus had in mind when he thought about the application of his ethics pronounced in the Sermon on the Mount.[40] So it is the church which God has chosen to advance His kingdom and no other institution on earth, and no other political community in the broader world. So, 'the church is the kingdom of heaven on earth. Though the church is not *identical* to the covenant of grace or the kingdom of heaven, it is precisely in the church that the covenant and kingdom are experienced until Christ returns.'[41] This is an important distinction since even the Westminster Confession of Faith can be misconstrued if read wrongly at this point. Notice what its chapter on the church says:

> The visible church, which is also catholic (that is, universal) under the gospel (that is, not confined to one nation, as it was before under the law), consists of all those throughout the world who profess the true religion, together with their children. It is the kingdom of the Lord Jesus Christ, the house and family of God, outside of which there is no ordinary possibility of salvation.[42]

A simplistic read of this paragraph would seem ostensibly to connect merely or equate the church with the KOG. However, this would be a mistake, as emphasized above, and that is not what the Westminster Assembly meant to communicate since both members of the Assembly and contemporaries of theirs would not have done so.[43] Rather, members of the Assembly identified the KOG with the 'proclamation of the gospel, with the coming of Jesus Christ, and with whatever else the passage and context might demand.'[44] Nevertheless, even though these two things are not equal, the church is certainly the kingdom of Christ. Yes, 'his kingdom is bigger than the church, but it certainly includes

---

39. Ibid., p. 298.

40. VanDrunen, *Living in God's Two Kingdoms*, p. 112.

41. Ibid., p. 116 [emphasis original].

42. Modern version, quoted in Chad Van Dixhoorn, *Confessing the Faith,* p. 338.

43. Ibid., p. 340.

44. Ibid., pp. 340-41.

the church, and God will cast a wide net to draw every kind of person into that church, into the kingdom of heaven, until his purposes are accomplished' (Matt. 13:47).[45]

One very important aspect of the relation of the church to the KOG is God's reign over His redeemed people.[46] Jesus made it clear that some will enter the kingdom (e.g., Mark 10:24, 23-25; Luke 18:17) and others will be cast out (Matt. 8:12; Luke 13:28). Paul did not mitigate his language with regard to some who will likewise not inherit the KOG (e.g., 1 Cor. 6:9; see also Gal. 5:21). This has important ramifications for what constitutes 'kingdom work.' As DeYoung and Gilbert suggest:

> Understanding that *kingdom* is a dynamic, relational word rather than a geographic one keeps us from thinking that 'extending the kingdom of God' is the right way to describe planting trees or delivering hot meals to the homeless. Sometimes people talk as if by renovating a city park or turning a housing slum into affordable, livable apartments, we are extending God's reign over that part or neighborhood. We're 'bringing order from chaos,' someone might say, and therefore expanding the kingdom. But as we've seen, the kingdom isn't geographical. Rather, it is defined relationally and dynamically; it exists where knees and hearts bow to the King and submit to him. And therefore you cannot 'expand the kingdom' by bringing peace and order and justice to a certain area of the world. Good deeds are good, but they don't broaden the borders of the kingdom. The only way the kingdom of God—the redemptive rule of God—is extended is when he brings another sinner to renounce sin and self-righteousness and bow his knee to King Jesus.[47]

DeYoung and Gilbert are quite clear in their book that such precise clarifications should not lead Christians into complacency, nor should it retard motivation of Christians for fighting against injustice and evil (in an appropriate context). Nevertheless, they don't pull their punches when they say that they fear 'that many church leaders are doing their people a disservice by leading them to hope too much for the betterment of society in "this present evil age," which still languishes in bondage and futility. Mission statements like "Transform the City and the World"

---

45. Ibid., p. 341.

46. Kevin DeYoung and Greg Gilbert, *What is the Mission of the Church?*, p. 121.

47. Ibid.

and "Change the City, Change the World" express a commendable desire, but simply go too far beyond what the Bible tells us we should expect to see in the world during this age, before Jesus returns.[48]

Charles Hodge emphasized similar teachings with respect to the KOG and the church, over a hundred years ago:

> As religion is essentially spiritual, an inward state, the kingdom of Christ as consisting of the truly regenerated, is not a visible body, except so far as goodness renders itself visible by its outward manifestations. Nevertheless, as Christ has enjoined upon his people duties which render it necessary that they should organize themselves in an external society, it follows that there is and must be a visible kingdom of Christ in the world. Christians are required to associate for public worship, for the admission and exclusion of members, for the administration of the sacraments, for the maintenance and propagation of the truth. They therefore form themselves into churches, and collectively constitute the visible kingdom of Christ on earth, consisting of all who profess the true religion, together with their children.[49]

For Hodge, the KOG is manifest in the members of Christ's church *not* when 'Christians are living in society to God's glory, this, too, is a manifestation of the kingdom of God,' as Keller asserted.[50] Keller argues that KOG work happens inside the church but also outside the realm of the church, in the culture. He says:

> Sometimes the Bible talks about the kingdom as though it operates inside the realms of the church alone; at other times it speaks as if it is outside the church, incorporating the entire world. Just as the biblical teaching on our fallenness gives us complementary truths that we must resolve to hold in balance—the curse and common grace—so too does the biblical teaching on Christ's redemption. His saving power is already at work, but not yet fully here. This saving power is at work in the gathered church, but it is not exclusive to the church .... We should expect healing from sin in all areas of life – private *and* public, within the church *and* out in culture. We must see the gathered church as the great vehicle for this restoration – and yet individual Christians out in the world can be said to be representatives of the kingdom as well. We cannot separate our spiritual or church life from our secular or cultural life. Every part of our life—vocational, civic, familial,

---

48. Ibid., pp. 129-30.
49. Charles Hodge, *Systematic Theology*, 2.604.
50. Keller, *Center Church*, p. 230.

269

recreational, material, sexual, financial, political—is to be presented as a living sacrifice to God (Rom. 12:1-2).[51]

I suggest that Keller's exhortation is not properly nuanced; rather, when Christians perform their spiritual duties as members of the church, *that* is when they manifest the KOG to the world according to Hodge and the scriptures. In other words, it is in their *sacred duties* (e.g., attending worship, praying), not in their *cultural duties*, that Christians manifest the KOG to the watching world. Since there is so much confusion in this area, before we move on in our discussion, it is worth our while to look at two Reformed luminaries in further detail who spent quite a bit of time engaging this very issue on the relationship of the church and the KOG: Geerhardus Vos and Herman Ridderbos.

## Geerhardus Vos on the Nature of the Kingdom of God and the Church, a Picture of a Biblical Theologian's Work in Progress

Vos had been criticized in reviews of *The Kingdom of God and the Church* for too closely identifying the KOG with the church; however, the case has been made that more careful readings of Vos do not allow such a critique. Vos' views were nuanced to be sure.[52] What is especially valuable for us to examine, given the subject of this book, is Vos' teaching on the KOG vis-à-vis liberal notions of the KOG that were prominent in his own day. Vos was especially concerned that those liberal notions undermined the historical reliability especially of the Gospel accounts.[53] I am not an expert on Geerhardus Vos, nor do I read Dutch, which I think would help extremely with an accurate assessment of his views;[54] nevertheless, there is a great need in our own circles to upright what has become a 'tilted' view on that biblical theologian's views on the KOG.

51. Ibid., p. 229.

52. See Danny Olinger's introduction to Geerhardus Vos, *The Teaching of Jesus concerning the Kingdom of God and the Church* (see Fontes Press, 2017) or the earlier version published by Wipf and Stock, 1998), especially pp. xxiii-xxv.

53. See Olinger, *Geerhardus Vos*, p. 128.

54. Here is a tremendous opportunity for a young scholar who knows Dutch, or is willing to learn to read Dutch, to assess responsibly Vos' views on this important subject. Perhaps there is a doctoral dissertation to be developed here?

There is no doubt that when one examines Vos' teaching (all his writings) on the KOG, it becomes evident that Vos was challenging the doctrine of the kingdom being represented in his own day by liberal social gospel preachers.[55] Vos may not have written as voluminously on the subject of the KOG as Ridderbos;[56] nevertheless, given his gifts of erudition and precision, Vos' views should be consulted frequently and regularly on this topic and perhaps given even equal consideration as to their value for thinking about this subject.[57]

If I were a betting man, then my bet would be that Vos had the social gospel of Walter Rauschenbusch (1861-1918), Professor of Church History in Rochester Theological Seminary, in mind when he wrote on our topic. Rauschenbusch was arguably the most important theorist of the famous social gospel movement in the early 1900s. Rochester functioned as the primary site for him to engage in sustained reflection on the kingdom of God for his entire career.[58] H. Sheldon Smith considered him 'the foremost molder of American Christian thought in his generation.'[59] His thought undoubtedly influenced Reinhold Niebuhr and Martin Luther King. Jr., as well.[60] He is someone with whom Vos would have been intimately familiar since they were contemporaries. Vos was concerned to offer a redemptive-historical look at the doctrine of the KOG in the midst of the liberal construals of the doctrine among contemporaries.[61]

The social gospel movement, the reader will recall from the discussion at the beginning of this book, was a response to the problems of industrialization and all the ills, as well as the wealth, that had occurred

---

55. This is especially the case with those who wanted to make the teaching on the kingdom entirely immanent, but also with regards to those that want to make the teaching on the kingdom entirely future.

56. Here I have in mind especially, Hermann Ridderbos, *The Coming of the Kingdom*, translated by H. de Jongste and edited by Raymond O. Zorn (Philadelphia, PA: Presbyterian and Reformed, 1962).

57. A point well made by Stonehouse in a review. See Olinger's introduction to *The Teaching of Jesus concerning the Kingdom of God*, p. xx.

58. Darryl Hart, *A Secular Faith*, p. 102.

59. Quoted in Ibid., p. 102.

60. Ibid., p. 103.

61. See Danny E. Olinger, *Geerhardus Vos: Reformed Biblical Theologian, Confessional Presbyterian* (Philadelphia, PA: 2018), pp. 123-25.

(extreme affluence for some, and severe harsh work conditions for others). In order to understand the influence of the liberal social gospel writers of Vos' day, one needs to describe and explore Rauschenbusch's views (see Chapter 1 of this book).

Before moving on to Vos' reflections upon this subject, it is worth asking why the OT prophets were so exercised about the problems of social injustice that they saw all around them. Doing so helps us to realize that *there really is something new* about the kingdom which Christ brings in contrast to the context in which the prophets were preaching. Let me explain.

In the Hebrew nation, the theocracy was of this world. Moreover, this theocracy was meant to typify the perfected KOG, something to be realized in the distant future when Christ comes a second time.[62] All their religious, national, social, and municipal affairs were of concern to the kings and especially the prophets. The prophets were covenant lawyers who had the solemn responsibility to hold the kings and the Israelites responsible to the stipulations of the covenant they had signed on to, so to speak. That theocracy could not 'coexist in time and place with any other national organization.'[63] *Therefore, we should expect that the prophets would be engaged with the social and civil life of the nation.* That was part and parcel of their job description since they were to maintain and sustain this unique and special theocratic situation among the people, the king, the surrounding nations and ultimately God.

However, the kingdom of Christ is different. It 'being designed to embrace all other kingdoms, can exist under all forms of civil government without interfering with any. It was especially in this view that Christ declared that his kingdom was not of this world.'[64] Once Christ comes and inaugurates the new covenant, we are no longer in a theocracy. Therefore, we should expect that the preaching on the KOG in the new covenant era subsequent to Christ's coming and Pentecost would be very different than it was in the time of the prophets.

Vos, in his early teaching on the subject of the KOG (1903), ended that book with a summary chapter called 'Recapitulation.' Here he listed

---

62. See Olinger, *Geerhardus Vos*, p. 152.

63. Hodge, *Systematic Theology*, 2. 605.

64. Ibid.

seven principles of teaching on the KOG. In his fifth point, he says: 'Jesus' doctrine of the kingdom as both inward and outward, coming first in the heart of man and afterwards in the external world, upholds *primacy of the spiritual and ethical* over the physical.'[65] Olinger comments at this point: 'The unseen realities of heaven constitute the essence of the kingdom of God. Liberalism tied the ethical solely to this world, which left no place for biblical faith and repentance. There is an ethical dimension to the kingdom, but it has to do with repentance from sin and faith in Christ.'[66]

Furthermore, one of his last published writings, which contains some of his most mature reflections on the topic of the prophets' preaching, seems to reflect clearly that Vos held very different opinions about the KOG from the liberal writers of his day, especially Rauschenbusch as described above. He says:

> The prophetic condemnation of the social sin of Israel does not have its deepest root in humanitarian motives. The humanitarian element is not, of course, absent. Nor could it be absent, for it is as old as the theocracy. The law takes the poor and defenceless under its special protection. It is in keeping with this, that the chief institutions of the theocracy, for example, that of the kingdom, bear a conspicuously humane, beneficent character. And we find this preserved and further developed in the prophets. Their rebuke of social sin attaches itself to the distinction between rich and poor, powerful and weak, a distinction that has been at all times the symptom and occasion, though not the cause, of social disease .... Not wealth and luxury in themselves the prophets attack .... His [Amos's] charge is that wealth and luxury such as were observable in his day render their possessors blind to all higher religious interests .... To the prophet it is the sinfulness of the wrong social conduct, to the modern social preacher it is too often the injuriousness to the social organism, that stands in the foreground. The prophets view the facts in their relation to God, as measured by the standards of absolute ethics and religion; the modern sociological enthusiast views them mainly, if not exclusively, in their bearing upon the welfare of man. What the prophets feature is the religious in the social; what many at the present time proclaim is the social devoid of or indifferent to the religious.[67]

---

65. Vos, *The Kingdom of God and the Church*, p. 103.

66. Olinger, *Geerhardus Vos*, p. 132.

67. Geerhardus Vos, *Biblical Theology: Old and New Testaments* (Grand Rapids, Michigan: Eerdmans, 1977), pp. 274-276.

It bewilders me to no end trying to understand why Keller didn't cite these later reflections as well as Vos' earlier writings. It is true that one can find places where Vos sounds transformationalist (and Keller is happy to quote these). This is probably due to the fact that Vos confirmed the supremacy of God in all things and this formed the foundation of our Lord's doctrine of the KOG.[68] Indeed, when just surveying Vos' writing on the KOG, one can find statements sprinkled here and there that might be construed under the category of cultural transformationalist; however, these statements are few and far between in his writings on the KOG.[69] Was Keller unaware of these later views of Vos? Did his goal to transcend the cut and thrust of debate over Christianity and culture move him to cite something from Vos that would seem more 'balanced' so that one's expression of Christianity can make room for cultic and cultural expressions of Christianity in this world? I really do not know. Perhaps there is yet another reason for this lacunae?

## Did Vos consistently maintain his views of Christ and Culture throughout his career?

My argument in this section of the chapter is that Tim Keller, in his book, *Center Church: Doing Balanced, Gospel-Centered Ministry in Your City*, has misrepresented Geerhardus Vos' view of the relationship between the KOG and the church. This is because Keller only gives a small representation of Vos' significant publications on this topic. In order to cite an author authoritatively, one should take into consideration the entire corpus of the author's work, especially if that survey represents significant, let alone nuanced shifts in the author's reflections. The latter would merely take a slice of time or topic out of the author's representative writings, whereas the former approach would take the totality of the author's views and seek to observe how the author had changed through time with respect to certain ideas.

Keller, in citing *The Teaching of Jesus Concerning the KOG*, represents Vos' teaching as saying that the KOG 'mainly operates through the church, but that it also operates through Christians who integrate their

---

68. Olinger, *Geerhardus Vos*, p. 130.

69. See, e.g., *A Geerhardus Vos Anthology*: The reader can even quickly skim the following work (though not as ideal as reading Vos completely): Danny E. Olinger (ed.), *A Geerhardus Vos Anthology: Biblical and Theological Insights Alphabetically Arranged* (Phillipsburg, NJ: P & R Publishing Company, 2005), especially pp. 165-75.

faith and their work.'[70] To support this claim, he cites the previous book. However, first of all, he cites the wrong pages for the book's quote,[71] and then he digresses into commentary on Vos' views, representing his comments as fairly representing Vos' views:

> Vos immediately makes it clear, however, that the institutional church should not have political power or control society through the state. So Vos states, *in summary*, that (1) the main way to see the kingdom forces of God at work is in the institutional church, whose main job is to minister through the Word and sacrament to win people and disciple them in Christ, and (2) when Christians are living in society to God's glory, this, too, is a manifestation of the kingdom of God. Without this *rare balance*, there is a tendency to see the kingdom as either strictly spiritual and operating within the church or mainly social and operating in the liberation movements out in the world. Vos's biblical balance will enable us to avoid imbalances in the cultural engagement and missional church debates in particular. I recommend reading his book carefully and in its entirety.[72]

I also recommend reading Vos' works in their entirety carefully. For example, it is true that in his earliest works, for example, his *Reformed Dogmatics*, he does make statements that sound as if they cohere with Keller's assessment, for Vos, even in his earliest writings, distinguishes between the KOG and the church in narrow and broad terms. He states:

> On the one hand, 'kingdom of God' is the narrower, and 'church' the wider concept. While the church has both a visible and invisible side, and so can often be perceived of an entire nation, the kingdom of God in its various meanings is the invisible spiritual principle. It is the lordship Christ exercises over our souls if we truly belong to Him, our submission to His sovereign authority, our being conformed and joined by living faith to His body with its many members .... On the other hand, the 'kingdom of God' or 'of heaven' is a broader concept than that of the church. In fact, it is presented to us as leaven that must permeate everything, as a mustard seed that must grow into a tree that with its branches covers all of life. Plainly, such a thing may not be said of the concept 'church.'[73]

---

70. Keller, *Center Church*, p. 229.

71. He cites pp. 162-63, when it is actually p. 83.

72. Ibid., p. 230.

73. G. Vos, *Reformed Dogmatics: Vol. Five, Ecclesiology, The Means of Grace, Eschatology*, trans. and ed. by Richard B. Gaffin, Jr. with Kim Batteau and Allan Janssen (Bellingham,

It would seem that Vos was still extending his thoughts on the relationship between the KOG and the church in similar trajectories when he wrote in 1903, in the book that Keller recommends:

> That Christ is King in this church and all authority exercised within the church-body derives from him is an important principle of church government, which those who endeavor to distinguish between the kingdom of God and the visible church do not always sufficiently keep in mind. From this, however, it does not necessarily follow, that the visible church is the only outward expression of the invisible kingdom. Undoubtedly the kingship of God, as his recognized and applied supremacy, is intended to pervade and control the whole of human life in all its forms of existence .... There is a sphere of science, a sphere of art, a sphere of the family and of the state, a sphere of commerce and industry. Whenever one of these spheres comes under the controlling influence of the principle of the divine supremacy and glory, and this outwardly reveals itself, there we can truly say that the kingdom of God has become manifest .... But we may safely affirm two things. On the one hand, his doctrine of the kingdom was founded on such a profound and broad conviction of the absolute supremacy of God in all things, that he could not but look upon every normal and legitimate province of human life as intended to form part of God's kingdom. On the other hand, it was not his intention that this result should be reached by making human life in all its spheres subject to the visible church ... [he admits the old covenant and the theocracy did do this][74]

This is one of Vos' earliest writings, however. Moreover, when you read all of Vos' writings in context on the subject of the KOG, what we discover is a moving away from a categorization like what Keller has given him and especially anything that might more closely align him with anything that smacks of the KOG as Rauschenbusch would construe things. In many respects, I think that a more careful read of Vos' take on the KOG can help people in the church recognize their kingdom responsibilities and duties. We need to think clearly and precisely in these areas so that people know what they are doing. Geerhardus Vos, when it comes to his thinking on the nature of the KOG and the church, is a picture of a Biblical theologian's work in progress. There is no doubt that when one

---

WA: Lexham Press, 2016), pp. 8-9. Or, see Vos' comments in *The Kingdom of God and The Church*, pp. 88-89.

74. See Vos, *The Kingdom of God and the Church*, pp. 88-89.

examines Vos' teaching on the KOG, it becomes evident that he was challenging the doctrine of the kingdom being represented in his own day. Vos, however, did not write as voluminously on the subject of the KOG in comparison with Ridderbos.[75]

## What about Ridderbos?

I treat Ridderbos and Vos as almost on equal terms when it comes to their comments on the KOG. N. B. Stonehouse compared Ridderbos' work to Vos' writing on the KOG.[76] Indeed it is remarkable that the two came to almost the same positions even though Ridderbos apparently was unaware of Vos' work when he wrote his own views on the KOG originally in Dutch. Arguably Ridderbos wrote more on the subject, as mentioned above; but because of Vos' tendency to write in precise language without verbosity, his ruminations are equally significant. Even so, where Ridderbos most closely touches on the issue of the relationship of the church to the KOG, his thoughts seem to align closely with the trajectory I'm arguing for:

> There can be no uncertainty about either the connection or the difference between these two fundamental notions: *The basileia* [kingdom] *is the great divine work of salvation in its fulfillment and consummation in Christ; the ekklesia* [church] *is the people elected and called by God and sharing in the bliss of the basileia.* Logically, the *basileia* ranks first, and not the *ekklesia*. The former, therefore, has a much more comprehensive content. It represents the all-embracing perspective, it denotes the consummation of all history, brings both grace and judgment, has cosmic dimensions, fills time and eternity. The *ekklesia* in all this is the people who in this great drama have

---

75. Here I have in mind especially *The Coming of the Kingdom*.

76. This discussion is found in Danny Olinger, *Geerhardus Vos: Reformed Biblical Theologian, Confessional Presbyterian* (Philadelphia, PA: 2018), pp. 134-35. Stonehouse wrote a review of the Dutch edition of Ridderbos' *The Coming of the Kingdom* (review of *De Komst van het Koninkrijk*, by H. N. Ridderbos, *WTJ* 14 [1952]). On p. 160, he writes: 'Broadly speaking the same conception of the significance and scope of the kingdom of God appears in both volumes, which is rather remarkable in view of the consideration that Vos's treatise evidently was not known to Ridderbos at the time that he wrote the work. If one takes in account, however, the fact that Ridderbos like Vos stands squarely in the stream of the Reformed traditions, sharing its convictions and insights, and is also a scholar of wide learning and rare exegetical skill, the larger measure of agreement will not appear as a bare coincidence. It is refreshing, nevertheless, to receive a new reminder that after fifty years Vos's fundamental perspectives and conclusions are by no means outdated.'

been placed on the side of God in Christ by virtue of the divine election and covenant. They have been given the divine promise, have been brought to manifestation and gathered together by the preaching of the gospel, and will inherit the redemption of the kingdom now and in the great future.[77]

Therefore, for Ridderbos as well as Vos, the KOG is a more comprehensive concept than the church. However, it is the church, and the church alone, that God has determined to be the distributor of the benefits of his kingdom and even to lay the foundation for its completion. Ridderbos does allow for a cosmic dimension to the KOG in the quote above (more on this below). Therefore, although the church should not merely be equated with the kingdom, it is through her members that the KOG is made manifest to the watching world. Moreover, *pace* the liberal view of the KOG that would view kingdom activity as fighting social injustice in the wide world, we have seen that the KOG is made manifest to the watching world when the church of God performs her duties prescribed by her Lord for the perfecting of the saints: ministering the Word by proclaiming the truth of the Gospel, administering the sacraments and church discipline, and caring for the poor, most especially in the church.

Finally, several ancillary questions remain before we move to the next chapter. What exactly is the goal of the KOG: does it include merely redeemed individuals or something significantly greater? When was this goal first envisioned in the mind of God? For the answer to the second of these questions, we return to the notion introduced in Chapter 1: the church was intentioned in the covenant of redemption, or the mind of God in the *Pactum Salutis*.

## The World to Come: the 'aionian-character' of the KOG

The kingdom of heaven, as VanDrunen says, 'as the full flowering of the redemptive kingdom, is an amazing reality. It was the original goal of the first Adam, but now Christ, the last Adam has become its king and made his people its citizens.'[78] There remains one important question for us to wrestle with before we leave this subject of the KOG and

---

77. Ridderbos, *The Coming of the Kingdom*, pp. 354-55.

78. David VanDrunen, *Living in God's Two Kingdoms*, p. 111.

its particular relationship to the church: the *aionian-character* of the KOG, its relationship to the church in the final outcome of things. By introducing this terminology, my goal is not to be over technical or introduce unnecessary doctrine. Rather, the choice of words that Paul, in particular, chooses is very selective. Vos rightly maintained that God himself was the primary teaching of the KOG, not the kingdom itself.[79]

By using *aionian-character*, we are picking up on a discussion that Geerhardus Vos has at the end of his book, *The Pauline Eschatology*.[80] The Greek word, *aionian* (used by Paul some fourteen times), can be traced back to the Hebrew word *'olam*.[81] The importance of these terms for the present discussion is that the present age represents the opposite of the world to come, the future 'aion' as expressed by the Rabbis so frequently. We engage in this discussion at this point in order to plumb the depths of the goal of the mission of the church. In other words, if the argument about the KOG is true as discussed above, i.e., that it is the new creation which is at least somewhat inaugurated now in the present but will be consummated in the future, then meditating on the future outcome of this new creation is not mere abstract speculation but becomes one of the most imminently practical subjects for the pilgrim saint living in this age. As Vos declares so eloquently:

> Eschatology ceases for those who have learned, and in principle experienced this, to be an abstract speculation: it becomes the profoundest and most practical of all thought-complexes because they, like Paul, live and move and have their redemptively-religious treasures in God.[82]

Vos identifies four actual elements that will unfold themselves in the future: the Spirit, life, glory, and the kingdom of God.[83] As the reader can imagine, we are most interested in the KOG element, but to unpack

---

79. That is why he insisted that one should always speak of either the Kingdom of God or the Kingdom of Heaven, but not merely 'the Kingdom.' See Olinger, *Geerhardus Vos*, p. 126.

80. See Geerhardus Vos, *The Pauline Eschatology*, foreword by Richard B. Gaffin, Jr. (first published 1930 by Princeton University Press and Reprinted by Presbyterian and Reformed, 1986; Phillipsburg, New Jersey: Presbyterian and Reformed, 1986), pp. 288-316.

81. Vos' work predates the definitive work done by E. Jenni on this Hebrew word and thus could have been strengthened by the insights which Jenni gave.

82. Ibid., pp. 293-94.

83. Ibid., p. 298.

this rich teaching of Scripture, we need also to talk about another integrated element with that doctrine, 'life'.

To understand what is promised in the future as consummate 'life' for the saint one needs to understand what was promised in the present world as a bountiful blessing, which signifies the greater blessing of life in heaven. Vos discusses the integral relation between mundane 'life' and the world to come, or 'eschatological life.'[84]

I have also discussed the symbolical value of 'life' in the OT, with all its material connotations of blessing, and its connection to eschatological life, or entitlement to heaven.[85] Some scholars have emphasized the fact that the new Jerusalem will be composed of the glorified saints and Scripture doesn't tell us much more than that. Others have emphasized that heaven will contain the glorified saints as well as transformed world cultural institutions, or in some manner the renewed heavens and earth. I will discuss, albeit briefly, some of the key passages below; however, my focus will be on what we can say with authority scripturally about the new age of the KOG in the world to come.

One passage that is often invoked to support this exegesis is Romans 8:19-25:

> For the creation waits with eager longing for the revealing of the sons of God. For the creation was subjected to futility, not willingly, but because of him who subjected it, in hope that the creation itself will be set free from its bondage to corruption and obtain the freedom of the glory of the children of God. For we know that the whole creation has been groaning together in the pains of childbirth until now. And not only the creation, but we ourselves, who have the firstfruits of the Spirit, groan inwardly as we wait eagerly for adoption as sons, the redemption of our bodies. For in this hope we were saved. Now hope that is seen is not hope. For who hopes for what he sees? But if we hope for what we do not see, we wait for it with patience (ESV).

Many Reformed luminaries have interpreted this passage (among others) as teaching about the resurrection of the sons of God and of them

---

84. Ibid., p. 306.

85. See the author's article, 'Leviticus 18:5 and Deuteronomy 30:1-14 in Biblical Theological Development: Entitlement to Heaven Foreclosed and Proffered,' pp. 109-46 in *The Law is Not of Faith: Essays on Works and Grace in the Mosaic Covenant*, edited by Bryan D. Estelle, J. V. Fesko, and David VanDrunen (Phillipsburg, NJ: P & R Publishing, 2009), especially pp. 116-19.

sharing in a renewed creation in the world-to-come.[86] Calvin himself seemed reluctant to speculate about the exact nature of the new creation, since the scriptures are relatively silent on the topic.[87] Even so, he talks about the kingdom of Christ in decisive terms such as *instauro, restituo*, and *renovatio*, words often translated interchangeably as 'renewal,' 'restoration,' and 'renovation.'[88] He often appealed to Acts 3:21; however, his *locus classicus* is Romans 8:19-21 when it comes to talking about the restoration of creation.

Others have emphasized that the continuity between the former world and the world-to-come is at precisely this point: the resurrection of the believers' bodies. It is primarily believers in the Lamb who provide the point of continuity between the former world and the new creation.[89] It is not without significance that Revelation 21:1-10 describes the New Jerusalem in terms of the congregation of the redeemed saints. Some interpret this passage as a literal interpretation of the physical description of the city of God descending from above, but this seems highly implausible. The 'bride of the lamb' (vv. 9-10), which John is shown in the next verses, is actually the 'eternal community of the redeemed' (21:2). Moreover, this is the bride identified by John, i.e., 'Come I will show you...' (v. 9) as the holy city Jerusalem (v. 10). Note that 21:3 emphasizes the corporate identity of the adopted people of God, thus the destiny of the whole elect people of God: *'Behold, the dwelling place of God is with man. He will dwell with them, and they will be his people, and God himself will be with them as their God.'*

We will avoid both of these extremes: the transformationalist impulse to accent the renewed cosmos on the one hand and what may be termed

---

86. See, e.g., Charles Hodge, *Commentary on the Epistle to the Romans* (1886; repr., Grand Rapids: Eerdmans, 1960); Herman Bavinck, *Reformed Dogmatics*, vol. 1, *Prolegomena*, ed. John Bolt, trans. John Vriend (Grand Rapids: Baker Academic, 2003), p. 445; Bavinck, *Holy Spirit, Church, and New Creation*, pp. 715-24; Douglas J. Moo, *The Epistle to the Romans*, NICNT (Grand Rapids: Eerdmans, 1996), p. 517; Beale, *New Testament Biblical Theology*, p. 257.

87. See, e.g., Tuininga, *Calvin's Political Theology*, p. 113.

88. Ibid., p. 113.

89. See, e.g., Meredith G. Kline, 'Death, Leviathan, and Martyrs: Isaiah 24:1-27:1,' in *A Tribute to Gleason Archer: Essays on the Old Testament*, ed. Walter C. Kaiser Jr. and Ronald F. Youngblood (Chicago: Moody Press, 1986), pp. 229-49, who sees Isaiah 24:1–27:1 as significantly influencing the apostle's discussion in Romans 9–11. A shorter summary of his arguments is found in David VanDrunen, *Living in God's Two Kingdoms*, pp. 63-71, 102-3.

as 'excessive individualism' on the other hand, which might limit the continuity between the old and the new to merely the resurrected bodies of the elect saints.

I find Vos' teaching to cohere with what we have discussed thus far and not to exceed the Scriptural teaching given heretofore frankly. As mentioned above, Vos mentioned four areas touching on the eternal estate. Here, I focus on the KOG. Imperishableness is part and parcel of the new 'life' mentioned above.[90] This is the great and central contrast between what we behold now and what we hope for in the future.

> A permissible paraphrase would be: the things that in this lower, preliminary, state engage our interest are transitory and corruptible; the things which in the present dispensation the believer cannot yet lay hold of by vision are the eternal, incorruptible realities.[91]

Vos also maintains here, as he does elsewhere, that this eschatological prospect was present from the beginning.[92]

Instructive in this regard is the fact that this 'life' is equated with the KOG in the teaching of Jesus. The reader will recall that when the rich young ruler approached our Lord, he asked him a question about how one may enter 'eternal life.' After Jesus answered, the disciples were flummoxed about the difficulty of anyone rich entering into eternal life, but Jesus answers his disciples in such a manner that he equates 'eternal life' with 'the kingdom God' (cf., Mark 10:23; Luke 18:24). No wonder that this becomes Paul's all-consuming passion. As Vos says, 'All Paul's labor was a most strenuous endeavor to bring the restlessly-temporal to where it would lose itself in the forever-undisturbable *aionian*. There is no passage in the Epistles indicative of an opposite trend or desire. There may be heavens in the plural numerically or structurally, but there is no succession of ages or worlds to come.'[93]

We may conclude this section therefore by noting that the accent of the scriptures with regard to the future age are on its incorruptible state. Based on Romans 8 and Revelation 21 (minimally), we may say with confidence that the New Jerusalem will be comprised of resurrected

---

90. Vos, *Pauline Eschatology*, p. 291.

91. Ibid., pp. 292-91.

92. Ibid., p. 304.

93. Ibid., p. 316.

saints. As far as the renewal of this world I have little to add and find that scripture by and large is silent on the issue even though many in the past have seen the transformation of this world as part of the world-to-come.

## Conclusion

In this chapter we explored the nature of the KOG and its relationship to the church. First, we traced some historical backgrounds, interacting especially with Calvin's seminal teaching on the KOG and his claim that its essential nature is spiritual.

Next, I traced the main points of a recent, clear, and simplified approach to the KOG by Professor Steven Baugh. Next, we discussed the relationship of the KOG to the church and saw that most have construed the concept of the KOG to be the larger category than merely the church. Nevertheless, the church is the sole institution on earth for carrying out the goals of the KOG.

As we began to trace the writings of some Reformed luminaries (especially G. Vos) on the topic of the KOG, we discovered how different and distinct his message was in contrast with the social gospel preachers of their own day, in particular Rauschenbusch. These differences became especially clear when we focused in upon the ministry of the prophets.

Finally, we looked forward to the 'aionian-character' of the KOG, its relationship to the church and the final outcome of things. Here, I leaned heavily on Vos' last chapter, 'the eternal state,' in his book, *The Pauline Eschatology*. Instead of focusing on the transformation of cultural matters from this temporal world in preparation for the world-to come, or emphasizing an excessive individualism, the corporate church should stick to its God-given job description: preparing the bride of Christ (individually and corporately) by the right administration of the means of grace and discipline in anticipation of entering the world to come.

# CHAPTER 11

# Primary Mission of the Church, Confessional Teaching

In this chapter our goal will be to examine confessional teaching on the primary mission of the church. I am assuming, and rightly so, that the Westminster Confession of Faith (WCF), 'one of the noblest uninspired expositions of Divine truth anywhere to be found,' was compiled by men 'who in an age of profound theological learning and great attainments in Divine truth were conspicuous among their contemporaries,' as Bannerman rightly asserts.[1] If the confessions and catechisms of our church do not teach the subject and see it as a derivative teaching of the Holy Scriptures, then perhaps this entire endeavor has been a misguided one and we should pack our bags, put our books away, and walk away from our overheated keyboards on our computers. However, such is not the case. What we will demonstrate in this chapter is that the biblical foundations are secure. What the church is not, as discussed in Chapters 4 through 9, are found in the confession as limiting boundaries provided by our Lord Himself. And positively stated, the very kinds of activities we have seen prescribed for the mission of the church throughout this project are the ones that the WCF takes pains to delineate.

---

1. Bannerman, *The Church of Christ*, p. 172.

# Chapter 20 of the WCF

Darryl Hart begins his massive treatment on the history of Calvinism is what seems—at first glance—like an odd place.[2] Describing a gathering of Christians in the home of the printer Christopher Froschauer, Hart describes what took place:

> Church teaching required Christians during the Lenten season to abstain from meat. In a bold act of defiance, comparable to flag burning today, the assembled ate the sausages served by the host. One of those present was the local priest, Ulrich Zwingli, who was surprised by the food and abstained from eating. Even so, Zwingli defended the choice of food the following month with a sermon entitled 'On the Choice and Freedom of Foods.' His reasoning was simple even if it captured a theme at the heart of the Swiss Reformation: if the Bible did not require a Lenten fast or specify foods to be avoided, then Christians were free to eat.[3]

Many times the notion of Christian liberty has been mishandled minimally and abused maximally. In other words, Christian liberty should not be used as a pretense in order to sin. Neither was the teaching ever about the church being freed 'to do things (such as create boards to which it could delegate the work of missions) about which Scripture is silent.'[4] Rather, with regard to the two kingdoms doctrine, Reformed theologians and confessions have insisted that Christian liberty is 'in regard to the justified individual, who was freed in the civil kingdom from any obligation to do things *contrary* to the teaching of Scripture and in the spiritual kingdom from an obligation to do things *beside* the teaching of Scripture.'[5]

This is why I begin this chapter by turning to the WCF, Chapter 20. This pristine statement about Christian liberty declares not only in paragraph 1 what Christ has purchased for us (freedom from the guilt of sin and bondage to Satan) but boldly proclaims in the next paragraph that 'God alone is Lord of the conscience and has left it free from the doctrines and commandments of men.'[6] Therefore, Christians must

---

2. D. G. Hart, *Calvinism: A History* (New Haven, CT: Yale University Press, 2013).

3. Ibid., p. 1.

4. VanDrunen, *Natural Law and the Two Kingdoms*, p. 258.

5. Ibid., p. 259 [emphasis original].

6. The quote is from the modern version in Chad Van Dixhoorn, *Confessing the Faith*, p. 262.

look to God's Word alone for direction and help in understanding the primary mission of the church. To follow a man-made polity without clear warrant from Scripture would be to bind the conscience of the sheep unduly.

## Chapter 23 of the WCF

Next, we begin with the chapter delineating the limits on the civil magistrate, then we move to chapters covering the role and responsibility of the church. It is also the chapter that has undergone the most revision through the centuries. The historic text (23.3) reads:

> The civil magistrate may not assume to himself the administration of the Word and sacraments, or the power of the keys of the kingdom of heaven: yet, he has authority, and it is his duty, to take order, that unity and peace be preserved in the church, that the truth of God be kept pure, and entire; that all blasphemies and heresies be suppressed; all corruptions and abuses in worship and discipline prevented, or reformed; and all the ordinances of God duly settled, administered, and observed. For the better effecting whereof, he has power to call synods, to be present at them, and to provide that whatsoever is transacted in them, be according to the mind of God.[7]

This teaching about the civil magistrate, especially in the first line, and what it is *not* to do in ecclesiastical matters seems clear enough. But, the notion prevalent at the time, that the magistrate had the responsibility to promote true religion in Scotland and England, was dominant. This is evident in the Scottish National Covenant (1638) and the Solemn League and Covenant (1643).[8] Nevertheless, this did not keep ministers from changing the language of the Confession in subsequent years. For example, in Scotland, already in 1647, the Assembly of the Church of Scotland (which ratified the WCF as the Confession of the Scottish Church) expressly excepted this point with regard to the magistrate's power to summon synods.[9] John Witherspoon in the eighteenth century led the church to revise a few paragraphs in the Confession at just this point since it seemed inconsistent with what was said elsewhere in the

---

7. The text of the Confession is taken from the best historical rendition as presented by VanDixhoorn, *Confessing the Faith*, p. 311.

8. See J. V. Fesko, *The Theology of the Westminster Standards*, p. 294.

9. Bannerman, *Church of Christ*, p. 179.

WCF. Later yet, American Presbyterians thought that the language about civil magistrates possessing the power to call synods or councils to be inconsistent with Scripture.[10] The divines at the Westminster Assembly cited examples from both the OT and the NT of such practice, and of course the Westminster Assembly itself had been called upon by Parliament to offer doctrinal advice. Nevertheless, even during the assembly there was tension between the House of Commons and the Assembly.[11]

Therefore, long before the Presbytery in Philadelphia revised the third paragraph of Chapter 23 of the WCF (1788), there had been rumblings in the American church against the notion of an establishment church, i.e., that the government should establish one church in a nation. Such unrest and uneasiness was in keeping with the biblical teaching that God established different governments in two distinct spheres: one civil and one ecclesial, as discussed earlier in this book. Therefore, they revised 23.3 to read: 'As Jesus Christ has appointed a regular government and discipline in his church, no law of any commonwealth should interfere with, prevent, or hinder their proper exercise among the voluntary members of any denomination or Christians, according to their own profession and belief.'[12] Today, Presbyterians in America accept this as their confession. Not only is this more coherent with our civil constitution, it is also more congruent, it seems to this author, with the teaching of Scripture. It also recognizes that Christ has given gifts to His church, namely, officers who administer the Word and sacrament, elders who rule, and finally deacons who serve the physical needs of Christ's sheep.

Also implemented in the 1788 revisions was the notion that the magistrate was the protector of the church, using a mixed metaphor taken from Isaiah 49:23, that the state is to be a 'nursing father' to the church, providing for her protection, declaring that it is the 'duty of the civil magistrates to protect the church of our common Lord', while not 'giving the preference to any denomination of Christians above the rest, in such a manner that all ecclesiastical persons whatever shall enjoy the

---

10. See Leah Farish, 'The First Amendment's Religion Clauses: The Calvinist Document that Interprets Them Both,' *JRS* 12 (2010): pp. 1-22, who argues that the revision of the WCF in 1788 had influence on the First Amendment's religion clauses.

11. See Van Dixhoorn's discussion, *Confessing the Faith*, pp. 312-15.

12. Ibid., p. 311.

full, free, and unquestioned liberty of discharging every part of their sacred functions, without violence or danger.' Romans 13:1-6 is often cited as a supporting proof text as well. In spite of the wisdom of such a recommended course of action, such an idea may be compatible with the Bible, but it may not be an idea directly taught in the Bible.[13] But God not only provides the human race with a society in which it is intended to thrive and live in neighborly concord, He also shows great concern for the corporate body of Christians He gathers together as well.

## The Headship of Christ

As I emphasized at the very beginning of this book, God exercises such watchful care over us that He doesn't just provide for us individually as Christians, but He gathers us into a society, and He provides everything necessary for our corporate life as well. Calvin, in his *Institutes of Christian Religion*, understood the profundity of this point for the sake of the community. He says:

> For as no city or township can function without magistrate and polity, so the church of God (as I have already taught, but am now compelled to repeat) needs a spiritual polity. This is, however, quite distinct from the civil polity, yet does not hinder or threaten it but rather greatly helps and furthers it. Therefore, this power of jurisdiction will be nothing, in short, but an order framed for the preservation of the spiritual polity.[14]

Within this society that God has called together, there must be officer-bearers. For every society must have office-bearers in order to have power of action and the authority to carry out policies. The difference between voluntary private societies in this regard is that office-bearers derive authority from the consent and permission of their members. Although the same is true in the church, an important distinction at just this point should not be ignored. The power 'of the Church is directly from God, being exercised and enforced, not only because of the permission or consent of its members, but because it is a positive Divine institution, apart from that consent.'[15] Indeed, the church of Christ is more than a

---

13. See Van Dixhoorn's discussion, *Confessing the Faith,* pp. 316-17.

14. John Calvin, *Institutes of Christian Religion* (Philadelphia, PA: Westminster Press, 1960), p. 1211 [Book iv., chap. 11.1].

15. Bannerman, *The Church of Christ,* p. 191.

voluntary society, and therefore the power of the church 'is not merely the surrender, under certain limitations, of the rights of all the members into the hands of a few for the good of society, but is rather the positive institution of Christ, having its origin and warrant directly from him. In other words, the source of Church power is not in the members, but in Christ.'[16]

The natural place to begin is Chapter 25 of the Confession, which is on the topic of the church:[17]

**25.1** The catholic or universal church which is invisible, consists of the whole number of the elect, that have been, are, or shall be gathered into one, under Christ the head thereof; and is, the spouse, the body, the fullness of him who fills all in all.

**25.2** The visible church, which is also catholic or universal, under the gospel (not confined to one nation, as before, under the law) consists of all those, throughout the world, that profess the true religion; and of their children: and is, the kingdom of the Lord Jesus Christ, the house and family of God, out of which, there is no ordinary possibility of salvation.

**25.3** Unto this catholic visible church, Christ hath given the ministry, oracles, and ordinances of God, for the gathering, and perfecting of the saints, in this life, to the end of the world: and does by his own presence and Spirit, according to his promise, make them effectual thereunto.

**25.4** This catholic church has been sometimes more, sometimes less visible. And particular churches, which are members thereof, are more or less pure, according as the doctrine of the gospel is taught and embraced, ordinances administered, and public worship performed more or less purely in them.

**25.5** The purest churches under heaven are subject both to mixture, and error: and some have so degenerated, as to become no churches of Christ, but synagogues of Satan. Nevertheless, there shall be always a church on earth, to worship God according to his will.

**25.6** There is no other head of the church, but the Lord Jesus Christ; nor can the Pope of Rome, in any sense, be head thereof; but is, that antichrist, that man of sin, and son of perdition, that exalts himself, in the church, against Christ, and all that is called God.

---

16. Ibid., p. 192.

17. The text of the Confession is taken from the best historical rendition as presented by Chad VanDixhoorn, *Confessing the Faith*, pp. 335-44.

The first and most important point for our topic to notice in this summary is the declaration that Christ is the head of the church. How important is the teaching for the primary mission of the church? Its importance cannot be overstated, as mentioned in Chapter 5. Not only does this teaching derive from the explicit language of Scripture, it is also 'sanctioned by the whole tenor of Scripture declarations.'[18] This doctrine is the rubric under which all the duties, privileges and blessings of the church are subsumed. As Bannerman puts it:

> All is derived from Him; and all emanates from Him as its source. Within the province of the Church, the Lord Jesus Christ is the only Teacher, Lawgiver, and Judge. If doctrine is taught, it is taught because He has revealed it; if ordinances are administered, they are administered in His name, and because they are His; if government is established and exercised, it is through His appointment and authority; if saving grace is dispensed, it is dispensed through the virtue and power of His Spirit; if a blessing is communicated, it is because He blesses.[19]

This teaching provides limits on the jurisdictional authority of the church and of her officers.[20] This was not just an American emphasis; this was the teaching of the Confession and is evident in the Disruption Controversy in Scotland in which Bannerman and William Cunningham played such important roles.

In Scotland, the established church was founded in 1560. It had been a 'pawn in political struggles between England and Scotland, and similar ones between the Crown and the English Parliament.'[21] William Cunningham (1805-1861) was a founder of the Free Church of Scotland. He believed that the very headship of Christ was at stake in the Disruption Controversy in Scotland (cf. 25.6 of WCF above). In 1843 many ministers left the established Church in Scotland to form the Free Church of Scotland.[22] What happened leading up to this precipitous

---

18. Bannerman, *The Church of Christ*, p. 194.

19. Ibid., p. 195.

20. Craig Troxel, '"Divine Right" Presbyterianism,' p. 136. Cf., Bannerman, *The Church of Christ*, p. 195; Thornwell, *Writings*, IV: pp. 162, 182, 192-93, 218-19, 236, 240, 473.

21. Darryl Hart, *A Secular Faith*, p. 47.

22. See 'Disruption,' in the *Oxford Dictionary of the Church*, p. 247. For a concise, detailed account of the events leading up to the disruption and into the years that followed, especially T. Chalmers' part, see Hart, *Calvinism: A History*, pp. 205-25.

event is fascinating. During the 'Ten Years Conflict' (1833-1843) two parties emerged. One party, the non-intrusionists, maintained the spiritual independence of the church against the intrusion of a minister on an unwilling congregation by a patron (often a landowner). The other party was content to have her ministers appointed by the patron or civil power. In 1834, the non-intrusionist party had the majority to pass the 'Veto Act' in their General Assembly which gave the right to congregations to reject the patron nominated minister.

William Cunningham found himself in the middle of the controversy when he published *The Defense of the Rights of the Christian People* (1840). The tumult tested these Scots to the core of their ecclesiological being as Craig Troxel says:

> One can hardly overstate how serious Cunningham was about the ecclesiological principles pertinent to the difficult ecclesiastical struggle he and others faced in the formation of the Free Church of Scotland. That struggle, it will be remembered, shook every minister in the Scottish Kirk to his ecclesiological bones. That is, it was the brand of controversy which forced theologians, ministers, and church members alike to scrutinize and stand behind their views of church power on those most fundamental of levels, the relationship between the church and state.[23]

What's interesting about examining this historical event from the vantage point of our topic is that these saints were forced by their social situation and circumstances to double down and think about, clarify, and stand for their convictions about what exactly the Scriptures teach on these matters of ecclesiology. For Cunningham, what mattered was the fact that Christ is the head of the church who authorizes her government and officers and empowers them to perform discipline in the church; the crucial Scriptural teaching about Christ's honor and dignity as the church's only head and ruler was at stake. He regarded the claim that the government of the church was based on natural principles which govern all independent societies as a fatal flaw in thinking. Rather, the government of the church is a *jus divinum*, a divine right revealed by the Scriptures. Because Christ is the sole head and ruler of the church, Cunningham maintained:

> It is only from Scripture that it can be proved to be in its nature and constitution a distinct and independent society; and the same Scripture that

---

23. Craig Troxel, '"Divine Right" Presbyterianism,' p. 151.

establishes this fundamental position, lays down certain general principles as to its constitution and government, its relation to Christ and His word, which, when fairly and honestly applied, exclude the civil power from all right of authoritative interference in the regulation of its affairs, and make it unlawful, as being a violation of duties which Christ has imposed, for the church to be a consenting party to any such interference.[24]

What has been said for Cunningham can be said for Bannerman as well: church power is regulated by the head of the church, i.e., the Lord Jesus. He alone is the origin and source of church power:

> Such, then, is the source of the power of the Church, – using the word power in its most comprehensive sense, to denote not merely a power to act in the way of authority and rule, but also, in addition to this, a power to act in every way in which it is competent for the Church as a Church to act; a power, namely, jurisdiction, in the way of administering word, and ordinance, and discipline, in the way of dispensing grace to its members. The source of all this power belonging to the Christian society is in the Lord Jesus Christ, as its ever present and ever living Head. This cardinal doctrine lies at the foundation of every other that concerns the Church of Christ, and ought to be guarded from those that would deny or derogate from it, with the utmost jealousy and care. It is so very explicitly and broadly laid down in Scripture, that few are found to controvert it in so many words, or expressly to deny that the Head of the Christian Church is Christ Himself. But without denying it in express terms, there are many systems of religious belief, and many societies bearing the name of Churches, that are found to trench upon this doctrine understood in its fullness and integrity, and practically to interfere with the rights and prerogatives that belong to Christ's Crown.[25]

This emphasis on Christ as head of His church, and the correlative teaching of all government in the church being derivative from this claim, is integrally related to the view of 'divine right' Presbyterianism as explicated by all these old school Presbyterian ministers. As Bannerman explains:

> In all that regards its life and doctrine, and ordinances, and grace, and authority; in short, in all that belongs to the Church as a peculiar society on earth, we recognize *Jus Divinum* – the presence and power of its Divine Head. All is derived from Him as its source. Within the province

---

24. William Cunningham, *Discussions on Church Principles*, p. 276.
25. Bannerman, *The Church of Christ*, pp. 199-200.

of the Church, the Lord Jesus Christ is the only Teacher, Lawgiver, and Judge .... In the language of the Confession of Faith, 'there is no other Head of the Church but the Lord Jesus Christ.'[26]

This then translates into the truth that ministers are limited in their powers, 'and polity.'[27] This truth and claim extends not just to their teaching but to the exercise of the government of the church as well. Again Troxel:

> What each of these men [Cunningham, Bannerman, Robinson, and Thornwell] articulated was that what is true of the church in her preaching and teaching capacities is true of her in her governmental and disciplinary capacities, they are both subsumed under, and hence limited in power by the authority and sufficiency of the Word.[28]

Again, it is difficult to overstate the importance of this confessional category:

> These men ultimately based their defense of the limits of church power upon the source of church power, the headship of Christ. All church power was established and is superintended by Christ, the supreme head of the church. This doctrine functioned for them as the most fundamental doctrine of all. It was the umbrella under which those other subsidiary principles were to be subsumed. Furthermore, the headship of Christ was recognized as the source of the church's derived power both as its founding head, but also as its presiding head.[29]

In other words, a society may have a head who is the founder but not the administrator of it. A founder may contribute to its origin and existence but then cease to be involved. Not so Christ! He is head of the church both as founder and administrator.[30] In this focus on the headship of Christ as the source and sustenance of the government of the church, it was Stuart Robinson and Bannerman that especially focused on the *munus triplex* (Christ as prophet, priest, and king) for the explanation of this doctrine.[31] But just as this concept of headship was important

---

26. Quoted in Troxel, '"Divine Right" Presbyterianism,' p. 149.
27. Ibid., p. 128.
28. Ibid., pp. 135-36.
29. Ibid., pp. 138-39.
30. Bannerman, *The Church of Christ*, pp. 198-99.
31. Troxel, '"Divine Right" Presbyterianism,' pp. 141, 163.

for Cunningham, Robinson, and Bannerman, so also it was equally important for Thornwell.[32] If Cunningham, Bannerman, Thornwell, and Robinson were all correct in their estimation of the importance of the headship of Christ for the doctrine of the church, then it is not surprising that the Divines turned back to this fundamental teaching when they expressed themselves on church censures in Chapter 30 of the WCF:

> **30.1** The Lord Jesus, as king and head of his church, has therein appointed a government, in the hand of church officers, distinct from the civil magistrate.

This headship of Christ over His church then factored in a huge way into the debates in America between Thornwell and Charles Hodge on the legitimacy of church boards: 'No other principle so contradicted the thought of Charles Hodge as the principle did in that controversy [over church boards].'[33]

## The Church Board Controversy between Hodge and Thornwell

The debate in the nineteenth century had to do with independent societies not under the direct control of the church, especially the General Assembly. These boards were especially for the purposes of missions and ministerial education. The position of Old School Presbyterians, though not all, at this time was '1) That the benevolent work of the church *must* be done by the church herself in her organized capacity; 2) That the benevolent work of the church *must not* be done by non-denominational Boards acting as agency of the church.'[34] When the debate broke out, just before the Civil War, it was primarily those from the border states and the South that were most engaged.[35]

It was Thornwell who primarily led the charge. He first made his views known in private letters but then read a carefully prepared paper at the Synod meeting in Augusta, Georgia, in 1840 which was published the

---

32. Ibid., p. 154.

33. Ibid., p. 169.

34. Kenneth Joseph Foreman Jr. quoted in Vance, 'The ecclesiology,' p. 171.

35. Ibid., p. 173.

following year in the *Baltimore Literary and Religious Magazine*. Thornwell did not change the substance of his views throughout his career.

For Thornwell, the church boards exercised power and discretion independent of church oversight. This ran contrary to his view that Christ endued only the Session, Presbyteries, Synods and General Assemblies with legitimate power.[36] In his view, the 'Assembly granted to boards what the constitution of the church had granted to presbyteries.'[37] Back and behind of his views was his notion of scriptural authority, which was discussed above. In other words, 'God had divinely revealed his will on these matters in his word. Thornwell understood this in the Puritan sense to mean that the church had no legislative and discretionary power. Church power, he believed, was only ministerial and declarative.'[38] This is in stark contrast to a Roman Catholic view of Church Power. By virtue of their claim to be the infallible interpreter of Scripture, and the fact that they make scripture, *de facto*, via their view of the canon as including the Apocrypha and their view of tradition, they in essence give the church magisterial power.[39] This was, in essence, the regulative principle applied to church organization just as it is applied to worship in *jure divino* Presbyterianism. For Thornwell, the whole debate, even his whole ecclesiology, can be whittled down to one theological question: whose will is to be done in the church?[40] What were Thornwell's motivations for pushing such a question?

It seems that part of his motivation was the recognition that human beings have a sinful propensity to abuse power.[41] However, another motivation, perhaps not so easy to detect, was the holiness of God: 'just as this attribute of God's character informed his [Thornwell's] piety and preaching so it also informed his understanding of the nature and exercise of ecclesiastical power.'[42] Even so, Thornwell was not so dogmatic about his position to break communion over this particular issue with his Presbyterian brothers, especially in the North. For

---

36. Ibid., p. 175.

37. Ibid., p. 176.

38. Ibid., p. 179.

39. Peck, *Notes on Ecclesiology*, p. 107.

40. Vance, 'The ecclesiology,' p. 223.

41. Ibid., p. 226.

42. Ibid.

Thornwell, polity belonged not to the *esse* of the church but to the *bene esse* of the church.'[43]

These views came to a head in a debate on the floor of the General Assembly in 1860, facing off against his opponent, Charles Hodge. For Thornwell, the issue struck at the vitals of legitimate power granted by Christ to the church. Charles Hodge wanted to permit church-controlled missions boards and voluntary societies. Thornwell and Robinson strongly disagreed.[44] In fact, it has been claimed that Thornwell's *jure divino* shines forth most clearly in his writings against fellow Old School Presbyterians at just this juncture.[45] Hodge's position is summed up in his Systematic Theology:

> How far the Church has discretionary power in matters of detail is a disputed point. By some all such discretion is denied. They maintain that everything concerning the organization, officers, and modes of action of the Church is as minutely laid down in the New Testament as the curtains, tassels, and implements of the tabernacle are detailed in the Old Testament. Others hold that while certain principles on this subject are laid down in Scriptures, considerable latitude is allowed as to the means and manner in which the Church may carry them out in the exercise of her functions. This latter view has always been practically adopted. Even the Apostolical Churches were not all organized precisely in the same way. The presence of an Apostle, or a man clothed with apostolical authority, as in the case of James in Jerusalem, necessarily gave to a Church a form which other churches where no Apostle permanently resided could not have. Some had deaconesses, others had not. So all churches in every age and wherever they have existed, have felt at liberty to modify their organization and modes of action so as to suit them to their peculiar circumstances. All such modifications are matters of indifference. They cannot be made to bind the conscience, nor can they be rendered conditions of Christian or ecclesiastical fellowship.[46]

For Thornwell and Robinson, 'the real issue was whether church government is of divine right, *jus divinum*, or whether the church is a human society governed by human wisdom, *jus humanum*.'[47] This was

---

43. Ibid., p. 228.
44. Ibid., pp. 187-88.
45. Cooper, 'Binding Bodies and Liberating Souls,' pp. 35-47, especially at p. 38.
46. Charles Hodge, *Systematic Theology*, 2. 606.
47. Troxel, '"Divine Right," Presbyterianism,' pp. 100-101.

the essential difference between Thornwell and Hodge: 'Thus, in contrast to Hodge's view that the church enjoyed considerable discretionary liberty, Thornwell viewed the church to be limited in its power by positive sanction, because church order was prescribed by Christ.'[48] This then was no trivial matter. 'Far from disagreeing over a mere semantic or trivial matter,' says Troxel, 'what divided Thornwell and Hodge involved the most fundamental, and therefore the most comprehensive of ecclesiological principles.'[49] For Thornwell, not only did church-appointed mission boards undermine *jure divino* Presbyterianism, but they were an 'affront to Christ's wisdom as sole Ruler of his kingdom.'[50] This, in short, was the essence of the debate:

> Each of these were carefully stated, the church has some discretionary privilege in matters of 'circumstance,' which pertain to the church's worship and government, as they are common to human society. But the church has no legislative or jurisdictional power of right that is inherent to the office. The church and her officers seek positive warrant for what is done in the church. The reason for this is because the head of the church has revealed his will for the church. Therefore, as Thornwell states, the church has no opinion, she has a creed.[51]

This, therefore, is where Troxel maintains that Hodge made a serious mistake. While praising Hodge for his long years of service in training thousands for the ranks of the ministry, especially in North America, and for his erudition in the areas of theology, Troxel does not withhold adulation. Nevertheless, in the area of ecclesiology, in Troxel's opinion, Hodge is found wanting. Hodge had greatly emphasized Pneumatology in his ecclesiology.[52] This, however, may have been his Achilles heel with respect to ecclesiology. Troxel summarizes:

> But, in effect, he made the Holy Spirit the head of the church because he considered the Spirit to be the source of church power. To ground all the privilege and prerogatives of the Church upon the indwelling of the Spirit, as Hodge did, is in effect to deny the ministry of Christ. The Holy Spirit

---

48. Ibid. p. 223.

49. Ibid., p. 226.

50. Cooper, 'Binding Bodies and Liberating Souls,' pp. 38-39.

51. Troxel, '"Divine Right," Presbyterianism,' p. 176.

52. See Alan D. Strange, *The Doctrine of the Spirituality of the Church,* pp. 132-74.

is not the head of the church any more than the Father is the head of the Church. That title, as such, is reserved exclusively for Christ.[53]

Indeed, in the debate between Hodge and Thornwell on the issue of church boards, Hodge may have done injury to his own views by referring to Thornwell's views on the subject as 'hyper-hyper-hyper-High Church Presbyterianism.' With this unrestrained rhetoric, Hodge was actually 'castigating the tradition passed down to him.'[54] Surely, Hodge, by claiming that 'where the Spirit is, *there* is the church,' actually opens himself up for serious critique.[55] Indeed, as Troxel summarizes, 'if the boards did operate in the way in which Thornwell claimed, and this was not denied by Hodge, then Thornwell must be declared the more consistent Presbyterian.'[56]

## The Role of the Church and State

The next area of confessional teaching that it is necessary to explore is the role of the church to the state, or vice versa. Bannerman wrote about the importance of a friendly relation that is necessary between the two.[57] The Westminster Confession is not short on words in this crucial area:[58]

**23.1** God, the supreme Lord and King of all the world, has ordained civil authorities to be, under him, over the people for his own glory and the public good. For this purpose he has armed them with the power of the sword for the defence and encouragement of those who are good, and for the punishment of those who do evil.

**23.2** It is lawful for Christians to hold public office when called to it. In such office they ought especially to maintain piety, justice, and peace, according to the wholesome laws of each commonwealth. For that purpose they may now, under the new testament, lawfully wage war upon just and necessary occasion.

---

53. Troxel, '"Divine Right" Presbyterianism,' p. 228.

54. Ibid., p. 222.

55. Ibid.

56. Ibid., p. 217.

57. Bannerman, *The Church of Christ*, p. 171.

58. Here we quote the modern rendition of the Confession which incorporates the changes prescribed by the American church in 1788, which more closely align with Scriptural teaching on the magistrate.

**23.3** Civil authorities may not assume to themselves the administration of the Word and sacraments, or the power of the keys of the kingdom of heaven, nor should they interfere in any way in matters of faith. Yet, as caring fathers, it is the duty of civil authorities to protect the church of our common Lord without giving preference to any denomination of Christians above the rest – doing so in such a way that all church authorities shall enjoy the full, free, and unquestioned liberty of carrying out every part of their sacred functions without violence or danger. As Jesus Christ has appointed a regular government and discipline in his church, no law of any commonwealth should interfere with, prevent, or hinder their proper exercise among the voluntary members of any denomination of Christians, according to their own profession and belief. It is the duty of civil authorities to protect the person and good name of all their people in such an effective manner that no person be allowed, either in the name of religion or unbelief, to offer any indignity, violence or injury to any other person whatever. They should also take care that all religious and ecclesiastical assemblies be held without interference or disturbance.

**23.4** It is the duty of people to pray for those in authority, to honour them, to pay them taxes or other revenue, to obey their lawful commands, and to be subject to their authority for the sake of conscience. Neither unbelief nor difference in religion makes void the just and legal authority of officeholders nor frees the people—church authorities included—from their due obedience to them. Much less does the Pope have any power or jurisdiction over civil authorities in their domains or over any of their people, nor can he deprive them of their domains or lives if he shall judge them to be heretics or on any other pretence whatever.

One more topic of great importance must be covered now, as recent events have shown it to be, and since we are not only talking about the power of the church in comparison with the power of the state; the relationship between the two is the question concerning what kind of responsibility the state bears for protecting the worship of the church. Calvin, for example, like all the magisterial Reformers thought that the state was responsible for the care of religion (*cura religionis*) 'and here Calvin was no different. After all, Christ is lord of *both* kingdoms, and both kingdoms must serve his purposes,' as Tuininga says.[59] 1 Timothy 2:2 became one of Calvin's favorite passages, since for him, it 'affirms the

---

59. Ibid., p. 280.

continuing responsibility of magistrates to defend and promote piety, worship, and doctrine.'[60] Indeed, from Calvin's viewpoint, he saw this as not merely an important function, but increasingly saw it as '*the most important function of civil government* .... to establish, protect, and promote Christ's spiritual kingdom.'[61] This same concern becomes manifest in WCF 23.

The original confessional statement claimed that the civil magistrate has a duty to defend and promote gospel truth; that 'he has authority, and it is his duty, to take order, that unity and peace be preserved in the church, that the truth of God be kept pure and entire, that all blasphemies and heresies be suppressed, all corruptions and abuses in worship and discipline prevented or reformed, and all ordinances of God duly settled, administered, and observed.' At this point the assembly cited a number of texts that show OT civil authorities and priests reforming society.[62] The problem, as Van Dixhoorn says, 'is that what is good for the old covenant people of God is not always good for the new.'[63] This dynamic—Israelite kings making sure the priests and Levites discharging their duties—does not carry over into the New Testament period since 'neither is any ruler or any nation responsible for the church.'[64]

Next, there was a second statement in the original language of the Confession that proved problematic since it claimed that the civil magistrate 'has the power to call synods, to be present at them, and to provide that whatsoever is transacted in them, be according to the mind of God.'[65] Here, the divines cite the example of good kings in Israel (Jehoshaphat and Hezekiah) and even a wicked king like Herod who called religious leaders to give them advice.[66] But the bitter irony here is that the Assembly came to realize the difficulties of having the state meddle in her affairs. Although the Assembly had been called

---

60. Ibid., p. 249.

61. Ibid., p. 251.

62. See Isa. 49:23; Ps. 122:9; Ezra 7:23; 25-28; Lev. 24:16; Deut. 13:5, 6, 10; 2 Kings 18:4; 233:1-26; 1 Chron. 15:12, 13: 34: 33.

63. See Van Dixhoorn, *Confessing the Faith*, p. 314.

64. Ibid.

65. See Ibid., p. 311.

66. See 2 Chron. 19:8-11 29 and 30; Matt. 2:4, 5.

by Parliament, 'Sharp conflict between assembly and Parliament characterized many months in 1645 and 1646, with the assembly eventually stating that they could not accept the changes made to their texts by the House of Commons, and the Commons charging the assembly with breaking the law.'[67]

## The Revisions in 1788 in the United States

Another point of contention swelling long before the revisions to the Westminster Confession in America in 1788 was the so-called 'establishment' of the church by or in a state. Indeed, this was increasingly recognized as a 'confusion of the two governments under God, the one churchly, the other civil.'[68] Therefore, because there was an increasing recognition that God had established not one, but two governments in two distinct spheres—for Christ's kingdom is not of this world as are civil governments (John 18:36)—the Philadelphia Assembly in 1788 changed the language of this chapter of the WCF, to suggest that the magistrate did have a responsibility to protect the church.

One of the primary prooftexts for this change was the passage from Isaiah 49:23. Isaiah 49 is a remarkable passage in many respects. First, there is the striking mixed metaphor of the government being 'as nursing fathers' in this new covenant passage. I say 'new covenant' since there is some significant continuity and disparity with the preceding chapters. Although the servant songs identify Cyrus, the Persian king, as fulfilling some functions of the servant songs, it is in chapters 49–53 where we see a sudden and striking shift, for the servant portrayed in these chapters truly and finally fulfills all that was predicated of the servant in these songs.[69] Chapter 48 of Isaiah was a literary foil to what follows in Isaiah 49. What Cyrus initially began in military fashion (48:14), the Messiah, a new Moses, will accomplish (anonymous in chapter 49, but clearly Christ in the following chapters). And with the realization of this new covenant, second exodus deliverance, Christ is Lord of both kingdoms (the civil and the religious), and both kingdoms—as Calvin saw and as was mentioned above—must serve His purposes.[70] Van Dixhoorn thinks

---

67. VanDixhoorn, *Confessing the Faith*, p. 315.

68. Ibid.

69. See Estelle, *Echoes of Exodus: Tracing a Biblical Motif*, pp. 169-72.

70. Tuininga, *Calvin's Political Theology*, p. 280.

this is strained exegesis; he states: 'The state must protect the church. This is an idea not incompatible with the Bible; it is not, as far as I can see, an idea from the Bible.'[71] He may have a point that appealing to Isaiah 49 to make this point is not immediately evident; nevertheless, I have tried to explain more of the context of the servant songs in Isaiah and to recognize that Calvin, together with the magisterial Reformers, may have recognized the good and necessary inference of this 'new covenant' and 'second exodus' passage applying to realities that we can now see unfolding in the church age with the global expansion of the church under the nurturing—although by no means always—and 'supportive' role of the state. When the state turns bestial, instead of supportive to the church's lawful efforts, the Confession of Faith gives us a right by way of humble petition to beseech her (and remind her) to mind her duty. Perhaps Calvin had more insight than we do, since he seemed to frequently appeal to 1 Timothy 2:1-3 to support this point.[72]

First, let it be clear that the Confession should be interpreted according to its context even as any other text should. When this method is accepted, it is clear that accusing the Divines of supporting the Erastian position is ludicrous at best. Bannerman set the agenda when he says:

> It may be conceded that, taken out of its connection, and viewed apart without reference to other statements in the Confession, and without regard to the use and meaning in their day of the somewhat technical language employed by the authors of it, the words do sound at first as if they ascribed to the civil magistrate a larger share of power *circa sacra* than we should now concede to him. But a very slight attention to the context, and to the real meaning of the language made use of, will be enough to remove all difficulty from the passage.[73]

In Chapter 23.3-4, the WCF says that it is the duty of the magistrate to protect the church. Often, Isaiah 49 and the language of the magistrate being a 'nursing mother' has been used in the history of confessions for the state to provide protection to the church. This might be a dubious notion without significant Scriptural support. Interestingly, something

---

71. VanDixhoorn, *Confessing the Faith*, p. 316.

72. In the OPC and the PCA, this proof text has been relegated to the next article in Chapter 23, emphasizing our duty as a church to pray for the magistrate.

73. Ibid., p. 173.

similar was penned in the Belgic Confession, Article XXXVI on the Magistracy (the civil government):

> We believe that our gracious God, because of the depravity of mankind, has appointed kings, princes, and magistrates; willing that the world should be governed by certain laws and policies; to the end that the dissoluteness of men might be restrained, and all things carried on among them with good order and decency. For this purpose, He has invested the magistracy with *the sword for the punishment of evil-doers and for the protection of them that do well.* Their office is not only to have regard unto and watch for the welfare of the civil state, but also to protect the sacred ministry,[74] that the kingdom of Christ may thus be promoted. They must therefore countenance the preaching of the Word of the gospel everywhere, that God may be honored and worshipped by everyone, as He commands in His Word. Moreover, it is the bounden duty of everyone, of whatever state, quality, or condition he may be, to subject himself to the magistrates; to pay tribute, to show due honor and respect to them, and to obey them in all things which are not repugnant to the Word of God; to supplicate for them in their prayers that God may rule and guide them in all their ways, and *that we may lead a tranquil and quiet life in all godliness and gravity.* Wherefore we detest the Anabaptists and other seditious people, and in general all those who reject the higher powers and magistrates and would subvert justice, introduce community of goods, and confound that decency and good order which God has established among men.[75]

Comparison of this modified version is a significant development away from a Christendom mindset that had previously existed in the church.[76]

---

74. At this point, it is worth noting that the original text read as follows: 'Their office is not only to have regard unto and watch for the welfare of the civil state, but also that they protect the sacred ministry, and thus may remove and prevent all idolatry and false worship, that the kingdom of antichrist may be thus destroyed and the kingdom of Christ promoted.' The Synod [CRC] of 1958 approved the following substitute statement which has been referred to other Reformed Churches accepting the Belgic Confession as their creed for evaluation and reaction: 'And being called in this manner to contribute to the advancement of a society that is pleasing to God, the civil rulers have the task, in subjection to the law of God, while completely refraining from every tendency toward exercising absolute authority, and while functioning in the sphere entrusted to them and with the means belonging to them, to remove every obstacle to the preaching of the gospel and to every aspect of divine worship, in order that the Word of God may have free course, the kingdom of Jesus Christ may make progress, and every anti-Christian power be resisted.'

75. Published by the board of publications of the Christian Reformed Church, Grand Rapids, MI.

76. See the discussion in David VanDrunen, *Natural Law and the Two Kingdoms*, p. 306.

Therefore, if the background of these confessional claims are that the state—in some kind of Erastian mode—has a responsibility to punish heretics, then we cannot disagree more. As Bannerman states in siding with the confession, 'Those who fought the battle of the Church's independence against the Erastians of their day with their learned and ready pens, and who further still had to contend with the Parliament of England, under whose authority they were assembled, on the very same question are not the men to be lightly, or without strong evidence, accused of justifying Erastianism or persecution.'[77] Further biblical warrant must be provided to demonstrate that this is the case in the new covenant era.

Chapter 23 of the Confession should be taken in tandem with Chapter 31, on Synods and Councils:[78]

**31.1** For the better governing and further edifying of the church, there ought to be such assemblies as are commonly called synods or councils. Overseers and other rulers of particular churches, by virtue of their office and power which Christ has given them for edification and not for destruction, have authority to appoint such assemblies and to convene together in them as often as they judge it expedient for the good of the church.

**31.2** Synods and councils have authority ministerially to decide controversies of faith and cases of conscience, to set down rules and directions for the better ordering of the public worship of God and the government of his church, and to receive and authoritatively act on complaints of maladministration in the church. If the decrees and decisions of these synods and councils are in accordance with the Word of God, they are to be received with reverence and submission, not only because of their agreement with the Word, but also because of the authority by which they are decided, as being an ordinance that God has appointed in his word.

**31.3** Since apostolic times, all synods and councils, whether general or particular, may err, and many have erred. Therefore, they are not to be made the rule of faith or practice, but are to be used as a help in regard to both.

**31.4** Synods and councils are to handle or conclude nothing but what pertains to the church. They are not to intermeddle in civil affairs which concern the state, except by way of humble petition in extraordinary cases,

---

77. Bannerman, *Church of Christ*, p. 173.
78. Again, we quote the modern form.

or by way of advice, for satisfaction of conscience, if they are required to do so by the civil authority.

There is a major difference here between the manner in which the modern version is written and the way in which it was originally composed in the seventeenth century. The focus is on the new phrase declaring that the assembly is a 'power which Christ has given.' As pointed out by Van Dixhoorn, this new statement is fully in accord with and coheres with earlier statements in the confession about Christ's headship (25.1).[79]

## Conclusion

In this chapter we have cited and explained briefly some of the major confessional statements regarding the relationship between the church and the state, and therefore the major confessional claims with regard to the primary mission of the church.

We have observed that these Divines were very jealous to keep apart things that do not belong together. In other words, they seemed to grasp that the church and state travel in different orbits and that these God-designed boundaries should be protected and respected. The church has a right to govern her institution and not have the state meddle in her affairs. Likewise, the state shares these perimeters within her institutions as well.

We also examined the controversy over independent church boards. This debate actually touches on the vitals of church government, its prescriptions and limitations. It also touches on the Spirituality of the Church (SOTC). The SOTC, as Professor VanDrunen reminds us, merely means that 'the church is a community specially created by Christ and His Holy Spirit, a community that is not defined by or identified with any existing institution or community of the common kingdom. As such the church does not usurp any of the "civil" functions of the common kingdom but devotes itself to exercising its distinctive "spiritual" functions as directed by the Lord Jesus in Scripture.'[80] Integrally related to this doctrine is the teaching of the ministerial authority of the church. This may be defined rather simply as well. VanDrunen again, says 'the officers of the church have authority only

---

79. See Van Dixhoorn, *Confessing the Faith*, p. 413.
80. David VanDrunen, *Living in God's Two Kingdoms*, p. 147.

to minister what the Word of God teaches, not to make up their own doctrines for believing or rules for living, no matter how compelling or wise they might seem to be. Ministerial authority stands in contrast to *legislative* authority, which leaders in the common kingdom possess. While the state, for example, has a broad discretionary power to *make* laws, the church has only the power to *declare* the laws and doctrines that already appear in Scripture.'[81] These teachings are directly related to the protection of the liberty of Christians. The church may only bind the conscience of believers in a way that Scripture binds the conscience of a believer. These nineteenth-century debates remind us of several important principles.

They remind us of what the SOTC is not. As mentioned previously, it does not mean that the church is antiphysical or antimaterial.[82] A few moments reflection on the activities of the visible church will disabuse anyone of that notion. But now I would like to ask the question as to whether it is merely a doctrine that is mostly a product of Southern Presbyterianism, which became a 'protective gesture' … 'mainly used to shield or prevent southerners from acting with justice towards African Americans in the nineteenth and twentieth centuries,' as Sean Lucas has suggested?[83] It is important, in my opinion, to maintain that the doctrine has been subject to abuse in the past (as will be discussed below). This has been the case in the history of the southern United States at times, and probably in other parts of the world as well. We should concede that the doctrine has been subject to abuse. However, it must be conceded that other views of Christianity and culture have as well: for example, activist Reformed world and life view transformationalism.[84]

The spirituality of the church, rightly understood and taught, is liberating for pastors and for God's people. In God's church, pastors do not need to be experts in all matters; only on one subject, ministering the Word of God. The doctrine of the spirituality of the church is not an abdication of social responsibility. Many people today are unaware that the principles limiting church power were already being discussed due

81. Ibid., p. 152.

82. Ibid., p. 146.

83. See Lucas, 'Owning Our Past: The Spirituality of the Church in History, Failure, and Hope.' http://rts.edu/.

84. Hart and Meuther, 'The Spirituality of the Church,' pp. 64-66.

to other precipitating social problems: especially the so-called voluntary societies (the debate between Hodge and Thornwell discussed above). These were essentially what we would call 'parachurch' organizations today. Embedded in the historical record was an active effort on the part of a colonization society to send black slaves back to Africa under the assumption that they would be able to succeed much better in that continent. The gross assumption was that those people who had become Christians would more effectively be able to 'Christianize their folk' as indigenous people rather than 'white' missionaries from Europe or North America. This was in part due to a notion of American exceptionalism, the notion that America came into existence to give birth to a whole new kind of world full of unprecedented freedoms and prosperity and that it was perhaps excepted from the normal course of the rise and fall of nations. During this time, the survival of the nation became paramount, even to men like Charles Hodge, who deplored slavery (even though he himself did employ slaves) and hoped for their gradual emancipation. Even so, the survival of the union and the nation were of paramount importance, as Alan Strange says:

> For Hodge, Thornwell, and most Presbyterians, Old and New School, the survival of the nation transcended all other concerns and was itself conceived as not merely a political conviction but rose to the level of a spiritual truism since the continued existence of the nation was the precondition of the continued existence and thriving of the American Presbyterian Church, at least as Hodge and company assumed at the time.[85]

Regardless of the merits of their cause, another seismic issue discussed in this chapter was whether such voluntary societies were even legitimately within the purview of the church's mission. Those debates brought important ecclesiastical principles to the debating floor for elucidation. Thornwell, holding to a 'divine right' Presbyterian view of church government, insisted the answer was no with regard to the independent boards. Hodge, on the other hand, remained open to the idea, even the idea of colonization of the blacks by moving them back to the continent of Africa as free men and women.

In the next chapter, we venture into a period of history where these principles were sharply tested.

---

85. Alan D. Strange, *The Doctrine of the Spirituality of the Church*, p. 338.

# CHAPTER 12

# Historical Studies

Mark Noll reminds us that 'warfare—the more cataclysmic the better—has often been the mother of theological profundity.'[1] If the preceding claim is true, and if many of the issues that touch on the primary mission of the church were hotly debated during the Civil War in the United States, then we would be foolish to ignore possible insights flowing from just before this period, and just after. Swords crossed. Bayonets were fixed. Heated debates occurred in the courts of the church over the proper role of church members and citizens of their countries. Votes were cast over issues this book has foregrounded.

Harriet Beecher Stowe's book, *Uncle Tom's Cabin,* was published in 1852,[2] suggesting indeed that the pen might just be mightier than the sword. Unfortunately, it didn't stop the battle at Antietam, or Sharpsburg if you wish: the bloodiest day (I think) in American history. It was said that the outcome of the war was already decided when Stowe published her book: it was that influential. The measure of its influence can be felt by the number of responses it received in the South, trying to 'set straight' that not all slaveholders were as cruel as Stowe's novel represented.[3] It was the

---

1. Quoted in Preston D. Graham, Jr. *A Kingdom Not of This World: Stuart Robinson's Struggle to Distinguish the Sacred from the Secular during the Civil War* (Macon, GA: Mercer University Press, 2002), p. 1.

2. It was serialized between 1851 and 1852; and then published in volume form in 1852.

3. As Peterson, *Ham and Japheth,* says: 'Judging from the angry response of Southerners, Stowe's attack touched a raw nerve. Almost without exception they expressed resentment that she had presented all slaveowners as morally corrupt tyrants. Interestingly, however, Stowe had never claimed that all slave-holders were tyrants, but only that the system of

first American novel to sell more than a million copies. To ignore that this happened during one of the most tumultuous periods in American history would be to stick our heads in the ground. Even as I write these words, the issue of racism in North America, if not around the world, is presently generating unprecedented levels of social strife. The number of books published on racism in recent years, both popular and academic, is one indicator that people are longing for answers.[4] Reformed churches in the modern era have erected study committees on the issue of race relations and generated more than a few Reports.[5] In my own denomination, civil rights was debated as early as the 1960s in the pages of the *Presbyterian Guardian*. One black pastor in the Orthodox Presbyterian Church commented how the church had made positive contributions to social reform in the past and urged the church to make positive reforms in the present with regard to the Civil Rights movement and the cause of African Americans. The article solicited many responses, including one by OT Professor E. J. Young that said the article failed to emphasize the gospel.[6]

---

slavery was not able the check the brutality of those who were' (Thomas Virgil Peterson, *Ham and Japheth: The Mythic World of Whites in the Antebellum South*, ATLA Monograph Series, No. 12 [Meteuchen, NJ: Scarecrow Press, Inc. and The American Theological Library Association, 1978], p. 51).

4. See, e.g., Ismael Hernandez, *Not Tragically Colored: Freedom, Personhood, and the Renewal of Black America* (Grand Rapids, MI: Acton Institute, 2016); David P. Leong, *Race & Place: How Urban Geography Shapes the Journey to Reconciliation* (Downers Grove, IL: IVP, 2017); Brenda Salter McNeil, *Roadmap to Reconciliation: Moving Communities into Unity, Wholeness and Justice* (Downers Grove, IL: IVP, 2015); John McWhorter, *Losing the Race: Self-Sabotage in Black America* (New York, NY: Harper Collins, 2001); John McWhorter, *Winning the Race: Beyond the Crisis in Black America* (New York, NY: Penguin, 2005); Dennis L. Ockholm (ed.), *The Gospel in Black and White: Theological Resources for Racial Reconciliation* (Downers Grove, IL: IVP, 1997); Jemar Tisby, *The Color of Compromise: The Truth about the American Church's Complicity in Racism* (Grand Rapids, MI: Zondervan, 2019); Jonathan Wilson-Hartgrove, *Reconstructing the Gospel: Finding Freedom from Slaveholder Religion* (Downers Grove, IL: IVP, 2018).

5. See, e.g., pcahistory.org/topical/race/NAPARC1977.html; http://www.opc.org/GA/race.html; faithpceChurch.org/race (the last reference contains many follow up studies and bibliographies). Details of the OPC's interaction with race can be found in Darryl G. Hart, *Between the Times: The Orthodox Presbyterian Church in Transition, 1945-1990* (Willow Grove, PA: The Committee for the Historian of the Orthodox Presbyterian Church, 2011), pp. 187-210. For a more recent discussion, see the many articles in *New Horizons* (May 2019).

6. See for details, Darryl G. Hart's review of Jemar Tisby's *The Color of Compromise: The Truth about the American Church's Complicity in Racism* in *Ordained Servant* 28 (2019): pp. 130-31.

Unfortunately, any doctrine or teaching in the church can be co-opted for evil purposes and with bad intentions. In the United States, that should not have become an excuse for hiding behind the skirts of the doctrine of the Spirituality of the Church (SOTC) as if it could be an excuse for the immense suffering of slavery, and the abuses of Jim Crow laws and segregation. In the United Kingdom, the British Empire began trading African slaves in 1562. The Abolition of Slavery Act was introduced in the British Empire in 1833. To state that the church's mission is spiritual does not automatically ameliorate the pain, injustice, and horror that many still feel about broken families, and generation after generation of lives stolen: 270 years of it as a British institution.

It is my opinion that today very few pause and think twice or deeply about the appropriateness of the church of Jesus Christ (in her official corporate capacity) being involved in all kinds of various causes: trying to improve the economic plight of those outside the church, Christian education, political causes of various kinds performed in the name of building the kingdom of God (KOG), just to name a few examples. One of the goals of this book has been to encourage people to think deeply about the primary mission of the church and of their own Christian involvement in cultural and social concerns. Christians should be involved in culture, and that is an appropriate and noble undertaking, but how? There are many issues today that people are confused over, and this book seeks to bring greater clarity and precision to our thinking on these matters.

This chapter will examine some of the most influential Old School Presbyterians during this period: James Henley Thornwell of South Carolina, Robert Lewis Dabney in Virginia, Charles Hodge in New Jersey, Stuart Robinson in Kentucky, and Samuel B. McPheeters of Missouri. It was during this period that Old School sensibility flourished in the United States and these men argued 'that the church had a unique commission to perform a task that was essentially spiritual in nature. At the same time they contended that to execute this mission the church had a specific means through the ordained ministry and oversight of ministers and elders meeting in delegated assemblies.'[7] During this time, the STOC doctrine flourished. After the 1869 merger of the Old and

---

7. D. G. Hart, *Calvinism: A History*, p. 250.

New School churches, this Old School sensibility became marginal.[8] When the Presbyterian church was fractured shortly afterwards into fundamentalist and modernist camps at the turn of the twentieth century over the issues of biblical criticism and evolution, the STOC experienced a further casualty.[9] Nevertheless, it was a crucial teaching during this period of the famous New Testament scholar, J. Gresham Machen.[10]

In this chapter, I will discuss those Old School luminaries. Moreover, I will comment briefly on slavery and the racism that was so prominent during this time (the latter still with us unfortunately). I will also comment on a much neglected and very interesting historical phenomena during these times: the issue of border-state pastors and what we can learn about the primary mission of the church from some of what took place with them during the Civil War, since lessons on the SOTC surface in the ill-treatment of them, particularly Samuel B. McPheeters.

Indeed, Southerners generally agreed that the church ought not to discipline her members that held slaves since the Bible itself did record instances of this. The problem, according to them, should be resolved politically. Charles Hodge, a moderate, complained that a civil discussion of the issue of slavery could no longer take place because of all the tensions that the abolitionists had injected into the situation.[11] Hodge was a leading figure for the Old School Seminary, Princeton, which had been established in 1812, and had become the bastion of the Old School in the North – the movement that tended to represent the strain of Scotch-Irish piety that put doctrine and confessionalism first as opposed to the 'New School' revivalism tradition, begun in the 1820s, evolving out of the Second Great Awakening with the rise of Charles Finney and its emphasis on emotion. Indeed, more influential for the hardening of positions than abolitionists were the revivalists, according to Ernest Trice Thompson, such as 'Charles G. Finney and his converts, Theodore Weld, Henry Ward Beecher, and his sister Harriet Beecher Stowe.' He continues: 'Religious evangelists insisted that all Slaveholders, even those who opposed the institution ... should

---

8. Ibid.

9. Ibid.

10. Ibid.

11. See Alan D. Strange, *The Doctrine of the Spirituality of the Church in the Ecclesiology of Charles Hodge.*

be expelled from the church, and they gradually aroused the North to a crusade which helped to make war almost inevitable.'[12] Not all, but unfortunately, many on both sides in the conflict at the outbreak of the Civil War—both blue and gray—became intent on convincing their congregants that God was on 'their' side, and political preaching abounded north and south of the Mason Dixon line.

Of course, even though this war happened over one hundred and fifty years ago, it has not quelled debate about race in this North American country and around the world as demonstrated by the recent protests and riots that emerged after the death of George Floyd. So we cannot touch upon the insights with regard to the mission of the church as debated during this time without raising the perilous issue of race.

The Civil War was about more than race; it was also about a fundamental difference of opinion over whether the Southern ideal of the sphere of the state is sovereign or whether state rule is limited and subordinate to the rule of the Federal government. But race and racial-based slave holding was a significant factor. Therefore, let me make a few preliminary comments about race before I discuss this period of history and its impact on thinking about issues of the primary mission of the church. My goal here is not to take a perilous step, but to bracket the issue of slavery from the primary mission of the church, which is spiritual.

Slavery in the South was race-based and therefore should be distinguished from other forms of slavery throughout history. This is a well-established fact. Moreover, if one looks at contemporary observers from 'the outside' during this period of history, then we can immerse ourselves in a little bit of 'objective' history. Of course, no history writing is completely objective; however, good history writing is somewhat objective. Let me explain. What is needed is objectivity. Neutrality is impossible, as explained so eloquently by noted American historian Thomas L. Haskell. What we need for good history writing is objectivity.[13] So, complete objectivity is impossible; however, to stand in another's shoes, so to speak, especially from this time, may help us to gain some perspective. Therefore, let's listen to Alexis de Tocqueville

---

12. Ernest Trice Thompson, *The Spirituality of the Church: A Distinctive Doctrine of the Presbyterian Church in the United States* (Richmond, VA: John Knox Press, 1961), pp. 22-23.

13. See Thomas L. Haskell, *Objectivity is Not Neutrality: Explanatory Schemes in History* (Baltimore, MD: The Johns Hopkins University Press, 1998), pp. 145-173.

(1805-1859). Tocqueville's analysis, *Democracy in America*, has been considered the 'standard source for generalizing about America.'[14] He travelled throughout the states, keeping his thoughts in writing which later would give birth to his two-volume work. The first was published in 1835. It gained recognition as a classic almost immediately.

Tocqueville was very interested in analyzing the effects of political liberty in France and in the United States. *Democracy in America* was considered a classic and so insightful into the 'American spirit' that it was actually required reading in many secondary schools throughout the United States for decades.[15] Tocqueville did not intend to enter into mere flattery of the burgeoning new democracy; rather, his goal was constructive criticism. He wrote two volumes, the second of which was published in 1840 and less well received than the first since it was perceived that he was too critical. In light of our current topic and the issue of slavery, his comments are less than laudatory based on his observations: slaveholding makes for lazy landowners.[16] Consider, for example, some of Tocqueville's observations:

> Thus it is that in the United States the prejudice rejecting the Negroes seems to increase in proportion to their emancipation, and inequality cuts deep into mores as it is effaced from the laws .... In the United States people abolish slavery for the sake not of the Negroes but of the white men .... The population of those provinces that had practically no slaves increased in numbers, wealth, and well-being more rapidly than those that had slaves .... But in all these circumstances the same fact stood out time and again: in general, the colony that had no slaves was more populous and prosperous than the one where slavery was in force .... So, the traveler who lets the current carry him down the Ohio till it joins the Mississippi sails, so to say, between freedom and slavery; and he has only to glance around him to see instantly which is best for mankind .... On the left bank of the Ohio work is connected with the idea of slavery, but on the right with well-being and progress: on the one side is degrading, but on the other honorable; on the left bank no white laborers are to be found, for they would be afraid

14. Louise Cowan and Os Guinness (eds), *Invitation to the Classics: A Guide to the Books You've Always Wanted to Read* (Grand Rapids, MI: Baker, 1908), p. 225.

15. Alexis de Tocqueville, *Democracy in America*, A new translation by George Lawrence (Garden City, NY: Anchor, 1969).

16. Apparently, I am in the good company of Thomas Sowell, of Stanford's prestigious Hoover Institute on this point.

of being like the slaves; for work people must rely on the Negroes; but one will never see a man of leisure on the right bank; the white man's intelligent activity is used for work of every sort.[17]

Of course this is just a perspective from one primary source. Undoubtedly it would be an overgeneralization to say that all Southern slaveholders were lazy. Counterexamples could be multiplied. Consider, for example, the fine example of the very productive, industrious, and highly generous plantation owner, lawyer and businessman John Jones Gresham.[18] He was the grandfather of J.G. Machen, about whom we will learn more below.

Many have recently claimed that the SOTC doctrine was merely a product of Southern Presbyterians in order to justify their slave-holding. The position argued in this book is that this is patently false, or at least such a claim is not the full picture. Some definitely abused this teaching of Scripture and even hid behind the skirts of this doctrine to justify racist pro-slavery customs and a pernicious way of supporting economic systems in the South during the nineteenth century; nevertheless, that does not mean we can throw the baby out with the bathwater. How could the church have slipped into such patent racism that contradicted the catholicity of the church? For example, when white American churches stationed 'color guards' at the doors of their churches in order to bar potential black worshipers and instead pointed them to suitable congregations on the other side of the tracks, someone needed to stand and cry 'Foul'! The church in the United States (both North and South) should feel ashamed for slipping into such practices.[19]

Nevertheless, the SOTC doctrine extends far back into the hoary past of the church long before the first shot was fired in April of 1861. Indeed, the notion of the SOTC in some sense 'extends back through the entire history of the church, even to biblical times.'[20] For example, with regard to Stuart Robinson, it is clear from the annals of history that his 'Scoto-American' ideas extend at least back to his college days at Amherst, long before the advent of the Civil War, and therefore the notion that it was

---

17. Tocqueville, *Democracy in America*, pp. 344-46 [Lawrence translation].

18. See Chapter 2 of Katherine Lynn Tan VanDrunen's unpublished doctoral dissertation, 'The Foothills of the Matterhorn: familial antecedents of J. Gresham Machen' (Ph.D. dissertation, Loyola University Chicago, 2006), pp. 36-103.

19. See Edmund Clowney, *The Church*, p. 97.

20. Strange, *The Doctrine of the Spirituality of the Church*, p. 4.

merely a Southern Presbyterian dogma are false.[21] Furthermore, even some of the most ardent defenders of the SOTC doctrine (Thornwell and Robinson) understood the grounds for it to be inherited from Scottish Presbyterianism, not merely motivated by race-based slavery. However, it must be noted that historically it is a fact that the Free Church of Scotland understood the independent notion of the church and the SOTC, and yet it also felt no hesitations about condemning slavery and encouraging the American church to do the same.[22]

Nevertheless, some Southern Presbyterian theologians held to fallacious notions about race. Today, the SOTC doctrine has become the scapegoat. Moderns often blame Southern pro-slavery of hiding behind the skirts of SOTC doctrine for the justification of slavery. While sometimes that claim may be justified, it was by no means the monolithic reason for pro-slavery advocates. As always, the argument presents itself in the most common garb: surface simplicity. However, the truer story lies beneath the surface. One of the primary texts of Scripture used by pro-slavery advocates had very little to do with the SOTC doctrine; rather, ironically, and sadly, it was the misinterpretation of the tale of Noah and his three sons that generated and influenced the subjugation of Africans into slavery, not only in the United States but around the world. This reality has been sadly neglected.

## The Myth of Ham in the Antebellum South

By and large, Southerners rejected polygenesis (the notion that blacks originated from a different species and were not fully human) since they interpreted Genesis literally and believed that all people descended from Adam and Eve. Moreover, if they denied this view, it would have implications for their view of original sin and redemption. So, if all people descended from Adam and Eve, and were therefore 'brothers and sisters,' then how could 'whites enslave blacks, especially black Christians.' This is the conundrum that faced many white Southerners. Many turned to the myth of Ham to find cognitive rest.[23]

The story of Noah and his sons is well-known. After the flood, Noah planted a vineyard; and after drinking some of the wine, he laid naked in

---

21. Graham, *A Kingdom Not of This World*, p. 38.

22. Ibid., p. 205.

23. Thomas Virgil Peterson, *Ham and Japheth: The Mythic World of Whites*, p. 109.

his tent (Gen. 9:22). Ham, the father of Canaan, looked upon his naked father (plausibly argued that this was an act of homosexual voyeurism), and when Noah 'awoke from his wine' he knew what his youngest son had done (9:24). The two older sons (Shem and Japheth) had carefully covered their father's nakedness without looking upon him. Noah's famous oracle (9:25-27) records a curse on Ham's son (Canaan), who would become a 'servant of servants' to his brothers.[24] Shem and Japheth would be blessed. At least part of the responsibility for the 'curse of Ham' can be found in Jewish tradition, where Jewish tradition had spoken of sex being banned in the ark, but Ham, a dog, and a raven transgressed the command and Ham's curse was that he was turned black.[25]

It would be hard to understate the importance of this oracle since it becomes a kind of index of major themes to be developed in subsequent biblical history.[26] It would also be hard to understate the importance of a gross and patently false *misinterpretation* of this text which suggested that black skin was part of this curse. Moreover, although the biblical curse of Noah was pronounced against Ham's son Canaan long ago, the text was misconstrued to link blackness with skin color (and allegedly imposed upon Ham's descendants) and further conflate this blackness with slavery and servitude. This became known as the dual curse of Ham.[27] Thus, the devastating claim was made that God had joined blackness and slavery. Some of the attempts to explain the connection between Noah's sons and black servitude have been embarrassing.[28] This unfortunate conflation

---

24. For a very creative restricting of the development of the compositional history of this section of Scripture, see David Frankel, 'Noah's Drunkenness and the Curse of Canaan: A New Approach,' *JBL* 140, no. 1 (2021): pp. 49-68.

25. See David M. Goldenberg, *Black and Slave: The Origins and History of the Curse of Ham*. Studies of the Bible and Its Reception, Vol. 10. Edited by Dale C. Allison, Jr., Christine Helmer, Thomas Römer, Choon-Leong Seow, Barry Dov Walfish, Eric Ziolkowski (Berlin/Boston: Walter de Gruyter, 2017), pp. 43-44.

26. See M.G. Kline, *Kingdom Prologue,* pp. 263-69.

27. The explicit link between 'blackness' and slavery/servitude occurs in a Syriac Christian work, known as *The Cave of Treasures*. It is a sixth–seventh century text at the latest, and probably dates back to the fourth or even the third century. See, Goldenberg, *Black and Slave*, p. 76.

28. See, e.g., Benjamin Braude, 'The Sons of Noah and the Construction of Ethnic and Geographical Identities in the Medieval and Early Modern Periods,' *The William and Mary Quarterly*, Vo. 54, No. 1 (Jan. 1997): pp. 103-42.

became the ideological foundation stone for enslaving blacks in Africa and deporting them from their homeland to places all around the world.[29] Indeed, there is evidence of black slaves throughout the Near East.[30] Egypt was the most egregious in its enforcement.[31] Migrated slaves were even immigrated into China.[32] This is not to say that the slaves in Greece and Rome and in the Ancient Near East were primarily black.[33] However, there is no doubt, based on the fact of history, that there were black African slaves in Rome and Greece.[34] However, it was when the dual curse idea began to appear that there was an exponential increase in the numbers enslaved from Africa.[35] It was the Muslim conquests, as a matter of fact, that increased subjugation in an exponential fashion.[36] There is indeed significant evidence to suggest that Muslims were responsible to a large extent for the influence of the curse of Ham in the Christian West,[37] although it would be wrong to attribute the double curse influence in the West merely to Islamic traditions.[38] The fact remains that it was actually the slave trade which drove the faulty exegesis of the biblical text.[39]

The Ham myth also gave grounding to the racism among antebellum, Southern Americans. Even more in America than in Europe, black slavery was justified through the double curse of Ham tradition.[40] Indeed, after 1830, the Ham myth became one of the chief citations of proslavery advocates upholding the South's peculiar institution of enslavement of blacks over and against abolitionist arguments.[41]

---

29. For the scholarly treatment of how this false interpretation came about, see Goldenberg, *Black and Slave*.
30. Ibid., pp. 82-83.
31. Ibid., p. 84.
32. Ibid., p. 83.
33. Ibid., p. 85.
34. Ibid., p. 83.
35. Ibid., p. 96.
36. Ibid., p. 96.
37. Ibid., pp. 120, 200.
38. Ibid., p. 134.
39. Ibid., p. 136.
40. Ibid., pp. 153, 201.
41. Peterson, *Ham and Japheth: The Mythic World of Whites*, p. 45.

There is no doubt that this 'dual curse myth of Ham' gave 'cultural depth to economics, politics, and racism in the Old South of America.'[42] Myth here is being used in a very precise manner. Even though myth often connotes 'unhistorical' to the modern man, I am using myth in a different sense. Myth may not be reduced to fiction; rather, myths may be expressions of truth, although a particular way of expressing truth.[43] Rather, myth is being used here to describe very broadly 'a narrative (story) concerning fundamental symbols that are constitutive of or paradigmatic for human existence.'[44] In other words, I am recognizing that religious symbols 'are narrated in myths or enacted in rituals' and that these myths help resolve cultural contradictions.[45] Thomas Peterson, quoting the influential sociologist Peter Berger, summarizes:

> Symbols are religious when they lodge everyday attitudes and mores within a universal frame of reference. Religion conveys profound significance to institutions and values by providing them with 'an ultimately valid ontological status,' writes Peter Berger, and 'by *locating* them with a sacred and cosmic frame of reference.' Analyzing the white Southern culture in its own terms involves, then, unpacking the system of meanings encompassed by the religious symbols that legitimated the people's values and validated their world view. And no story was more symbolically persuasive in resolving certain tensions between white Southerners' racial values and their most fundamental religious beliefs than was the myth of Ham. Southern versions of the Ham myth placed the institution of slavery squarely within the context of divine purpose.[46]

Therefore, Peterson sets forth the following definition of myth based on the American versions of Noah and his three sons: myth is a '*narrative irreducible to fact or fiction, whose language conveys the passive voice, the imperative mood, and the continuous progressive tense.*'[47] Let me explain.

First, that the myth of Ham exists in the liminal space between fact and fiction empowers it to strengthen values and the South's peculiar

---

42. Ibid., p. ix.

43. Ibid., pp. 127-28.

44. Bernhard Batto, quoted in the author's *Echoes of Exodus: Tracing a Biblical Motif*, p. 117.

45. Peterson, *Ham and Japheth: The Mythic World of Whites*, p. 4.

46. Ibid., pp. 4-5.

47. Ibid., p. 123.

institution of slavery. Second, that the myth of Ham functioned in the passive voice means it was superintended by God, according to the pro-slavery argument. Third, that the myth of Ham suggests the imperative mood means it implies enduring commands: they prescribe 'a pattern of human behavior, but also prescribe a people's social actions and their social values.'[48] This imperative mood conveys (allegedly) 'God's laws for regulating the relationship between blacks and whites in America and consequently legitimized slavery and black subordination in the antebellum South as divine ordinances.'[49] Fourth, that the mythic language suggests the *continuous progressive tense*, as Peterson claims, needs further explanation. The continuous progressive tense is not recognized in standard English, but linguists do note its usage in 'black English.' For example, '*They be fooling around*' indicates generality, repeated action, or existential state, according to linguists.[50] Therefore, since the myth of Ham had a continuous progressive tense, it had a universalizing effect so that even 'when myths seemingly take place in a supposedly historical period (as does the Ham myth, for example), the time is so far removed that it is not susceptible to historical investigation.'[51] Thus, the racial diversity and role sets established in the minds of Southern pro-slavery people was a mythic expression of the outworking of the progenitor pattern established in the story of Noah and his sons.[52] Finally the myth is narrative in the sense that 'myths portray archetypal patterns of human behavior.'[53] This becomes important in the South before the Civil War since the arguments of abolitionists in the North were forcing Southern pro-slavery advocates to defend their customs, beliefs, and institutions.[54] The Ham myth provided grist for the mill of such defense, anchoring the practice of slavery in a primordial past.[55]

For example, this was the case for Robert Lewis Dabney (1820-1898). Dabney was a Southern Presbyterian minister and educator, having served

48. Ibid., pp. 125.
49. Ibid.
50. Ibid., p. 133.
51. Ibid., p. 126.
52. Ibid.
53. Ibid.
54. Ibid., p. 127.
55. Ibid.

on the faculties of Union Theological Seminary in Virginia, the University of Texas, and Austin Theological Seminary.[56] He was Virginia's leading Presbyterian theologian.[57] Dabney also served as chaplain for Stonewall Jackson in the Civil War.[58] For example, Dabney argued that the biblical text (Gen. 9) provided support for the enslavement of blacks.[59] Even so, Dabney did not consider that the Ham text should be regarded as the primary force in the proslavery argument.[60] Nevertheless, it was instrumental. It probably contributed to their deplorable exegesis of so-called household ethics passages in the NT as well. Dabney's views were representative of an entire Southern culture, where the 'everyday values of the society, codified in customs and laws, encouraged by racial attitudes, and enforced by social institutions became intellectually and emotionally persuasive when they fit neatly into the Southerners' picture of the universe [i.e., their worldview].'[61] Southerners may have reconciled in their own minds how they could subjugate blacks to enslavement; however, in the end pro-slavery Southerners argued that blacks were inferior to whites.[62]

First, let it be conceded at the start that the American form of slavery was race-based. Therefore, when arguments are made about slavery represented in the Bible and America's peculiar institution, which was race-based slavery, this point should be conceded. That there was slavery in the ancient Near East and in Greco-Roman culture, and that the institution is 'recognized' in the Old and New Testaments, cannot be denied.[63] Furthermore, descriptions of such slavery should be contextually aware.

---

56. For a recent bibliography, see Sean Michael Lewis, *Robert Lewis Dabney: A Southern Presbyterian Life* in the series, *American Reformed Biographies*, D. G. Hart and Sean Michael Lewis eds. (Phillipsburg, NJ: P & R Publishing, 2005).

57. Peterson, *Ham and Japheth: The Mythic World of Whites*, p. 21.

58. See R. L. Dabney, *Life and Campaigns of Lieut.- Gen. Thomas J. Jackson* (Harrisonburg, VA: Sprinkle, 1977).

59. David M. Goldenberg, *Black and Slave*, p. 233. This is based on Dabney's *A Defense of Virginia, (and through Her, of the South,) in Recent and Pending Contests against the Sectional Party* (New York, 1867), pp. 101-04.

60. Peterson, *Ham and Japheth: The Mythic World of Whites*, p. 102.

61. Ibid., p. 114.

62. Ibid., p. 119.

63. See the author's entry under 'Slavery' in *The Baker Expository Dictionary of Biblical Words*, Mark Strauss and Tremper Longman III eds. (Grand Rapids, MI: Baker Academic,

What is race and what is a racist? The word 'race' has undergone a huge change in meaning in the last fifty years or so.[64] Until the middle of the last century, the term 'race' was used in Europe and even occasionally in the United States, with what we would call today 'an ethnic group, that is to say, a group defined primarily by linguistic and other cultural, historical, and some sense geographical criteria.'[65] But social scientists took the word, which had a common and imprecise meaning, and gave it a very precise meaning. Now, the term for anthropologists became 'a group of people sharing certain visible and measurable characteristics, such as hair, pigmentation, skull measurements, height, and other physical features.'[66] In current usage in the United States, 'race' is used 'exclusively to denote such major divisions as white, black, Mongolian, and the like. It is no longer applied to national, ethnic, or cultural entities, such as the English or the Irish, the Germans or the Slavs, or even the Japanese, who are now seen as being part of a much larger racial grouping found in East Asia.'[67] In the ancient world, although there was a great diversity of people— Egyptians, Sumerians and Akkadians, the Israelites and the Arameans, the Hittites, the Medes, and the Persians and even later, the Greek and the Romans—there was no great racial difference (in the modern sense) represented. In other words, in the material culture left behind—friezes and pictorial representations—physical features play a minor role.[68]

The word 'racist' has been used in so many different contexts and in so many different ways in our modern context, that it has become very imprecise.[69] In this chapter, 'racist' refers 'to the belief that the black

2021); K.C. Hanson, 'Slavery' and S. S. Bartchy, 'Slavery,' in *The International Standard Bible Encyclopedia*, Four Volumes edited by Geoffrey W. Bromiley (Grand Rapids, MI: Eerdmans, 1988), p. 4. The language of 'recognized' is merely historically descriptive, not suggesting that slavery of the American type is proscribed or prescribed by the Bible, or specifically how American race-based slavery was to be most wisely ended, a topic that is way beyond this monograph and one I will leave to readers to formulate their own opinions.

64. Bernard Lewis, *Race and Slavery in the Middle East: An Historical Enquiry* (New York/Oxford: Oxford University Press, 1990), p. 16.

65. Ibid.

66. Ibid.

67. Ibid., p. 17.

68. Ibid.

69. Peterson, *Ham and Japheth: The Mythic World of Whites*, p. 65. See e.g., the recent article published by the linguist, John McWhorter, 'Words Have Lost Their Meaning,' *The Atlantic* (March 31, 2021).

race was inherently inferior to the white.'[70] This was not always the case in the world, especially in the ancient world.[71] Bernard Lewis, praised as one of the world's foremost Islamic scholars, claims that a negative attitude toward black skinned people first happened after the death of Muhammad (632 A.D.) and the ensuing Arab conquest of Africa.[72] Moreover, one must concede that everyone's attitude toward race grows out of a myriad of factors, as David Torbett's contrast between Charles Hodge and Horace Bushnell demonstrates. Attitudes towards race and slavery in the nineteenth century 'Arose from a constellation of theological method, normative principles, anthropological assumptions, predominant loyalties, and interpretations of changing circumstances.'[73]

After the discussion above by B. Lewis, we can say that categories of race now assume that 'peoples of the world can be categorized into a handful of distinct groups based primarily upon shared physical features associated with particular geographical regions – features such as skin color, hair texture, or the shape of eyes, nose, or mouth.'[74] As VanDrunen rightly observes: 'Saying even this much provokes serious questions about the validity of "race."'[75] VanDrunen continues to note the many problems with making race a criterion for making legal distinctions between one person and another.[76] He concludes that 'race is an illegitimate basis on which to exclude someone from participation in institutions or from equal justice under the Noahic covenant.'[77] More below on this topic below.

Indeed, the story of the American Presbyterian Church's reaction to slavery is a long one with many details. It is sufficient to register at this point that, in 1818, a strong statement condemning slavery was made. It begins:

> We consider the voluntary enslaving of one part of the human race by another, as a gross violation of the most precious and sacred rights of human

---

70. Ibid.
71. Cf. Lewis, *Race and Slavery in the Middle East.*
72. Ibid., pp. 22-25, 26, 37, 40-41.
73. David Torbett, *Theology and Slavery,* p. 130.
74. VanDrunen, *Politics after Christendom,* p. 190.
75. Ibid.
76. Ibid., pp. 191-92.
77. Ibid., p. 192.

nature; as utterly inconsistent with the law of God, which requires us to love our neighbor as ourselves, and as totally irreconcilable with the spirit and principles of the gospel of Christ …. It is manifestly the duty of all Christians who enjoy the light of the present day, when the inconsistency of slavery, both with the dictates of humanity and religion, has been demonstrated, and is generally seen and acknowledged, to use their honest, earnest, and unwearied endeavors, to correct the errors of former times, and as speedily as possible to efface this blot on our holy religion, and to obtain the complete abolition of slavery throughout Christendom, and if possible, throughout the world.[78]

This was American Presbyterianism's most famous condemnation against slavery.[79] This clarion call by the General Assembly of 1818 went unheeded and, curiously, opinions hardened in the South and the North. Some, like Thompson, see the years of 1830-31 as the real dividing line, when 'from 1830 on, the North became steadily more opposed to slavery.'[80] Some, like Charles Hodge, were concerned to hold the union of the church and the nation together and thought that Southern Presbyterian slaveholders would listen to the voice of reason and educate their slaves with a view to preparing them for freedom.[81] During the decades following the General Assembly pronouncement, Hodge published two essays, one in 1836 and one in 1851. His essay of 1836 was edited without his knowing it, to make it appear that he was pro-slavery. As a matter of fact, although he did not consider slaveholders worthy of excommunication, he did see that the whole issue was tied up with the question of race.

## Charles Hodge[82]

Hodge has been mentioned many times in this book already. His life and career are quite remarkable. After attending Princeton, he was later

78. Quoted in Strange, *The Doctrine of the Spirituality of the Church*, p. 188.

79. Paul C. Gutjahr, *Charles Hodge: Guardian of American Orthodoxy* (Oxford/New York: Oxford University Press, 2011), p. 169.

80. Ernest Trice Thompson, *The Spirituality of the Church*, pp. 22-23.

81. Strange, *The Doctrine of the Spirituality of the Church*, p. 192.

82. For book-length treatments of Hodge, see the biography by his son, A. A. Hodge, *The Life of Charles Hodge* (New York: Charles Scribner's Sons, 1880; reprinted by Banner of Truth, 2010). Also note the excellently written biography by Paul C. Gutjahr (Oxford/New York, Oxford University Press, 2011) and finally Andrew Hoffecker, *Charles Hodge:*

groomed to become one of her first Professors in biblical languages, then in Old and New Testaments, and finally he worked in Systematic Theology. After settling down in his career at Princeton, marrying and starting a family, he spent two years in Europe in order to strengthen his knowledge of modern foreign languages and especially in order to learn the new and very influential theological and biblical trends coming out of countries there, in particular, Germany. Hodge is one example of a Northern Presbyterian minister and theologian that applied the doctrine of the spirituality of the church to events in his own day.[83] As the foremost biographer of Hodge says, 'No single American professor trained more graduate students in any field than did Hodge during the nineteenth century.'[84]

Hodge's unhappy solution to the problem of slavery was colonization of the slaves. This becomes an important factor for debates in the ensuing decades. Hodge told his readers that 'they [the slaves] are men; their colour does not place them beyond the operation of the principles of the gospel, or from under the protection of God.'[85] Therefore, 'the master and slave belong to different races, [this] precludes the possibility of their living together on equal terms.'[86] For Hodge, the solution was that they should separate, and thus he supported African colonization. Moreover, he concluded that a right understanding of the power and authority of the church meant that the church should not pronounce more than the scriptures. Slavery, according to him, was not sinful, 'but slaves should be treated as those made in the image of God.'[87] These thoughts of Charles Hodge were crystallized in an important article written in an important article on abolitionism in 1844, the year before another landmark

---

*The Pride of Princeton* (Phillipsburg, NJ: P & R Publishing, 2011). Also important, in addition to his *magnum opus*, namely, his three-volume *Systematic Theology*, is Charles Hodge, *Discussions in Church Polity: From the Contributions to the 'Princeton Review,'* selected and arranged by the Rev. William Durant (New York, NY: Charles Scribner's Sons, 1878). Alan Strange, *The Spirituality of the Church*, pp. 49-87, provides a very nice summary of the life of Charles Hodge.

83. For a lengthy and well-written exploration of this theme, see Strange, *The Doctrine of the Spirituality of the Church*.

84. Gutjahr, *Charles Hodge*, p. 213.

85. Quoted in Strange, *The Doctrine of the Spirituality of the Church*, p. 195.

86. Ibid., p. 196.

87. Ibid.

General Assembly in 1845. Hodge was growing increasingly opposed to abolitionism, especially with the kind that was marked by atheistic humanism and paid little attention to the Bible.[88] Slavery was not *malum se* (evil in itself), but he did acknowledge the need for reform.[89] After all, how could one condemn a practice that is not condemned in Scripture? This was the bottom line on the American form of slavery for Hodge: 'slavery *in se* [in itself] was not unbiblical, though problematic in its American form, warranting much regulation.'[90]

One of the most interesting debates in the Presbyterian Church during these tumultuous years surrounded a resolution by Dr Gardiner Spring. The General Assembly met in Philadelphia in 1861 and was composed of mostly delegates with Northern sympathies. As is customary in Presbyterian General Assemblies, the moderator from the previous year is invited to give the opening sermon. With great irony, Dr Spring chose as his text John 18:26: 'My kingdom is not of this world' (usually a passage chosen to defend a two kingdoms view). At the end, on Saturday morning, May 18, Dr Spring offered a resolution, 'that a Special Committee be appointed to inquire into the expediency of this Assembly making some expression of their devotion to the Union of these States, and their loyalty to the [Federal] Government [of the United States]; and if in their judgment it is expedient so to do, they report what that expression shall be.'[91] Immediate opposition arose, and Hodge was not in the least satisfied with the ensuing actions of the assembly. In short, the debate ensued for days, and 'a determination on the part of the assembly to say something affirmative about the Union and offer support for the U.S. government' was not acceptable to Hodge.[92] Indeed, 'Hodge and those with him continued to resist these efforts yet continued to experience defeat.'[93] At the end of the day, Hodge's efforts did not carry the day, and 'Hodge's

---

88. Ibid., p. 219. However, Strange notes that Hodge could have paid better attention to the development of Redemptive History, since the slavery of foreigners by the Israelites was part of their particular period, which included *cherem* warfare in their conquest of Canaan.

89. Ibid., p. 198.

90. Ibid., p. 219.

91. Quoted in Strange, *The Doctrine of the Spirituality of the Church*, p. 242.

92. Ibid., p. 244.

93. Ibid.

committee' lost by a vote of 128 to 84.[94] At question here is whether the church has a 'prophetic voice' towards the culture, a topic which will be taken up in more detail below. Hodge did not object, according to Strange, that the church of the Lord Jesus Christ does have a 'prophetic voice,' where appropriate. However, in this instance:

> Hodge did not contest the right of the church to give prophetic witness on a matter that might have political consequences – for example, in the case of Sabbath observance or the acknowledgement of the Christian faith in the public schools. What he contested in the action of the General Assembly in the Gardiner Spring resolutions was the right of the church to decide for its members to whom their allegiance belonged, whether to the Union and the Federal Government or to their states and the government of the Confederate States of America.[95]

To be precise, Hodge put it like this:

> We make this protest, not because we do not acknowledge loyalty to our country to be a moral and religious duty, according to the word of God, which requires us to be subject to the powers that be; nor because we deny the right of the Assembly to enjoin that, and all other like duties, on the ministers and churches under its care; but because *we deny the right of the General Assembly to decide the political question, to what government the allegiance of Presbyterians as citizens is due, and its rights to make that decision a condition of membership in our church.*[96]

In short, Hodge thought the matter was clearly beyond the proper jurisdiction of the General Assembly of the Presbyterian Church. So Hodge crossed his Rubicon and argued clearly for the SOTC, even against the majority of his Northern brethren. He became much appreciated for this stance among his Southern colleagues in the ministry. Even in the North, Hodge's stance was seen to be as strong as McPheeter's (discussed below) with regard to the case for non-intervention of the church in political matters.[97] However, the consequences for Hodge were much less serious than they were for McPheeters.

This is not to say that Hodge completely opposed the corporate church speaking to matters that may indirectly have political consequences. For

---

94. Ibid., p. 245.

95. Ibid., pp. 246-47.

96. Quoted in Strange, Ibid.

97. See, e.g., Van Dyke, *The Spirituality and Independence of the Church*, p. 34.

Hodge, Strange contends, 'church action must be "purely political" to violate the spirituality of the church – not merely an action that has some political consequence.'[98] For example, the church may preach against laws that forbid slaves to read, or a 'church judicatory may pass a resolution calling for allowing slaves to be taught to read. Political consequences may attach to such actions, but Hodge was not concerned about that. He did not want the church to take actions that were political *simpliciter*.'[99]

## James Henley Thornwell

James Henley Thornwell (1812-1862) lived a short, but productive and influential life as a pastor-churchman, college president and seminary professor. He has been described by American historian George Bancroft as 'the most learned of the learned.'[100] Thornwell was voluminous in his literary output but found writing cumbersome.[101] Given the attention that he attracted from his northern counterpart, Charles Hodge, he was Southern Presbyterianism's 'most intellectually gifted and vocal leader.'[102] He was sickly for much of his youth and into his adult life.[103] He was known for his superb skill at argumentation.[104]

---

98. Strange, *The Doctrine of the Spirituality of the Church*, p. 317. This is a principle that Strange takes pains to demonstrate was Hodge's view in his monograph in multiple places over and against what Strange considers to be the more extreme views of the SOTC by some of Hodge's contemporaries (e.g., Thornwell and Robinson) and modern authors as well. See, e.g., pp. 321, 336.

99. Ibid.

100. Quoted in Gutjahr, *Charles Hodge*, p. 289.

101. John Lloyd Vance, 'The ecclesiology of James Henley Thornwell: An Old South Presbyterian theologian' (Ph.D. dissertation, Madison, NJ: Drew University, 1990), 4.539-46; S. Scott Bartchy, *First-Century Slavery and the Interpretation 1 Corinthians 7:21*, SBLDS 11 (Atlanta, GA: Scholars Press, 1973). For a full length treatment of Thornwell's life, theology, and work, see James Oscar Farmer Jr., *The Metaphysical Confederacy: James Henry Thornwell and the Synthesis of Southern Values* (Macon, GA: Mercy University Press, 1986); Brian T. Wingard, '"As the Lord Puts Words in Her Mouth:" The Supremacy of Scripture in the Ecclesiology of James Henley Thornwell and Its Influence Upon the Presbyterian Churches of the South' (Ph.D. dissertation, Philadelphia, PA: Westminster Theological Seminary, 1992); Christopher C. Cooper, 'Binding Bodies and Liberating Souls: James Henley Thornwell's Vision for a Spiritual Church and a Christian Confederacy,' *The Confessional Presbyterian* Vol 9 (2013): pp. 35-47.

102. Gutjahr, *Charles Hodge*, p. 288.

103. Vance, *Ecclesiology of Thornwell*, p. 5.

104. Ibid., p. 7

Unfortunately, for some, he was a staunch supporter of Southern society, and some believe he had the ability to prevent the Civil War but didn't.[105] Indeed, many have failed to benefit from the ecclesiology of Thornwell because they were not able to get past his defense of Southern slavery.[106] Vance has offered a sober assessment:

> One must not, of course, dismiss or minimize Thornwell's views on slavery no matter how kind and considerate he might have treated his own slaves; or, that he made important distinctions which modified his views on slavery, distinctions his critics often fail to mention. Thornwell's views on this subject are unacceptable by contemporary standards, and, a fortiori, were unacceptable by the most morally sensitive of his own time.[107]

Even so, Vance continues describing Thornwell's ecclesiology and enjoins a sympathetic reading despite Thornwell's shortcomings in this area.[108] He was such a good preacher that he was compared to Chrysostom, although his preaching was characterized as condensed and technical, perhaps overshooting the average person in the pew.[109] Thornwell maintained the doctrine of justification as central to his theology.[110]

Not only was he a consummate churchman; he was also an educator that held several positions at South Carolina College: he served as instructor, professor, chaplain and finally as president.[111] He replaced Thomas Cooper, the rationalist, when Cooper was forced to resign in 1834. Thornwell led the institution to become more friendly to Calvinist theology.[112] He had a reputation as the consummate leader that had won the esteem of his colleagues. His ability to lead so effectively, it was widely rumored, lay in his character: he was honest and fair in his

---

105. Ibid., pp. 7-8. For another view, see Farmer's, *The Metaphysical Confederacy*, who argues that the aggression of the North forced Southern intellectuals to mount a defense of Southern society based on their orthodox faith, a conservative approach to societal change and the idealization of their society.

106. Ibid., p. 9.

107. Ibid., p. 12.

108. Ibid., p. 13.

109. Ibid., pp. 17-18.

110. Ibid., p. 20.

111. Ibid., p. 23.

112. Peterson, *Ham and Japheth, The Mythic World of Whites*, p. 19.

work there and this inspired trust and confidence.[113] His writings can be characterized as having a philosophical cast, even outstripping Hodge according to some in this respect.[114]

This was in contrast to many others, even Old School Presbyterians (e.g. C. Hodge in the North and Breckinridge in the South) who believed the church was best situated to influence causes like education and slavery. Whereas Hodge believed that the church should be guided by general principles, or *jure humano* (by human right) as discussed below, Thornwell claimed and followed consistently that 'the Bible is our only rule, and that where it is silent we have no right to speak.'[115] Thornwell saw no place for the church to influence politics declaring, 'It is not the distinctive province of the Church to build asylums for the needy or insane, to organize societies for the improvement of the penal code, or the arresting of the progress of intemperance, gambling or lust.'[116] Whereas Hodge saw that the church possessed an 'interpretive flexibility' on ecclesiastical, political matters, the existence of voluntary societies and denominational boards, Thornwell argued that such structures had no place in scripture and therefore no place in the church, claiming that 'God had laid down in the Scripture a form of Church government, for which we are not at liberty to depart ... we can no more create a new office, or a new organ for the church, than we can create a new article of faith.'[117] Thornwell held that the corporate church held no role in political problems of the day. These two heavyweight ecclesial giants found themselves at odds in print and on the floor of the General Assembly, especially in 1845 and 1860. In addition to the above issues, they locked horns especially on the issue of the validity and recognition of Roman Catholic baptisms.

Alan Strange has made the argument that Thornwell modified his SOTC doctrine, coming out of the debates with Hodge in 1859-60, and that Thornwell never went in the direction of declaring the state 'secular' in his efforts to protect the orbits of the church and the state

113. Vance, *Ecclesiology of Thornwell*, p. 26.

114. Ibid., p. 30.

115. Quoted in Gutjahr, *Charles Hodge*, p. 291.

116. Quoted in Marcus John McArthur, *Render unto Lincoln: Disloyalty and Clergy in Civil War Missouri* (Unpublished manuscript, 2015), p. 33.

117. Quoted in Gutjahr, *Charles Hodge*, p. 292.

as distinct. For Strange, this is very different than moderns who argue (as do Thornwell's successors according to Strange) for the SOTC's concomitant, the secularity of the state.[118] The gist of Thornwell's nuanced views is well expressed by Wingard:

> Thornwell did not deny that the Scriptures contained principles which Christians ought to make use of in their relationships with the civil magistrate (and every other area of life), rather he maintained that the Church as a court of Jesus Christ, while she could point out these general principles, it has no right to presume to dictate the specific application of those principles in ways not specifically mandated by the Word of God ... declaring the right as a judicatory to extrapolate from general principles by making specific applications which depended upon her own opinions of matters.[119]

Now we move on to some interesting examples of 'border state' pastors during the Civil War.

## Stuart Robinson

Born in Ireland, on November 14, 1814, Stuart Robinson's story is a fascinating one. His father preceded the family to America, in hopes of etching out a better living for his family whom he would send for later. He was injured in one of his arms early in childhood, probably dropped by his nurse. Stories differ about how this happened; nevertheless, this left him with a permanent disability. After immigrating to Virginia, Stuart's mother died. Now his father, suddenly saddled with five children, recognized this was a great burden and so he entrusted his son to the care of a pious German farmer called Andrew Troutman. Troutman recognized early on that Stuart, due to his handicap, would be unfit for a career of manual labor, and so the Troutmans entrusted Stuart to the care of a Presbyterian pastor, Rev. James M. Brown, realizing that Stuart might be better suited and trained for a vocation of the mind. Brown nurtured him for the ministry. An even more significant influence during this time was his coming under the influence of Dr William Henry Foote, an instructor of the academy in Romney, Virginia. It was under Foote's influence that the Old School sympathies of the

---

118. See Strange, *The Doctrine of the Spirituality of the Church*, pp. 250-57.
119. Wingard, 'As the Lord Puts Words in her Mouth,' p. 270.

'Scoto-American' idea of the church in relation to the state took root in Robinson.[120] His later education at Union Seminary and Princeton, institutions of the Old School, would only further solidify and nourish his convictions.[121]

Leading up to the Civil War, Robinson gained notoriety for his eloquence on matters of ecclesiology. This led to his appointment by the General Assembly to Danville Seminary in Kentucky. His magnum opus on the topic was published in 1858, entitled *The Church of God as an Essential Element of the Gospel*.[122] Robinson connected his views with the Scottish Reformation; indeed, so much so, that the whole of the Scottish church's *Second Book of Discipline* was reprinted in the back of Robinson's book. He saw the American experiment with its separation of church and state as an opportunity to complete what the Scottish Presbyterians had begun.[123]

It was during this time that a growing controversy was occurring between Robinson and Robert J. Breckinridge, the uncle of Vice President John C. Breckinridge. The flash point occurred where Robinson argued for the SOTC doctrine whereas Breckinridge argued for 'the church's responsibility in "all aspects of human life," including the growing political controversy between the states.'[124] Probably in response to some of the growing tensions with Breckinridge at Danville, Robinson accepted a call to the Second Presbyterian Church in Louisville, Kentucky in the spring of 1858. The makeup of this church was a perfect fit for Robinson's ecclesiology, since it had on its rolls members that were sympathetic to the 'union,' immigrants from New England, and others heavily invested in businesses of the South and keenly in favor of the South. Some of the members were even blacks who were slaves. Thus, the congregation had an air of ambivalence

---

120. Graham, *A Kingdom Not of This World*, p. 37.

121. Ibid.

122. Stuart Robinson, *The Church of God as An Essential Element of the Gospel, and The Idea, Structure and Functions Thereof. A Discourse in Four Parts, With An Appendix, Containing the more important symbols of Presbyterian Church Government, Historically Arranged and Illustrated* (Joseph M. Wilson, 1858. Reprint, Willow Grove, PA: The Committee on Christian Education of the Orthodox Presbyterian Church, 2009). (Hereafter, *The Church*.)

123. Graham, *A Kingdom Not of This World*, p. 29.

124. Ibid., p. 31.

with regard to contemporary political problems.[125] However, this would change during the war and in the city, due to its mixed sympathies, and resulted in an atmosphere there that can only be described as pandemonium, and full of social contention. Suspicion ran high everywhere within the city walls, so to speak.[126]

The initial years of Robinson's ministry were prosperous in every way; however, in spite of the relocation from Danville Seminary to Louisville, the tensions between the two theologians' ecclesiological positions grew as Breckinridge moved from a semi-spirituality and mostly apolitical stance towards views that saw the church's ministry and mission as directly relevant to the politics of the state.[127] However, for Robinson, 'advancing the kingdom of Christ did not call for saturating public life with religious ideals, persuading church leaders to take stands on questions of political moment.'[128] For Robinson, 'The civil realm ... was a "sphere under God." But Robinson demonstrated no interest in American exceptionalism on this score. The United States might be under God, but so was every other nation on the planet, which meant that they all had equal access to the laws and norms of the created order and to human reason to try to figure out the best means for restraining wickedness and protecting the welfare of citizens.'[129] This raises a crucial and timeless insight that Robinson's arguments and life raise, which Hart eloquently summarizes:

> Robinson demonstrated an important axiom in Protestant experience with American politics: the higher (i.e., more religious or spiritual) one's view of the ministry of the church, the more realistic one's assessment of the possibilities of politics; conversely the higher (i.e., more religious or spiritual) one's view of the state, the less unique the nature and purpose of the church.[130]

So prescient and insightful were Robinson's views, that it cost him dearly. He took flak from both sides. Even his fellow Southerners criticized him

---

125. Ibid., p. 32.

126. Ibid., pp. 43-45.

127. Ibid., p. 33.

128. Darryl Hart, *A Secular Faith*, p. 118.

129. Ibid., pp. 118-19.

130. Ibid., p. 119.

when he could not (as a minister) endorse the Confederacy, and he took criticism from Union soldiers as well. During the outbreak of the war, the previous mixture of Northern and Southern sympathies that produced a natural soil in which Robinson's apolitical views could prosper, became a location of nothing short of pandemonium, as mentioned above. The climax of this surd evil culminated with ministers required to take oaths of allegiance to the Union, most infamously in 'Order Number 61,' in 1864, an act that caused much alarm among border-state ministers.[131]

In short, during the war, ministers in the border-states, who appeared to be dissenting from the cause of the Union, were either jailed or exiled. Some were forced into exile. Others voluntarily did so. Such was true of Robinson as well. While travelling to visit his terminally ill brother out of the state, he received correspondence from friends that it was dangerous to return to Louisville and so he voluntarily exiled himself to Toronto, Canada, where he lived for the duration of most of the war and maintained a fruitful ministry especially among students and citizens in Toronto.[132] His wife Mary remained in Louisville during this time, suffering indignities by undisciplined troops while she tried to protect their property. The property of the *True Presbyterian* (press, type, and papers) was confiscated in 1864 and was never to appear again under that name; however, after the war under a new title, *Free Christian Commonwealth*, it did appear.

The very fact that Stuart Robinson was in a border-state contributed to what made his view of the church as spiritual and apolitical a threat. In other words, as Graham adroitly points out, the situation may have been better for Robinson if he had resided in a truly committed Northern or Southern state. But *because* he resided in a border-state, his views became suspect and less palatable to some.[133]

## The Case of Samuel B. McPheeters

Samuel McPheeters was born on September 18, 1819, in Raleigh, North Carolina, destined to become the center of a great controversy

---

131. Graham, *A Kingdom Not of This World*, p. 51. Robinson, in exile, denounced with deep concern the substance and abuses of Order Number 61, and shortly thereafter the *True Presbyterian* was confiscated. For details, see Ibid., pp. 55-56.

132. Ibid., pp. 53-54.

133. Ibid., p. 62.

forty years later. He died in 1870, reaching only fifty-one years after enduring a period of tremendous personal, professional turmoil and suffering, hearsay, speculation and slander. Border-state pastors suffered tremendously during the Civil War. Border States throughout the Civil War were Missouri, Kentucky, Maryland and West Virginia, and Delaware less so. There was a high degree of division in these states in matters related to the Civil War. Although these states were geographically within the Union, they often had many citizens that were sympathetic to Southern causes. Also, residing in many of these states were enthusiastic Unionists, sometimes army troops of the Union, and sometimes Copperheads (those in the Union who were nonetheless sympathetic to the cause of the Confederacy).

McPheeter's personal story is representative of the hardship that took place among Presbyterian churches during the war. To illustrate how bad it was, one has only to observe how many Presbyterian churches went into nonexistence during that time. One Presbyterian pastor, George Miller, wrote that 'the effects of the war upon our churches will be readily seen in the fact that between 1861 and 1866, one half of all the churches on the roll became utterly extinct not appearing afterward on the role of either Assembly.'[134] McPheeters made a perilous attempt to maintain the apolitical nature of the church in his own border-state. Indeed, as a commissioner to the General Assembly in 1862, he joined Stuart Robinson by protesting a paper by Breckinridge because 'it was inconsistent with the nature of the church and the proper functions of its judicatories to express any judgment on political questions.'[135] There was a minority among the leadership in his own church that actively sought his removal and succeeded in spite of the fact that only a minority opposed McPheeters in his own presbytery. He appealed to the General Assembly in 1864 but failed and was removed from office. It brought him into the center of political and ecclesiastical strife, military intervention, ultimately a personal meeting with President Lincoln himself, exile and banishment from his pulpit, his state and home, and ultimately probably contributed to a premature breakdown of his health.[136]

---

134. Quoted in Ibid., p. 65.

135. See A. Strange, *The Doctrine of the Spirituality of the Church*, p. 286.

136. He was by no means the only one since extant sources say that some 120 clergymen faced some kind of interference from Federalists during or immediately after the war. Cf.,

Some were incensed at the injustices levied against McPheeters. None was a more ardent supporter, and more clearly demonstrated the principles at stake, than Rev. Henry J. Van Dyke, the pastor of First Presbyterian Church in Brooklyn. Van Dyke was a supporter of slavery and published a famous pro-slavery sermon in spite of the fact that he was the pastor of that church.[137] Van Dyke provides a stark contrast to another preacher in Brooklyn, Henry Ward Beecher (yes, related to the famous novelist, his sister), who was renowned for being one of the most vocal opponents of slavery in the North at the time. In a famous speech delivered in the Synod of New York on October 18th, 1864, Van Dyke sets forth his case towards the end of his long speech:

> Stript of all forms and technicalities, and regarded, as it would appear in a court of equity, upon its real merits, the whole proceeding, from its inception to its consummation, amounts to this, that a minority of a congregation, urged on by political zeal and abetted by the interference of a secular power, has been able to deprive the majority of the minister of their choice, whom even his enemies admit to be a faithful and able servant of Christ, proscribing and branding him as a disloyal man, simply because he is supposed to entertain political opinions about which the bible and our standards have nothing to say.[138]

Even a moderate voice, like Charles Hodge, who strove to exercise sympathy to all sides during this tumultuous time, after analyzing the case concluded that McPheeters was 'free from all charge or suspicion of disloyal conduct in word or deed' and that 'the highest national authorities' had cleared him of all charges; and moreover that McPheeters had the 'full confidence' of the 'great body' of his congregation, presbytery, and was one of the 'most devoted Union men of St. Louis.'[139] So, Hodge was disappointed in the outcome of the vote at the General Assembly; nevertheless, he also thought that McPheeters

---

Marcus John McArthur, *Render unto Lincoln: Disloyalty and Clergy in Civil War Missouri* (Unpublished manuscript, 2015), p. 5.

137. The sermon was *The Character and Influence of Abolitionism: A Sermon Preached in the First Presbyterian Church, Brooklyn on Sabbath Evening, Dec. 9th, 1860* (New York: G. F. Nesbit & Co., 1860). See Strange, *The Doctrine of the Spirituality of the Church*, pp. 315, for details.

138. Henry J. Van Dyke, *The Spirituality and Independence of the Church: A Speech Delivered in the Synod of New York, October 18th, 1864* (New York, 1864).

139. Quoted in Strange, *The Doctrine of the Spirituality of the Church*, p. 288.

had made some grave mistakes along the way and that this was the origin of his problems.[140]

## J. Gresham Machen[141]

Fast forward to the next generation. These same principles elucidated by these other Old School men, were stated eloquently by J.G. Machen (1881-1937), the founder of the denomination in which I serve:

> The responsibility of the church in the new age is the same as its responsibility in every age. It is to testify that this world is lost in sin; that the span of human life—nay, all the length of human history—is an infinitesimal island in the awful depths of eternity; that there is a mysterious holy living God, Creator of all, Upholder of all, infinitely beyond all; that he has revealed himself in his Word and offered us communion with himself through Jesus Christ the Lord; that there is no other salvation, for individuals or for nations, save this, but that this salvation is full and free, and that whosoever possesses it has for himself and for all others to whom he may be the instrument of bringing it a treasure compared with which all the kingdoms of the earth—nay, all the wonders of the starry heavens—are as the dust of the street.[142]

Machen learned this Old School doctrine from his mother, Minnie Gresham Machen, who was arguably the chief influence in his life.[143] Baltimore, the place where he was raised, was the home of many displaced Southerners after the civil war.[144] Machen was raised in an affectionate

---

140. Ibid.

141. Much has been written on Machen; however, the best works describing his life, influences upon him, and his work include Darryl Glenn Hart, '"Doctor Fundamentalis" An Intellectual Biography of J. Gresham Machen, 1881-1937' (Ph.D. Dissertation, The John Hopkins University, 1988); ibid., *Defending the Faith: J. Gresham Machen and the Crisis of Conservative Protestantism in Modern America* (Baltimore, MD: The John Hopkins University Press, 1994); Katherine Lynn Tan VanDrunen's unpublished doctoral dissertation, 'The Foothills of the Matterhorn: familial antecedents of J. Gresham Machen,' (Ph.D. dissertation, Loyola University Chicago, 2006).

142. J. Gresham Machen, 'The Responsibility of the Church in Our New Age,' *The Presbyterian Guardian* 36:1 (January 1967), p. 13. Machen, a Professor at Princeton Theological Seminary, was a staunch defender of orthodoxy in his day. This led him to found Westminster Theological Seminary in 1929 and the Orthodox Presbyterian Church in 1936. He was born into a home that reflected the aristocratic south [see, D. G. Hart, 'Doctor Fundamentalis,' pp. 27-28]. Some of the consequences of this influence will be discussed below in the book.

143. Katherine VanDrunen, 'The Foothills of the Matterhorn,' p. 160.

144. Ibid., p. 156.

family that was thoroughly Southern and valued their Southern identity. In this home, the Christian faith was of the utmost importance and education was an essential aspect of life.[145] The SOTC was an Old School doctrine to which Minnie Machen was cordially attached and often showed up in her journals, especially when she related abuses coming forth from the pulpit.[146]

As a young Christian, I became aware of the teaching of J.G. Machen (or as his friends called him at Princeton's exclusive eating and social clubs, 'Das,' or as his students at Princeton called him, 'Dassie'). A pastor put several first edition copies of his books into my hands. I read eagerly, and since Machen was a budding mountaineer (like myself) and took a courageous stand against the liberalism of his day, he instantly became one of my heroes. Additionally, having been raised in a mainline church that was constantly taking pains to address social matters at the expense of addressing sin and orthodox answers for a sin-cursed world, it was at the feet of Machen, so to speak, that I first heard lucid teaching on the subject of the SOTC. I had found my home. Machen's life and vocation is well known and recited in many popular works, so I'll not rehearse well-trodden ground here.

Nevertheless, more recently it has come to the attention of the public eye that Machen wrote a letter in 1913 to his mother about his institution's (Princeton) plan of integration for students at Princeton. As Hart has recounted it, Machen thought that 'if a black man were to take up residence in Alexander Hall, Machen wrote, he would consider moving out, which would have been "a great sacrifice to me."'[147]

Of course this is disappointing to hear. Yes, Machen had clay feet. He was a mere (although great) man who it seemed was afflicted with notions of white supremacy in his own day. Perhaps it is good that we talk about this, it might save us from our undue adulation of heroes of the faith and from our tribalism, which so often afflicts our conservative churches with the stench of division. Yet, that does not mean we have nothing

---

145. Ibid., p. 161.

146. Ibid., pp. 183-84.

147. Quoted in Darryl G. Hart, 'The Unpardonable Sin?' a review of Jemar Tisby's, *The Color of Compromise: The Truth about the American Church's Complicity in Racism* in *Ordained Servant* 28 (2019): pp. 130-31. (First published electronically at https://opc.org/os.html?article_id=754&issue_id=146.)

to learn from Machen and it especially doesn't mean that we should not cite, quote, or allude to him and his teachings, let alone remove plaques, pictures, or statues honoring him at our institutions. Even so, this unpleasant fact about the letter to his mother does demonstrate how hurtful and damaging such things can be, not only in the past but in our present generation as well. This leads me to explore the fascinating story of another Princeton grad, Francis James Grimké. It seems that Princeton had regressed instead of progressing on the difficult issue of race relations by the time 'Das' arrived in her esteemed halls.

## The Case of Francis Grimké

Francis James Grimké (1850-1937) is worthy of mention in this study of the primary mission of the church for several reasons. He was an important figure in American Christianity at the time, often referred to affectionately (not pejoratively) as the 'Black Puritan.'[148] The term was employed because he was much loved as a leader of black Presbyterians but also because of his emphasis on the need of character for both white and black Christians.[149] Moreover, he kept rigid standards for his own moral conduct and expected the same of others as well.[150] Additionally, he thought one's religion should 'spill over' into all of life so it should be reflected especially in human relations.[151]

Grimké was a student at Princeton (due to the generosity of his aunts, famous abolitionists) after attending Lincoln and Howard Universities during these tumultuous years after the Civil War. At Lincoln he graduated as valedictorian. At Howard, he studied law like his brother but eventually dropped those ambitions in response to his sense of call to the ministry.[152] This was a unique time in the history of Presbyterianism, since there was a concern immediately following the Civil War to raise up a 'native ministry' lest 'thousands of Negroes [in the south] be lost

---

148. Louis B. Weeks III, 'Racism, World War I and the Christian Life: Francis Grimké in the Nation's Capital,' in *Black Apostles: Afro-American Clergy Confront the Twentieth Century* (Boston, Mass: G. K. Hall & Co., 1978), pp. 57-75, especially pp. 70-71.

149. Ibid., pp. 68-70.

150. Darryl M. Trimiew, *Voices of the Silenced: The Responsible Self in a Marginalized Community* (Cleveland, OH: The Pilgrim Press, 1993), p. 51.

151. Weeks, 'Racism, World War I and the Christian Life,' p. 71.

152. Trimiew, *Voices of the Silenced*, p. 50

to Presbyterianism.'[153] Later, he was actually offered the presidency of Howard University but declined. While studying at Princeton, where he matriculated in 1875, he was considered an outstanding student, who, according to Charles Hodge, was 'equal to the ablest of his students.'[154] Significantly, Grimké's three year tenure at Princeton coincided with the final years of Charles Hodge's career.[155] A.A. Hodge labelled him 'a very able man, highly educated, of high character, and worthy of all confidence.'[156] He also won the confidence of the president of the College, James McCosh.[157] It is important to remember that Grimké was a very accomplished and well-educated clergyman, but not a professional theologian.[158]

In his first year at Princeton, Grimké experienced little, if any, racial prejudice.[159] This may be attributed to the culture created by Grimké's black predecessor, Matthew Anderson, who was to become one of Grimké's closest friends.[160] Anderson, a black man from a free Negro family residing in Pennsylvania, applied to Princeton in 1874 and was accepted. The schools seem to have not realized he was black, and when he first showed up, Dr McGill tried to place him in residence with a black family in town; however, Anderson insisted on residing in the dormitory. One year later, Grimké and two other black students matriculated. The test came due to the relationship between the seminary and her elder university institution. All students had access to the university library and classes. One of the most popular classes among the seminarians was a history of philosophy class, offered by the president, James McCosh. Usually, the undergraduates welcomed the students from the seminary; however, when Culp (one of the black students from the Seminary with the darkest skin)

---

153. Henry Justin Ferry, 'Francis James Grimké: portrait of a black puritan,' (Ph.D. diss. Yale University, 1971), p. 77.

154. Quoted in David Torbett, *Theology and Slavery*, p. 179.

155. Ferry, 'Francis James Grimké,' p. 86.

156. Weeks, 'Racism, World War I and the Christian Life,' p. 59.

157. Ibid.

158. Trimiew, *Voices of the Silenced*, p. 56.

159. See *The Works of Francis J. Grimké*, edited by Carter G. Woodson (Washington D.C., Associated Publishers, 1942) 4 vols., at vol. 1, p. 526.

160. Ferry, 'Francis James Grimké,' p. 92.

appeared in the class, apparently it became a 'minor *cause celebre*.'[161] Several Southern students in McCosh's class protested the presence of the black students, but McCosh insisted that he would not exclude any student from his class on the basis of color.[162] In short, McCosh and many friends of Culp encouraged him to remain in the class, which he did, and truth and justice (forever on the scaffold) prevailed.[163] The following year, Grimké himself took the class with no tumult or problems whatsoever.

Even so, forty years later, the situation had changed, and Grimké made his protest known in strident terms. I will quote at length what he writes because it helps us capture the passion and pain that this pastor felt about his alma mater:

> Princeton is not only the oldest, but the greatest of our theological schools. The work to which it is especially devoting itself is the preparation of men for the gospel ministry – the preparation of men to go out and proclaim the unsearchable riches of grace in Christ Jesus to a perishing world. In a school like that you would expect to find the highest type of Christianity, the finest expressions of the spirit and teachings of Jesus Christ; you would expect, if anywhere in the world, men of all races would be received on terms of perfect Christian equality, it would be in a theological seminary – in one of the schools of the prophets. And yet, what is the fact as to this seminary? The color line is drawn in it, so far as the dormitories are concerned. There is no disposition now to allow colored students to occupy rooms within these buildings. It did not use to be so. Forty years ago when I entered the seminary, there were three other colored students, making four in all, and we all occupied rooms within the dormitories. Things have since changed; prejudice has so increased that the color of a man's skin now shuts him out of these buildings. It is a shame that it should be so. It is a shame that, at the very fountain head of theological training in the great Presbyterian Church, race prejudice should be allowed to assert itself, and to thrive. Who is responsible for this? Is it the President of the seminary? Then he is not fit to be President. Are the professors responsible for it? Then they are not fit to be professors. They may have the scholarship, the technical knowledge, but the higher qualification, the mind that was in Jesus, the spirit and the temper of the great Teacher, without which mere scholarship counts for

---

161. Ibid., p. 94.
162. Ibid.
163. Ibid.

nothing, they are sadly lacking in. Are the Directors responsible for it? Then they are not fit to be Directors in a school of this kind.[164]

He was a former slave himself, the son of a black slave and her white master. He was emancipated when his father died; however, later his half-brother tried to enslave him again, so he fled. After joining a Confederate regiment in order to serve as a valet for a Confederate army officer, he was later spotted by the same half-brother when marching through his former town, arrested and thrown into prison where he almost died. His mother fortunately rescued him and nursed him back to health. This saved his life, but his half-brother guardian sold him to another Confederate army officer, and he served under him for the duration of the war.[165] Undoubtedly, and understandably, these experiences profoundly shaped his subsequent life and his utter disgust for racism in whatever form it was found.

After graduation he went on to pastor a black congregation for many years in the Washington D.C. area. Hence, being a pastor of a well-known church in a predominately white denomination inside the beltway left him and his congregation in a constant state of tension within his denomination.[166] There was no true integration in his day; rather, the church was a 'church within a church' in a denomination that was unabashedly racist.[167] His brothers and sisters in the denomination remained segregationist. Even so, he refused to leave; he remained and played the role of the gadfly.

He married a remarkable woman, Charlotte Forten, on December 19, 1878. From all reports, they shared a wonderful marriage, but the same could not be said for Grimké's public life. Weeks describes:

> As a black clergyman in an essentially white denomination, as a black citizen in a nation dominated by white thinking, Grimke fought continually the insidious presence of political and religious racism. Throughout his life, although specific issues and the Christian response to each varied immensely, he remained consistently in favor of the full enfranchisement of black America.[168]

---

164. *Works of Francis J. Grimké*, p. 526.

165. See, for details, Trimiew, *Voices of the Silenced*, pp. 49-50.

166. Ibid., p. 55.

167. Ibid.

168. Ibid., p. 60.

Much of his ministry coincided with the proliferation of Jim Crow laws, which of course legalized racial segregation, especially in Southern states, that included not only racial segregation but restrictions on voting and even in some cases banned interracial marriage. During this time, he was known for combatting systemic racism, especially during World War I by protesting the segregation of troops. I have already addressed the issue of the complexity of addressing 'systemic injustice' in a society. However, Jim Crow laws provide a good example of 'systemic' injustice. In other words, this was more than merely the malice of individuals he was combatting; rather, it was systematized injustice, perhaps even allowing or incentivizing malicious individuals to be racist!

Grimké has been largely neglected by historical scholarship which has merely focused on his founding of the American Negro Academy or the National Association for the Advancement of Colored People.[169] At the core of Grimké's arguments and rhetoric for systemic change were ideas he learned at Princeton, ironically enough: a belief in the unity of humankind – the idea 'that all human beings are essentially similar and essentially equal in God's eyes: "With God a white skin carries no more weight than a black skin, or skin of any other hue."'[170]

Interestingly, at Princeton, during his time there as a student, Grimké received little, if any, racial prejudice in the dormitories where he roomed.[171] During this time he studied under luminaries like Charles Hodge, Archibald Alexander Hodge, Caspar Wistar Hodge, and William Henry Green. He learned later that the idea of segregation among students was encouraged by his beloved alma mater and he was crushed and wrote and spoke vigorously against it. In 1908, he wrote to his own presbytery: 'If there is any one thing that Jesus himself desired to accomplish, more than others it was to break down these artificial and anti-Christian walls of separation. When will the church of Jesus Christ cease its hypocritical cant about religion, and begin to live it, in spirit and truth?'[172] However, like most social gospel preachers, the 'central purpose of Dr Grimké's life was the application

---

169. Ibid., especially at p. 57.
170. Torbett, *Theology and Slavery*, p. 180.
171. Grimké's works, I. p. 526.
172. Ibid., IV, p. 115.

of the Gospel to the social order, particularly in regard to the elevation of his people.'[173]

Grimké unfortunately could be quite militant in his thoughts and actions, which unfortunately cost him dearly because he was precluded from publishing in denominational periodicals.[174] His views on Christian religion in America (and not just Presbyterians) was expressed in militant and dim terms, for example: 'So far as the color line is concerned, white American Christianity has been and still is absolutely rotten, utterly alien from the spirit and principles of the religion of Jesus Christ .... Jesus came to break down the walls of separation and to make us brethren .... but the American Church has been, and is now doing all in its power to produce the very opposite effect ....'[175]

For Grimké, miscegenation was no obstacle, since he was honored when asked to officiate at the wedding of his friend, Frederick Douglass, to Miss Pitts, who happened to be white. He delighted in being asked.[176] For Grimké, participation of blacks in World War I (which he opposed since he thought the war was merely to insure white supremacy throughout the world) was unconscionable since the same black man who was to spill his own precious blood on behalf of the nation would not be allowed to 'enter a single restaurant, eating place, or hotel on Pennsylvania Avenue and get a sandwich, or a glass of milk simply because of the color of his skin.'[177] This filled the pastor with 'bitterness and hostility.'[178] Grimké could have definitely helped his cause and message before, during, and after the war if he had used more tempered speech.

There is no doubt, based on Grimké's works, that he thought the only solution to the hatred of racism was the Christian gospel.[179] Even so, sometimes he could act with such stridency that, as Trimiew states it, 'Grimké understood rejecting racism in general and white supremacy in particular was at the heart of the Gospel. Accordingly, a responsible self, a follower of Jesus, had to hold to, and to also give evidence of,

173. Torbett, *Theology and Slavery*, p. 167.

174. Weeks, 'Racism, World War I and the Christian Life,' p. 61.

175. Quoted in Ibid., pp. 61-62.

176. Ibid.

177. Quoted in Ibid., p. 66.

178. Ibid.

179. Ibid., p. 68.

being "no respecter of persons." For this reason, Grimké regarded most white Christians as borderline heretics.'[180] However, Grimké was definitely a communitarian and believed that a privileged education and giftedness entailed helping the less fortunate in his community.[181] Even so, Grimké has been criticized for his, perhaps, over-confidence in capitalism.[182] Most Americans, says Trimiew, 'did not have a college education, well-educated aunts to help them [with tuition], and degrees from outstanding universities.'[183]

I am not aware of anywhere in the published writings of Grimké where he referred directly to the segregationist sympathies of J. Gresham Machen, who wrote to his mother in a personal letter in 1913 sharing his concern about a black man taking up residence in Alexander Hall (at Princeton), as mentioned above. Perhaps he was unaware. Nevertheless, he was aware of some segregationist sympathies on the part of some at Princeton.

## Conclusion

We have covered much in this chapter. Not only did we deal with such luminaries in the nineteenth and twentieth centuries as Charles Hodge, Thornwell, Stuart Robinson, Samuel B. McPheeters and J. Gresham Machen, I tried to engage the difficult social issue of slavery that so perplexed Reformed luminaries in the North and South during the nineteenth century.

As a biblical scholar, I found myself fascinated (and saddened) by the influential and mistaken so-called 'myth of Ham' which so many people had been duped by for many centuries. Thankfully, in recent years, much good research and many interesting monographs and articles have taken pains to explain this historical phenomenon. In the next chapter, we move on to discuss the very nature of church power. As we move towards the conclusion of this book, we will move slowly from more theoretical discussions to practical application. For example, in the next chapter, I deal with a recent debate in church courts on women in the

---

180. Trimiew, *Voices of the Silenced*, p. 62.
181. Ibid., p. 54.
182. Ibid., p. 60.
183. Ibid.

military. Far from irrelevant, what we observe in these recent debates is that the principles associated with the primary mission of the church, yeah even expressed as the SOTC, will not go away but keep raising their head.

# PART FOUR

# CHAPTER 13

# The Glorious King and Head of the Church: The Nature of Church Power

In the previous chapter we examined a period of history that demonstrated the flourishing of Old School Presbyterianism in America, in both the North and the South before the conflagration of the Civil War that left more men dead than any other war in the history of the United States. That chapter began to uncover one of the most important principles in church government: the nature of ecclesiastical power. As Craig Troxel has shown in his exquisitely argued unpublished dissertation: '*Jus divinum* [divine right] Presbyterianism has been an unusually rich blessing for the Reformed tradition. But despite its profitable contributions, the doctrine of the church and church power are still in need of further reformed consequent exposition.'[1]

We saw in a previous chapter that these debates on the legitimacy of independent church boards manifested themselves most vividly in the use of extra-biblical bodies such as voluntary societies and boards of governance within the Presbyterian church during the nineteenth century. Therefore, while it may seem like an oblique turn in our argument, this subject actually shucks to the very cob of the issue of the primary mission of the church and its various permutations even down to contemporary times. We will again touch on the debate over church

---

1.  A. Craig Troxel, '"Divine Right" Presbyterianism,' p. 249.

boards to make clear what the real differences of opinion were, which are integrally related to the topic of the primary mission of the church.

Then, so that we do not become too abstract, but demonstrate again how these issues keep emerging in contemporary problems, we shall shift to look briefly at another case debated recently on the floor of General Assemblies about whether women should serve in military combat units; in short, the issue has been called 'women in combat.' Reformed denominations have wrestled over the issue of church power and the appropriateness of the church, as a corporate church, addressing the civil government over this contentious issue. In the course of my argument, I hope to resurrect an important exegetical, theological, and ecclesiological principle that has been lost on the church in modern times: the important teaching of the headship of Christ over the church.

## The Nature of Church Power

Stuart Robinson, the border-state pastor in the nineteenth century who was introduced in the last chapter, has made one of the most pristine and clear statements on church power in his book, *The Church of God as an Essential Element of the Gospel.*[2] In this book, Robinson's apologetic for the church is 'essentially a statement of the sufficiency of Scripture and its outworking for the government of the Church.'[3] He discusses four elements of church power: the source of church power; the delegation and vesting of church power; the mode of exercise of church power; and the limits of church power. I will briefly describe each of these following Robinson's order and then reflect on the historical background to these views before proceeding to our illustrations of how they work out (or not) in the church by discussing the issue of 'women in combat' which has been a contemporary matter for serious deliberation and debate in some Reformed and Presbyterian churches.

The origin of church power for Robinson is unilateral, top down from its source. He states: 'The source of all Church power is primarily Jesus Christ, the Mediator.'[4] Although Jesus Christ is the source of

---

2. Stuart Robinson, *The Church of God as an Essential Element of the Gospel* (Philadelphia: Joseph M. Wilson, 1858; repr., Willow Grove, PA), p. 61.

3. Troxel, '"Divine Right" Presbyterianism,' p. 88.

4. Robinson, *The Church of God*, p. 61.

power, He 'vests' or delegates his power to men. This power is vested in the whole body, both elected officers and the people. That is why in my first chapter, I cited Chapter 3.1 of the PCA Book of Church Order, which says, as the reader will recall:

> That power which Christ has committed to His Church, vests in the whole body, the rulers and the ruled, constituting it a spiritual commonwealth. This power, as exercised by the people, extends to the choice of those officers whom He has appointed in His church.[5]

Robinson makes the point forcefully, that the power of the church is not considered as an aggregate of individuals in the church, nor as the office-bearers apart from the people; rather, 'power is vested in the Church as an organic body, composed of both rulers and ruled.'[6] See, e.g., Romans 12; 1 Corinthians 12; Ephesians 4:4.

Nevertheless, the administration (or mode) of this power is through the officers. This was the case in the OT theocracy (e.g., judges and kings) and in the NT through apostles.[7] In the NT, elders always act in a plurality, never alone.[8] They are representatives of the people, but they are not separate from the commonwealth of the people who selected them. This is why we should demur from applying the term 'clergy' to the ministers and 'laity' to non-officers in the church. They are not a caste separate from the people of the congregation. This is one of the things that so exercised Thornwell when Hodge used such terminology, i.e., 'clergy.' Thornwell asserted that Hodge had slipped into prelacy:

> Now, according to Dr Hodge, the people, as contradistinguished from the clergy, are *one* of the organs of government, or, if not a whole organ, a part of one. If they are not a hand, they are a finger. They have a *substantive part* in *government*, in a sense in which they do not have a substantive part in preaching or in dispensing the sacraments. Dr Hodge divides the church into two castes, with separate and even antagonistic interests; and government—although he repudiates the notion that all power is joint—is the joint product of two factors. The division is thoroughly Popish, though the use of it is not.[9]

---

5. PCA *Book of Church Order*, pp. 3-1.
6. Robinson, *The Church of God*, p. 62.
7. Ibid.
8. Ibid., p. 65.
9. Thornwell, IV, p. 273.

To promote conceptual clarity, there is no hierarchy among the people here as if God determined that there would be bishops in His church. Nor is this the Roman Catholic practice of vesting church power in the clergy vis-à-vis the people. Rather, church power is vested in the people as a whole and a distinction needs to be made between essential and effective power at just this point.

This distinction is that church power is '*in primo actu*, in the church as a body, an organic whole; the people and the rulers are the organ of election.'[10] With regard to the officers of the church, power is '*in actu secundo*, or as to its exercise.'[11] Not only does this distinction separate Presbyterians, with regard to polity, from Roman Catholics or Anglicanism, it also makes them distinct from New England Congregationalists.[12] This is clear from the writing of the famous Scottish theologian and a delegate to the Westminster Assembly, Samuel Rutherford (c. 1600-1661), who wrote in refutation of a well-known proponent of the Congregational theory, who assert that 'that all power resides in church-members, in the brotherhood, and that they delegate this power to whom they elect to bear office; these office-bearers being deputies or proxies of the people, and doing only in the matter of government what the people themselves might of right do.' But as Rutherford says and Thomas Peck comments:

'The church which Christ, in his gospel, hath instituted, and to which he hath committed the keys of his kingdom; the power of binding and losing the tables and seals of the covenant; the offices and censures of his church; the administration of all his public worship and ordinances, is a company of believers meeting in one place every Lord's day for the administration of the holy ordinances of God to the public edification' (*Right of Presbyteries*, ch. 1, sec. 1, prop. 1). In answer to this, Rutherford contends that 'the keys,' the power of binding and losing, are not given to the company of believers, considered as an unorganized assembly, but to the organized church, an assembly under officers of their own choice; and this organized body is the 'subject' of ecclesiastical power in *actu primo*, and that the presbyters are the

10. T. E. Peck, *Notes on Ecclesiology*, p. 167.

11. Ibid.

12. For a more detailed discussion of the biblical lexemes (OT and NT) and biblical passages supporting these distinctions and how errors of prelacy crept into the church, see Ibid., pp. 163-71.

'subject' of the power of government in *actu secundo*, or, as our *Confession of Faith* (xxx.1) expresses it, the Lord Jesus is king and head of his church, and hath therein *appointed a government in the hands of church officers*, distinct from the civil magistrate. The rulers of the church, therefore, although the representatives of the people, are not their deputies or proxies; are not responsible to them, though elected by them; but are responsible to Jesus Christ, who has ordained the constitution of the church, created these offices, and defined their functions.[13]

This is why the Erastian system (where the civil magistrate appoints ministers and oversees discipline in the church) was considered such an egregious mistake by our Scottish brothers. This was the ground motive for the Disruption Controversy in the Church of Scotland and the eventual birth of the Free Church of Scotland. The church has a right to choose its own officers (Acts 6:3; cf. Acts 6:5; Acts 14:23; Titus 1:5); however, once they are chosen, they are not accountable to the people, unless of course they are found derelict in discharging their duties or fall into moral turpitude. In short, the officers are responsible to their head and king, Jesus Christ, and not to the people.

So, we have seen that power in the church in regard to its origin derives from its head, the Lord Jesus Christ. Also, as Robinson asserts, this power is vested in the whole organic church. Moreover, the mode of this power is through the elected office-bearers of the church, who administer the Word of God, the sacraments, and discipline as representatives of Christ. Finally, this power is limited in the mode of its exercise: it is wholly spiritual.[14] As Professor Troxel states succinctly: 'Church power is spiritual not only because it is so in contrast to civil power, but also because it is inherently spiritual in its mode and end.'[15]

But where did these Old School Presbyterians derive their ideas on church government? In this next section of this chapter, I will briefly discuss the genesis of these ideas in the Scottish church and at the Westminster Assembly. In contrast to Maddex, who was mistaken about the origin of the SOTC doctrine being primarily a Southern, or border-state phenomena, it is clear from the historical record that its origin was primarily from Scotland, and secondarily from England.

---

13. Ibid., pp. 168-69.

14. Robinson, *The Church of God*, p. 69.

15. Troxel, '"Divine Right" Presbyterianism,' p. 64.

## Historical Background: The Scottish Reformation, Westminster, and Presbyterianism in the United States

The most immediate background for the development of the spirituality of the church (SOTC) doctrine in the United States was the Scottish Reformation. It is to Scotland that the Presbyterian and Reformed churches in America owe a great debt of gratitude. In the last chapter, I challenged the claims of Sean Lucas (who was depending on the research and writing of Maddex) with regard to the origination of the doctrine of the SOTC. In this chapter, I will briefly trace the development of the SOTC during the period that can be credited with the triumph of Presbyterianism in the English-speaking world: it is to Scotland, not England, that we should turn our attention, particularly to John Knox (c. 1514-1572).

Early in his ministry, Knox raised the issue of the proper definition of the church. The essence of this issue was the proper nature of authority. As Richard L. Greaves states it in his well-researched book, 'Perhaps the most crucial doctrine of the Reformation, the question of the authority and place assigned to Scripture determined the nature of the theology, polity, and worship of the Reformed church.'[16] Even in his first sermon in St. Andrews, Knox has raised the issue of how to define the church. He went on in his career to define the church by the marks of a true church.

Knox's contrarian spirit was manifesting itself already in 1550, when he was preaching in Berwick that the 'mass is idolatry and he was refusing to use vestments or to have the people kneel in the communion service.'[17] Early on in his career, Knox was placed in exile and he had to wait, therefore, until his return in 1559 before his desires for reform could be put into practice.[18] When he returned from exile, the Great Council of the realm appointed Knox and five colleagues to commit to writing their judgments on the reformation of religion. Knox was probably the leader of the group, called the six 'Johns.'[19] The *First Book*

---

16. Richard L. Greaves, *Theology and Revolution in the Scottish Reformation*: Studies in the Thought of John Knox (Grand Rapids, MI: Eerdmans, 1980), p. 4.

17. Ibid., p. 5.

18. Vance, 'The ecclesiology ...,' p. 105.

19. Ibid. Also see Greaves, p. 7.

*of Discipline* was published in 1560. The *Scots Confession* was presented to the Scottish Parliament in August of 1560.[20] The third document, *The Book of Common Order* (1556) was the work of John Knox alone, while in exile.[21] It is here that the 'regulative principle of worship' was explicitly embraced, and whether one 'considers doctrine, worship, or polity, in Scotland, after Knox, all things were subject to a biblical test in matters ecclesiastical.'[22]

In these documents, Knox wanted to develop a definition of the church that was fundamentally spiritual, rather than visible in nature.[23] This was, in part at least, to come to a true definition of the church from scripture alone vis-à-vis the Roman Catholic Church. What's of great interest to us here, and germane to our discussion of the primary mission of the church, is that Knox saw no room for any mere mortal to be head of the church:[24]

> As king and head of the church it is his office to guide, rule, and defend the church, and to make its laws. Such laws are expressed in Scripture and must be obeyed in every detail. The church does not have the power to overlook or alter these laws, nor does it have the right to formulate additional laws of its own.[25]

Even so, at the time in which Knox came into leadership in the Church of Scotland, the church membership was hardly in a position of being a moral exemplar. This did not deter Knox from pressing his point: the marks of a true church are not merely the holiness of her membership, but the true marks of the church (right preaching of the Word of God, the right administration of the sacraments, and discipline of her members) are the true notes of a recognizable church of God.

Moreover, and germane to our topic, the doctrine of the church as expressed by Knox and coauthored in the *Scots Confession* reflects his thinking on the primary mission of the church. For Knox, the invisible church is the true indicator of the elect of God.[26] Moreover,

---

20. Ibid.
21. Vance, p. 105.
22. Ibid., p. 107.
23. Greaves, p. 47.
24. Ibid., p. 48.
25. Ibid.
26. Ibid., p. 50.

in opposition to any earthly vicar, the sole head of the church is Christ alone, 'who has never delegated his authority to an earthly vicar.'[27] During this time, Knox engaged the writings of a Jesuit, James Tyrie, and emphasized 'the importance of the spiritual nature of the church, insisting that it is composed only of the godly elect, and therefore in its visible manifestation has to be holy.'[28]

A number of very important Presbyterian principles had been introduced by Knox; however, it was under the leadership of Andrew Melville (1545-1622) that the General Assembly at Edinburgh adopted the Second Book of Discipline on April 24, 1578 (he was moderator on that occasion). This was a bold move, because it completely removed power over the church by the king and declared that the church has one head, Christ, and 'all church power and authority are derived from him and exercised in his name.'[29] Reading the 'Second Book' of discipline, an emphasis on the SOTC is evident.[30] Early on in the document, the notion is set forth: 'For this power ecclesiastical flowes immediatlie from God, and the Mediator Jesus Christ, and is spirtuall, not having a temporall heid on earth, bot onlie Christ, the onlie spirtuall king and Governour of his kirk' (I.10).[31] The notion of the spiritual rule in the church is permeated through the document, beautifully balanced and interwoven throughout. Indeed, in several places the document warns against mixing the spiritual and civil jurisdictions. This is to be the concern not only of lawfully gathered assemblies as a whole, but the moderator of the assembly in particular. The importance of the 'Second Book' can hardly be overstated with regard to the church in Scotland and in the United States.[32]

The reform movements we have been describing in Scotland, together with the reform movements by English Puritans, culminated in the

---

27. Ibid.

28. Ibid.

29. Vance, p. 108.

30. A copy, found in 'Compendium of the Laws of the Church of Scotland,' which is made to conform in its arrangement and in sense to the *authenticated* copy found in the Book of the Universal Kirk, is located as an appendix in Stuart Robinson, *The Church of God as an Essential Element of the Gospel*, pp. 119-49.

31. This paragraph is numbered as I.5 in some editions.

32. Vance, p. 109.

Westminster Assembly (1643). Scotland sent four commissioners, two of whom, Samuel Rutherford (1600-1661), who was mentioned earlier and George Gillespie (1613-1649), who, in spite of his youth—for he was the youngest member of the Assembly—defended the principles on church government found in the Second Book of Discipline.[33]

Most members of the Assembly were English, and a large majority were open to the *jus divinum* principles of church government; however, it was the Scots who were thorough-going *jure divino* Presbyterians and 'played a role in the Assembly out of proportion to their number.'[34] Of course there were debates with regard to how strict subscription should be to the Confession and catechisms produced by the Assembly. Nevertheless, it was the Scots, according to every evidence, that were more strict than most of the English members of the Assembly.[35]

James Henley Thornwell, discussed at length in the last chapter, was definitely an Old School Presbyterian of the Old South. In the South, there was great potential for a massive European Roman Catholic immigration in the nineteenth century.[36] Thornwell's major concern with Roman Catholic views was theological and ecclesiological.[37] With regard to his ecclesiology, it must be seen against the backdrop of the Reformation, which then found its way into Britain, America, and especially the American South. Historical studies have demonstrated that Thornwell depended not as much on ideas for his ecclesiology derived from the New World, but from the Old World of Europe, a notion that upends the arguments of Maddex, and of Sean Lucas who depended on the scholarship of Maddex as claimed previously.[38] Indeed, the main sources for Thornwell's ecclesiology were Calvin ... the Scottish 'Second Book of Discipline,' [and] upon the Westminster Standards, plus others such as Samuel Rutherford, George Gillespie, and John Owen.'[39]

---

33. Ibid., p. 110.

34. Ibid., p. 112.

35. Ibid., pp. 117-18.

36. Ibid., pp. 132-33.

37. Ibid., p. 134.

38. Ibid.

39. Ibid., p. 135. He depended less on the Westminster standards for his ecclesiology, for he considered them not sufficiently clear on Presbyterian polity.

Thornwell applied his prodigious gifts to questions of ecclesiology throughout his ministry. This became a focal point for theologians around the world in the nineteenth century, as Philip Schaff wrote:

> The great central theme of the Present around which all religious and theological movements revolve, is the *Church Question*. This is admitted by the most intelligent and learned men of the age, in the old world as well as in the new. No one can deny ti [sic] without showing, either that he is destitute of the gift of historical observation, or that he trembles for the existence of his own unchurchly position, and would fain quiet his well grounded fear by self-illusion.[40]

Thornwell took up this question very earnestly since it 'went to the heart of what the church is and what the church does.'[41]

But the main and governing principle of Thornwell's ecclesiology is that Christ is the head of the church and in this it must be said that 'his thought is thoroughly Christocentric.'[42] This Reformation principle is 'a song which the English puritans never tired of chanting, and a principle which is exalted in the Scottish Second Book of Discipline, [it] is an emphasis running through and dominating entirely Thornwell's ecclesiology.'[43] For Thornwell, Christ's headship must be placed in the context of covenant theology.[44] Sadly, this important insight about the headship of Christ has been sadly lacking in modern treatments on the church, including Reformed writers. For R.B. Kuiper, e.g., no other topic loomed larger; however, the teaching has not received the attention it deserves.[45] It is exactly here that a 'representative principle is operative in Thornwell's

---

40. Quoted in Ibid., p. 142.

41. Ibid., p. 144.

42. Ibid., p. 146.

43. Ibid.

44. Ibid., p. 148.

45. R. B. Kuiper's, *The Glorious Body of Christ: A Scriptural Appreciation of the One Holy Scripture* (Grand Rapids, MI: Eerdmans, 1966; repr. Banner of Truth Trust, 1967), p. 91. Nevertheless, in this book the doctrine receives only six pages (pp. 91-96); or, Edmund P. Clowney's, *The Church*, where reference to the headship of Christ is only referenced incidentally with an allusion to Ephesians 4:13, 15 or the WCF 25.1, but never unpacking the ramifications of the doctrine specifically for the mission and polity of the church. On p. 146, Clowney refers to the headship of Christ but in the context of nurture, making no comments with regard to its importance for polity in the church beyond the nurture of the Christian.

thought at its most fundamental level, the headship of Christ.[46] To state the importance of this principle for Thornwell cannot be understated:

> This principle is consistently applied at every other level of the church. Others have equally affirmed that Christ is the only and great Head of the church, but few if any have so logically and so consistently applied it to the nature and mission of the church as Thornwell did.[47]

For Thornwell, this meant that Christ as king must be integrally related to Christ as head.[48] Moreover, the role of this king and head as lawgiver, is integrally related to the law which He promulgates in his plenary, infallible Word, the holy Scriptures.[49] Moreover, since the Bible was a revelation of God's revealed will, it was a law pertaining to faith and practice of believers.[50] His position was clear: 'whatever the Bible teaches, explicitly or implicitly, is "law" in church.'[51] It was these ecclesiological tenets that were elaborated upon and applied in the church board controversies, which will be discussed now.[52]

## The Primary Reason for Church Power: Illustrated by the Debates over Independent Boards

The primary reason for limits on church power is due to the source of church power: the headship of Christ over His church. Ultimately, great ecclesiologists like Cunningham, Bannerman, Thornwell, and Robinson all grounded their views on church power in the headship of Christ. As mentioned previously, this primarily flowed from a commitment to *jure divino* theology: practices in the church, even the polity of her government, must be sanctioned by the Bible. As the great Scottish theologian, Cunningham, wrote:

> The Calvinistic section of Reformers, following their great master, adapted a stricter rule, and were of opinion that there were sufficiently plain indications in Scripture itself, that it was Christ's mind and will that nothing should

---

46. Vance, p. 149.
47. Ibid.
48. Ibid., pp. 157-58.
49. Ibid., pp. 159-64.
50. Ibid., p. 164.
51. Ibid., p. 165.
52. Ibid., p. 167.

be introduced into the government and worship of the Church, unless a positive warrant could be found in Scripture.[53]

This is in contrast to the view that the church is allowed to do anything not condemned in Scripture. Assuming that disagreement can be a great achievement, the real point at issue between Hodge and Thornwell on this particular issue is a regulative one. In other words, for Thornwell, the regulative principle applies to church government as well as to worship in the church. At the end of the debates (both on the floor of the General Assembly and in the ensuing debates in their respective periodicals, which were later published in great detail in their respective journals), the real issue has to do with what Scripture commands. Hodge thought he was defending liberty by maintaining that there should be a level of discretion in the church regarding government and rule:

> According to the old, and especially the genuine American form of government prescribed or instituted in the New Testament, so far as its general principles or features are concerned, there is a wide discretion allowed us by God, in matters of details, which no man or set of men, which neither civil magistrates nor ecclesiastical rulers can take from us. This is part of that liberty with which Christ has made us free, and in which we are commanded to stand fast.[54]

Hodge, it may be argued, was committed to rule in the government of the church by *jure humano* (by human right). James Bannerman describes the position:

> The form of government for [the] Church should be left to the discretion and judgment of its members, and should be adjusted by them to suit the circumstances of the age, or country, or civil government with which they stand connected .... there is no scriptural model of Church government set up for the imitation of Christians at all times, nor any particular form of it universally binding .... Christian expediency, guided by a discriminating regard to the advantage and necessities of the Church at the moment, is the only rule to determine its outward organization, and the only directory of Church government.[55]

---

53. Quoted in Thornwell, 4.249.

54. Charles Hodge, *Discussions in Church Polity* (New York, NY: Charles Scribner's Sons, 1878), p. 131.

55. James Bannerman, *The Church of Christ*, 2:202. Quoted in Guy Waters, *How Jesus Runs The Church*, p. 42.

Hodge grew weary of Thornwell being like a pit-bull locked on a bone with regard to the issue of church boards, exclaiming, 'The Church is getting tired of such-splitting. She is impatient of being harassed and impeded in her great operations by such abstractions.'[56] He seemed to think that Thornwell's views were of a particular Southern *iure divino* [divine right] stripe.[57] Later, in his summary of the speeches on the floor of the General Assembly in 1860, Hodge wrote:

> As to the principle that everything must be prescribed in the word of God as to the government and modes of operation of the church, or be unlawful, it was urged that no Church ever existed that was organized on that principle. Every Church that pleaded a *jus divinum* for its form of government, was content to claim divine authority for the essential elements of their system, while they claimed a discretionary power as to matters of detail and modes of operation; that it was absurd to do more than this with regard to our own system. The great principles of Presbyterianism are in the Bible; but it is preposterous to assert that our whole Book of Discipline is there.[58]

Hodge, it may be stated, even grew exasperated and called Thornwell's concept of Presbyterianism 'hyper-hyper-hyper High Church Presbyterianism.'[59] Thornwell disagreed, however. He did not want to deny discretionary power: 'We only limited and defined it.'[60] As Thornwell says:

> We want the reader distinctly to apprehend the point at issue. It is not, as Dr Hodge represents it, whether the church has *any* discretion—that is conceded on both sides—but, what is the measure or limit of that discretion? We hold it to be the *circumstances* connected with commanded duties, and hence affirm that whatever is not enjoined is prohibited. He holds that it pertains to the actions themselves, and maintains that whatever is not prohibited is lawful.[61]

Thornwell was a firm believer in *jure divino* (divine right) ecclesiology. The church may not do whatever it deems wise in its polity; rather, there

---

56. Hodge, *Discussions in Church Polity,* p. 132.

57. Strange, *The Doctrine of the Spirituality of the Church*, p. 172.

58. Ibid., p. 440.

59. Quoted in Vance, p. 184.

60. Thornwell, 4.245.

61. Thornwell, 4.251.

must be clear sanction in the Bible not only for her worship but for her doctrine and practice. Bannerman, a leading Scottish theologian of the time, defines *jure divino* government in the following manner:

> The form and arrangement of ecclesiastical government have not been left to be fixed by the wisdom of man, nor reduced to the level of a question of mere Christian expediency, but have been determined by Divine authority, and are sufficiently exhibited in Scripture .... In respect of its government and organization, as well as in respect of its doctrine and ordinances, the Church is of God, and not of man .... Scripture, rightly interpreted and understood, affords sufficient materials for determining what the constitution and order of the Christian society were intended by its Divine Founder to be. In express Scripture precept, in apostolic example, in the precedent of the primitive Churches while under inspired direction, and in general principles embodied in the New Testament, they believe that it is possible to find the main and essential features of a system of Church government which is of Divine authority and universal obligation. They believe that the Word of God embodies the general principles and outline of ecclesiastical polity, fitted to be an authoritative model for all Churches, capable of adapting itself to the exigencies of all different times and countries, and, notwithstanding, exhibiting a unity of character and arrangement in harmony with the Scripture pattern. Church government, according to this view, is not a product of Christian discretion, nor a development of the Christian consciousness; it has been shaped and settled, not by the wisdom of man, but by that of the Church's Head. It does not rest upon a ground of human expediency, but of Divine Appointment.[62]

To promote conceptual clarity, let us observe the insights of a younger colleague of Thornwell, Thomas Peck, who became a Professor at Union Theological Seminary. He called Hodge's position, the Latitudinarian one. He says, 'The Latitudinarians (I use the word for want of a better) hold a *discretionary* power in the church, limited only by the prohibitions of the word; whatever is not prohibited, or contradicted by what is commanded, is lawful, is a matter of Christian liberty, the church has power to order or not according to her views of expediency.'[63] His descriptions of Hodge's position is helpful to narrow in on the precise differences.

---

62. Bannerman, *Church of Christ*, 2:202. Quoted in Waters, *How Jesus Runs the Church*, p. 43.

63. Peck, *Notes on Ecclesiology*, p. 108.

Peck continues to describe Hodge's position, saying, that he contends that general principles are laid down in Scripture, but details are left to the discretion and wisdom of the church. This does seem to be a fair description of Hodge's view since he says:

> There are fixed laws in the Bible, according to which all healthful development and action of the external Church are determined. But as within the limits of the laws which control the development of the human body, there is endless diversity among different races, adapting them to different climes and modes of living, so also in the Church. It is not tied down to one particular mode of organization and action, at all times and under all circumstances .... A Christian ... may believe and do a thousand things not taught or commanded in the Scriptures. He cannot rightfully believe or do anything contrary to the word of God, but while faithful to their teachings and precepts, he has a wide field of liberty of thought and action. It is precisely so with regard to the organization of the Church.[64]

Thornwell denied that he was introducing and developing a new doctrine of the church; rather, he claimed that he was the faithful expositor of Presbyterianism:

> Our doctrine was precisely that of the Westminster Standards, of John Calvin, of John Owen, of the Free Church of Scotland, and of the noble army of Puritan martyrs and confessors. 'The whole counsel of God,' say the Westminster Divines, 'concerning all things necessary for His own glory, man's salvation, faith, and life, is either expressly set down in Scripture, or by good and necessary consequence may be deduced from Scripture: unto which nothing at any time is to be added, whether by new revelations of the Spirit, or by traditions of men.' This is clearly our doctrine of the law of positive conformity with Scripture as the measure of the Church's duty.[65]

Peck takes aim at Hodge's construal of liberty, however. With precise distinctions, he cuts to the very core distinctions. He says, 'This is obviously a very unsatisfactory rule. What are "general principles"?' He continues by referring to Thornwell:

> General principles may be either 'regulative' or 'constitutive.' Regulative principles define only ends to be aimed at, or conditions to be observed; constitutive determine the concrete form in which those ends are to be

---

64. Hodge, *Discussions on Church Polity*, p. 122.
65. Thornwell, 4.245.

realized. Regulative express the spirit, constitutive, the form of a government. It is a regulative principle, for example, that all governments should be administered for the good of their subjects; it is a constitutive principle that power should be lodged in the hands of such and such officers, and dispensed by such and such courts. Regulative principles define nothing as to the mode of their own exemplification; constitutive principles determine the elements of an actual polity.[66]

This is why Peck says that if Hodge's general principles are regulative, then he is a latitudinarian.[67]

It is clear that Thornwell did hold to a *jure divino* Presbyterianism throughout his career, and moreover it seems clear, given the outline of the evidence in this chapter, that Thornwell was indeed correct to connect his church theory with that of Calvin, with Scottish and English divines, and with Westminster.[68] Having read both sides of the argument from these major Old School stalwarts, it does seem to this writer that Thornwell made the better arguments and presented his case more logically and forcefully than Hodge, in spite of the fact that the 1860 General Assembly voted overwhelmingly in favor of Hodge's position. We could also turn to other topics of debate between the two, e.g., the role of elders or the legitimacy of Roman Catholic baptisms, but we have chosen to limit our discussion to church boards which is sufficient to demonstrate the differences between these two Old School giants.

Gutjahr, in his bibliography of Hodge, represents the debate as demonstrating degrees of 'biblicism.' In other words, which giant was most fundamentally committed to the Bible as the source of knowledge and piety. He says, for example:

His [Hodge] approach to many ecclesiastical matters evince a pronounced flexibility. Hodge pales in comparison as a conservative biblical constructionist when set against Thornwell, a man so tied to what appeared—or did not appear—in the Bible that even Hodge considered his biblical hermeneutic to be untenable 'superlative high churchism.' Next to Thornwell, Hodge comes across as a biblically [sic] pragmatist who believed that it was simply impossible to decide every issue by Thornwell's 'Thus Saith the Lord' principle of adjudication. A million different practical and

66. Thornwell, 4.252.

67. Peck, *Notes on Ecclesiology*, p. 109.

68. Vance, p. 189.

cultural considerations led Hodge to assert that 'Christ has, in his infinite wisdom, left his church free to modify her government, in accordance' with certain general scriptural principles. Hodge argued that churches must be governed by general principles rather than hard and fast rules that apply equally to all congregations in every situation.[69]

However, this commends itself, unfortunately, by the most popular of credentials: surface simplicity. The essence of the logic and the substance of the argument lie beneath the surface at the more substantive level. The real issues at hand were the topics of church power, the limits of church government, the declarative power of the church vis-à-vis the lack of legislative power.

As Craig Troxel says, the Old School, especially in the South, considered the doctrine of the headship of Christ over the church to be the most fundamental ecclesiological principle of all.[70] Perhaps one of the most helpful sources to display this is Bannerman's well-established division of church power.[71] Bannerman and Stuart Robinson thought that the notion of Christ's headship should be articulated in terms of the *munus triplex*, that is to say that its importance for the church's understanding and practice of doctrine, worship, and government should be informed in terms of Christ's prophetic, priestly and kingly headship.[72] Bannerman stated:

> … the proper offices of Christ, as head of his believing body, are personal, incommunicable, and perpetually to be exercised by himself. He has not devolved on the church, or on any parties in the church, offices and powers that once centred in himself; because, although no longer on earth, but in heaven, he still continues to occupy these offices and to exercise these powers himself personally towards his believing people. Unseen and absent in the body, Christ is still the real head of his church, no less than when he was on earth; and all the offices implied in that headship, he continues to discharge in person, and not by delegate, to his people. Prophet, priest, and king to his people once, Christ has appointed and permitted no mortal successor to himself in these characters, and it is in vain that we look to the church now for the human administration of such offices. The visible

---

69. Gutjahr, *Charles Hodge*, p. 291.

70. Troxel, '"Divine Right" Presbyterianism,' p. 185.

71. James Bannerman, *The Church of Christ*, vol. 1, pp. 277-78.

72. Troxel, '"Divine Right" Presbyterianism,' p. 184.

church on earth, in short, is *not* the human embodiment of the offices and powers of its invisible Head.[73]

Craig Troxel's nomenclature on the right side of the following chart is an attempt to make the same division in language more accessible:

| Potestas | Bannerman's nomenclature | Troxel's suggestion[74] |
|---|---|---|
| Δογματικα | Doctrine | Doctrine |
| Διατατικη | ordinances | Worship |
| Δακριτικη | discipline and government | government |

This position was derived from Scripture itself ultimately, but these men also understood their position to be a confessional one. As Chapter 30 of the WCF states: 'The Lord Jesus, as King and Head of his church, hath therein appointed a government, in the hand of church officers, distinct from the civil magistrate.' For these Old School ministers, the Scriptures were sufficient for not only doctrine and worship but for the very government of the church as well. This flowed from the headship of Christ. In other words, the so-called regulative principle (the church may only do that which is prescribed by God) applied not just to worship but to the very government of the church as well. Any breach of this principle entailed a reduction of the headship of Christ over His church since He is Lord and King of His bride.

God has provided pastors for the edification of the saints. Calvin's emphasis on the noble calling of pastors is jarring in our present climate:

> The work of pastors, therefore, is nothing less than 'the edification of the church, the everlasting salvation of souls, the restoration [*reparatio*] of the world, and, in fine, the kingdom of God and Christ.' Through preaching and teaching, faithful pastors 'renovate the world, as if God formed the heaven and earth anew by their hand.'[75]

## Women in Combat

For many readers this may seem like a strange logic gap in a chapter on the prescribed bounds of church power: jumping from a nineteenth-century debate over independent church boards to a modern one associated with a

---

73. Bannerman, quoted in Troxel, '"Divine Right," Presbyterianism,' p. 252 [emphasis Bannerman's].

74. Ibid., p. 116.

75. Tuininga, *Calvin's Political Theology*, p. 195.

squabble in a few churches associated with the North American Presbyterian and Reformed Council (NAPARC).[76] However, at issue was exactly the principles we have been speaking about above: the proper authority and power of the church as designated by her head, the Lord Jesus Christ, and the constant theme that has surfaced throughout this book, namely, the relationship between the church and the state. Therefore, far from being a tangential discussion, the matters that came to the fore in this issue are exactly the same matters with which this book is concerned.

I will focus on how the debate unfolded in my own denomination: the Orthodox Presbyterian Church (OPC).[77] At the 65th General Assembly of the OPC, at the request of the PRJC (the Presbyterian and Reformed Joint Commission on Chaplains and Military Personnel), the GA erected a committee of three members 'to study and report back to the 66th General Assembly biblical guidance on the subjects of women in the military and combat, limiting its inquiry to the biblical and moral issues that are properly the concern of the church.'[78] A Report was submitted to the 66th General Assembly; however, the Assembly returned the Report to the committee and added two more members. The debate, study, and discussion resulted ultimately in two different Reports (referred to below as Report 1 and Report 2) and was finally voted upon by the 68th General Assembly.

This debate went on for several years in the OPC, as it did in other Reformed denominations.[79] The author happened to be a commissioner

---

76. The churches associated with one another in order to advise, cooperate, and counsel one another on various matters include not a few churches in North America: the Associate Reformed Presbyterian Church, Canadian Reformed Churches, Free Reformed Churches of North America, Heritage Reformed Congregations, Korean-American Presbyterian Church, the Orthodox Presbyterian Church (OPC), the Presbyterian Church in America (PCA), the Reformed Church in the United States (RCUS), the Reformed Presbyterian Church of North America, The Reformed Church of Quebec, and the United Reformed Churches.

77. This same issue exercised the Presbyterian Church in America, which erected its own study committee, for at least four consecutive General Assemblies.

78. For details, see the *Minutes of the Sixty-Eighth General Assembly: May 30th-June 6th, 2001* (Willow Grove, PA: Orthodox Presbyterian Church, 2001), pp. 258-84. All other references to this Assembly are based on this reference.

79. For example, in the PCA, the discussion was protracted over at least four consecutive General Assemblies roughly contemporaneous with the discussions in the OPC. The Bible Presbyterian Church also weighed in on this issue. The RCUS came out with a position paper on this topic in 1996.

at the last assembly that it was dealt with and deliberated on the floor (the 68th). Needless to say, as the minutes of the General Assembly mention: 'At the heart of our problem is a significant difference in the hermeneutical positions of the committee members.'[80] The main issues, it can fairly be said, were over exegesis, hermeneutics, the WCF's notion of 'general equity' (19.4), and the propriety of the corporate church addressing the civil government on this issue.

## Comparing and Contrasting Report 1 and Report 2

In what follows I hope to be as generous as possible (and as conscience allows) in the description of the contents of these two Reports and the vigorous debate that ensued on the floor of the 68th General Assembly. Nevertheless, the reader should know upfront that I believe the Assembly erred by voting in favor of Report 1 over Report 2 for numerous reasons. Churches, even godly ones, may and do err, as the WCF affirms (cf., 25.5; 31.3). Moreover, a protest was filed at the Assembly to which 42 commissioners out of 141 assigned their names (in addition to numerous negative votes being recorded, when the original vote was taken). This is something our church polity allows for in the OPC.[81] My understanding from the historian of the OPC was that this was the largest amount of signatories on a Protest ever filed in the history of the denomination.

Report 1 is ten pages, single spaced, and the final form is represented in the Minutes (pages 260-70). The authors of the Report were George W. Knight III (Chairman) and Robert B. Needham. They suggest that the scriptural and confessional evidence should lead the church to be opposed to any draft of women into the military, that the church should be opposed to the placing of women into combat roles, and that no chaplain ordained by the OPC should be 'required to advocate, support, or agree with any philosophy and effort to include women in military combatant units, nor can he be required by any superior line or staff officer to teach or advocate such a philosophy and effort, nor shall he be forbidden to provide the biblical counsel contained in this report.'[82] They

---

80. Ibid., p. 258.

81. The contents of the Protest (lodged on Tuesday afternoon, June 5th, 2001) are recorded on pp. 45-46 of the *Minutes of the Sixty-Eighth General Assembly*, p. 45-46. The contents of the Response to the Protest may be found on pp. 51-52 in the same minutes.

82. Ibid., p. 270.

claim that they sought to give a faithful summary of Scriptural teaching on the matter (primarily from the OT) and they almost immediately cut right to the core of the debate by describing their view of the 'general equity' clause in 19.4 of the WCF. They appeal to an explanation of the Divines for the Sabbath Day observance (LC 120) by appealing to the use of 'equity' there by the Divines, i.e., 'the reasons annexed to the fourth commandment, the more to enforce it, are taken from the equity of it, God allowing us six days of seven for our own affairs, and reserving but one for himself in these words, Six days shalt thou labour, and do all thy work.' From this internal evidence within the Catechism, they understand the sense to be that the divines are appealing to the 'equity (or justness) in God's demand and doing so by appealing to that which rises above the Jewish character of the form in which the command is given.'[83]

Next, they appeal to the intended meaning of the Divines by noting how the second part of the phrase—'further than the general equity thereof may require' WCF (19.4)—appears in the extant writings of four writers somewhat contemporaneous to the time of the Westminster Assembly or shortly (relatively speaking) afterwards, who comment on the phrase in the Confession. They conclude, summarizing the expositors, with the statement: 'the intent of the Confession's statement, we may summarize that "general equity" is an expression of the "law of nature, common to all nations" and that it is "universal and permanent."'[84]

Next, an appeal is made to the Apostolic use of Scripture. Numerous passages are cited, but the gist of the argument is that Paul (and others) cite OT passages (even ones that are non-didactic) and that these 'written for our instruction.'[85] Following this an appeal is made to Chapter 31 of the WCF to claim that this section gives 'warrant to the church to address this case of conscience and to adopt conclusions "consonant to the Word of God," but at the same time reminds us of other important truths.'[86] Appealing to the Form of Government (FOG), the authors state that although rulings of the General Assembly cannot be made a rule of faith for believers nor may they bind consciences; nevertheless,

---

83. Ibid., p. 259.
84. Ibid., p. 260.
85. Ibid., p. 261.
86. Ibid.

if statements of the GA are declarative of the Word of God, they are to be received with deference and submission since they are made by the highest adjudicatory of the church and [allegedly] consonant with the Word of God.[87]

Next, Report 1 addresses the possible objections made on the basis of the Westminster Standards, especially Chapter 31.4. The blunt question asked is 'What is the warrant for an assembly of a church to be making a pronouncement on this matter relating to the civil authority?'[88] Following this, the authors of Report 1 cite an extended quote from Professor John Murray that they claim supports the findings of their Report and the legitimacy of making their appeal to the civil government.[89] Next, they have a section on Scriptural teaching regarding foundational principles with regard to sexual distinctions, arguing in effect for greater physical strength of males and warning of the dangers of placing women in combat roles with a 'high probability of being captured and thereby being placed in danger of rape.'[90] Following this, they cite examples from Judges 4 and 5 and other OT examples and proof texts that support their claim that women should not be put in the way of harm. They follow this with a short section on the NT in which the authors of Report 1 see great continuity with the OT passages already cited and argue that the NT is virtually silent on the issue.[91]

Report 2 is divided into three sections: I. What are the Biblical and Moral issues? II. What Issues are Properly the Concern of the Church? III. What Biblical Guidance can be Given to the Church? Report 2 argues that the issues are not sufficiently set forth in God's Word in such a manner that allows the church to make a declarative statement on the topic.[92]

Under the first heading they address the hermeneutical question. They suggest that Report 1 employs a hermeneutic that is 'contrary to what Scripture and the subordinate standards teach.'[93] Report 1 uses a

---

87. Ibid.
88. Ibid.
89. Ibid., pp. 262-64.
90. Ibid., p. 265.
91. Ibid., p. 269.
92. Ibid.
93. Ibid.

number of Scriptures from the Pentateuch that take place in the context of the conquest of Canaan, and in the context of Israel's *cherem* warfare (complete annihilation) with her enemies. But these passages may not be simply lifted out of their scriptural context in order to apply to the present ethical questions presented to the church. This is a fundamental point of hermeneutical difference between Report 1 and Report 2. The authors of Report 2 were clearly relying on an axiomatic hermeneutical teaching of Geerhardus Vos here: namely, the 'principle of periodicity.'

The principle of periodicity teaches that every application of scripture must respect the covenantal context in which it was originally given. This is clearly stated in Vos' *magnum opus*:

> The method of Biblical Theology is in the main determined by the principle of historic progression. Hence the division of the course of revelation into certain periods. Whatever may be the modern tendency towards eliminating the principle of periodicity from historical science, it remains certain that God in the unfolding of revelation has regularly employed this principle. From this it follows that the periods should not be determined at random, or according to subjective preference, but in strict agreement with the lines of cleavage drawn by revelation itself. The Bible is, as it were, conscious of its organism, it feels, what we cannot always say of ourselves, its own anatomy. The principle of successive Berith-makings, as marking the introduction of new periods, play a large role in this, and should be carefully heeded.[94]

This fundamental hermeneutical difference in approach between the two Reports can hardly be overstated. For example, Report 2 says: 'A more consistently post-resurrection hermeneutical perspective leads to different conclusions [than Report 1] regarding the proper use of the passages.'[95] For example, the authors here claim that when these passages are viewed in the context of *herem* warfare, which was unique to Israel, the 'exclusion of women from combat is seen as typological.'[96] By this they mean that in the New Covenant, those devoted to destruction in Holy War are the nations, not taking their lives in this present case, but bringing them to faith through the Gospel. The New Covenant, the authors contend, is not

---

94. Geerhardus Vos, *Biblical Theology: Old and New Testaments* (Grand Rapids, MI: Eerdmans, 1948), p. 25. This quote will appear in a new printing, entirely reset in 1975 and published also by Eerdmans (1977) can be found on p. 16.

95. *Minutes*, p. 272.

96. Ibid.

identified with any national army; rather, with the 'Church militant. In this church, both men and women put on the whole armor of God, that they may stand in the evil day, and having done all to stand (Eph. 6).'[97] In the New Covenant, both men and women go forth as a holy priesthood (1 Pet. 8-20) to proclaim the gospel of light.[98] In the New Covenant, the *cherem* warfare continues (in a sense) under God as the 'divine warrior', but now God's people go forth with the 'sword of the Spirit' in order to proclaim the gospel of grace and disciple the nations.[99] With regard to women in this endeavor, the Old Testament office of priesthood has been expanded in the New, with the only prohibition to women not to occupy the office of teaching and ruling in the church.[100] Even the sign of circumcision, which was exclusively applied to males in the Old Covenant, is fulfilled in the New Covenant with the circumcision made 'without hands, by putting of the body of the flesh by the circumcision of Christ, having been buried with him in baptism, in which you were also raised with him through faith in the powerful working of God, who raised him from the dead (Col. 2:11-12).'

Next, Report 2 turns to the interpretation of WCF 19.4: 'To them also, as a body politick, he gave sundry judicial laws, which expired together with the state of the people, not obligating any other now, further than the general equity thereof may require.' As the authors of Report 2 claim, 19.4 suggests that, in the first place, the Mosaic civic code does not have any force for modern application except when it can be demonstrated that in its *general* equity' it is still to apply, but not in its specific application.[101] Therefore, they contend that the burden of proof is on those who argue from the Mosaic civic code to demonstrate that the 'general equity' of the code still applies to all governments at all times. The authors of Report 2 suggest that Report 1 has in no ways met this threshold. As the authors of Report 2 say, 'The key difference between disagreeing parties [here] centers upon how we understand and apply the phrase 'general equity' in Conf. 19.4.'[102]

---

97. Ibid. Also cf., 2 Cor. 10:3-5.

98. Ibid. Also cf., Gal. 3:28.

99. Ibid., p. 274.

100. Ibid.

101. Ibid., p. 275.

102. Ibid.

Report 2 then embarks on a historical and philological discussion of the meaning of 'general equity.' Since Report 1 talks about the NT being 'virtually silent' on the subject, and then makes the claim via the words of Charles Hodge that this 'leaves the Old Testament rule of duty on this subject still in force,' then why (the authors of Report 2 ask) is this not applied in other situations in which the NT is virtually silent?[103] For example, 'What would we consider to be the "equity" of: a woman's redemption if she is not pleasing to her husband (Exod. 21:8); a man who refuses to marry his brother's widow (Deut. 25:5-10; a newly married woman found not to be a virgin (Deut. 22:13-21); the dedication of the first-born male (Exod. 13:2, 12; Num. 3:13; 8:17)?'[104]

Next, Report 2 addresses the topic of 'What issues are Properly the Concern of the Church?'[105] The authors claim that the church should only address issues of faith in light of her responsibility to exercise the 'keys of the kingdom of heaven' and not just any moral, ethical, or cultural issue. The authors are clear to state that they believe this topic is truly a moral and ethical issue; however, the precise question before the church is whether '"the inclusion of women in combatant units" is clearly "contrary to the Word of God" and is an issue which the church in her corporate expression must adjudicate because it encumbers her corporate vocation.'[106] They appeal to WCF 31.4 and claim that the only extraordinary occasion when a church should appeal to the civil magistrate is when the state has impinged upon the church's ability to exercise the power associated with the keys of the kingdom and, then, only by way of humble petition.[107]

Report 2 appeals to the spiritual nature of church power, suggesting that the church's vocation is confined to 'considering those matters which pertain to her doctrine, worship, and government (Conf. 31.3).'[108] Whereas Report 1 had appealed to Professor Murray in an effort to bolster their case, Report 2 marshals quotes from Professor Machen in order to strengthen their case suggesting that the church, *in its corporate*

---

103. Ibid., p. 277.
104. Ibid.
105. Ibid., pp. 277-81.
106. Ibid., p. 277. Emphasis original.
107. Ibid., p. 278.
108. Ibid., p. 279.

*capacity*, has no business making official pronouncements upon the political and social questions of the day.[109] Indeed, in the next section they explicate the ministerial nature of church power by appealing to the Form of Government of the OPC, which quotes the WCF:

> All church power is only ministerial and declarative, for the Holy Scriptures are the only infallible rule of faith and practice. No church judicatory may presume to bind the conscience by making laws on the basis of its own authority; all its decisions should be founded upon the Word of God. 'God alone is Lord of the conscience, and hath left it free from the doctrines and commandments of men, which are, in anything, contrary to his Word; or beside it, if matters of faith, or worship' (Conf. XX.2).[110]

Thus the authors of Report 2 warn of the far reaching implications of the other Report asking whether Report 1's content has really reached the threshold of understanding clearly the teaching of God's Word on this topic such that the church is willing to bind the consciences of her people.

In the final section of Report 2, they ask 'What Biblical Guidance can be Given to the Church?'[111] Report 2 actually appeals to a communication distributed to the committee by the Chair of the Presbyterian and Reformed Joint Commission on Chaplains and Military Personnel (the committee that originally asked for advice), claiming that a majority of chaplains would actually deal with this issue in person rather than have a denominational statement staking out a position![112] Furthermore, the notion of 'combatant units' vis-à-vis 'non-combatant positions' is outdated World War II military doctrine that doesn't even apply in modern military doctrine where there is no such distinction.

In conclusion, Report 2 concludes that the OPC should not speak *qua* church (i.e., in her corporate capacity) to the issue of women in combat. In short, they should definitely not do so based upon appeals to Israel's theocratic civil law, and moreover they should not do so since this would violate the church's spiritual nature and ministerial task. Rather, they recommend that the GA merely remind 'church

---

109. Ibid., p. 280.
110. Quoted in Ibid.
111. Ibid., pp. 281-82.
112. Ibid.

members of their covenantal obligations (e.g., marital, parental, and ecclesiastical) when considering joining, enlisting, or re-enlisting in military service.'[113]

It should be evident to the reader by now why this case in the church was taken up in this chapter: it is very much concerned with the primary mission of the church, its power and the limits on its power, the legitimacy of the church in her corporate capacity officially addressing the civil magistrate, and of course hermeneutics and exegetical methods for interpreting the mission of the church in any culture in which she finds herself. In this author's view, Report 2 made a better ecclesiological argument; moreover, their argument was more responsible biblically and hermeneutically. Report 1 was completely unconvincing as a theological argument to this author when he was present as a commissioner at the General Assembly, and it remains so after reviewing the debate with students for years. Report 2 was much more helpful on this issue and seems to use better theological rationale for what it recommends (and doesn't recommend) and represents unalloyed historic Presbyterianism with regard to its ecclesiological claims. Alas, good arguments don't always win the day in the courts of the church. It is remarkable, nevertheless, that Report 1 won the vote at the General Assembly when the argument of Report 2 was far superior.

Therefore, in spite of the fact that Report 1 was received by the church, one of the authors of Report 2 co-authored a journal article with another OPC minister in the following year in the *Westminster Theological Journal* in order to explain further the history of the phrase 'general equity' as it had been used in the two reports submitted to the General Assembly.[114] This was a welcome contribution to secondary resources on this important issue since ministers especially were limited to scant resources.[115]

---

113. Ibid., p. 282.

114. A. Craig Troxel and Peter J. Wallace, 'Men in Combat Over the Civil Law: "General Equity" in *WCF* 19.4,' *WTJ* 64 (2002): pp. 307-18.

115. Report 1 and 2 both appealed to the Secondary Standards use of the word and phrases and Report 2 appealed to the helpful and oft-quoted article by Sinclair Ferguson, 'An Assembly of Theonomists? The Teaching of the Westminster Divines on the Law of God,' in William S. Barker and W. Robert Godfrey, Editors, *Theonomy: A Reformed Critique* (Grand Rapids, MI: Zondervan Academic, 1990). Besides this, however, not much was available heretofore to the interested minister.

This article was a helpful addition to ongoing discussion about hermeneutical and exegetical application of passages from the Pentateuch (and elsewhere in Scripture) to ethical and moral issues. However, certain erroneous matters need to be clarified since their history of the term *equity* may have been flawed, and thus hindered rather than helped their argument.[116] Troxel and Wallace were partially correct in their survey of the use of equity when they noted that courts of equity were established to remedy injustices that could occur for a plaintiff or a defendant at law. But equity courts and law courts had different rights and remedies so that equity courts were not established because one could not find justice in the court of law; rather, an equity court has the power to afford a plaintiff what he sought. For example, one could seek an injunction in an equity court but not in a law court. Likewise, one could seek monetary remedies in a law court but not in an equity court. The fact of the matter is that one may seek 'equity' not merely due to perceived unfairness in the application of the law; rather, an equity court has the power to supply the remedy one seeks (e.g., small claims courts providing 'equitable remedies' up to $5,000). While the separation of law courts and legal courts continued for a time in America, Troxel and Wallace claimed that the tendency in the U.S. recently has been to collapse law and equity, although it still remains a live issue as illustrated (according to them) by the voting recount debacle in the 2000 U.S. presidential election.[117] But here their claims didn't comport with the facts and weakened their argument on the history of the term 'equity.'

The reader will recall that the presidential election between Bush and Gore was so close in the state of Florida that electoral votes were in dispute. The Supreme Court upheld the decision of Florida's Secretary of State, Katherine Harris, to certify hand recounts from certain counties in Florida. The drama was high. Troxel and Wallace maintained that this was an equity decision; however, that was not the case. The Supreme Court ruled that she in fact had constitutional and statutory power to act as she did and, moreover, being an executive and not a judicial court, it is not proper to apply 'equity' to her actions in this case.

---

116. In what follows I am dependent on the argument of William C. Godfrey, Esq. in an unpublished paper he submitted in my class at Westminster Seminary California, 4/21/2010.

117. Troxel and Wallace, 'Men in Combat,' pp. 310-11.

## Conclusion

In this chapter I have focused on the nature of church power. It was argued that the headship of Christ ruling over His church is a crucial rubric for understanding every fundamental topic in ecclesiology. We looked at the history of this crucial teaching and its influence on North American ecclesiology. We also drilled down deeper into the independent church board controversy as a crucial example of how church power works out in practice in a topic of debate within the church. Finally, we looked at a modern debate that has exercised Presbyterian and Reformed Churches—women in the military and combat—to demonstrate the practical relevance of thinking about church power and its manifestation in the modern period.

In the next chapter, we compare and contrast church power with state power and discuss the interrelationship of these two spheres which this book has been so engaged with.

CHAPTER 14

# Primary Mission of the Church: The Nature of Church Power and State Power and their Inter-relationship

The church, to be sure as we saw in the last chapter, has been granted power. And the origin of her power is from the head and king of the church, the Lord Jesus Christ. But where is the origin of power for the state? And can looking at how the state and the church differ with regard to power (and therefore authority) help us to understand the distinct mission of the church? Yes.

Therefore, in this chapter, I will give primary attention to the distinctions between church power and the power vested in the state. We will follow the outline of the discussion on this topic in Thomas Peck's *Notes on Ecclesiology*.[1] Peck begins this section by noting: 'We may obtain a still clearer view of the nature and extent of church power ... by comparing it with civil power, and considering the relations of the two organizations to which these powers belong.'[2] Peck is exactly right.

---

1. T. E. Peck, *Notes on Ecclesiology* (Richmond, VA: Presbyterian Committee of Publication, 1892).

2. Ibid., p. 119.

## The Israelite Theocracy

In Chapter 2 (Genesis Foundations), we noted that we had neither the church nor the state in the modern sense; however, we did observe that Cain and his lineage started cities and so we saw in seed form what would later become governments. Peck notes that it was in the theocratic period of ancient Israel that civil power and ecclesiastical power began.[3] In the period of Moses and the nation of Israel, the state and ecclesiastical power were not totally separated, nor confounded.[4] Rather, what was there was the *peculiar* calling of the nation of Israel. These people, distinct from all the peoples of the earth, was to be a 'treasured possession among all peoples, for all the earth is mine; and you shall be to me a kingdom of priests and a holy nation' (Exod. 19:5-6). As I emphasized in Chapter 2, this priestly task is for the redeemed, and them alone, and is not to be practiced outside of the redeemed community. Such an inclination often goes hand in hand with the state turning bestial. As Peck writes: 'Any nation that boasts that it is a "kingdom of priests," is ... in rebellion against God. Israel was not, in this respect, a model or pattern for civil communities, but a type of the church of God under the gospel.'[5]

In Israel, therefore, we have a shadowy type of the church. Alliances that Israel was forbidden to form with other nations are shadowy types of the kinds of alliances that the church is forbidden to form with civil governments.[6] Peck offers a lovely and eloquent meditation on this point:

> God was the sovereign of Israel in the sense of being their lawgiver, which he is of no other nation. He was their husband, and the husband of no other. Transgression in them was adultery as well as treason. They were the inheritance of God, and he was their inheritance. He was their landlord and they were his tenants. Their taxes were acknowledgements of his goodness and of his proprietorship in the land and in its fruits. Nor was he an absent proprietor. He dwelt among them. When they dwelt in tents, he dwelt in a tent with them. When they lived in houses, he dwelt in a house among them. They were his family, and he the father and head. None of these

---

3. Ibid., p. 121.
4. Ibid., p. 124.
5. Ibid., p. 124.
6. Ibid., pp. 124-25.

things are true of any other nation, nor can they be. They are all true of the Christian church, the body of Christ, and eminently true of her as the substance of which Israel was the shadow.[7]

A moment's reflection upon the offices in Israel will reinforce in our minds the peculiar character of the theocracy of Israel, as well as demonstrate to us that the power of the state and the ecclesiastical power were not entirely separate, but that a special relationship was inherent.

For example, even when God allowed the Israelites to have a king, that king was never to meddle in the affairs of the faith, or the worship offered in the cult. Although he was required to keep a copy of the law, it was the special office of the priests and Levites to read it publicly.[8] When a king did arrogate to himself the duty of a priest, the punishment was dire (e.g., Uzziah being smitten with leprosy, cf. 2 Chron. 26:16-23). Of course David intended and Solomon built the temple, but this came about by a prophet speaking in the name of God, and not in their legal exercise of their royal function.[9] The prophets were the supreme mouthpiece of God in Israel. When God suffered the people their request and granted them a king, God increased the number and importance of the prophets so that the king and the people would remember that their true King was God Himself, and thereby He would restrain the people's apostasy. G. Vos recognizes this point, as does Peck: 'The king was subject to the prophet, because the government was a theocracy, and all civil and social arrangements were subordinate to the religious, as the shell is subordinate to the kernel, or the body the soul.'[10]

This peculiar commonwealth of Israel, as has been mentioned, was a shadowy type of the church age since the relationship between offices within the commonwealth and the role settings with regard to coming under the authority of God alone is but an adumbration of the church age to come:

> As men and as citizens, priests and prophets were under obligation to obey the king; but as priests and prophets, they were subject to God alone, the head of the theocracy; a foreshadowing of the precise relations of the office-bearers of the church under the gospel of the civil power.[11]

---

7. Ibid., p. 125.
8. Ibid., p. 125.
9. Ibid., p. 126.
10. Ibid., p. 127.
11. Ibid.

This is remarkable, as Peck perceptibly states: a nation and theocracy in the ancient Near East actually had public offices and a form with a distinction between civil and sacred functions (cf. 2 Chron. 19: 8-11)![12] It was not an entire separation; nevertheless, 'We find the sacerdotal functions given to a separate order of officers, and the whole ministry of the tabernacle to a particular tribe; while the elders, the representatives of the patriarchal system, seem to have continued the exercise of civil functions.'[13]

## The Early Church Age

After the return from exile of the Jewish people, which was beggarly compared to the glorious age of the monarchy, we come to the era of the church which escaped 'the trammels of the Hebrew state and ... [they] assume a separate and independent existence.'[14] Many of the Jews did not understand that the Israelite monarchy and theocracy would find its fulfillment (not replacement) in the church of Jesus Christ. Some of the Jews, because of this misunderstanding, even asserted more and more 'an attitude of bitter hostility to it [the state, i.e., the Roman empire].'[15] Our Lord softened this abrupt transition between the theocracy and the church age by allowing a forty-year period to ensue before the total collapse of the temple and 'petrified' Judaism.[16]

Although Domitian (A.D. 81-96) was not the first emperor to persecute Jews or Christians, his terror apparently grew hot. Previous emperors did not take divine titles to themselves; not so Domitian. He styled himself as 'Master and God' and made oaths obligatory. When prominent Jews and Christians refused, third century historians seem to indicate that this raised the ire of Domitian and persecution came.[17] In subsequent years, Christianity became a capital offense and martyrs for the cause of Christ became more numerous.[18] Thus, the spirit of Nebuchadnezzar was manifest

---

12. Ibid.

13. Ibid.

14. Ibid., p. 128.

15. Ibid.

16. Ibid.

17. Henry Chadwick, *The Early Church: The story of emergent Christianity from the apostolic age to the foundation of the Church of Rome* (London: Penguin Books, 1967), pp. 28-29.

18. Ibid., pp. 29-30. The reader will recall that the term Erastian (first introduced in Chapter 1 above) finds its genesis in the name Thomas Erastus, who maintained that

in those 'legitimate' successors. Thus, the conflict of the ages continued as the war raged between the seed of the woman and the seed of the serpent.

But the winds of change were on the horizon. Constantine (A.D. 306-37) was the first Roman emperor to convert to Christianity. Peck gives his rule a rather negative read: with regard to his interference in ecclesiastical affairs, he says that 'we find the germ of Erastianism' in Constantine's rule.[19] A more nuanced reading might suggest that he had an approach of 'studied restraint' since he considered himself an 'overseer of those outside' (ἐπίσκοπος τῶν ἐκτός).[20] However, as often happens, his epigones took his ideas further: especially his son Constantius didn't fear to tread on ecclesiastical power:

> Boldly thrusting himself into theological controversy, in his desire to impose upon the ecclesiastical authorities a modification of the Nicene formula, he argued that, as the divine repository of imperial power, his authority was paramount in Church as well as state; and, in declaration, 'my will must be considered binding' (ὅπερ ἐγὼ βούλομαι, τοῦτο κανὼν νομιζέσθω), he assumed a more than papal infallibility.[21]

However, in the course of subsequent years, this action of merely intermeddling took a backseat to swinging to the opposite extreme. Still holding to the union of the spiritual and the temporal (i.e., the civil), a new change developed with the Carolingian line of monarchs (a.d. 752) and 'ambitious attempts to revive the Roman empire in the West. In order to secure the patronage and assistance of the church, they conferred civil authority and territory upon ecclesiastics, and the people himself became a feudatory of Pepin (752-58), Charlemagne (768-814), and their successors in the holy German Roman empire.'[22] And what was to become of this trend?

---

the magistrate is responsible for lawful discipline in the church. This became influential in England, and the fact that Elizabeth I was determined to be the supreme governor of the church, together with other factors (especially in Scotland), gave rise to Puritanism's influence in Presbyterian, Congregational, Baptist and Separatist churches to push for an independence and separation of church and state, especially in America.

19. Peck, *Notes on Ecclesiology*, p. 132.

20. Eusebius quoted in Charles Norris Cochrane, *Christianity and Classical Culture: A Study of Thought and Action from Augustus to Augustine* (London/New York: Oxford University Press, 1940), pp. 186-87.

21. Ibid., p. 187.

22. Peck, pp. 133-34.

The new trend evolved into wars between popes and emperors, which made for a tumultuous world during the whole of the middles ages as the church gained more and more power, first under the direction of Hildebrand (1073-1085) and Innocent III (1198-1216). As Southern states it:

> The theory of supreme political authority committed to the pope by Christ was an integral part of the papal plentitude of power, at least in the eyes of the thirteenth-century popes. If this went, everything else was shaken. But supreme political power could not be exercised by the pope in person: for this he must have deputies, and the most important of these deputies was the emperor.[23]

Innocent III extended the deplorable exercise of indulgences to Crusaders promising them rewards in heaven for good works performed.[24] Boniface VIII (1294-1303) took it even further and granted individual indulgences for those who visited the church of the Holy Apostles in Rome.[25] As the church gained more and more power, it reached 'the summit of its audacity' under Boniface VIII.[26] He 'attached more importance to his secular sovereignty' than any pope.[27]

## The Reformation

However, then 'came the earthquake of the Reformation.'[28] Yet it was far from dissolving the union that had grown between the church and state. Instead, a grasp of the significance of the spiritual kingdom of Jesus Christ and the entailments for the church age of a necessary separation and independence of the civil sphere from the church only made progress by baby steps at the beginning.[29] Luther saw it dimly, Calvin more clearly.[30] For Luther, as Robinson said in a speech in Cincinnati, November 8, 1866:

---

23. R. W. Southern, *Western Society and the Church in the Middle Ages* (London: Penguin Books, 1970), p. 145.

24. Ibid., p. 137.

25. Ibid., p. 138.

26. Peck, *Notes on Ecclesiology*, p. 134.

27. Southern, *Western Society and the Church in the Middle Ages*, p. 149.

28. Peck, *Notes on Ecclesiology*, p. 134.

29. Ibid., pp. 134-35.

30. For an overview of Calvin's two kingdoms application to the civil and ecclesiastical realm, see David VanDrunen, *Natural Law and the Two Kingdoms*, pp. 69-93.

Luther had some glimpses of the grand truth that the spiritual kingdom of Jesus Christ is something separate from and independent of the civil government ordained of God the Creator in the hands of Caesar; but, driven to shelter himself under the protection of the monarch who was ambitious to rid himself of the authority of the pope, yet equally jealous of such an *imperium in imperio* as a completely organized spiritual government in the hands of the church, Luther was obliged, as he thought, to sacrifice a part of the spiritual prerogatives of the church for protection against the power of the pope.[31]

Both Luther and Calvin had a two kingdoms theology; however, 'it is Calvin's emphasis on the visible expression of the kingdom of Christ in the outward ministry of the Church that most practically distinguishes his two kingdoms theology from that of Luther.'[32] Peck claims that since Calvin was French instead of German, he was able to see more of the truth.[33] Matthew Tuininga in his lengthy and excellent study concurs and agrees that while Calvin's theology was influential it was especially his political theology that had influence:

> It was his political theology, so uniquely applicable to a context in which state and church were separated, that distinctly shaped the French church. In contrast to Melanchthon or Bullinger, Calvin stressed the distinction between the church and the political order, and he provided a model for a range of autonomous church government functions through the offices of pastor, elder, and deacon.[34]

This is a great beneficial relevance that Calvin has for Christians today. It is important to recognize that Calvin lived long before political liberalism emerged, so 'Calvin's relevance for contemporary Christian public engagement lies not in his political actions or opinions but in his political *theology*.'[35] Remarkably, the chapters on the civil government in the *Institutes* changed little between 1536 and 1559, unlike the chapters on Christ's spiritual government.[36] Calvin's influence was felt far and

---

31. Quoted in Peck, *Notes on Ecclesiology*, p. 134.
32. Tuininga, *Calvin's Political Theology*, p. 185.
33. Ibid., p. 135.
34. Tuininga, *Calvin's Political Theology*, p. 84.
35. Ibid., p. 355.
36. Ibid., p. 228.

wide, including in Holland, but especially in Scotland. It was Knox's influence, and the development of Melville's *Second Book of Discipline*, as I argued in Chapter 12, that profoundly influenced the church in the United States.

Thus, the Scotch and Scotch-Irish were the main instruments in molding the Presbyterian Church in the United States, as argued in a previous chapter. Stuart Robinson, adapting Melville's language, said that 'there be two republics in this nation, one of the civil republic of the United States, of which the man in the White House is the head; and the other the spiritual commonwealth, of which Jesus Christ is head, with which the man in the White House has nothing to do, *but to protect the persons and property of its subjects*, as that of other citizens.'[37] As Peck seems to indicate by his own historical context, the church was forced in the nineteenth century to come to terms with its own teaching about their only head and king, Jesus Christ.[38] Given the pressures upon her in the second half of the nineteenth century, she was 'compelled by the assaults of her adversaries to study her own nature and to define her relation to that other ordinance of God, the state.'[39]

Having traced through history the ebbs and flows of the relationship between church and state, Peck then burrows down into dogmatic reflections of the similarities and distinctions between the relations of the church and the state. He notes:

> The church and the state agree in these three points: 1st, That they are ordained of God; 2nd, That they are ordained for his glory; 3rd, That they are ordained for the good of mankind. They differ in the following points: 1st, In the aspects and relations in which God is contemplated by them respectively as the *source* of power; 2nd, In the aspects in which man is contemplated by them respectively as the *object* of power; 3rd, In the rule which they are to be respectively guided in the exercise of power.[40]

Significantly, at this very point, Peck claims that the principles stated above flowed from and are entailed in a recognition of the different ways in which God rules the world. I have emphasized this point from

---

37. Quoted in Peck, *Notes on Ecclesiology*, p. 137 [emphasis mine].
38. Ibid., p. 138.
39. Ibid.
40. Ibid.

the very beginning of the body of this book (see, e.g., the early pages of Chapter 2 where I cite Professor Guy Waters). God is the source of both kingdoms, the civil and the religious, although He deigned to rule them with the following important distinction that bears repeating: 'I observe that the state is the ordinance of God, considered as Creator, and, therefore, the moral governor of mankind, while the church is an ordinance of God, considered as the Savior and Restorer of mankind.'[41]

## The Fundamental Difference Between Church Power and State Power

Next, Peck notes that contemplating man as the *object of power* is what matters most and then he makes a fine distinction with regard to noting that the state is for man as man, whereas the church is for man as sinner. This may sound like he is merely stating the obvious; however, paying attention to the ebb and flow of redemptive history is what his insights unlock since the state is in place for the whole of mankind, but the church is a government of grace and exercises its power for the body of Christ.[42]

Peck brings us back to the garden of Eden in order to contemplate what would have been needful if humans had not fallen: having passed the probation, parents would have still needed to *direct* their children in the way of righteousness, but they would not have needed *restraint*, for if Adam had obeyed in the covenant of works, he would have been confirmed in righteousness and his children (presumably he and Eve would parent in response to 'Be fruitful and multiply') would have had no danger of going astray. Before the fall into sin, there was no need for restraint, after the fall, there is: 'Hence arose a government of *force*.'[43] For Calvin, and for many Reformed theologians following in his wake, this involved a fundamental distinction with regard to the use of the law:

> Thus while there is an element of truth to the claim that Calvin identified the objective of political order in light of the same ideal of righteousness as he did the spiritual kingdom of Christ, it is crucial to emphasize that, in Calvin's view, whereas the spiritual kingdom is involved in the *restoration*

---

41. Ibid., p. 139.

42. Ibid.

43. Ibid., p. 140 [emphasis original].

*of true righteousness* (the spiritual use of the law), the civil order is involved in the *restraint of outward unrighteousness* (the civil use of the law).[44]

This is a fundamental difference between the state and the church with regard to their function. The state considers humans beings only outwardly; however, the church has to deal with the realm of the spirit.[45] As Peck says, the ministry of the church is to be a servant of the Word, in charity:

> Its sanctions are not corporeal, involving the exercise of brute force, but only moral and spiritual, appealing to the judgment, the faith, the conscience of its members. It knows nothing of the sword, the dungeon, the lash, pecuniary fines, etc., etc., but only of argument, exhortation, admonition, censure, etc., etc., Its great function is to teach, to convince, to persuade, 'to bear witness to the truth.' Its triumphs are the triumphs of *love*; it drags no reluctant captives at the wheels of its chariot; the design of its ordinances, oracles, ministry, is through the efficacious operation of the Holy Ghost to bring its captives into hearty sympathy with its king, and so to give them a share in the glory and exultation of the triumphs of the king .... Its only sword is the sword of the Spirit, which is the word of God. Its discipline is not the punishment of an avenging judge, asserting the unbending majesty of the law, but the discipline of a tender mother, whose bowels yearn over the wayward child, and who inflicts no pain, except for the child's reformation and salvation. The authority of his kingdom is spiritual.[46]

Therefore, the power that the church ministers is spiritual. The power that the state 'ministers' is magisterial. Calvin, although he could not completely extricate himself from the 'thralldom of "the spirit of the age",'[47] nevertheless saw the fundamental difference of the pastor's office as that of serving: 'Ministers may not rule in an "authoritative manner in the church [*imperio ecclesiae regimini*] but are subject to Christ's authority [*Christi imperio subesse*]." They are "servants, not masters [*ministros, non dominos*]." Thus the church's authority is *ministerial* rather than *magisterial*, spiritual rather than political.'[48]

---

44. Tuininga, *Calvin's Political Theology*, p. 323.

45. Peck, *Notes on Ecclesiology*, p. 143.

46. Ibid., pp. 143-44.

47. Ibid., p. 135.

48. Tuininga, *Calvin's Political Theology*, p. 199.

This is why the church and state differ so much with regard to the guidance of their God-ordained power: their constitutions differ radically. That of the church is divine revelation, that of the state is 'by human reason and providential events.'[49] This brings us to the very core of their differences: the church's only constitution is the revealed will of God, and she is only allowed to declare what has been declared to her and govern her polity according to the prescriptions of that divine revelation; but the state may adopt whatever organization she wishes for herself, and its power is magisterial and imperative.[50]

Consequently, since the state was ordained by God (as Creator and moral Governor of the universe) for man as man, so to speak, 'it has nothing to do with any principles of religion but those that belong to man as man: to wit, the being of God and a moral government.'[51] To grant the state any power over Christ's kingdom in the church is a travesty of His order of creation following the fall; therefore 'to give it any power over the truths of revealed religion, and over the records which contain those truths, is to confound it with the church, or what is practically the same thing, to abolish the church, except as an auxiliary of the state, in its preserving order.'[52]

So where will the Christian statesman in our congregations find light? He will find it wherever it is evident, he will find it from the study of the classics and from modern erudite statesmen, he 'will seek light from every possible quarter.'[53] Peck comments eloquently:

> The true statesman will seek light from every possible quarter. As he will enlarge his views by the study of the political writings of Plato, Aristotle and Cicero, and by the study of the great historians of Greece and Rome, as well as those of modern states, so he will not neglect the laws of Moses, nor the striking biblical histories in which the operation of those laws is exemplified. And in many points of civil regulation he will find that the Bible sustains the conclusions of reason and experience.[54]

---

49. Peck, *Notes on Ecclesiology*, p. 144. Statement of the Assembly (1861) quoted.
50. Ibid., p. 145.
51. Ibid., p. 146.
52. Ibid.
53. Ibid., p. 150.
54. Ibid., pp. 150-51.

## Are Politics Secular and non-Religious?

I argued previously that there are limitations on church power and state power. Furthermore, I argued that the church is restricted from inter-meddling in the civil sphere. Likewise, the state is restricted from meddling in the sphere of the church. Following the discussion above, it may seem that we are left with nothing more than to conclude that the state is secular and that the church is religious, and never the two should meet.

Alan Strange has categorized Darryl Hart of doing just that: 'While it is the case that, in more recent years, those who would vie for the spirituality of the church might have as its concomitant the secularity of the state.'[55] My reading of Hart's book is different. One way to cut the difference here is to precisely define 'secular.' Is Hart using it in an Augustinian way or according to French Revolutionary connotations? Hart would demur from the latter, since he says that Thornwell clearly thought the state was ordained by God, and 'What Christian didn't?'[56] Hart's argument is rather that 'attempts to employ the sacred and eternal for the common and temporal end up trivializing the faith.'[57] For Hart, 'the state or civil order … derived its authority from the created order and its rule from the "light of nature."'[58] Moreover, 'the state and the church had different ends. The state's was to restrain evil and cultivate social order; the church's was to save a remnant of the human race for the world to come.'[59] Additionally, as Hart maintains: 'The United States might be under God, but so was every other nation on the planet, which meant that they all had equal access to the laws and norms of the created order and to human reason to try to figure out the best means for restraining wickedness and protecting the welfare of citizens.'[60] This

---

55. See Strange, *The Doctrine of the Spirituality of the Church*, p. 252. In footnote 96 on this page, he argues that 'Hart not only argues for the institutional separation of church and state … but for a secularized state, which is something that neither Hodge nor Thornwell would argue for and, in fact, as can be see [sic] herein, argued against. This is important to note here because Hart and others claim that their doctrine of the spirituality of the church is the successor to Thornwell's doctrine. While there are certainly points of clear continuity, Thornwell's rejection of a secularized state reveals clear discontinuity.'

56. Private correspondence, 8/04/2020.

57. Darryl Hart, *A Secular Faith*, p. 12.

58. Ibid., p. 118.

59. Ibid.

60. Ibid., pp. 118-19.

hardly sounds like the kind of secularistic canvas onto which Strange is trying to paint Hart.

Nevertheless, this does beg a question. Would some other language than 'secular' bring more agreement among allies who are convinced that the SOTC and historic notions of the primary mission of the church deserve a seat on the bus? How can we best talk about such categories, which have a very noble pedigree in our Reformed and Presbyterian churches?

Perhaps a way forward can be observed in the project of VanDrunen. In his recently published book on political theology, he proposes a constructive case for engagements with politics in terms of the Noahic covenant.[61] Rather than offer the idea that the political community has no religious base whatsoever, VanDrunen's tome suggests that the Noahic covenant is the foundation for political community.[62] This does not entail that political communities are religiously free; rather, political communities – no matter what their religious commitments – are under obligation to God to perform the ethical obligations of God according to the Noahic covenant.[63] Essentially, VanDrunen's book is one long argument that the Noahic covenant has been neglected for helpful grist for the political theology mill. This, of course, would put all political endeavors – whether Christian, Muslim, Jewish or whatever – under the aegis of God's rule in the Noahic covenant.

## Does the church exercise a prophetic word towards culture?

For the reader who has been paying close attention to the argument of this book, it will not be difficult to guess the answer from my perspective: the prophetic mission of the church is to declare to the world that they are engulfed in sin, and unable to extricate themselves except through the saving grace of God. Perhaps addressing this question directly will bring clarity.

As has been stated clearly, our responsibility in this age of the church is different than it was for the Israelite theocracy. The last great

---

61. David VanDrunen, *Politics after Christendom: Political Theology in a Fractured World* (Grand Rapids, MI: Zondervan Academic, 2020).

62. Ibid., p. 197.

63. Cf., Chapter 2 of this book.

prophet of the Old Testament period was John the Baptist. He was the messenger of ultimatum, calling Israel to repent at the inauguration of Christ's coming, in such a manner that his baptism was a 'sign of eschatological judgment.'[64] It was expected in the prophetic office of the Old Covenant that prophets addressed the society, *since it was a theocracy*, and the prophets played the role of gathering legal briefs in order to indict the people and the king for their shortcomings in failing to live up to the stipulations of the Mosaic Law. Of course, this is not all that they were – they were also heralds of the New Covenant to come. Nevertheless, they were like lawyers, bringing their lawsuit on behalf of God to the people. That office has ceased. Christ is the ultimate prophet who has heralded the good news of his Gospel. We are no longer in a theocracy. These distinctions need to be kept in mind when we talk about the church's alleged prophetic role in the common grace cultures where God places her. As M.G. Kline reminded us years ago: a hermeneutical muddle can occur when 'simplistic appeals to features in the life of theocratic Israel [are made] to determine the functions of the common grace state.'[65]

Nevertheless, there are constant clarion calls from Christians and ministers for the church, the corporate church, to address social justice issues. This is a virtual leitmotif in Alan Strange's book on Hodge's view of the SOTC. Strange takes great pains to demonstrate that Hodge held to a far more moderate view of the SOTC than his Southern colleagues by 'not keeping the church from engaging in her prophetic task to declare the whole counsel of God to all, in and out of the church.'[66] It is the clarion call of several influential books in the Reformed community.[67] More recently, pastors are suggesting that 'social justice is an important subject that should not be ignored either by the church

---

64. M. G. Kline, *By Oath Consigned: A Reinterpretation of the Covenant Signs of Circumcision and Baptism* (Grand Rapids, MI: Eerdmans, 1968), p. 51.

65. See M. G. Kline, *Kingdom Prologue*, p. 179.

66. Alan Strange, *The Doctrine of the Spirituality of the Church*, p. 321. Earlier in the book, he calls Robinson and Thornwell's views the 'radical spirituality of the church wing' (see p. xxiii). (See also pp. xx, xxiv, 5, 13, 127, 150, 230-231, 237, 246, 262).

67. See, e.g., Steve Corbett and Brian Fikkert, *When Helping Hurts: How to Alleviate Poverty without Hurting the Poor … and Yourself* (Chicago, IL: Moody, 2009) and Harvie M. Conn, *Doing Justice and Preaching Grace* (Grand Rapids, MI: Zondervan, 1982).

*corporately* or the Christian privately.'[68] While I appreciate the caveats that are often included in such statements,[69] such statements fuel the tendency to create 'fuzzy boundaries' with regard to job descriptions for the corporate church, as I have been arguing throughout this book. We don't see the Scriptures speaking on a number of complex social issues, such as 'slavery, economic inequality, imperial military actions, immigration policy, and a host of other social and political concerns.'[70] Even on so important an issue as abortion, she (the church) may not speak publicly on a bill pending before Congress on such a weighty issue as abortion for all kinds of reasons.[71] However, the first and most important reason is that her authority is ministerial and declarative and therefore church courts and ministers in their official capacity are to only handle 'ecclesiastical' matters.[72] This is not ghettoizing the Gospel; it is merely calling on Christians to give respect to the job descriptions that God has laid out in Scripture.[73] Moreover, perhaps we should pause and consider whether such clarion calls for the corporate church addressing issues of social injustice in her *corporate capacity* actually do more harm than good. In other words, is it a regression on the part of the church with regard to recognizing her job description or is it forward thinking? Is it a 'desire for the church to be relevant and influential in socially evident ways'?[74]

Therefore, consider how this 'plays out' among some of the major figures we have been engaging. For Thornwell:

> The object of Christian ministry, the ministry that belongs to the church, is not to reform society or fix the many ills that are common among men in a fallen, yet temporal world. Rather, a minister of the church exists 'to persuade men to be reconciled to God through Christ, to persuade

---

68. See Eric B. Watkins, 'The Color of Preaching,' *New Horizons* (May 2019): pp. 4-5 [emphasis mine].

69. Ibid.

70. Guy Waters, *How Jesus Runs the Church*, p. 69.

71. Ibid., pp. 68-69.

72. Ibid., pp. 66-70.

73. Ibid., p. 70.

74. See D. G. Hart's addressing this issue in *Between the Times: The Orthodox Presbyterian Church in Transition, 1945-1990* (Willow Grove, PA: The Committee for the Historian of the Orthodox Presbyterian Church, 2011), pp. 185-210.

them to accept of the blessed Saviour in all His offices, and to rest upon Him and Him alone for 'wisdom and righteousness and sanctification and redemption.'[75]

Hodge, on the other hand, according to Alan Strange, opposed the SOTC when it was adduced to muzzle the prophetic voice of the church or to keep the church 'from addressing matters in civil society that he believed appropriate for the church.'[76]

It seems to this author that the church should respect the God-given boundaries allotted to the state and the state should exercise great care not to transgress the 'cultic' boundaries of the church. Theological confession is assigned to the church and nowhere else. In the realm of the state, God has given political equality and therefore, as believing citizens of a common grace culture with unbelievers, we should strive to be good neighbors and the church corporately should not impinge on the rights of unbelievers. Ideally, the state should just perform her God-given duties and discharge them well. So how is the church to influence society for the better?

By the voting of individual citizens, citizens with informed views that vote responsibly. Moreover, we should pray earnestly as a corporate church for our civil leaders and the magistrate wherever the Lord has placed us, especially in these extraordinary and difficult times (1 Tim. 2:1 and following).

---

75. Thornwell (Vol. IV, p. 565) quoted in Christopher C. Cooper, 'Binding Bodies and Liberating Souls,' pp. 35-47, especially at p. 40.

76. Strange, *The Doctrine of the Spirituality of the Church*, p. 262. Also see the preface and pp. xxiv, 13, 230-31, 236-37, 246, 263, 280,316-17, and 321.

CHAPTER 15

# Conclusion

I want to draw a conclusion to this book by returning to the Scriptures. After laying the Scriptural foundations, we have seen in several chapters what the primary mission of the church *is not*. It is not to be construed as is often done along transformational lines, i.e., as if the mission of the church was making our culture a more Christian place. This will run against so many trends in the modern church, especially in America. Why? In short, because in just the past two decades, the number of members in churches has dropped from seventy percent to fifty percent. According to Shadi Hamid, a regular contributor to *The Atlantic*, this is largely because what was once *religious* belief has now been channeled into *political* belief.[1] Adherents of 'wokeism' are challenging the narratives about the exceptionalism of America's founding. Definitions of racism have altered in order to include a 'systemic' aspect, and people expect the corporate church to weigh in.[2] The charge of 'silence is complicity' is rampant.

Along transformational lines, the most extreme forms are illustrated by liberation theologies and theonomy. A 'softer' version of the same model is evidenced in the followers of Kuyper and Dooyeweerd. But if the argument of this book holds, then the mission of the church is not even to be categorized along the recent lines of 'missional' theological trends, as evidenced in N. T. Wright's work, for example.

---

1. Shadi Hamid, 'America Without God,' *The Atlantic* (April 2021 issue, although published online on March 10, 2021).

2. Hermina Dykxhoorn, 'Living in a Woke World: And Just What That Means,' *Christian Renewal,* May 1 (2021): pp. 24-26.

Rather, what we observed in the next four chapters – in the 'what it is' section of the book, where we considered the nature of the kingdom of God (especially in the NT), the confessional teaching (especially of WCF 20, 23 and 31), and various historical studies of certain Old School Presbyterians who emphasized that Christ is the only head of the church and the ramification of the *iure divino* church polity – is that the church is a missions agency, given a specific task on this earth. This can be stated in negative terms by clarifying what the mission of the church is not. For example, it is not the same as the state or civil sphere. The mission can and should be stated positively as well. Not only did we attempt to set this forward with biblical justification and evidence, but in the last three chapters we set forth what such a vision of the primary mission of the church should look like with respect to the church, politics, and education. Although limited and restrained, she has been given a particular charter and job description by her Lord, and that should be followed assiduously. Otherwise, fuzzy boundaries result.

And now, in this conclusion, we return to scripture to illustrate from Paul's preaching at Athens what the primary mission of the church should look like (Acts 17:16-34). As Kevin DeYoung and Greg Gilbert have said: 'A study of mission would seem incomplete without a glance at the missionary par excellence of the New Testament: Paul the apostle to the Gentiles.'[3] Of course, Paul was concerned to 'remember the poor' (Gal. 2:10). Moreover, he recognized the importance of loving one's neighbor (Rom. 13:10). Even so, when the gospel was first declared in this cultural and political center of Athens, it was done with utter simplicity and profundity. To illustrate this, I want to take you back to Athens, so to speak, on that day and ask a number of questions. By doing so, we can observe, through a very vivid illustration, what the primary mission of the church is. Paul, as the apostle to the Gentiles, is our supreme example here. He embodies the primary mission of the church in his own ministry to the Gentiles. Of course, that is not to gloss over his unique position as the apostle to the Gentiles; however, there is something essential about what he does in Athens that illustrates the ongoing primary mission of the church even in the wake of his powerful ministry.

---

3. DeYoung and Gilbert, *What is the Mission of the Church,* pp. 59-60.

## What would Paul have seen in Athens?

Athens, especially the Acropolis, is almost ineffable. I had the privilege of being in that city for almost a week in the Spring of 2019. To walk in the vicinity of the Acropolis, let alone to see her ramparts lit up, is a remarkable sight to behold.

Going back two millennia, Paul would have seen and experienced a city with a long history and a very noble pedigree of ideas attached to it. In order to understand what he did in Athens on that day, it may be worthwhile to trace some history of Athens. The Acropolis, in particular, was probably built to celebrate the victory of the Athenians over the Persians. In fact, there was a bronze statue known as *Athena Promachos*, 'Athena the Defender,' at the base of which read inscription, 'the Athenians set this up from the spoils of the Medes' (i.e., the Persians). This monumental statue was started around 465 B.C., but completed somewhere between 458-455 B.C. A writer from the second century, Pausanius, wrote that the point of the spear she held and the crest of her helmet on the statue were visible to mariners from miles away as they approached by sea. The statue was probably taken to Constantinople many years later, where it disappeared.

The goddess Athena appears as the personification of wisdom when she stops Achilles from his killing in the Iliad. In the Odyssey, the second most important epic of the Greeks, Athena is equated with the wisdom and the cunning of Odysseus as he escapes one difficulty after another. Chiefly, however, she is the protector and patron of Greek heroes, and Athena would have retained pride of place on the Acropolis.

If Paul had shown up four centuries earlier, the Acropolis would have been in many ways a very unified place; not that it wasn't so when he arrived. What do I mean by a unified place? The unity of the place would have been felt in its architecture and its planning, in the iconography and themes that would surround one as they made their way around the Acropolis. One major theme that a person would experience could be found in the introductory pediment on the Acropolis. There, one would have seen Heracles being led towards Zeus and Hera to be immortalized. What was engraved at exactly this point becomes a paradigm for civilization, especially Western civilization: *a person is immortalized by the works he or she leaves behind!* Athens had set the cultural agenda for centuries to come.

The unified impression would have also come from the religious cults found on the slopes of the Acropolis as well as on its summit. The entrance would have been marked by cyclopean walls, rising over four meters in many places. Moreover, that person would have been impressed by the number and variety of votive offerings. That probably would have impressed him most of all. There would have been many marble statues and gifts (*algama*) dedicated to Athena. Not just rich marble; also terracotta figurines would have been everywhere since those are the offerings that the poor could afford. Indeed, the ancient record has left an accurate presentation of the religious atmosphere of the place. In the first century A.D., Petronius, a contemporary writer from Nero's court said satirically, 'It was easier to find a god at Athens than a man.'

Unfortunately, we know from the annals of history, that during the Hellenistic period (500-300 B.C.), much of the gold that adorned many of the statues in Athens was stripped from them. And during this period, Athens becomes a kind of college town. It would have been like Cambridge, Massachusetts, where some prestigious centers of learning are. So, in other words, visiting Athens in Paul's day would have been like visiting Harvard or MIT in our own day.

In 86 B.C., Athens was sacked by the Roman general Sulla. Much of the city was destroyed in the process. Nevertheless, Athens remained a very important cultural center. In 31 B.C., Octavian defeated Mark Antony and Cleopatra, and Athens became a provincial capital. But Athens in the Roman era was still a cultural and intellectual center. The temple of Olympian Zeus had been begun by Pisitratus in the sixth century B.C.; now it was finally finished. Athens was a cultural center, but now it had become a political center as well.

We know that the Roman emperor, Augustus himself, commissioned a small temple in 27 B.C. It was an elegant little temple. It was dedicated to Roma and Augustus. Why is this so symbolic and so important? Now this temple told the world, so to speak, that Athens (formerly the cultural center of the ancient world) had been absorbed into the surrounding Roman empire. Augustus wanted to recreate the 'golden age' of Athens in Rome. Everything that had been the glory of Greece, now was to be assimilated, 'politicized' so to speak, into the imperium of Rome, the supreme power of Rome. Athens was now being exploited for her ideas and her ideals. But today the little temple consists of just a few remains, the base of columns which tourists hardly notice as they pass by in the modern period. Unless you know what to look for, or have a reliable guide, you could almost miss the bases of the remaining columns which are overshadowed by the majestic remains and reconstructions of the Parthenon. How the flower fades! It is here one day and gone the next. Kingdoms and nations perish.

In short, what do we have in Athens when Paul was there for the first time? We have a conflation of power politics and prestigious ideas. We have the most noble seminal achievements of the Western world mixed with the political ambitions of Rome, all of this with a religiosity that soaked the entire city, but especially the Acropolis. It was into that context, that evocative atmosphere, that the apostle Paul speaks and preaches, which leads to my next question.

## Where was it that the apostle Paul spoke publicly?

The simple answer to that question is that the apostle spoke and proclaimed the Gospel wherever he went in the city. He proclaimed the Gospel first in the synagogue, then in the *agora* (i.e., the market place). But finally, and most significantly, he proclaimed the Gospel at the Areopagus.

There is a debate among archeologists and biblical scholars about what the reference to the Areopagus is. Some think that it was merely a topographic reference. Others think it is a reference to a court, a place where judicial cases were tried. The Areopagus was a hill near the Acropolis (on the side of the mount). In ancient times, we know that a council met there. In fact, its ancient function was a homicide court that was bound by rigid cultic traditions, and it met on that hill on the side of the Acropolis.[4] The place to which they took Paul was the Areopagus, probably both a topographical reference, in this author's opinion, on a hill, but also and more importantly a place where court meetings and proceedings often took place. Sometimes there were judicial proceedings there. Sometimes there was merely an exchange of ideas; however, it was always a court or place marked by religious overtones.

---

4. See Hemer, 'Paul at Athens: A Topographical Note,' *NTS* 20 (April 1974), pp. 341-50.

In Roman times, it was an important place for supervising morals and education as well. But whether hill or court, the real point of the narrative in its own historical context is to recognize that the Areopagus was always a court, and a meeting place with religious overtones. Now we can focus our beam of inquiry even sharper and more precisely.

## What did Paul say and to whom did he say it? Moreover, how did he say it?

Taking up the latter question first, we should be particularly struck by the courtesy of his approach. He was not bombastic. He was not arrogant. Nevertheless, he did not shirk from a firm proclamation of the truth.

Here Paul speaks into the context of the intellectual elites of ancient Athens. There were at least two groups that can be identified. First, there was the Epicureans, those well-known atheistic materialists for whom pleasure in this life is the chief end. Then there were the Stoics. These folk belonged to that celebrated school of lofty and severe pantheists for whom the universe itself was considered to be under the law of iron necessity. Furthermore, for them, if matters don't go your way, then you are expected to keep a stiff upper lip and by all means do not wear any of your emotions on your sleeve. It was the expectation of having an iron jaw in the midst of the iron law of necessity. Now we are at the crux of the matter.

Think about this. Here is a situation that is somewhat like Paul visiting Harvard, the Sorbonne, or Yale, or the University of Chicago. All of them are centers of culture and learning. But it's even more than that. Imagine taking Harvard yard and plopping it down right in the middle of the Mall in Washington DC with all its statuary, its amazing museums, and the political buzz in the air. Mix in the New York Met museum of art or the British museum for good favor. Such is the cultural milieu in which the apostle finds himself.

Recorded for us in holy Scripture is the divinely inspired oracle of God with respect to what He wanted His apostle (or by way of extension, the church) to say in such a situation. So what was it that God wanted the church to do and say in a context where the most significant power politics are being mixed with the best and most excellent products of the culture of human beings apart from and without God?

400

To that very simple question, we have a very simple answer. First, Acts 17:18-19 clearly gives the content of what the apostle preached, 'Jesus and the resurrection.' But it is really in verses 24 and following that we have the fuller context of his proclamation.

He uses the statue dedicated to the 'unknown god' as his platform. God is the same yesterday, today and tomorrow, he says. In other words, God has often been in the business of taking the language and cultural products of human beings and subverting them for His honorable purposes. He turns them on their head. But Paul doesn't just give them Jesus and the resurrection in his preaching. He gives them so much theology that entails and supports Jesus and the resurrection. What he does is give them a mini lesson in Systematic Theology. In verses 23b-24, he says 'This I proclaim to you ... the God who made the world and all things in it, since He is Lord of Heaven and earth, does not dwell in temples made with hands ...' Now, there is the doctrine of creation. But he is just warming up.

In verse 25, Paul continues his theologically-based sermon by saying, 'neither is He served by human hands, as though He needed anything, since He Himself gives to all life and breath and all things.' Now there is the self-existence of God, His 'aseity' as some have expressed it, or His 'self-origination.'

In verse 26, the apostle continues, 'and He made from one, every nation of mankind to live on all the face of the earth ...' Now there is the doctrine of the federal headship, the representative headship of Adam. He goes on in verse 26: 'having determined their appointed times, and the boundaries of their habitation.' Now there is the doctrine of God's providence and sovereignty. Paul is saying that one God, the living and true God, lives and resides in august royalty over them.

Then, in verses 27-28, the apostle continues: 'that they should seek God, if perhaps they might grope for Him and find Him, though He is not very far from each of us ...' Now, there is the immanence and presence of God, or better yet, the omnipresence of God.

And the apostle seems to be implying in verses 26-27 that their problem is not God's distance from us, but our distance from him! Then, the apostle continues in verse 28: 'for in Him we live and move and exist, even as some of your own poets have said, 'For we are his offspring ...' (here he quotes Aratus or possibly Cleanthes). Now there is the doctrine of common grace, and the apostle is using pagan language and poetry for divine theological purposes.[5]

Then, the apostle continues, honing in with his sharpened two-edged sword, in verse 29: 'Being then the offspring of God, we ought not to think that the Divine Nature is like gold or silver or stone, an image formed by the art and thought of man.'

Now there is the Creator/creature distinction. There is Romans chapter 1, with the rebelliousness of man hidden in studious courtesy. Can one even doubt at this point that the apostle's hands and arms were not pointing, and his eyes were not looking, to those rich and luxurious and symbolically freighted works surrounding him and the audience?

Now in verses 30-31 comes the hammer blows of elegant rhetoric, followed by the cymbals of the trumpeting word of God: 'Therefore, having overlooked the times of ignorance, God is now declaring to men that all everywhere should repent, because He has fixed a day in which He will judge the world in righteousness through a Man whom He has appointed, having furnished proof to all men by raising Him from the dead.'

Now there is the glorious free offer of the gospel, the final judgment, the session and the eventual second visitation of Christ, and most of all the resurrection. Here is where the apostle turns the discussion from philosophical subtleties to personal responsibility.

Here's the point: *What does God want us to say and do (as a church, following his preaching example) in the context where the most powerful politics are being mixed in with the best cultural and intellectual products of the human race? What does Almighty God want his church, as the church*

---

5. Aratus lived about 270 B.C. The fuller quote from *Phenomena 1-5* reads:
    'From Zeus let us begin; him do we mortals never leave unnamed; full of Zeus
    Are all the streets and all the market-places of men; full is the sea and the heavens
        thereof; always we all have need of Zeus. For we are his offspring.'

    Cleanthes wrote later:
    'the image and the echo only of thy eternal voice.'

These are Ralph Stob's translations, from *Christianity and Classical Civilization* (Eerdmans, 1950), p. 62. Stob makes a fine argument for the view that Paul would have read these poets and that he was not just parroting some snatch of poetry that would have been floating around at the time. His justification is based on the fact that 'Tarsus was unique among the cities of antiquity. More than others it was the meeting place of East and West. In it there was all that which was typically oriental [i.e., middle eastern], but also the Hellenic spirit had entered in marked degree.'

*corporately but especially through her ordained officers, to say in such a context?* He wants us to proclaim a robust theology which culminates in the bold, but courteous, proclamation of the work and ministry of the human/divine mediator: Jesus Christ.

## Why did Paul Say It?

One clear reason from our text is because the apostle was moved, indeed, he was indignant about all the idolatry he experienced. My former NT colleague, S. M. Baugh, thinks that Paul hoped for better from the Athenians and was sorely disappointed. But Paul had a jealousy for the worship of the Almighty God burning in his bosom. Another reason Paul said what he said is that his whole presentation of Christ was situated in the context of his systematic theology. There is no anti-intellectualism on the part of the apostle here.

But there is another important reason for which he said what he said. It is not explicitly said in the text, but it is safely assumed. First, there were others in the audience besides those erudite philosophers. More were present than those Epicureans and Stoics. And even those Epicureans and Stoics, even the most powerful Roman politician who may have been present, needed to hear his message.

After all, did those intelligent learned philosophers have wives and children? Probably some of them did. And if they did, then they were poignantly aware of the fact that they had sometimes set a bad example before their beloved children, especially those pleasure-seeking Epicureans! Here's my point: there is hardly anything that weighs on a conscience more than the weight of knowing that you may have set a bad example for a little one. Moreover, there could have been a hundred different reasons why their consciences were weighed down.

Did those intelligent philosophers ever wake up in the morning (or, even in the middle of the night) and wonder if they had wasted their lives? There are few things that weigh on a conscience like a wasted life. Remember, the city of Athens and her citizens thought from ancient times of Pericles' idea, that a person's works which he or she leaves behind is what makes them immortal. Contrary to this, Paul comes in preaching and teaching that what makes a person immortal is actually something outside of themselves and their works, an alien righteousness found in another.

## What was the effect of Paul saying what he said?

When God speaks, people must listen. God's command to repent here was not a mere invitation: it was a command. In other words, these were not some new, mere scraps of knowledge that the apostle was sloppily weaving together for the insatiably intellectually curious. This is preaching with covenantal teeth attached. Think of Isaiah 55:11-12: 'For as the rain and snow come down from heaven, and do not return there without watering the earth, and making it bear and sprout, and furnishing seed to the sower and bread to the eater, so shall my word be which goes forth without succeeding in the matter for which I send it.'

Here is a plea to understand and obey, not just another new tidbit of brain food for their insatiable mental appetites. The conversion of the woman and others seems to demonstrate that there was a crowd that day, and an interested gallery of listeners. They seemed to have had a tender conscience.

We have powerful weapons in our hands. We have God's Word, and we have the pristine clarity of the theology of the Reformation bequeathed to us. Why should we search for anything else for our mission? Now we find ourselves in this pagan post-Christian world with very similar opportunities to proclaim this life-giving theology into an atmosphere where many people are ignorant of these basic biblical truths. Here in the speech of Paul is an unparalleled model for preaching the Gospel and witnessing to the truth in the context of a lost world.

## Conclusions and Practical Applications

Just because the church should stay out of civil affairs does not mean that individual Christians should be socially uninvolved. I have tried to argue in this book that the church has a particular job description. I think I have found myself most closely aligned with the ecclesiology of Thornwell for whom:

> The church not only should not but also need not attempt to reform society for the advancement of the gospel because the church prescribed by Christ is sufficient, irrespective of outside social structures, and provides the best means available for the spiritual task that Christ has given it.[6]

---

6. Cooper, 'Binding Bodies and Liberating Souls,' pp. 35-47, especially at p. 41.

My hope is that the reader has picked up that I think making 'private' opinions public and ministerial declarations, especially from the pulpit, should be distinguished. Throughout this book, for example, I have attempted to register my disgust, dismay, and denouncement of various forms of racism as they have manifested themselves in recent history: Southern race-based slavery, the hypocrisy of apartheid practices (even in the name of Reformed Christianity), and Princeton devolving into segregationist practices. As a Seminary Professor, who trains people from all over the world and who in many cases will return to serve in many corners of the world, I have a responsibility to train my students to combat racism wherever it may raise its ugly head. That means one thing for my Israeli students, another for those who may return to Turkey, Nigeria, or China, and the list goes on.

However, I have done so as a 'private citizen' and a human being, not in my official office as speaking 'for the church' corporately. Other Christians should do the same. It is no wonder that folks speak out and are bewildered why the church does not speak to such systemic injustice; however, the church acting in her capacity as the corporate church should be very, very wary of doing so publicly, especially from the pulpit, given the restrictions upon her with regard to her declarative authority. That there is such a thing as 'systemic injustice(s)' cannot be denied, as I have mentioned above. Apartheid in South Africa and legalized Jim Crow laws in the Southern U.S., with their policies that institutionalized racism, perhaps even incentivizing malicious people (who are racist either inside or outside of conscious awareness), are easy examples. Nevertheless, one orthodox Christian may have one opinion about how to address a complex social issue while another orthodox Christian may have another. Hopefully, the corporate church can communicate confessional unity, with exegetical diversity, and without necessarily having unanimity of complex social problems. Let individuals debate the merits of their case about whether there are extra-legal 'systems' or policies that have been or are racist. However, I maintain, this is not the purview of the church in her corporate capacity.

Rather, the real issue is about how to actualize these feelings and thoughts into charitable service to one's neighbor while still respecting the 'job descriptions' laid out in scripture for the corporate church and for the individual Christian whatever his or her calling may be. One of the goals of the R.E.D.S. (Reformed, Exegetical and Doctrinal Studies) is that each new volume would explore 'pastoral implications so that they contribute to the church's theological and practical understanding of God's word.'[7] Although this book has tried primarily to lay out theoretical foundations (also within the aims of this series), how odd would it be to conclude a book on the primary mission of the church without some practical suggestions about how to concretize some of the principles and the historical position set forth in it? So allow me to set out some suggestions for individual Christians that may want pastoral application in light of this book's argument.

My experience has been that it is an especially difficult mountain to climb for those who have lived privileged lives to truly empathize with others who have not; but it is not impossible. Consider, for example, the Rafiki foundation.[8] Here, individual Christians join together with their financial resources and hard-earned skills in order to serve those who have not: through medicine, education, catechetical instruction and such. Such an organization seems like a viable model that still coheres and respects the principles outlined above in this book for the primary mission of the church. The reason being is that these are the acts of *individual* Christians for the sake of improving the plight of those less fortunate or bereft of basic medical needs, for example.

My wife and I worked for many years in experiential education programs in part designed to work with inner city kids, prison inmates, and handicapped clients. These were Christian programs and although they derived some financial support from the church, they were not a direct ministry of the corporate church; and yet they were often highly effective, even as an alternative to incarceration. These are just a couple of examples. Many more could be cited.

My main point in this monograph, however, as has been mentioned repeatedly, is that the church should stick to her corporate job description. But that doesn't restrict ministers, and individual Christians who are laity, from speaking out, voting, and even peaceful protesting. One thing that we should conclude after surveying so many biblical

---

7. From the series preface at the beginning of each volume, Matthew Barrett and J. V. Fesko.

8. https://www.rafikifoundation.org/rafiki-story

406

passages, so much doctrine on ecclesiology, and so much application of the principles explored throughout history, is that many of the issues we touched upon are tremendously complex. No wonder so many well-meaning Christians differed over some of the issues we engaged. And that should make for a good dollop of humility to be infused into our conversations, especially with brothers and sisters in Christ, on some of these topics. As George Marsden says in his influential book: 'Like many fascinating things, however, most of history is too complex to be susceptible either to genuinely comprehensive treatment or to definitive scientific analysis. In the final analysis it can be understood and illuminated only by sympathetic insight.'[9]

Dare I say that the church today is as much as ever faced with similar historical issues that she has faced, as outlined in some of the history covered previously. On the one side are those (often labelled progressives) who desire that the mission of the church should have, as a fundamental aspect and goal of its mission, social reform and that the preaching of the gospel must have direct social consequences and application. On the other side are those who want to emphasize that the primary mission of the church is about sharing the good news of the gospel, meaning the preaching of the life and message of Jesus Christ, who was born of a woman, under the law, in order to fulfill all righteousness so that he might deliver us from captivity to our sins and make us sons of God.

I have tried to emphasize throughout this book that pressures to redefine the spiritual nature of the church and her mission are afoot. Those of us, like myself, who want to remind the church of her biblically mandated mission are often labelled (at best) as complicit in the social ills round about us since we are not willing to address such social malaise from the pulpit, or in our Sunday school classes. Purposeful quietism does not necessarily entail complicity in the sinful structures or practices that are all around us; rather, it may be because we see it as our very sacred duty to discharge that we stick to our God-given job description. That may not prevent us from choosing a more appropriate venue to discuss such controversial matters, such as through writing books or through appropriate educational avenues.

---

9. George M. Marsden, *Fundamentalism and American Culture*, p. vi.

Of course that should not limit us as *individual* Christians from doing our part as we are able and have opportunity to mitigate injustices, to ameliorate suffering, and to speak boldly, wisely, and with humility into the unjust and sinful situations of the culture and communities in which we find ourselves.

I have argued in this book, from the very beginning (see Chapter 2), that the Lord's church was born out of heaven itself. Following Stuart Robinson, I argued that the legitimate church of Jesus Christ finds her genesis before the beginning of creation in the Trinitarian covenant known as the *Pactum Salutis*. If my discussion holds, that fact should be enough to spark an interest and engage each child of God in the topic of the primary mission of the church. In other words, our hearts should be warmed with affection towards the triune God by realizing that God had the interest of his very own elect in mind, even before the beginning of the world! He had already designed and intended what he would ultimately implement for the perfecting of his saints. Not only had he intended to call those who were truly his own, but he would also implement what was necessary to transform his kingdom of priests, readying them for the world to come.

Moreover, in his Word, the Bible, he has left us numerous passages from many parts of both testaments, so giving us instruction by word and example how this would be carried out: the earliest chapters of Genesis, the Patriarchs, Noah's covenant, Joseph and Daniel in the courts of foreign magistrates, and numerous New Testament passages, instruct us in diverse ways how we ought to live out our pilgrimage as earth-dwellers until we die and go to heaven or until his own Son comes again to bring us to our everlasting abode.

I have suggested throughout this book at various places that the so-called social gospel has made a resurgence and is alive and well, popular, and persuasive to some in the church. Consequently, I have seen things that should not exist in the church of Christ. For example, friendships have been sullied and fractured because one party thought the other was not 'woke' enough and therefore, dissatisfied, they severed ties with their own church and deep friends. We must hit the pause button, however, and ask why? Sadly, I think that we in the church must first take the log out of our own eye and ask if this present emphasis on social justice may arise, at least in part, from some of the unpaid bills of the church. Let me explain.

Could it be, for example, that the social justice warriors have flourished presently due to the vacuous spaces that the church has left open by particularizing and denouncing certain sins (e.g., homosexuality) while not condemning others (e.g., greed, avarice, white collar crime, which are addressed in various places of Scripture as well)? The so-called obvious deeply-serious sexual sins have often been highlighted to the neglect of others that may be less conspicuously so. Consequently, people are deeply disturbed, even angry, when they don't see the church 'calling out' white collar crime for example, or obvious abuses of power in the civil realm. Not all sins are equally heinous, this is true. Biblically, it is somewhat easy to demonstrate that some sins are more egregious than others. Nevertheless, that shouldn't stop the church, as the corporate church, from denouncing all sinful actions (as long as she does so based on Scriptural declarative power), no matter how subtle or less overt they may be.

A chief question that arises from this study is whether a rigorous application of the mission of the church presented above (or the SOTC if you will), with its attendant restraint in the church addressing social issues (e.g., abortion, or prayer in public schools), will inevitably lead to secularism. I would say the answer is no. I have made the point above in this monograph that the church does have a moral duty to address issues that Scripture addresses. Moreover, there may be indirect consequences for the political realm that flow from the faithful preaching and teaching of Scripture. This stated most clearly in Alan Strange's rewritten dissertation on Charles Hodge and in his book reviews as well:

> That we must preach the ethical imperatives of Scriptures is patent. Paul's teaching, for instance, is fraught with such. But how one does it properly, even prophetically (in challenging wickedness in both the church and wider society), without doing it politically, and I mean by this without doing it in a way that divides persons of the same confession, is a challenge. We must not preach a political or social message. That is not to say that preaching God's Word may never have political or social *implications*. It does mean, however, that we should be guided by a healthy spirituality of the church, one that understands the spiritual character and calling of the church as an institution. A proper spirituality of the church distinguishes itself from

the world, while giving itself to the world, holding out Jesus Christ as the only hope of a needy and dying world.[10]

If a reader has ploughed carefully through the argument of this book, she may have learned some new things. Mental furniture may have been moved from what was customary or expected. And one may be left with a feeling of 'what now'? Such a person may be a Christian with a deep desire to relieve pain and suffering in the world. One may be tempted (wrongly I would suggest) that a Christian shouldn't be concerned about a well-ordered society or happiness in the mundane existence. Nothing could be further from the truth!

10. Alan Strange, review of Eric Watkins, *The Drama of Preaching: Participating with God in the History of Redemption* (Eugene, OR: Wipf and Stock, 2016) in *Ordained Servant* (April 2018). Strange also claims that Hodge recognized that faithful preaching may have political consequences as well. See, Strange, *The Doctrine of the Spirituality of the Church*, pp. 246, 237.

# Bibliography

Alter, Robert. *The Art of Biblical Narrative.* New York: Basic Books, 1981.

Arnold, B. T. 'The Use of Aramaic in the Hebrew Bible: Another Look at Bilingualism in Ezra and Daniel,' *Journal of North West Semitic Languages* 22/2 (1996): pp. 1-16.

Armerding, Carl E. *Theology of Liberation.* Phillipsburg, New Jersey: P & R, 1979.

———, 'Wordplay and Narrative Techniques in Daniel 5 and 6,' *JBL* 112/3 (1993): pp. 479-85.

Arrupe, Pedro, S. J. 'Marxist Analysis by Christians,' *Catholic Mind* (September, 1981).

Bacon, Francis. 'Of Revenge,' in *The Oxford Book of Essays: Chosen and Edited by John Gross.* Oxford: Oxford University Press, 1991.

Bahnsen, Greg. *Theonomy in Christian Ethics.* Phillipsburg, N.J.: Presbyterian and Reformed, 1984.

Bannerman, James. *The Church of Christ: A treatise on the nature, powers, ordinances, discipline and government of the Christian Church.* Carlisle, PA: Banner of Truth, 1960.

Bartchy, Scott S. *First-Century Slavery and the Interpretation 1 Corinthians 7:21,* SBL Dissertation Series 11. Atlanta, GA: Scholars Press, 1973.

Bartchy, S. S. 'Slavery' in *The International Standard Bible Encyclopedia*, four vols, edited by Geoffrey W. Bromiley (et al.). Grand Rapids, MI: Eerdmans, 1988: pp. 4.539-46

Baskwell, Patrick. 'Kuyper and Apartheid: A Revisiting,' *Harvard Theological Review* 62/4 (2006): pp. 1269-1290.

Baugh, S. M. *The Majesty on High: Introduction to the Kingdom of God in the New Testament* (self published, 2017).

Bavinck, Herman. *Reformed Dogmatics: Holy Spirit, Church, and New Creation.* 4 volumes. John Bolt ed. Grand Rapids, MI: Baker Academic, 2008.

Beale, G. K. *The Temple and the Church's Mission: A Biblical Theology of the Dwelling Place of God.* Downer's Grove, IL: IVP, 2004.

———, *A New Testament Biblical Theology: The Unfolding of the Old Testament in the New.* Grand Rapids, MI: 2011.

Bell, Jr., Daniel M. *Liberation After the End of History: The Refusal to Cease Suffering,* London and NY: Routledge, 2001.

Bellis, Alice Ogden, and Joel S. Kaminsky (eds.) *Jews, Christians, and the Theology of the Hebrew Scriptures.* Society of Biblical Literature Symposium Series. Atlanta: Society of Biblical Literature, 2000.

Benjamin, Walter W. 'Liberation Theology: European Hopelessness Exposes the Latin Hoax,' *Christianity Today* (March 5, 1982).

Berkhof, Louis. *Systematic Theology.* Fourth Revised and Enlarged Edition. Grand Rapids, MI: Eerdmans, 1941.

Berlin, Adele. *Poetics and Interpretation of Biblical Narrative.* Sheffield: Almond Press, 1983.

Boesak, Allan. *Black and Reformed: Apartheid, Liberation, and the Calvinist Tradition,* edited by Leonard Sweetman. Maryknoll, NY: Orbis Books, 1984.

Bonino, Jose Miguez. *Doing Theology In A Revolutionary Situation.* Philadelphia: Fortress Press, 1975.

———, *Toward a Christian Political Ethics.* Philadelphia: Fortress, 1983.

Brakel, Wilhelmus à. *The Christian's Reasonable Service,* 4 vols., trans. Bartel Elshout. Ligonier, PA: Soli Deo Gloria, 1992-95. originally published in 1700.

Bratt, James D. ed., *Abraham Kuyper: A Centennial Reader*. Grand Rapids, MI: Eerdmans, 1998.

Braude, Benjamin. 'The Sons of Noah and the Construction of Ethnic and Geographical Identities in the Medieval and Early Modern Periods,' *The William and Mary Quarterly*, Vo. 54, No. 1 (Jan. 1997): pp. 103-42.

Breen, Quirinus. *Christianity and Humanism: Studies in the History of Ideas*. Grand Rapids, MI: Eerdmans, 1968.

Brichto, Herbert Chanan. *Toward a Grammar of Biblical Poetics: Tales of the Prophets* , New York: Oxford University Press, 1992.

———, *The Names of God: Poetic Readings in Biblical Beginnings*. New York: Oxford University Press, 1998.

Brown, Raymond. *The Death of the Messiah*. 2 Volumes. New York: Double Day, 1994.

Burkett, Randall K. and Newman, Burkett. *Black Apostles: Afro-American Clergy Confront the Twentieth Century*. Boston, Mass: G. K. Hall & Co., 1978.

Calvin, John. *Commentaries on the First Book of Moses called Genesis* (Grand Rapids, Michigan: 1948).

Chadwick, Henry. *The Early Church: The story of emergent Christianity from the apostolic age to the foundation of the Church of Rome*. London: Penguin Books, 1967.

Chaplin, Jonathan. *Herman Dooyewerd: Christian Philosopher of State and Civil Society*. Notre Dame, IN: University of Notre Dame Press, 2011.

Cochrane, Charles Norris. *Christianity and Classical Culture*: *A Study of Thought and Action from Augustus to Augustine*. London/New York: Oxford University Press, 1940.

Conn, Harvie M. 'Theologies of Liberation: An Overview.' Pages 327-394 in *Tensions in Contemporary Theology*. Edited by Stanley N. Gundry and Alan F. Johnson. Grand Rapids, Michigan: Baker, 1976.

———, *Doing Justice and Preaching Grace*. Grand Rapids, MI: Zondervan, 1982.

Coppes, Leonard. 'The Discussion of the Theology of the Diaconate,' pp. 427-34 in *Between the Times: The Orthodox Presbyterian Church in Transition, 1945-1990*. Willow Grove, PA: The Committee for the Historian of the Orthodox Presbyterian Church, 2011.

Corbett, Steve and Brian Fikkert, *When Helping Hurts: How to Alleviate Poverty without Hurting the Poor ... and Yourself*. Chicago, IL: Moody, 2009.

Cowan, Louise and Os Guinness (eds), *Invitation to the Classics: A Guide to the Books You've Always Wanted to Read*. Grand Rapids, MI: Baker, 1908.

Csikszentmihalyi, Mihaly, 'Marx: A Social-Psychological Evaluation,' *Modern Age* 2 (1967): pp. 272-82.

Clark, R. S. 'Reconstructionism,' in *New Dictionary of Christian Apologetics* (eds. Campbell Campbell-Jack, Gavin J. McGrath and C. Stephen Evans (eds.) Downers Grove, Illinois: InterVarsity Press, 2006.

Clowney, Edmund. *The Church*, Contours of Christian Theology, Gerald Bray (ed.) Leicester, Intervarsity, 1995.

Cooper, Christopher C. 'Binding Bodies and Liberating Souls: James Henley Thornwell's Vision for a Spiritual Church and a Christian Confederacy,' *The Confessional Presbyterian* 9 (2013): pp. 35-47.

Cunningham, William. *Discussions on Church Principles: Popish, Erastian, and Presbyterian*. Edinburgh: T and T Clark, 1863.

Dahl, Nils Alstrup. *Jesus in the Memory of the Early Church*. Minneapolis, MN. Augsburg, 1976.

Davis, Bill. 'Contra Hart: Christian Scholars Should Not Throw in the Towel,' *Christian Scholars Review* 34 (2005): pp. 187-200.

DeHart, Paul J. *The Trial of the Witnesses: The Rise and Decline of Postliberal Theology*, Oxford: Blackwell, 2006.

Dennison, James T. Jr., *The Letters of Geerhardus Vos* (Phillipsburg, New Jersey: P & R Publishing, 2005).

DeYoung, Kevin and Greg Gilbert, *What is the Mission of the Church?: Making Sense of Social Justice, Justice, Shalom, and the Great Commission*. Wheaton, IL: Crossway, 2011.

Dooyeweerd, Herman. *A New Critique of Theoretical Thought: The Necessary Presuppositions of Philosophy.* 4 volumes; trans. David H. Freeman and William S. Young (Philadelphia, PA: Presbyterian and Reformed, 1953-1958).

————, *In the Twilight of Western Thought: Studies in the Pretended Autonomy of Philosophical Thought.* Nutley, NJ: The Craig Press, 1972.

————, *Roots of Western Culture: Pagan, Secular, and Christian Options.* Trans. by John Kraay; Mark Vander Vennen and Bernard Zylstra (eds). Toronto: Wedge, 1979.

Driver, S. R. *An Introduction the Literature of the Old Testament.* Edinburgh: T & T Clark, 1961.

Dumbrell, William J. 'Genesis 2:1-17: A Foreshadowing of the New Creation,' in *Biblical Theology: Retrospect and Prospect* (IVP, 2002).

Dykxhoorn, Hermina. 'Living in a Woke World: And Just What That Means.' *Christian Renewal*, May 1, (2021): pp. 24-26.

Edmondson, Mika. *The Power of Unearned Suffering: The Roots and Implications of Martin Luther King, Jr.'s Theodicy.* Lanham, MD: Lexington Books, 2017.

Estelle, Bryan. 'The Use of Deferential Language in the Arsames Correspondence and Biblical Aramaic Compared,' *MAARAV* 13.1 (2006).

————, 'The Covenant of Works in Moses and Paul,' in *Covenant, Justification, and Pastoral Ministry: Essays by the Faculty of Westminster Seminary California.* R. Scott Clark (ed.). Phillipsburg, PA: P & R, 2007.

————, Review article of Kenneth L. Gentry, *Covenantal Theonomy: A Response to T. David Gordon and Klinean Covenantalism. Ordained Servant,* 16/5, 2007.

————, J. V. Fesko, and David VanDrunen (eds). *The Law is Not of Faith: Essays On Grace and Works in the Mosaic Covenant.* Phillipsburg, New Jersey: P & R, 2008.

————, *Echoes of Exodus: Tracing a Biblical Motif*. Downer's Grove, IL: Intervarsity Academic, 2018.

415

————, 'Motifs and Old Testament Theology,' *Unio Cum Christo: Studies in Old Testament Biblical Theology* Vol. 5, No. 1 (April, 2019): pp. 27-44.

Farish, Leah. 'The First Amendment's Religion Clauses: The Calvinist Document that Interprets Them Both.' *Journal of Religion & Society*, 12 (2010): pp. 1-22.

Farmer, James Oscar Jr., *The Metaphysical Confederacy: James Henry Thornwell and the Synthesis of Southern Values.* Macon, GA: Mercy University Press, 1986.

Ferry, Henry Justin. 'Francis James Grimke: portrait of a black puritan,' Ph.D. diss. Yale University, 1971.

Fesko, J. V. *The Trinity and the Covenant of Redemption.* Fearn, Ross-shire: Mentor, 2016.

————, *The Theology of the Westminster Standards: Historical Context and Theological Insights.* Wheaton, IL: Crossway, 2014.

————, *Death in Adam, Life in Christ: The Doctrine of Imputation.* Reformed, Exegetical and Doctrinal Studies. Fearn, Ross-shire: Mentor, 2016.

————, *Reformed Apologetics: Retrieving the Classic Reformed Approach to Defending the Faith.* Grand Rapids, MI: Baker Academic, 2019.

————, *The Covenant of Works: The Origins, Development, and Reception of the Doctrine*, OSHT, Richard A. Muller ed. Oxford, Oxford University Press, 2020.

Fewell, Danna Nolan. *Circle of Sovereignty: A Story of Stories in Daniel 1–6*, Journal for The Study of Old Testament Supplement Series 72, David Clines and Philip Davies (eds). Sheffield, Almond Press, 1988.

Folmer, M. L. *The Aramaic Language in the Achaemenid Period: A Study in Linguistic Variation*, Orientalia Lovaniensia Analecta 68. Leuven: Peeters, 1995.

Frame, John. *The Amsterdam Philosophy: A Preliminary Critique, Papers by John Frame and Leonard Coppes.* Phillipsburg, NJ: Harmony Press, n.d.

————, 'Towards a Theology of the State,' Westminster Theological Journal 51 (1989): pp. 199-226.

Frankel, David. 'Noah's Drunkenness and the Curse of Canaan: A New Approach.' Journal of Biblical Literature 140, no. 1 (2021): pp. 49-68.

Fromm, Erich. Marx's Concept of Man: With a translation from Marx's 'Economic and Philosophical Manuscripts by P. B. Bottomore. New York: Frederick Unger Publishing Co., 1961.

Garr, Randall. In His Own Likeness: Humanity, Divinity, and Monotheism. Culture and History of the Ancient Near East Series 15; Leiden: Brill, 2003.

Gentry, Peter J. and Stephen J. Wellum, Kingdom Through Covenant: A Biblical-Theological Understanding of the Covenants. Wheaton, IL: Crossway, 2012.

Ginsberg, H. L. 'Composition of the Book of Daniel,' Vetus Testamentum 4 (1954): pp. 246-75.

Godfrey, Robert W. and William Barker (eds). Theonomy: A Reformed Critique. Grand Rapids, MI: Zondervan, 1990.

Goldenberg, David M. Black and Slave: The Origins and History of the Curse of Ham. Studies of the Bible and Its Reception, Vol. 10. Edited by Dale C. Allison, Jr., Christine Helmer, Thomas Römer, Choon-Leong Seow, Barry Dov Walfish, Eric Ziolkowski. Berlin/Boston: Walter de Gruyter, 2017.

Gordon, T. David. 'Response' Modern Reformation May/June 2002, 48. This clarification to Gordon's original article, 'The Insufficiency of Scripture.' Modern Reformation (Jan-Feb, 2002): pp. 18-23.

————, 'Critique of Theonomy: A Taxonomy,' Westminster Theological Journal 56 (Spring, 1994): pp. 23-43.

Graham, Preston D. Jr. A Kingdom Not of This World: Stuart Robinson's Struggle to Distinguish the Sacred from the Secular during the Civil War. Macon, GA: Mercer University Press, 2002.

Greaves, Richard L., *Theology & Revolution in the Scottish Reformation: Studies in the Thought of John Knox*. Grand Rapids, MI: Christian University Press, 1980.

Greenberg, Moshe. 'Hebrew *segullah* and Akkadian *sikiltu*,' *Journal of the American Oriental Society* 71 (1951): pp. 172-74.

Greenstein, Ed. 'Theory and Argument in Biblical Criticism.' *Hebrew Annual Review* 10 (1986): pp. 77-93.

Gropp, Douglass M. 'The Language of the Samaria Papyri: A Preliminary Study,' *Maarav* 5-6 (1990): pp. 169-187.

———, 'Imperial Aramaic,' in *The Oxford Encyclopedia of Archaeology in the Near East* ed. Eric M. Meyers; 5 vols.; Oxford: Oxford University Press, 1997, pp. 3.144-146.

Grimké, Francis J., *The Works of Francis J Grimké,* edited by Carter G. Woodson, Washington D.C., Associated Publishers, 1942, 4 vols.

Gutierrez, Gustavo. *A Theology of Liberation.* Translated and edited by Sister CaridaInda and John Eagleson (Maryknoll, New York: Orbis Books, 1973).

———, *A Theology of Liberation: 15ᵗʰ Anniversary Edition with a new introduction by the Author.* Translated and edited by Sister Caridad Inda and John Eagleson. Maryknoll, NY: Orbis, 1988.

Gutjar, Paul C. *Charles Hodge: Guardian of American Orthodoxy.* Oxford/New York: Oxford University Press, 2011.

Hafemann, Scott (ed.). *Biblical Theology: Retrospect and Prospect.* Downer's Grove, Illinois: Intervarsity Press, 2002.

Hagner, Matthew 1–13. Word Biblical Commentary 33A. Waco: Word, 1993.

Hamid, Shadi Hamid, 'America Without God,' *The Atlantic* (April, 2021 issue, although published online on March 10ᵗʰ, 2021).

Hart, Darryl Glenn. '"Doctor Fundamentalis" An Intellectual biography of J. Gresham Machen, 1881-1937' (Ph.D. Dissertation, The John Hopkins University, 1988.

————, 'The Spirituality of the Church, the Westminster Standards, and Nineteenth-Century American Presbyterianism.' In *Calvin Studies*. VIII: Presented at The Colloquium on Calvin Studies, held January 26-27, 1996, at Davidson College and the Davidson College Presbyterian Church, Davidson, North Carolina. [Edited by] John H. Leith.

————, and John R. Muether, 'The Spirituality of the Church' *Ordained Servant* Vol. 7, No. 3 (July, 1998): pp. 64-66.

————, *The University Gets Religion: Religious Studies in American Higher Education*. Baltimore, MD: The John Hopkins University Press, 1999.

————, 'Christian Scholars, Secular Universities, and the Problem with the "Antithesis,"' *Christian Scholars Review* 30 (2001): pp. 383-402.

————, *The Lost Soul of American Protestantism*. American Intellectual Culture Series, Jean Bethke Elshtain, Ted V. McAllister, Wilfred M. McClay (eds.). Oxford/New York: Rowman & Littlefield Publishers, 2002.

————, *A Secular Faith: Why Christianity Favors the Separation of Church and State*. Chicago, IL: Ivan R. Dee, 2006.

————, *Between the Times: The Orthodox Presbyterian Church in Transition*, 1945-1990. Willow Grove, PA: The Committee for the Historian of the Orthodox Presbyterian Church. 2011.

————, *Calvinism, A History*. New Haven, CT: Yale University Press, 2013.

————, 'The Unpardonable Sin?' a review of Jemar Tisby's, *The Color of Compromise: The Truth about the American Church's Complicity in Racism* in *Ordained Servant* 28 (2019): pp. 130-33. First published electronically at https://opc.org/os.html?article_id=754&issue_id=146

Haskell, Thomas L. *Objectivity is Not Neutrality: Explanatory Schemes in History* Baltimore, MD: The Johns Hopkins University Press, 1998.

Hays, Richard B., Stefan Alkier, and Leroy A. Huizenga, (eds). *Reading the Bible Intertextually*. Waco, TX: Baylor University Press, 2009.

Held, Moshe. 'A Faithful Lover in an Old Babylonian Dialogue,' *Journal of Cuneiform Studies* 15 (1961): pp. 11-12.

Helm, Paul. *John Calvin's Ideas*. Oxford, 2004.

C. J. Hemer, 'Paul at Athens: A Topographical Note,' *NTS* 20 (April, 1974): pp. 341-50.

Henry, Carl. *God, Revelation and Authority*. Waco, Texas: Word Books, 1979.

Hernandez, Ismael. *Not Tragically Colored: Freedom, Personhood, and the Renewal of Black America*. Grand Rapids, MI: Acton Institute, 2016.

Hess, Richard and David Tsummra (eds.). *I Studied Inscriptions from Before the Flood*. Winona Lake, IN: Eisenbrauns, 1994.

Hodge, A. A. *The Confession of Faith: A Handbook of Christian Doctrine Expounding The Westminster Confession* (Carlisle, PA: The Banner of Truth Trust, 1958).

———, *The Life of Charles Hodge*. New York: Charles Scribner's Sons, 1880, reprinted by Banner of Truth, 2010.

Hodge, Charles. *Systematic Theology*, 3 Volumes. Grand Rapids, MI: Eerdmans, 1982.

———, *Discussions in Church Polity*. New York, NY: Charles Scribner's Son, 1878.

Hoffecker, Andrew. *Charles Hodge: The Pride of Princeton*. Phillipsburg, NJ: P & R Publishing, 2011.

Ingersoll, Julie J. *Building God's Kingdom: Inside the World of Christian Reconstruction*. Oxford: Oxford University Press, 2015.

Joüon, Paul. *A Grammar of Biblical Hebrew*. Translated and Revised by T. Muraoka. Editrice Pontificio Istituto Biblico, Roma, 1991.

Kalsbeek, L. *Contours of a Christian Philosophy: An Introduction to Herman Dooyeweerd's thought*. Bernard and Josina Zylstra, eds. Toronto: Wedge, 1975.

Keele, Zach. 'A Biblical Theology of Justice,' *Modern Reformation* (May/2020).

Keesmaat, Sylvia C. *Paul and His Story: (Re)Interpreting the Exodus Tradition.* Journal for the Study of the New Testament Supplement Series 181. Sheffield: Sheffield Academic Press, 1996.

Keller, Timothy. *Center Church: doing balanced, Gospel-centered ministry in your city.* Grand Rapids, MI: Zondervan, 2012.

Kitchen, K. A. 'The Aramaic of Daniel,' pp. 31-79, in Wiseman, *Notes on some problems in the Book of Daniel* (cf., below under Wiseman).

Kirk, J. Andrew. *Liberation Theology.* Atlanta: John Knox Press, 1979.

Kline, Meredith G., *Kingdom Prologue: Genesis Foundations for a Covenantal Worldview* (Overland Park, KS: Two Age Press, 2000).

———, 'Abram's Amen.' *Westminster Theological Journal* (1968/69): pp. 1-11.

———, 'Oracular Origin of the State,' in *Biblical and Near Eastern Studies: Essays in Honor of William Sanford LaSor* (Grand Rapids, Michigan: Eerdmans, 1978).

———, *God, Heaven, and Har Magedon*: *A Covenantal Tale of Cosmos and Telos. (*Eugene, OR. Wipf and Stock, 2006).

———, *Genesis: A New Commentary.* (Peabody, Mass. Hendrickson, 2016).

Kuiper, R. B. *The Glorious Body of Christ*: *A Scriptural Appreciation of the One Holy Scripture.* (Grand Rapids, MI: Eerdmans, 1966; repr. Banner of Truth Trust, 1967).

Kutscher, E. Y. *Current Trends in Linguistics*, 6 (1970), pp. 399-403.

Kuyper, Abraham. *Lectures on Calvinism* (Grand Rapids, MI: Eerdmans, 1931).

———, *De Gemeene Gratie.* Kampen: J. H. Kok, 1945. Originally published in 1902-04.

Leeman, Jonathan. *Political Church: The Local Assembly as Embassy of Christ's Rule.* (Downers Grove, IL: IVP Academic, 2016).

Legaspi, Michael C. *Wisdom in Classical and Biblical Tradition* (Oxford/New York: Oxford University Press, 2018).

Lenglet, A. 'La structure littéraire de Daniel 2-7,' *Biblica* 53 (1972): pp. 169-170.

Leong, David P. *Race & Place: How Urban Geography Shapes the Journey to Reconciliation.* (Downers Grove, IL: IVP, 2017).

Levinson, Jon D. *Sinai & Zion: An Entry into the Jewish Bible* (San Francisco: Harper and Row Publishers, 1985).

Lewis, Bernard. Bernard Lewis, *Race and Slavery in the Middle East: An Historical Enquiry.* (New York/Oxford: Oxford University Press, 1990).

———, *What Went Wrong: Western Impact and Middle Eastern Response.* (New York: Oxford, 2002).

Longacre, Robert E. *Joseph: A Story of Divine Providence: A Text Theoretical and Textlinguistic Analysis of Genesis 37–48.* (Winona Lake, IN: Eisenbrauns, 1989).

Lyon, David. *Karl Marx: A Christian Assessment of His Life and Thought* (Downers Grove: Intervarsity Press, 1979).

Lucas, Sean Michael. *Robert Lewis Dabney: A Southern Presbyterian Life.* American Reformed Biographies. D.G. Hart and Sean Michael Lewis eds. Phillipsburg, PA: P & R, 2005.

———, 'God and Country American Style.' *Westminster Theology Journal* 69 (2007): pp. 185-97.

———, *For a Continuing Church: The Roots of the Presbyterian Church in America.* Phillipsburg, PA: P & R, 2015.

———, 'Owning Our Past: The Spirituality of the Church in History, Failure, and Hope.'

http://rts.edu/. https://journal.rts.edu/article/owning-our-past-the-spirituality-of-the-church-in-history-failure-and-hope/

Machen, J. G. 'The Responsibility of the Church in Our New Age,' *The Presbyterian Guardian* 36:1. January, 1967.

———, 'The Importance of Christian Scholarship,' in *Education, Christianity, and the State: Essays by J. Gresham Machen,* edited by John W. Robbins (Jefferson, MD: The Trinity Foundation, 1987).

Maddex, Jack P. 'From Theocracy to Spirituality: The Southern Presbyterian Reversal on Church and State,' *Journal of Presbyterian History (1962-1985)*, Vol. 54, No. 4 (Winter, 1976): pp. 438-57.

Marsden, George M. *Fundamentalism and American Culture*: *The Shaping of Twentieth-Century Evangelicalism 1870-1925*. (Oxford/New York: Oxford University Press, 1980. This book was later expanded and revised in *Understanding Fundamentalism and Evangelicalism*. Grand Rapids, MI: Eerdmans, 1991.

————, *The Outrageous Idea of Christian Scholarship*. Oxford/New York, Oxford University Press, 1997.

Marx, Engels. *On Religion*. Moscow, Progress Publishers, 1957.

McArthur, Marcus. *Render unto Lincoln: Disloyalty and the Clergy in Civil War Missouri*. PhD diss., University of St. Louis, 2015.

McNeil, Brenda Salter. *Roadmap to Reconciliation*: *Moving Communities into Unity, Wholeness and Justice*. Downers Grove, IL: IVP, 2015.

Matthews, Kenneth A. *Genesis 1–11:26* (The new American Commentary 1A; Broadman & Holman Publishers, 2001).

McDonald, Jeffrey S. 'J. Gresham Machen and the Culture of Classical Studies,' *WTJ* 82 (2020): pp. 95-119.

McVicar, Michael J. *Christian Reconstruction: R. J. Rushdoony and American Religious Conservatism*. Chapel Hill, NC: The University of North Carolina Press, 2015.

McWhorter, John. *Losing the Race*: *Self-Sabotage in Black America*. New York, NY: Harper Collins, 2001.

————, *Winning the Race*: *Beyond the Crisis in Black America*. New York, NY: Penguin, 2005.

————, 'Words Have Lost Their Common Meaning,' *The Atlantic* (March 31st).

Mills, Lawrence. *The Jew in the Court of the Foreign King*: *Ancient Jewish Court Legends*, Harvard Dissertations in Religion 26 (Minneapolis, MN: Fortress, 1990).

Miranda, Jose Poririo. *Marx and the Bible: A Critique of the Philosophy of Oppression.* Trans. John Eagleson; New York: Orbis Books, 1974.

Moltmann, Jurgen. *Theology of Hope: On the Ground and the Implications of a Christian Eschatology.* Translated by James W. Leitch. New York: Harper and Row, 1967.

————, 'An Open Letter to Jose Miguez-Bonino,' *Christianity and Crisis* 35, n. 5 (March 29, 1976), pp. 57-63.

Montgomery, J. A. *A Critical and Exegetical Commentary on the Book of Daniel.* New York: Charles Scribner's and Sons, 1927.

Morey, Robert A. *The Dooyeweerdian Concept of the Word of God.* Phillipsburg, NJ: Presbyterian and Reformed, 1974.

Moser, Tyler. 'To Speak Well in Two Languages: The Book of Job in the Theology of Gustavo Gutiérrez.' MAHT thesis, Westminster Seminary California, 2020.

Nash, Ronald H. *Poverty and Wealth: The Christian Debate Over Capitalism* (Westchester: Crossway Books, 1986).

Neusner, Jacob. *A Rabbi talks with Jesus: An Intermillennial, Interfaith Exchange.* New York: Doubleday, 1993.

Nickoloff, James B (ed.) *Gustavo Gutiérrez: Essential Writings.* Minneapolis, MN: Fortress, 1996.

Noegel, Scott B (ed.). *Puns and Pundits: Word Play in The Hebrew Bible and Ancient Near Eastern Literature.* Bethesda, MD: CDL Press, 2000.

Noll, Mark A. *The Scandal of the Evangelical Mind.* Grand Rapids, MI: Eerdmans, 1994.

North, Gary. *The Dominion Covenant.* Institute for Christian Economics, 1987.

————, *Marx's Religion of Revolution: The Doctrine of Creative Destruction.* Nutley: Craig Press, 1968.

Nunez, Emilio A. *Liberation Theology.* Chicago: Moody Press, 1985.

Ockholm, Dennis L. (ed.), *The Gospel in Black and White: Theological Resources for Racial Reconciliation.* Downers Grove, IL: IVP, 1997.

Olasky, Marvin (ed). *Freedom, Justice, and Hope.* Westchester, Illinois: Crossway Books, 1988.

Peck, T. W. *Notes on Ecclesiology.* Richmond, VA: Presbyterian Committee on Education, 1892.

———, 'Church and State,' *Southern Presbyterian Review* 16:2 (Oct. 1863): pp. 121-144.

Perkins, Harrison. *Catholicity and the Covenant of Works: James Usher and the Reformed Tradition*, OSHT, Richard A. Muller ed. (Oxford, Oxford University Press, 2020).

Peterson, Thomas Virgil. *Ham and Japheth: The Mythic World of Whites in the Antebellum South.* Metuchen, NJ: The Scarecrow Press, 1978.

Pixley, George V. *On Exodus: A Liberation Perspective.* trans. by Robert R. Barr. Maryknoll, New York: Orbis, 1987

John Petrov Plamenatz, *Karl Marx's Philosophy of Man.* Oxford: Clarendon Press, 1975.

Ratzinger, Joseph. *Instruction On Certain Aspects of the 'Theology of Liberation.'* Printed in the U.S.A. by the Daughters of St. Paul; 50 St. Paul's Ave., Boston, MA. O2130.

Rauschenbusch, Walter. *Christianity and the Social Crisis.* New York: Hodder & Stoughton, 1907.

———, *Christianizing the Social Order.* New York, NY: The Macmillan Company, 1926.

Rabinowitz, Jacob 'Grecians and Greek terms in the Aramaic Papyri,' *Biblica* 39 (1958): pp. 76-82.

Robertson, O Palmer. *The Christ of the Prophets.* Phillipsburg, New Jersey: P & R, 2004.

Robinson, Stuart. *The Church of God as an Essential Element of the Gospel, and the Idea, Structure, and Function in Four Parts.* Willow Grove, PA: The Committee on Christian Education of the Orthodox Presbyterian Church, 2009.

Rowley, H. H. 'The Unity of the Book of Daniel,' in *The Servant of the Lord and Other Essays on the Old Testament.* London: Lutterworth, 1952: pp. 237-268.

Sarna, Nahum M., *The JPS Torah Commentary: Genesis*. Philadelphia, PA: Jewish Publication Society, 1989.

Scobie, Charles H. H. *The Ways of Our God: An Approach to Biblical Theology*. Grand Rapids, MI: Eerdmans, 2003.

Segovio, Fernando F. *Decolonizing Biblical Studies: A View from the Margins*. New York: MaryKnoll, Orbis, 2004.

Segundo, Juan Luis. *Theology and the Church: A Response to Cardinal Ratzinger and a Warning to the Whole Church*. Translated by John W. Diercksmeier. San Francisco: Harper and Row, 1970.

Seitz, Christopher R. *Figured Out: Typology and Providence in Christian Scripture*. Louisville, KY: Westminster John Knox Press, 2001.

Seufert, Michael. 'Refusing the King's portion: A reexamination of Daniel's dietary reaction in Daniel 1,' *Journal for the Study of the Old Testament* 43/4 (2019): pp. 644-60.

Shea, William. 'Further Literary Structures in Daniel 2-7: An Analysis of Daniel 4,' *Andrews University Seminary Studies* 23 (1985): pp. 29-52.

———, 'Further Literary Structures in Daniel 2–7: An Analysis of Daniel 5, and the Broader Relationships within Chapters 2-7,' *AUSS* 23 (1985): pp. 277-95.

Skillen, James. 'The Pluralist Philosophy of Herman Dooyeweerd,' in Jeanne Heffernan Schindler, ed., *Christianity and Civil Society: Catholic and Neo-Calvinist Perspectives* (Lanham: Lexington Books, 2008): pp. 97-114.

Smith, Frank Joseph. *The History of the Presbyterian Church in America: The Continuing Church. Movement*. Manassas, VA: Reformation Educational Foundation, 1985.

Smith, Morton Howison. *Studies in Southern Presbyterian Theology*. Jackson, MS: Presbyterian Reformation Society, 1962.

———, *Commentary of the Book of Church Order*. Greenville, SC: Greenville Seminary Press, 1990.

Sobrino, Jon S. J., *Christology at The Crossroads*. trans. John Drury; New York: Orbis Books, 1978.

————, *Jesus in Latin America*. New York: Orbis Books, 1987.

Southern, R. W. *Western Society and the Church in the Middle Ages.* London: Penguin Books, 1970.

Stevenson, Leslie. *Seven Theories of Human Nature.* New York: Oxford University Press, 1987.

Stob, Ralph. *Christianity and Classical Civilization.* Grand Rapids, MI: Eerdmans, 1950.

Strange, Alan D. *The Doctrine of the Spirituality of the Church in the Ecclesiology of Charles Hodge.* Reformed Academic Dissertations. Phillipsburg, PA: Presbyterian and Reformed, 2017.

Sugirtharajah, R. S. *The Postcolonial Biblical Reader.* R. S. Sugirtharajah (ed.) Blackwell Publishing, 2006.

————, *The Bible in the Third World: Precolonial, Colonial, and Post-Colonial Encounters.* Cambridge University Press, 2001.

Thompson, Ernest Trice. *The Spirituality of the Church: A Distinctive Doctrine of The Presbyterian Church in the United States* (Richmond, VA: John Knox Press, 1961).

Thornwell, J. H. *The Collected Writings of James Henry Thornwell*, four volumes. Edinburgh; Carlisle, PA: Banner of Truth Trust, 1974.

Tocqueville, Alexis de, *Democracy in America*, A new translation by George Lawrence Garden City, NY: Anchor, 1969.

Torbett, David. *Theology and Slavery: Charles Hodge and Horace Bushnell.* Macon, GA: Mercer University Press, 2006.

Tisby, Jemar. *The Color of Compromise: The Truth about the American Church's Complicity in Racism.* Grand Rapids, MI: Zondervan, 2019.

Trimiew, Darryl M. *Voices of the Silenced: The Responsible Self in a Marginalized Community.* Cleveland, OH: The Pilgrim Press, 1993.

Troxel, Craig. "'Divine Right" Presbyterianism and Church Power,' Ph.D. dissertation, Westminster Theological Seminary, 1998.

Troxel, Craig A. and Peter J. Wallace, 'Men in Combat Over The Civil Law: "General Equity" in *WCF* 19.4,' in *Westminster Theological Journal* 64 (2002): pp. 307-318.

Tucker, Robert C. *Philosophy and Myth in Karl Marx* (Cambridge: Cambridge University Press, 1961).

Tuininga, Matthew. *Calvin's Political Theology and the Public Engagement of the Church: Christ's Two Kingdoms*, Cambridge Studies in Law and Christianity, John Witte, Jr., editor. Cambridge: Cambridge University Press, 2017.

Tuttle, Gary A (ed.) *Biblical and Near Eastern Studies: Essays in Honor of William Sanford LaSor.* Grand Rapids, Michigan: Eerdmans, 1978.

Ursinus, Zacharias. *Commentary of Dr Zacharias Ursinus on the Heidelberg Catechism.* Translated from the Original Latin by the Rev. G.W. Willard. Phillipsburg, NJ: Presbyterian and Reformed, 1852.

Vance, John Lloyd. 'The ecclesiology of James Henley Thornwell: An Old South Presbyterian theologian.' Ph.D. dissertation, Madison, NJ: Drew University, 1990.

Van Der Toorn, Karel. 'Theology, Priests and Worship in Canaan and Ancient Israel,' *Pages 2044-52 in CANE.*

VanDixhoorn, Chad. *Confessing the Faith: A Reader's Guide to the Westminster Confession of Faith.* Carlisle, PA: Banner of Truth, 2014.

VanDrunen, David. 'Natural Law in Early Calvinist Resistance Theory,' *Journal of Law and Religion.*

————, 'The Importance of the Penultimate: Reformed Social Thought and the Contemporary Critiques of the Liberal Society,' *Journal of Markets and Morality* 9, No. 2 (Fall, 2006): pp. 219-49.

————, 'The Context of Natural Law: John Calvin's Doctrine of the Two Kingdoms,' *Journal of Church and State* 46 (2004): pp. 503-525.

————, *Living in God's Two Kingdoms: A Biblical Vision for Christianity and Culture.* Wheaton, IL: Crossway, 2010.

————, *Natural Law and the Two Kingdoms: A Study in the Development of Reformed Social Thought.* John Witte, General editor. Grand Rapids, Eerdmans, 2010.

———, *Divine Covenants and Moral Order: A Biblical Theology of Natural Law*. Emory University Studies in Law and Religion. John Witte, General editor. Grand Rapids: Eerdmans, 2014.

———, 'Power to the People: Revisiting Civil Resistance in Romans 13:1-7 in Light of the Noahic Covenant,' *Journal of Law and Religion* 31, no. 1 (March 2016): pp. 4-18

———, *Politics after Christendom: Political Theology in a Fractured World*. Grand Rapids, MI: Zondervan Academic, 2020.

VanDrunen, Katherine Lynn Tan, 'The Foothills of the Matterhorn: familial antecedents of J. Gresham Machen,' Ph.D. dissertation, Loyola University Chicago, 2006.

Van Dyke, Henry J. *The Spirituality and Independence of the Church: A Speech Delivered in the Synod of New York, October 18$^{th}$, 1864*. New York, 1864.

Vanhoozer, Kevin J. *The Drama of Doctrine: A Canonical Linguistic Approach to Christian Theology*. Louisville, KY: Westminster John Knox, 2005.

van Prinsterer, G. Groen. *Unbelief and Revolution: A Series of Lectures in History Lectures VIII & IX*. Edited and translated by Harry Van Dyke in collaboration with Donald Morton. Amsterdam, The Groen van Prinsterer Fund, 1975.

Van Prinsterer, Groen. *Lecture Eleven from Unbelief and Revolution* (Amsterdam: The Groen Van Prinsterer Fund, 1973).

———, *Lectures Eight and Nine from Unbelief and Revolution* (Amsterdam: The Groen Van Prinsterer Fund, 1975).

Van Til, Henry R. *The Calvinist Concept of Culture*. Grand Rapids, MI: Baker, 1959.

Vos, Geerhardus. *Biblical Theology: Old and New Testaments*. Grand Rapids, MI: 1948.

———, *The Pauline Eschatology*. Princeton University Press, 1930. The book was later published by Presbyterian and Reformed, with a foreword by Richard B. Gaffin, Jr. Phillipsburg, NJ: Presbyterian and Reformed, 1979.

Vree, Dale. 'Ideology versus Theology: Case Studies of Liberation Theology and the Christian New Right,' in *Christianity Confronts Modernity*. Peter Williamson and Kevin Perrotta (eds.). Ann Arbor, Michigan: Servant Books, 1981.

Waltke, Bruce with Cathi J. Fredericks. *Genesis: A Commentary*. Grand Rapids, MI: Zondervan, 2001.

Ward, Rowland S. *Foundations in Genesis: Genesis 1-11 Today* (Wantirna, Victoria: New Melbourne Press, 1998).

Warnock, Raphael G. *The Divided Mind of the Black Church: Theology, Piety, & Public Witness*. Religion, Race, and Ethnicity Series, Peter J. Paris, General Editor. New York, NY: New York University Press, 2014.

Waters, Guy Prentiss. *How Jesus Runs the Church*. Phillipsburg, NJ: Presbyterian & Reformed, 2011.

Watkins, Eric B. 'The Color of Preaching,' *New Horizons* (May, 2019): pp. 4-5.

Webster, Ransom Lewis. 'Geerhardus Vos (1862-1949): A Biographical Sketch,' *Westminster Theological Journal* 40 (1978): pp. 304-317.

Weeks III, Lewis. 'Racism, World War I and the Christian Life: Francis Grimke in the Nation's Capital,' in *Black Apostles: Afro-American Clergy Confront the Twentieth Century*. Boston, Mass: G. K. Hall & Co., 1978.

Weeks, Stuart. *Early Israelite Wisdom*. Oxford. Oxford University Press, 1994.

Weigl, Michael. *Die aramäischen Achikar-Sprüche aus Elephantine und die alttestamentliche Weisheitsliteratur*, Beihefte zur Zeitschrift für die alttestamentliche Wissenschaft 399 (Berlin: de Gruyter, 2010).

Wenham, Gordon J. 'Sanctuary Symbolism in the Garden of Eden Story,' pp. 399-404 in *I Studied Inscriptions from Before the Flood* (ed. Richard S. Hess and David Toshio Tsummra; Winona Lake, Indiana: Eisenbrauns, 1994).

———, *Genesis 1–15*. Word Biblical Commentary 1. Waco, Texas: Word Books, 1987.

Weston, Paul. *Lesslie Newbigin: Missionary Theologian, a Reader.* Compiled and introduced by Paul Weston. Grand Rapids, MI: Eerdmans, 2006.

Wilkins, Steve and Douglas Wilson, *Southern Slavery As It Was.* (Moscow, ID: Canon Press, 1996).

Wills, Lawrence M. *The Jew in the Court of the Foreign King*: *Ancient Jewish Court Legends.* Harvard Dissertations in Religion 26. Minneapolis, MN. Fortress, 1990.

Wilson-Hartgrove, Jonathan. *Reconstructing the Gospel*: *Finding Freedom from Slaveholder Religion.* Downers Grove, IL: IVP, 2018.

Wilson, Lindsay. *Joseph Wise and Otherwise: The Intersection of Wisdom and Covenant in Genesis 37–50.* Carlisle: Paternoster, 2004.

Wingard, Brian. '"As the Lord Put Words in her Mouth:" The Supremacy of Scripture in the Ecclesiology of James Henley Thornwell and Its Influence upon the Presbyterian Churches of the South.' Ph.D. dissertation, Philadelphia, PA: Westminster Theological Seminary, 1992.

Wiseman, D. J. 'Some Historical Problems in the Book of Daniel,' Pages in *Notes on some problems in The Book of Daniel.* London, Tyndale Press, 1965: pp. 9-18.

Witsius, Herman. *The Economy of the Covenants between God and Man: Comprehending a Complete Body of Divinity*, 2 vols., trans. William Crookshank 1822; reprint, Phillipsburg: P&R, 1990.

Wright, N. T. *The Climax of the Covenant: Christ and the Law in Pauline Theology.* Minneapolis, MN: Fortress Press, 1991.

———, *The Day the Revolution Began: Reconsidering the Meaning of Jesus's Crucifixion.* San Francisco: HarperOne, 2016.

———, *Surprised by Hope: Rethinking Heaven, the Resurrection, and the Mission of the Church.* New York, HarperOne, 2008.

———, *Paul and the Faithfulness of God.* Christian Origins and the Question of God 4. Minneapolis: Fortress, 2013.

Wolters, A. L. 'Untying the King's Knots: Physiology and Wordplay in Daniel 5,' *Journal of Biblical Literature* (1991): pp. 117-22.

————, 'The Riddle of the Scales in Daniel 5,' *Hebrew Union College Annual* (1991): pp. 155-77.

Yamauchi, Edwin. *Greece and Babylon: Early Contacts Between the Aegean and the Near East.* Grand Rapids, MI: Baker, 1967.

# Subject Index

# Scripture Index

442

*Also available in the REDS series...*

R.E.D.S.
REFORMED,
EXEGETICAL
AND
DOCTRINAL
STUDIES

MENTOR

# FOR THE MOUTH OF THE
# LORD HAS SPOKEN

## THE DOCTRINE OF SCRIPTURE

GUY PRENTISS WATERS

SERIES EDITORS J.V. FESKO & MATTHEW BARRETT

ISBN 978-1-5271-0607-9

# For the Mouth of the Lord Has Spoken

## The Doctrine of Scripture

### Guy Prentiss Waters

There is no book better than the Bible. It is God's own word. He breathed it into existence. He does wonderful things in and by it. But there is hardly a book more assailed, mocked, and assaulted than the Bible. New Testament Professor Guy Prentiss Waters delves into the doctrine of Scripture. Addressing the revelation, inspiration, inerrancy, sufficiency and perspicuity of the Bible, he also engages with what some other prominent theologians had to say on the subject.

*What can be more important than understanding the Book that God gave us? Dr. Guy Waters thoroughly, carefully, and winsomely sets before us the riches of the doctrine of Scripture. He alerts us to faulty thinking of the past and the present and also commends to us a faithful and orthodox view of the Bible, the very words of God, which are life itself.*

Stephen J. Nichols
President, Reformation Bible College, CAO Ligonier Ministries,
Sanford, Florida

**CLASH OF VISIONS**

**POPULISM AND ELITISM IN NEW TESTAMENT THEOLOGY**

**ROBERT W. YARBROUGH**

SERIES EDITORS J.V. FESKO & MATTHEW BARRETT

R.E.D.S.
REFORMED,
EXEGETICAL,
AND
DOCTRINAL
STUDIES

MENTOR

ISBN 978-1-5271-0391-7

# Clash of Visions

## Populism and Elitism in New Testament Theology

### Robert W. Yarbrough

Each year thousands die for the Jesus they read about in the Bible. At the same time scholars worldwide reject central truths of the Book. Here is an analysis of two contrasting approaches to biblical interpretation: one which has encouraged many to abandon the Christian heritage, the other which has informed the largest numeric increase of professing Christians in world history in recent generations and which is projected to continue.

*This is a book that every Christian student should read before studying at a non–evangelical institution. Even those at Bible–believing institutions (including seminaries) will benefit, since they will likely be reading books by 'elitists' and may at some point study under them in graduate school. I found the book riveting and had a hard time putting it down. The two appendices about the life–pilgrimage of two 'populist' theologians are worth the price of the book.*

G. K. Beale
Professor of New Testament and Biblical Theology, Westminster
Theological Seminary, Philadelphia, Pennsylvania

# Christian Focus Publications

Our mission statement —

STAYING FAITHFUL

In dependence upon God we seek to impact the world
through literature faithful to His infallible Word, the Bible.
Our aim is to ensure that the Lord Jesus Christ is presented as
the only hope to obtain forgiveness of sin, live a useful life and
look forward to heaven with Him.

Our books are published in four imprints:

## CHRISTIAN
## FOCUS

Popular works including biographies, commentaries, basic doctrine and Christian living.

## CHRISTIAN
## HERITAGE

Books representing some of the best material from the rich heritage of the church.

## MENTOR

Books written at a level suitable for Bible College and seminary students, pastors, and other serious readers. The imprint includes commentaries, doctrinal studies, examination of current issues and church history.

## CF4•K

Children's books for quality Bible teaching and for all age groups: Sunday school curriculum, puzzle and activity books; personal and family devotional titles, biographies and inspirational stories — because you are never too young to know Jesus!

Christian Focus Publications Ltd,
Geanies House, Fearn, Ross-shire,
IV20 1TW, Scotland, United Kingdom.
www.christianfocus.com